THE EU CITIZENSHIP DIRECTIVE

THE EU CITIZENSHIP DIRECTIVE

A Commentary

ELSPETH GUILD
STEVE PEERS
JONATHAN TOMKIN

OXFORD
UNIVERSITY PRESS

OXFORD
UNIVERSITY PRESS

Great Clarendon Street, Oxford, OX2 6DP,
United Kingdom

Oxford University Press is a department of the University of Oxford.
It furthers the University's objective of excellence in research, scholarship,
and education by publishing worldwide. Oxford is a registered trade mark of
Oxford University Press in the UK and in certain other countries

First Edition published in 2014

Impression: 1

Published in the United States of America by Oxford University Press
198 Madison Avenue, New York, NY 10016, United States of America

British Library Cataloguing in Publication Data
Data available

Library of Congress Control Number: 2013948379

ISBN 978–0–19–870523–9

Printed and bound in Great Britain by
CPI Group (UK) Ltd, Croydon, CR0 4YY

PREFACE

Directive 2004/38, the citizens' Directive, seeks to give effect to the cornerstone of the status of European Union citizenship: the right of European Union citizens to move to and reside in any Member State of their choosing.

As the case-law of the Court of Justice of the European Union illustrates, Union citizens and their family members may wish to spend time in other Member States for a variety of different reasons, whether for short stays or long-term residence, whether as tourists, visitors, students, entrepreneurs, workers, service providers or recipients, or indeed, for no particular purpose at all. Crucially, and for the first time, the movement of all such diverse categories of persons is regulated by a single overarching Union legislative instrument.

Since its provisions took effect on 29 April 2006, the citizens' Directive has proven to be a fertile ground for litigation, generating increasing, dynamic, and rapidly evolving case-law. References to the Court of Justice from national courts have sought clarification and interpretation of a range of the Directive's provisions concerning the nature and scope of free movement and residence rights, the rights of third-country national family members of Union citizens and the extent to which beneficiaries of free movement rights are entitled to equal treatment in the host Member State, particularly as regards accessing social allowances. Yet, despite the Directive's novelty, its provisions may also be regarded as forming a part of a continuum of measures building on past free movement legislation and codifying an extensive body of case-law of the Court of Justice spanning over 50 years.

It becomes clear that a fully informed reading of the citizens' Directive and the movement and residence rights, for which it provides, implies an understanding of the Directive's historical, legislative, and jurisprudential context. This book has been written to facilitate such an understanding.

Our approach in this book has been to provide a comprehensive Article-by-Article commentary upon the citizens' Directive. Each chapter traces the legislative development of the Directive's provisions. Special emphasis is placed on highlighting the connections and interactions between the Directive's constituent provisions so as to permit a global appreciation of the system of free movement rights to which the Directive gives effect. Each provision is annotated containing a detailed analysis of the case-law of the Court of Justice as well as of related measures impacting upon the Directive's interpretation including European Commission reports and guidelines on the Directive's implementation.

The book is practice-oriented and we have afforded special attention to identifying key issues liable to emerge in the application of the Directive, and have advanced views on the best approaches to dealing with such issues in the light of existing case-law of the Court of Justice and the nature of legal reasoning in the Union legal order.

While the review of the chapters has been collective, primary responsibility for writing the chapters has fallen on different members of the team. Professor Elspeth Guild, Radboud University Nijmegen, co-authored the Introduction and was primarily responsible for Chapter 4 (Permanent Residence) and Chapter 6 (Restrictions on Free Movement Rights). Professor Steve Peers, of the University of Essex, co-ordinated this project, co-authored the Introduction and was primarily responsible for Chapter 1 (General Provisions) and Chapter 7 (Final Provisions). He further contributed sections relating to Schengen in Chapter 2 (Exit and Entry) and the sections on retention of residence rights in Chapter 3 (Right of Residence). Jonathan Tomkin, Member of the European Commission's Legal Service, is primarily responsible for Chapter 2 (Exit and Entry), Chapter 3 (the Right of Residence), and Chapter 5 (Provisions Common to the Right of Residence and the Right of Permanent Residence). Views expressed by Mr Tomkin are his own and are not necessarily those of the European Commission.

We have endeavoured to state the law as of 20 July 2013, although it has been possible to take account of some case law from September 2013.

Finally, we wish to thank our editors, Alex Flach, Sujitha Karthikeyan, and Clare Kennedy of Oxford University Press for their enthusiastic encouragement of this project, as well as to our ever understanding and supportive families. In particular, Elspeth Guild expresses her thanks to Didier for his love and support. Steve Peers thanks his wife—Pamela Chatterjee—and children Kiran, Isabella, Serena, and Sophia for their love and support. Jonathan Tomkin thanks his family Vera, Julia, Richard, Magda, Jeanie, Alex, and Adam, for their love and support, manifested, not least, in a ready and regular exercise of free movement rights.

EG SP JT
January 2014

CONTENTS

Contents

TABLE OF CASES

EFTA COURT

EUROPEAN COURT OF HUMAN RIGHTS

TABLE OF LEGISLATION

3) NATIONAL LAW

LIST OF ABBREVIATIONS

CFR	Charter of Fundamental Rights
CJEU	Court of Justice of the European Union
CMLRev	Common Market Law Review
CRC	Convention on the Rights of the Child
CYELS	Cambridge Yearbook of European Legal Studies
EAW	European Arrest Warrant
EC	European Community
ECHR	European Convention on Human Rights
ECtHR	European Court of Human Rights
ECR	European Court Reports
EEA	European Economic Area
EEC	European Economic Community
EFTA	European Free Trade Association
EJML	European Journal of Migration and Law
ELJ	European Law Journal
ELRev	European Law Review
EPL	European Public Law
EU	European Union
EUConst	European Journal of Constitutional Law
ICCPR	International Covenant on Civil and Political Rights
LIEI	Legal Issues of Economic Integration
MJ	Maastricht Journal of European and Comparative Law
OECD	Organisation for Economic Cooperation and Development
OJ	Official Journal
OUP	Oxford University Press
Rev Aff Eur	Revue d'Affaires Européene
TEU	Treaty on European Union
TFEU	Treaty on the Functioning of the European Union
UK	United Kingdom
UN	United Nations
WHO	World Health Organization
YEL	Yearbook of European Law

INTRODUCTION

This book examines European Union Directive 2004/38 on the right of citizens of the Union and their family members to move and reside freely within the territory of the Member States.[1] This Directive (which we refer to in this book as 'the citizens' Directive', or 'Directive 2004/38') gives effect to the right which EU law provides to all EU citizens and their family members (as defined) of any nationality to move, reside, and exercise economic activities if they so choose on the territory of any EU Member State. The right to move and reside anywhere in the EU is a right which is accorded to Union citizens by virtue of Articles 20(2)(a) and 21 of the Treaty on the Functioning of the European Union (TFEU) and enshrined in Article 45 of the EU Charter of Fundamental Rights. The right as expressed in what is now Article 21 TFEU has been interpreted as having direct effect.[2] The Directive also gives effect to the specific rights of free movement of persons which are found in Articles 45 (free movement of workers), 49 (the right of establishment, more commonly understood as the right of self-employment as regards natural persons), and 56 (the right of service provision). These Articles have also been found to have direct effect.

The right of free movement of persons in their capacities as workers, self-employed persons, or service providers straddles two of the four fundamental freedoms of the European Union—free movement of persons and services. These freedoms were inscribed in the original European Economic Community (EEC) Treaty with a transitional period by which time these freedoms had to be achieved. In 1961 the EU first adopted implementing legislation towards free movement of workers—Regulation 15/61. This was followed in 1964 by a deepening of the rights of workers in Regulation 38/64. According to the recital in the preamble to the first Regulation, the objective is the abolition of all discrimination based on nationality between workers of the Member States as regards work, pay, and other conditions of work. The objective requires also the elimination of waiting periods and other restrictions which constituted an obstacle to free movement by the end of the transitional period. The first stage of the transitional period lasted two years (similarly to that of the transitional arrangements for nationals of the 2004 Member States).[3]

---

[1] [2004] OJ L 158/77, and corrigenda ([2004] OJ L 229/35, [2005] OJ L 197/34, and [2007] OJ L 204/28). All references in this book are to this Directive, unless indicated otherwise.

[2] Case C-413/99 *Baumbast and R* [2002] ECR I-7091.

[3] E Guild, *European Immigration Law* (Kluwer Law International, The Hague 2000), 110–120, which examines in depth the Regulation in comparison with the subsidiary legislation under the EEC Turkey Association Agreement.

Until 1990, the free movement right was limited to EU citizens and their family members who were exercising economic activities—workers, self-employed persons, or service providers or recipients. Only those pensioners who had exercised an economic activity in the host State for more than three years gained a right of residence not dependent on economic capacities. The status of service recipient, however, became increasingly unclear as the Court of Justice of the European Union (CJEU) was requested to interpret the scope of Article 56. A high water mark came in 1989 when the Court held that a tourist visiting a Member State's capital for a short holiday qualified as a service recipient for the purposes of claiming an entitlement to non-discrimination in relation to nationals of that State.[4] This line of decisions sits slightly uncomfortably with jurisprudence regarding students and the extent of their claims to non-discrimination, given that students spend an even longer period on the territory and have a greater effect on the economy of the host State than tourists.[5] In 1990, the EU institutions adopted three Directives, one each on the right of residence of students, pensioners, and the economically inactive. The European Parliament challenged the first of these Directives on the grounds that the wrong legal base had been used (and won).[6] The result was quite a hotchpotch of measures covering a variety of situations which often intersected or were otherwise intertwined.

The introduction of the status of citizenship of the Union as a formal status in the EC Treaty by means of the Maastricht Treaty (entering into force in 1993) provided an excellent opportunity to consolidate the law into one coherent measure. After lengthy negotiations, including two false starts,[7] this opportunity was realized on 29 April 2004 with the adoption of the Directive. The following Monday, 1 May 2004, ten Member States joined the EU and their nationals immediately became beneficiaries of the new Directive (once the transposition period ended on 1 May 2006). It built on the previous measures in accordance with the teleological approach of the Union, adding new rights but not limiting or reducing existing ones.[8] Directive 2004/38 replaced all the previous Regulations and Directives covering the field with some exceptions.[9]

---

[4] Case 186/87 *Cowan* [1989] ECR 195.

[5] See Case 197/86 *Brown* [1988] 3205, in which the Court did not assess students' position from the perspective of recipients of services, and Case C-109/93 *Wirth* [1994] ECR I-6447, in which the Court concluded that higher education courses financed out of public funds and tuition fees were not 'services' for the purposes of the Treaty at all.

[6] Case C-295/90 *Parliament v Council* [1992] ECR I-4193.

[7] Before the Maastricht Treaty, see COM(1988) 815 ([1999] OJ C 100/6 and 8), on which discussions ceased in 1992. Afterwards, see COM(1998) 394 ([1998] OJ C 344/12), on which discussions never even began. Both proposals concerned the legislation regarding the free movement of workers only.

[8] See case law beginning with Case C-127/08 *Metock* [2008] ECR I-6241, para 59, in which the CJEU held that since recital 3 in the preamble to the Directive states the objective to 'strengthen the right of free movement and residence of all Union citizens', it followed 'that Union citizens cannot derive less rights from that Directive than from the instruments of secondary legislation which it amends or repeals'.

[9] Certain rights of workers are to be found in Regulation 492/2011 ([2011] OJ L 141/1) which replaced Regulation 1612/68 in 2011.

The background to the Directive

The first measures giving effect to the right of free movement of workers as provided for in the Treaty were adopted in 1961. Regulation No 15/1961[10] set out key principles governing freedom of movement for workers and was accompanied by a Directive regulating entry, employment, and residence.[11] Regulation 15/61 set out how migrant workers of the Member States gain access to the labour market, how job offers are coordinated, and which bodies within the Member States are responsible for the execution of the duties. Member States were permitted to retain a preference for their own nationals in respect of any job offer for a maximum of three weeks (Article 1). If no national worker could be found within that period, then a national of any other Member State was entitled to take the job and the state was under a duty to authorize that employment. Where an employer nominated a worker national of another Member State for a job, then the three weeks' waiting period did not apply.

Article 2 of the Regulation set out the mechanisms by which the worker obtained security of access to the labour market and residence. This was in incremental steps according to the length of employment. After one year's employment on the territory of another Member State, the worker was entitled to an extension of his or her work permit for the same job. After three years' employment, the worker was entitled to change employer and take any other employment for which he or she was qualified. On completion of four years' employment the worker was entitled to free access to the labour market under the same conditions as nationals of the host State. After five years' employment, where the individual had worked for between eight and twelve months per year with permission, the worker was entitled to any paid employment of his or her choice. The use of the eight- to twelve-month period was clearly designed to seek to include as many seasonal workers as possible and to avoid that workers who were issued only short-term work permits of less than a year became excluded from the possibility of obtaining free access to the labour market. The Regulation also provided that periods of employment completed before its entry into force counted towards the calculation of the one-, three-, four-, and five-year periods.

The Regulation also took care to ensure that Member States were restricted as regards denying workers rights on the basis of absences. Migrant workers tend to return to their countries of origin for holidays, periods of festivals, or when they are ill or pregnant. Family emergencies may require them to spend substantial periods

---

[10] Regulation 15 of 16 August 1961 on initial measures to bring about free movement of workers within the Community (1961 OJ 57/1073, hereinafter 'Regulation 15').

[11] Council Directive of 16 August 1961 on administrative procedures and practices governing the entry into and employment and residence in a Member State of workers and their families from other Member States of the Community (1961 OJ 80/1513, hereinafter 'the 1961 Directive').

in their country of origin although they may plan to return and resume their life in their host country as soon as possible. The Regulation therefore provided, at Article 7, that absences of forty days or less as well as annual holidays, absences on account of illness, maternity, accident at work, or industrial injury must be counted as part of the period of regular employment. Involuntary unemployment, long absences on account of illness, and the completion of military service were specifically excluded from the calculation of the time periods, so as not to prejudice the acquisition of rights.

The Regulation specifically provided for equal treatment with own nationals for EU migrant workers as regards conditions of work, employment, remuneration, and dismissal. The Regulation also provided protection for the family members of EU migrant workers. Articles 11 to 14 defined family members in a more limited manner than that contained in the current Directive 2004/38.[12] Only spouses and children under twenty-one could accompany or join workers in the host State. The worker was obliged to have regular employment (though no minimum salary level was required) and adequate housing for the family. Family members were entitled to take employment on the same conditions as applicable to the principal. The children of migrant workers were entitled to equal treatment in access to vocational training and apprenticeships. Further, in order to protect migrant workers, the Regulation included a standstill clause which prohibited the introduction of any measures which would have the effect of further restricting access to the labour market and treatment of migrant workers from other Member States and their family members.

The second stage of the transitional period for free movement of workers occurred two years later and was accompanied by the adoption of a new Regulation 38/64 which was designed to further progress the integration of the EU labour market. In the preamble to this Regulation, one finds references to different categories of workers—permanent, seasonal, and frontier. For the first time the situation of workers who are the employees of service providers and as such sent across EU borders is mentioned (an issue which is still, in 2013, a matter of concern in some Member States).[13] As regards access to the labour market, at this stage of the realization of free movement of workers, the three weeks' period during which employers may prioritize recruitment of nationals of the host Member State has been removed. Subject to only very limited reservations, the procedures on changing employment also vanish—as soon as the individual was admitted to the labour market he or she was entitled to change job. Once a worker had been regularly employed in a Member State for one year and wished to continue

---

[12] C Urbano de Sousa, 'Le droit des membres de la famille du citoyen de l'Union europééne de circuler et de séjourner sur le territoire des états membres, dans la directive 2004/38/CE' in J-Y Carlier and E Guild, *The Future of Free Movement of Persons in the EU* (Bruylant, Brussels, 2006), 103–126

[13] J Y Carlier, *La condition des personnes dans l'union europééne* (Larcier, Brussels, 2007).

employment in the same field or where a worker had been employed for two years or twenty-seven months over the preceding three years as a seasonal worker or twenty months over the preceding three years in whatever occupation, then no restrictions could be applied to his or her access to the labour market of the host State. Migrant workers no longer needed to seek extensions of their work permits. Regulation 38/64 extended the class of family members entitled to join the EU migrant worker to include all dependent relatives in the ascending and descending lines of the worker and or his or her spouse. Also, at this point the right to facilitation for other family members appears in EU law. Admission to the host State of other family members, who were either dependent on the worker (or his or her spouse) or lived under the same roof as the worker, had to be facilitated. For the first time, the Regulation states clearly that the nationality of the family members is irrelevant to the exercise of the right. No change was made to the conditions for admission or the right to employment for family members. However, the children of migrant workers were expressly now entitled to take courses of general education.

In 1968, Regulation 1612/68 was adopted which replaced the previous rules providing a clear set of rights for migrant workers.[14] At the same time, Directive 68/360 was adopted which provided the rules on procedures for the treatment of EU migrant workers.[15] Directive 73/148 on the rights of the self-employed was finally adopted in 1973.[16] What is particularly important about Regulation 1612/68 is just how little it changed the ground rules of free movement of workers. While all waiting times for admission to the labour market vanished, and the rights of family members were widened, the structure remained consistent and provided the basis for Directive 2004/38. Interestingly, Directive 64/221 which set out the rules of exclusion and expulsion of migrant workers, and which had been adopted in 1964,[17] continued to apply until the citizens' Directive was adopted in 2004.[18]

Who are citizens of the Union?

It is not possible to introduce Directive 2004/38 fully without first giving some consideration to its intended beneficiaries—the nationals of the Member States. From six Member States in 1957, in 2012 there were twenty-seven and in 2013 Croatia joined the EU, making that figure twenty-eight. The EEC was established

---

[14] [1968] OJ L 257/2.
[15] [1968] OJ L 257/13.
[16] [1973] OJ L 172/14.
[17] [1964] OJ L 56/850.
[18] M Condinanzi, A Lang, and B Nascimbene, *Citizenship of the Union and Freedom of Movement of Persons* (Martinus Nijhoff, Leiden, 2008).

in 1957 with six Member States: Belgium, France, Germany, Italy, Luxembourg, and the Netherlands. According to EU law, it is for each Member State to designate who its nationals are. The UK has changed its designations a number of times since its accession to the EU. However, once an individual is recognized as a citizen of a Member State, he or she is also automatically a citizen of the Union.[19] How an individual acquired citizenship of a Member State makes no difference to the acquisition of EU rights on the basis of the TFEU or Directive 2004/38 or otherwise.[20] Similarly, if a Member State withdraws citizenship from an individual, his or her EU citizenship will also be extinguished—provided such withdrawal has been taken place in accordance with requirements provided for in Union law.[21]

On the basis of EUROSTAT's statistics,[22] the population of those original six Member States from 1957 looks like this:

Country	Population 2010 (millions)
Belgium	10.8
France	64.7
Germany	81.8
Italy	60.3
Luxembourg	0.5
Netherlands	16.6
TOTAL	234.7

In 1973, Denmark, Ireland, and the United Kingdom joined the European Union. No transitional provisions applied to the free movement of workers notwithstanding fears in some EU countries of an influx of migrant workers.[23]

Country	Population 2010 (millions)
Denmark	5.5
Ireland	4.5
UK	62.0
TOTAL:	72.0

In 1981, Greece became a Member State and for the first time since 1957, transitional restrictions on free movement of workers were applied which were not lifted until 1 January 1988. No transitional restrictions were placed on the

---

[19] Art 20 TFEU.

[20] Case C-369/90 *Micheletti and Others* [1992] ECR I-4239; Case C-200/02 *Chen and Zhu* [2004] ECR I-9925.

[21] Case C-135/08 *Rottmann* [2010] ECR I-1449. On these issues, see further the commentary on Art 2(1) of the Directive in Chapter 1.

[22] See <http://epp.eurostat.ec.europa.eu/cache/ITY_OFFPUB/KS-SF-11-038/EN/KS-SF-11-038-EN.PDF> visited 6 August 2012.

[23] W Bohning, *The Migration of Workers in the United Kingdom and Western Europe* (OUP, Oxford, 1972).

self-employed and service providers and recipients. The current population of Greece is 11.3 million.

In 1986, Spain and Portugal became Member States and once again there was a delay in the realization of free movement of workers according to Article 56 Accession Treaty until 1 January 1993. However, the delay was lifted on 1 January 1992.

Country	Population 2010 (millions)
Portugal	10.6
Spain	46.0
TOTAL	56.6

In 1995, Austria, Finland, and Sweden joined the EU, but no transitional restrictions were applied to free movement of workers. A free movement regime had been established with the EU under the EEA Agreement the preceding year, so no transitional arrangements were appropriate.

Country	Population 2010 (millions)
Austria	8.4
Finland	5.4
Sweden	9.3
TOTAL	23.1

The year 2004 saw the single largest expansion of the EU with ten new States joining: Estonia, Cyprus, Czech Republic, Latvia, Lithuania, Hungary, Malta, Poland, Slovakia, and Slovenia.[24] Two States were not subject to any transitional restrictions on free movement of workers: Cyprus and Malta. All the rest of the 2004 Member States were subject to transitional restrictions on free movement of workers which permitted the EU 15 (those States which were already part of the EU before 2004) to apply restrictions under national law on movement of workers for a period of two years starting from 1 May 2004. At the end of the first period of two years, ie by 1 May 2006, the EU 15 had to notify the European Commission whether they intended to continue to apply restrictions on movement of workers after that date. If they did, then they could continue to apply restrictions on workers from the EU 8 for a further three years until 1 May 2009; a long stop of 1 May 2011 applied under specific circumstances of a threat or actual serious disruption to the labour market. It was invoked only by Austria, Germany, and the UK.

---

[24] On the legal issues arising from immigration after the most recent enlargements, see, from a large literature, S Currie, *Migration, Work and Citizenship in the Enlarged European Union: Law and Migration* (Ashgate, Farnham, 2008).

Country	Population 2010 (millions)
Czech Republic	10.5
Cyprus	0.8
Estonia	1.3
Latvia	2.2
Lithuania	3.3
Hungary	10.0
Malta	0.4
Poland	38.2
Slovakia	5.4
Slovenia	2.0
TOTAL	74.1

One of the striking things about the Member States that acceded in 2004 is that with only the exceptions of the two Mediterranean islands, the populations have struggled to remain static over the past twenty years and in fact in a number of the States there has been population decline.[25]

On 1 January 2007 Bulgaria and Romania joined the EU. Their nationals are subject to the same transitional arrangements as the EU 8, namely, the formula of two years restrictions on free movement of workers according to national decision, followed by a notification by the other Member States of an extension for a further three years and then a final two-year period if there is a declaration of a serious disruption (or threat thereof) to the domestic labour market. Restrictions on Bulgarian and Romanian workers may continue until 1 January 2014. As with the previous enlargement, nationals of these countries are entitled to move for the purposes of self-employment, service provision, and receipt (subject to sectoral limitations on services in Austria and Germany).

Country	Population (2010) (millions)
Bulgaria	7.6
Romania	21.5
TOTAL	29.1

With the addition of Croatia, which joined the EU in 2013, and which has a population of 4.4 million, the EU has a current total of 506.9 million inhabitants, less than half of whom live in one of the original six Member States. The meaning of free movement of persons has not only moved on in terms of a consolidation of the content of the right for EU citizens, but also been completely transformed by the enlargement processes of the EU. When free movement of workers was first realized it was designed around a total population of 233.2 million persons. Now more than double that number either have acquired free movement rights or are in

---

[25] R Cholewinski, R Perruchaud, E MacDonald, *International Migration Law: Developing Paradigms and Key Challenges* (T M C Asser, The Hague, 2007).

the process of doing so. Further, free movement and residence is no longer limited to those exercising economic activities, thus virtually the total EU population is eligible to exercise the right to move and reside (see Chapter 3 regarding the exceptions). This is quite a change to the shape of EU free movement and its beneficiaries.

Do citizens of the Union use their rights; if so, how and where?

According to the EU's statistical office, in 2011 12.8 million EU citizens were living in a Member State other than that of their underlying nationality.[26] This equals 2.5 per cent of the EU 27 population. This figure is in fact dwarfed by the number of third-country nationals living in the EU which accounts for 20.5 million people, or 4.1 per cent of the EU's population. Of course, with each enlargement the first figure increases and the latter figure diminishes as regards those persons who are nationals of the State joining the EU. For EU citizens moving and residing in a Member State other than that of their underlying citizenship, three Member States are the most popular destinations:

Member State	EU citizens residing in but not holding the nationality of the host State (000)
Germany	2,628.3
Spain	2,329.2
UK	2,061.4

After these three preferred destinations come France and Italy, almost tied with approximately 1,339,200 (France) and 1,334,800 (Italy) EU residents. No other Member State has more than a million nationals of other Member States living there. However, when one considers EU citizens from other Member States as a percentage of the population, the picture is very different.

Member State	Percentage of resident EU citizens not holding the nationality of the host State
Luxembourg	37.2
Cyprus	12.5
Belgium	6.8
Ireland	6.5
Spain	5.0

In no other Member States does the percentage of EU citizens resident but not citizens exceed 5 per cent of the population. When researchers consider the impact of EU mobility on host Member States, it is always useful to remember that two sets of figures are critical. The impact of EU citizens exercising their free movement right of residence depends also on the number of people who are not exercising the

---

[26] Eurostat newsrelease STAT/12/105, 11 July 2012.

right. If one compares these figures with the corresponding ones on third-country nationals resident in EU Member States, the picture is somewhat different. The top three are:

Member State	Third-country nationals resident in the host State (000)
Germany	4,570.6
Spain	3,325.5
Italy	3,235.5

As a percentage of the total population the situation looks like this:

Member State	Percentage of third-country nationals resident in the host State as % of population
Latvia	16.6
Ireland	14
Cyprus	7.4
Spain	7.2
Greece	7.1

In no other Member State does the percentage exceed 7 per cent. Of course, these figures are explained by history, laws on acquisition of citizenship, and State succession. The point to be made here is that often those Member States which are most interested in mobility and migration-related issues are not those most affected by either of the two—in terms of absolute numbers of foreigners or percentage of foreigners as part of the whole population.

What does free movement of persons mean?

By establishing a right for EU citizens, and their third-country national family members, to move and reside anywhere in the EU, the relationship of EU citizens and their families to the immigration authorities of the Member States has changed fundamentally. Instead of entry, residence, and exercise of economic activity on the territory of the State being a prerogative of nationals of that State and thereafter as regards everyone else a matter of choice by the authorities of the State, EU citizens have a right to all three. Member State authorities are prohibited from interfering with the rights of EU citizens to move, reside, and exercise economic activities unless they can justify the interference on the basis of the limited grounds permitted in EU law itself—public policy, public security, or public health (see Chapter 6).

As regards third-country nationals who are not related to an EU citizen exercising a free movement right, Member State immigration authorities are entitled to set the rules as they wish, subject to the impact of EU immigration law (and their protection obligations under international law). Almost without exception, they wish to maintain a discretionary control over the arrival, residence, and economic activities of third-country nationals at least over the first five years of their residence. Thus, for instance, the UK authorities chose, in 2011, to introduce quotas for highly skilled migrant workers and in 2012 to introduce new income requirements for family reunification of British citizens and permanent residents with third-country national family members. Because the people affected by these changes are third-country nationals, the changes are at least on their face lawful even if, as some commentators have calculated, two-thirds of British citizens would not be able to meet the new income requirement to sponsor their spouse to live with them in the UK and thus enjoy family life.[27]

Because free movement of persons is one of the four founding freedoms of the EU it is not available for structural reform. A Member State which no longer wishes to comply with the right of citizens of the Union to move, reside, and exercise economic activities anywhere in the Union (either by prohibiting their departure or their arrival) beyond the very limited scope which is permitted by the Directive (see Chapter 6) at the moment has no option but to consider withdrawal from the EU (unless all the Member States were able to agree on an amendment to the Treaties as regards free movement of persons).

What do EU citizens think about their rights?

Leaving aside those EU citizens who exercise their free movement rights, what do the people of the EU in general think of these rights—do they favour them or worry about the consequences? According to a Eurobarometer survey published in 2010,[28] 60 per cent of EU citizens consider that people moving within the EU is a good thing for EU integration, 50 per cent consider it is a good thing for the labour market, and 47 per cent think it is good for the economy in general. People living in the EU 15 (those Member States which formed the EU before 1 May 2004) are more positive about the benefits of intra-EU mobility than those living in the EU 12 (who have joined between 2004 and 2007). Those who are most convinced of the benefits of mobility are the Danes (77 per cent consider it beneficial) followed by the Swedes (76 per cent), and the Irish (71 per cent). The least convinced are the Cypriots of whom only 31 per cent think it is beneficial, followed by the Italians (31 per cent). The British were at the slightly above the middle of the scale in viewing mobility as beneficial (51 per cent). However, across the EU people are more convinced that mobility is a good thing for individuals but less sure that it is beneficial for families.

---

[27] A Travis, 'Stark choice under new immigration rules: exile or family breakup', *The Guardian*, 8 June 2012.
[28] See <http://ec.europa.eu/public_opinion/archives/ebs/ebs_337_en.pdf> visited 6 August 2012.

A minority of EU citizens, according to the same Eurobarometer survey, consider that moving abroad would improve their work chances (39 per cent) but of those who do think it would improve their work chances only 30 per cent actually envisaged moving abroad. At the two extremes were Latvians, 76 per cent of whom think their work chances would be improved by moving, whereas only 12 per cent of Austrians agree with the statement. However, of those who would envisage moving abroad to work the highest percentages were: 64 per cent of Germans and 51 per cent of Finns. The choices of where people who participated in the study wanted to go are perhaps somewhat surprising. The top four were:

USA	21%
UK	16%
Australia	15%
Spain	13%

The bottom four were:

Brazil	2%
South Africa	3%
Denmark	3%
Ireland	4%

Of these choices, Ireland is among the most surprising, as it has among the highest percentages of EU citizens who are not Irish citizens living there. It is unclear what this may mean as regards the experiences of those who have exercised their mobility rights. The other surprising aspect of the choices of EU citizens is the relative indifference that they reveal about the benefits of EU free movement of persons. However, as the study shows in great detail, there is a long and uncertain road between the expression of a preference, the decision to move, preparation to do so, and actually carrying out the act. We will now leave the realities of EU mobility and the preferences of its citizens and return to the law which regulates mobility in the EU.

Understanding the Directive

The Directive was adopted three years after the CJEU held for the first time that Union citizenship is destined to become the fundamental status of nationals of the Member States.[29] It affirms this view in recital 3 in its preamble and states that this objective makes it necessary to codify the instruments dealing separately with workers, self-employed persons, students, and others. The objective is to simplify and strengthen the right of free movement and residence of all Union citizens.

---

[29] Case C-184/99 *Grzelczyk* [2001] ECR I-6193.

The right of free movement, according to the Directive, includes the right of all Union citizens and their family members of any nationality to exercise that right under objective conditions of freedom and dignity. This may be understood as referring back to the EU Charter of Fundamental Rights, Article 1 of which establishes a right to dignity which is clarified in the explanations as not only a fundamental right in itself but as constituting the real basis of fundamental rights.[30] The Directive's approach to facilitating the exercise of free movement rights is set out in the recitals, each of which corresponds to a section of the operational provisions of the Directive. The overarching scheme of rights provided for are as follows:

- a period of entry and residence without formalities for three months;
- a qualification regarding becoming an unreasonable burden on the social assistance system of the host Member State;
- for periods longer than three months the possibility for Member States to apply administrative procedures and to fulfil a specific mobility right;
- EU provisions on family members—their definition and rights to accompany or join an EU citizen exercising a mobility right;
- permanent residence after five years' residence in the host Member State fulfilling the substantive conditions after acquisition of which no further conditions may be applied;
- a general right to equal treatment and a prohibition on discrimination on the basis of nationality within the scope of the Directive;
- restrictions on the right of mobility are limited to those which can be justified by the State authorities on the basis of public policy, public security, or public health;
- after acquiring permanent residence Union citizens gain enhanced protection against expulsion and even greater protection after ten years or where they are minors;
- a high level of procedural safeguards apply;
- no ban on re-entry can be permanent;
- a right for Member States to guard against abuse of rights and fraud;
- a safeguard provision for more favourable provisions which may exist in national law; and
- a statement to the effect that the Directive respects the EU Charter of Fundamental Rights.

In the following chapters we will examine each of the provisions of the Directive and provide a clear analysis in light of all relevant judicial pronouncements on the meaning and application of them. We will take into account the reports from the European Commission on the Directive's implementation in the Member States,[31]

---

[30] [2007] OJ C 303.
[31] COM(2008) 840; see also the guidance on the Directive (COM(2009) 313).

and academic and doctrinal positions on the meaning of provisions which are contentious or otherwise in need of further clarification. This book is designed to assist everyone who seeks to understand the meaning of EU mobility and the rights of citizens of the Union.

The chapters follow the structure of the Directive, which is divided into chapters as follows:

(a) chapter I (Articles 1–3): general provisions;
(b) chapter II (Articles 4–5): right of exit and entry;
(c) chapter III (Articles 6–15): right of residence;
(d) chapter IV (Articles 16–21): right of permanent residence;
(e) chapter V (Articles 22–26): provisions common to the right of residence and the right of permanent residence;
(f) chapter VI (Articles 27–33): restrictions on the right of entry and the right of residence on grounds of public policy, public security, and public health; and
(g) chapter VII (Articles 34–42): final provisions.

The Directive in context

While the focus of this book is on the legal interpretation of the citizens' Directive, it is necessary to consider the Directive also in its broader context. The historical context (in terms of the development of the legislation on the free movement of persons and the successive enlargements of the Union) has been considered above. But there is also a legal context, a territorial context, a social and economic context, and a human rights context.

Legal context

The focus of this book is on a specific secondary legislative measure—the citizens' Directive. However, the subject matter of the Directive is also affected by other primary and secondary measures, most notably the Treaty rules on citizenship of the Union and the free movement of persons (all of which were referred to already above), and secondary law on other aspects of the free movement of persons, in particular legislation on the free movement of workers,[32] the coordination of social security,[33] and the recognition of qualifications.[34] A full analysis of these other measures is beyond the scope of this book, although the book does refer to

---

[32] Reg 492/2011, [2011] OJ L 141/1.
[33] Reg 883/2004, [2004] OJ L 166/1.
[34] Directive 2005/36, [2005] OJ L 255/32.

these other sources where relevant, and summarize some of their content.[35] In particular, it should be emphasized that although the citizens' Directive focuses on the equality of EU citizens who move to other Member States, the free movement provisions also prohibit non-discriminatory obstacles which pose a barrier to free movement.[36] Furthermore, the concept of EU citizenship is broader than the subject matter of the citizens' Directive, not only in the broader sense that the concept of citizenship encompasses more generally the relationship between the EU integration process and institutions and the general public,[37] but also in the narrower sense that the formal concept of EU citizenship also includes provisions on voting in municipal and European elections, consular protection, and rights relating to citizens' initiatives, petitions, complaints to the EU Ombudsman, and contact with the EU institutions.[38]

Territorial context

While the concept of EU citizenship is unique to the nationals of the EU's Member States, the citizens' Directive is not. Since it replaced legislation relating to the free movement of persons which also applied to the third States which are party to the European Economic Area (EEA)—namely, Norway, Iceland, and Liechtenstein—it was in time extended to nationals of those States as well, with certain adaptations.[39] As a result, it has been interpreted by the EFTA Court, which has jurisdiction over the interpretation of EU internal market measures which have been extended to those three associates of the EU.[40]

Furthermore, although the Directive has not been extended to any other third States, a broadly similar comprehensive regime for the free movement of persons also applies between the EU and Switzerland.[41]

---

[35] For instance, see the commentary on Art 2(1) in Chapter 1 (as regards the Treaty rules on citizenship), on Art 12(3) in Chapter 3 (as regards Reg 492/2011), and on Art 24 in Chapter 5 (as regards Reg 492/2011 and the Treaty provisions on citizenship and free movement).

[36] See, for instance, Case C-415/93 *Bosman* [2005] ECR I-4921.

[37] See the EU citizenship report (COM(2013) 269, 8 May 2013).

[38] Arts 22–24 TFEU. From a huge literature, see J Shaw, 'Citizenship: Contrasting Dynamics at the Interface of Integration and Constitutionalism', in P Craig and G De Burca, eds, *The Evolution of EU Law*, 2nd edn (OUP, Oxford, 2011), 575.

[39] EEA Joint Committee Decision 158/2007. [2008] OJ L 124/20.

[40] Case E-4/11 *Clauder*, judgment of 26 July 2011; Case E-15/12 *Wahl*, pending. See Chapters 4 and 6 respectively.

[41] [2002] OJ L 114. For analysis, see S Breitenmoser, 'Sectoral Agreements between the EC and Switzerland: Contents and Context' (2003) 40 CMLRev 1137 and S Peers, 'The EC-Switzerland Agreement on Free Movement of Persons: Overview and Analysis' (2000) 2 EJML 127.

Social and economic context

Until the adoption of the citizens' Directive in 2004, the most important legislation which governed the free movement of EU citizens had been Regulation 1612/68 (and the accompanying Directive 68/360). Both measures had been adopted in 1968 and their core provisions had not been amended since. Between 1968 and 2004 (and a fortiori 2013), the social and economic context of the free movement of persons has changed profoundly, quite apart from the doubling in population of the Union discussed above. Whereas the drafters of the 1968 legislation could assume that most families consisted of married couples: a male breadwinner, with a wife focusing on unpaid work in the family home and several children, in the meantime the divorce rate has soared, far more married women work outside the home in the paid labour market, and many couples do not get married at all.[42] Relationships between same-sex couples, which attracted hostility (and in some cases criminalization) in 1968, have been legitimated in the form of civil partnerships or marriage in a growing number of Member States. In 1968, long-standing full employment, high growth rates, and favourable demographics sustained policies of encouraging immigration and the expansion of the welfare state in EEC Member States. Now, high unemployment, low (or negative) growth, and deteriorating demographic outlooks have led to concerns about controlling immigration and related attempts to limit access to social welfare. The citizens' Directive attempts to address the growth in divorce, unmarried couples, and same-sex relationships, and with its consolidation and strengthening of the rights of EU citizens and their family members (especially third-country national family members), there is inevitably tension about the degree of recognition to afford to newer forms of family relationships and the impact of the Directive on the control of immigration and the cost of the welfare State. Indeed, at least some EU citizens resent mobility from other Member States as well, particularly after the recent large enlargements of the EU. The legal rules governing these issues are explored in depth throughout this book.

Human rights context

Finally, within the scope of the EC (now EU) legal order, fundamental rights have long been protected as general principles of Community law. These rights are now recognized in the EU's Charter of Fundamental Rights (see Article 6(1) TEU), although the general principles are still referred to also in Article 6(3) TEU. The EU is also obliged to accede to the European Convention on Human Rights

---

[42] See generally L Hantrais, 'What is a Family or Family Life in the European Union?', in E Guild, ed, *The Legal Framework and Social Consequences of Free Movement of Persons in the European Union* (Kluwer, The Hague, 1999), 19.

(Article 6(2) TEU), although it has not yet done so. The Charter is relevant to this book in particular as regards its Article 7 (corresponding to Article 8 ECHR, on the right to private and family life) and Article 47 (the right to a fair trial and effective remedy).[43] However, this book does not examine the Charter issues in detail, given that in most respects the Directive provides for higher standards and more detailed rules than the ECHR.[44] It should be noted that the Charter is only relevant where there is a link to EU law, although the CJEU sometimes refers to Member States' human rights obligations even outside the scope of the EU legal order.[45]

---

[43] See particularly Chapters 1 and 6 as regards the former right, and chapter 6 as regards the latter.

[44] See the critique of the ECHR standards in Chapters 1 and 6. The point is relevant since the interpretation of Art 7 of the Charter is in principle the same as Art 8 ECHR: see Art 52(3) of the Charter, as interpreted (for instance) in Case C-400/10 PPU *McB* [2010] ECR I-8965.

[45] See, for instance, Case C-256/11 *Dereci*, judgment of 15 November 2011, not yet reported.

1

GENERAL PROVISIONS

A. Function

The general provisions of the citizens' Directive (Articles 1–3) state its purpose and define its territorial and personal scope. Essentially, the Directive applies to EU citizens and their family members who move to another Member State. This might at first seem like a straightforward definition, but immediately questions arise. Who determines if a person is an EU citizen at all? What about dual citizens of two Member States, or of one Member State and a non-Member State (a 'third State')? What is the position of EU citizens who move to one Member State, and then return to their home Member State? Is it fair to develop a regime for EU citizens who move to another Member State, if that means that EU citizens who stay in their own country ('static' EU citizens) are worse off by comparison (the phenomenon of 'reverse discrimination')? Which family members should have the right to move with the EU citizen, and what conditions (if any) should be attached to their movement?

These questions have been partly addressed in the case law of the Court of Justice, but its answers remain controversial and have raised a number of further questions in turn. In particular, when interpreting these key provisions of the Directive, there is an inevitable tension between the EU objective of promoting the free movement rights of EU citizens on the one hand, and many Member States' objective of controlling immigration from third States on the other.

B. Historical development

All EU legislation providing for rights for EU citizens (or rather, originally, nationals of Member States) to enter and reside in the territory of another Member State has consistently addressed the position of the family members of those citizens, for the obvious reason that a large majority of EU citizens are either part of a family already or intend to develop a family life later. So a right to move which only applied to (say) workers, but not to their family members, would not be very effective at achieving its aim of facilitating the free movement of workers. The most significant prior legislation in this field—Regulation 1612/68 on the freedom of movement of workers—therefore permitted a wide category of family members to install themselves with the worker on liberal terms, and also expressly provided for those family members' access to employment and education.[1] So did the legislation on self-employed persons and service providers or recipients,[2] on persons who ceased their economic activity,[3] and later (to a lesser extent) on the persons who were not carrying out economic activities at all.[4] The legislation regulating the derogations from the free movement of nationals of Member States also applied to those persons' family members.[5]

The relevant provisions of the prior legislation were the subject of considerable jurisprudence, much of it concerning the admission and status of family members who were third-country nationals. This case law was partly intertwined with the question of whether the prior rules on the free movement of various categories of Member States' nationals could only be invoked where those nationals had moved between Member States, and if so, precisely what sort of actions constituted movement between Member States. To some extent, this case law was integrated into the citizens' Directive, but that Directive still left some important questions outstanding, partly because it was ambiguous and partly because there was much important case law during the negotiation of the Directive (2001–2004) and during its transposition period (2004–2006). The relevant case law on the prior legislation is therefore integrated into the commentary on Articles 2 and 3 below.

C. Interrelationship of Articles 1–3 with other provisions

Since these provisions determine the personal and territorial scope of the rest of the Directive, they are closely related to all of it. But they have a more specific relationship with the provisions which define the material scope of the Directive, ie the conditions that persons have to fulfil to exercise the rights of residence (Articles 6 and 7, in Chapter III) and permanent residence (Article 16, in Chapter IV). As regards family members in particular, in general they are covered by all the provisions of the Directive, if they accompany or join the EU citizen who is the primary right-holder (Article 3(1)), but several provisions set out specific rules for them, as

---

[1] Arts 10–12 of that Reg, [1968] OJ L 257/2. See also Art 1 of Directive 68/360, [1968] OJ L 257/13.

[2] Art 1(1)(c) and (d), Directive 73/148, [1973] OJ L 172/14.

[3] Art 1, Reg 1251/70, [1970] OJ L 142/24, and Art 1, Directive 75/34. [1975] OJ L 14/10.

[4] Art 1(2) of Directives 90/364 and 90/365 ([1990] OJ L 180/26 and 28), and Art 1 of Directive 93/96 ([1993] OJ L 317/59).

[5] Art 1(2) of Directive 64/221 ([1964] OJ 56/850). The prior legislation is discussed in more detail in the commentary on Arts 2(2) and 3(2), below.

regards: visas (Article 5(2), in Chapter II); the right of residence (Article 7(1)(d), (2), and (4), in Chapter III); administrative formalities (Articles 9–11 and 20, in Chapters III and IV); their status after the end of a family relationship (Articles 12 and 13, in Chapter III); and permanent residence (Articles 16(2), 17(3) and (4), and 18, in Chapter IV). Also, the 'abuse of rights' provision (Article 35, in Chapter VII) largely concerns the status of third-country national family members.

D. Other relevant rules

First of all, although the definition of EU citizens—the most important definition as regards the personal scope of the citizens' Directive—is referred to in Article 2(1) of this Directive, the main source of this definition is Article 20 TFEU.[6] Similarly, the key issue as regards the territorial scope of the legislation—its limitation to cases where EU citizens have moved between Member States—is linked to EU citizens' right to move and reside freely, as set out in Article 21 TFEU.[7] Moreover, the CJEU's interpretation of each of these Treaty provisions has resulted in the creation of categories of EU citizens and/or their family members who derive rights from the Treaty which do not fall within the scope of the Directive, even though in some respects at least these rights are comparable to those in the Directive.[8] Furthermore, the children of EU citizen migrant workers and their parent carers also derive rights similar to those in the Directive from a separate legislative act, a Regulation on the free movement of workers.[9] Finally, these provisions of the citizens' Directive are also linked to the EU–Turkey association agreement, which must be interpreted in accordance with EU free movement law,[10] and to EU immigration law, most notably Directive 2003/86 on family reunion for third-country nationals and Directive 2003/109 on the rights of long-term residents.[11]

E. Analysis—Article by Article

Article 1—Subject

This Directive lays down:

(a) the conditions governing the exercise of the right of free movement and residence within the territory of the Member States by Union citizens and their family members;

---

[6] See further the commentary on Art 2(1) below.
[7] See further the commentary on Art 3(1) below.
[8] See further the commentary on Art 3(1) below.
[9] See further the commentary on Art 12(3) below.
[10] See, for instance, Case C-451/11 *Dülger*, judgment of 19 July 2012, not yet reported.
[11] Respectively [2003] OJ L 251/12 and [2004] OJ L 16/44. On the links with the citizens' Directive, see respectively Joined Cases C-356/11 and C-357/11 *O and S*, judgment of 6 December 2012, not yet reported, and Case C-40/11 *Iida*, judgment of 8 November 2012, not yet reported, both discussed in the commentary on Art 3(1) below.

(b) the right of permanent residence in the territory of the Member States for Union citizens and their family members;

(c) the limits placed on the rights set out in (a) and (b) on grounds of public policy, public security or public health.

Unlike the first provisions of some EU legislation, Article 1 of the citizens' Directive is a straightforward description of the content of the Directive, and so does not appear to add anything to its interpretation. Article 1(a) corresponds to the provisions of chapter III of the Directive; Article 1(b) corresponds to the provisions of chapter IV of the Directive; and Article 1(c) corresponds to the provisions of chapter VI of the Directive. The CJEU has only briefly mentioned Article 1, and did not draw any significant conclusions from its wording.[12] It is hard to imagine that it ever would do.

Article 2—Definitions

For the purposes of this Directive:

(1) 'Union citizen' means any person having the nationality of a Member State;

Although the Directive does not refer to this expressly, Union citizenship is defined in the EU's primary law, namely, the Treaties. While the definition of EU citizenship does not therefore stem from the citizens' Directive, nevertheless this definition is of obvious primordial importance to the Directive, and so should be considered in some detail in that specific context. There are three separate, but closely connected issues here: (a) the acquisition and loss of EU citizenship; (b) mutual recognition of national citizenship decisions; and (c) the position of dual citizens, either of two Member States or of a Member State and a third State. Due to its close connection with Article 3(1) of the citizens' Directive, concerning its territorial scope (ie the need to move between Member States in order for the Directive to apply), the position of persons who are dual citizens of two Member States is considered as part of the commentary on that provision.

Acquisition and loss of EU citizenship

The starting point is Article 9 TEU, which states that:

Every national of a Member State shall be a citizen of the Union. Citizenship of the Union shall be additional to and not replace national citizenship.

Article 20(1) TFEU then essentially repeats these provisions, with the addition of the statement that 'Citizenship of the Union is hereby established'. Article 20(2) TFEU then lists the rights of EU citizens, and Articles 21–25 TFEU elaborate

---

[12] Case C-434/09 *McCarthy* [2011] ECR I-3375, paras 33 and 36, noting simply that Art 1(a) sets out 'conditions' for the exercise of free movement rights, and that the Directive applies only where free movement has taken place. See also Joined Cases C-424/10 and C-425/10 *Ziolkowski and Szeja*, judgment of 21 December 2011, not yet reported, para 36.

further upon these rights.[13] When the formal legal concept of EU citizenship was first introduced into the Treaties, in the original Treaty on European Union (known generally as the Maastricht Treaty), the Member States' representatives attached the following declaration to that Treaty:

> The Conference declares that, wherever in the Treaty establishing the European Community reference is made to nationals of the Member States, the question whether an individual possesses the nationality of a Member State shall be settled solely by reference to the national law of the Member State concerned. Member States may declare, for information, who are to be considered their nationals for Community purposes by way of a declaration lodged with the Presidency and may amend any such declaration when necessary.

Furthermore, a decision of the Heads of State and Government of the Member States, meeting within the European Council, adopted a Decision in 1992, concerning certain problems raised by Denmark as regards ratification of the TEU ('the Edinburgh Decision'). This Decision stated that the Treaty rules on EU citizenship give Member States' nationals 'additional rights and protection', but they 'do not in any way take the place of national citizenship', and again, '[t]he question whether an individual possesses the nationality of a Member State will be settled solely by reference to the national law of the Member State concerned'.[14] The notion that States are entirely competent to define their own nationals is also rooted in international law.[15]

The possession of the nationality of a Member State raises issues of how such nationality can be acquired or lost, and the loss of nationality can be either involuntary or voluntary (ie by means of denunciation). Since the issue of denunciation of nationality is linked to the CJEU case law relating to dual citizens of two Member States, it is considered separately below.[16]

The first ruling of the Court of Justice on nationality issues was *Micheletti*.[17] In this case, one Member State's authorities were reluctant to recognize the nationality of another Member State which Mr Micheletti had acquired, given that he was also (and initially) a national of a third State. The CJEU started by recognizing that '[u]nder international law, it is for each Member State, *having due regard to Community law*, to lay down the conditions for the acquisition and loss of nationality'.[18] While in principle this ruling was consistent with the declaration attached to the TEU (which had been signed and was being ratified at the time of the *Micheletti* judgment, although the Edinburgh Decision had not yet been

---

[13] On the right to move and reside freely in particular, see further the commentary on Art 3(1) below. On the citizenship provisions in the Treaty generally, see the introduction.

[14] [1992] OJ C 348/1.

[15] See Art 3(1) of the Council of Europe Convention on Nationality.

[16] See the commentary on Art 3(1) below.

[17] Case C-369/90 [1992] ECR I-4239.

[18] Case C-369/90 [1992] ECR I-4239, para 10 (emphasis added).

adopted), the CJEU left the door slightly ajar for possible scrutiny of Member States' nationality laws, by hinting that Community (now EU) law might place some constraints on national sovereignty, rather than confirming that nationality was determined 'solely' by national law.

However, it took nearly twenty years before the Court began to elaborate on such constraints. In the meantime, in the judgment in *Kaur*, the Court strengthened the principle that Member States could define their own nationals, referring to a 'principle of customary international law' to this effect, in accordance with which the UK has 'defined several categories of British citizens whom it has recognised as having rights which differ according to the nature of the ties connecting them to the United Kingdom'. The rights of these persons were defined in a declaration to the UK's Treaty of Accession, which was updated later following changes in British nationality law, but other Member States 'were fully aware of its content and the conditions of accession were determined on that basis', and that declaration did not deprive anyone of any EU law rights, for '[t]he consequence was rather that such rights never arose in the first place for such a person'.[19]

This judgment proved to be the high-water mark of national control over nationality law in the Court's jurisprudence. More recently, in the case of *Rottmann*, the Court began to outline the limits to such national control, as regards a person who (unlike Ms Kaur) *had* enjoyed the status of EU citizenship, but then was deprived of it.[20] Mr Rottmann was an Austrian citizen and resident by birth, who later moved to Germany following the start of an investigation against him for serious fraud. He applied for and obtained German nationality, with the result that he lost Austrian nationality. But once the German authorities found out about the previous proceedings in Austria, which Mr Rottmann had not disclosed to them, they began the process of withdrawing his German nationality; and it did not appear that he met the criteria for the reacquisition of Austrian nationality either.

The CJEU began by agreeing that in line with the declaration to the TEU and the Edinburgh Decision, Member States had competence to determine who their nationals were. However, even if a matter falls within national competences, the exercise of those competences must have due regard to EU law. In this case, the 'situation of' an EU citizen who 'is faced with a decision withdrawing his naturalisation, adopted by the authorities of one Member State, and placing him, after he has lost the nationality of another Member State that he originally possessed, in a position capable of causing him to lose the status' of EU citizenship conferred by the Treaties 'and the rights attaching thereto falls, by reason of its nature and its consequences, within the ambit of European Union law'. Therefore the CJEU could rule on the 'conditions in which a citizen of the Union may, because he loses his nationality, lose his

---

[19] Case C-192/99 [2001] ECR I-1237, paras 19–27.
[20] Case C-135/08 [2010] ECR I-1449.

status of citizen of the Union and thereby be deprived of the rights attaching to that status'. While the obligation for national law in this area to have due regard to EU law 'does not compromise the principle of international law previously recognised by the Court' that Member States 'have the power to lay down the conditions for the acquisition and loss of nationality', it 'enshrines the principle that, in respect of citizens of the Union, the exercise of that power, in so far as it affects the rights conferred and protected by the legal order of the Union', such as 'in particular' a withdrawal of naturalization as in the *Rottmann* case, 'is amenable to judicial review carried out in the light of [EU] law'.[21]

In Mr Rottmann's case, a withdrawal of nationality due to deception could be compatible with EU law, since it was in the 'public interest' and 'it is legitimate for a Member State to wish to protect the special relationship of solidarity and good faith between it and its nationals and also the reciprocity of rights and duties, which form the bedrock of the bond of nationality'. Withdrawal of nationality on such grounds was provided for by international law, in particular the 1961 Convention on the Reduction of Statelessness and the European Convention on Nationality. It was therefore up to the national court to determine the proportionality of the decision in light of national and EU law. On this point, the national court had to 'take into account the consequences that the decision entails for the person concerned and, if relevant, for the members of his family' as regards the loss of EU citizenship rights, assessing 'in particular, whether that loss is justified in relation to the gravity of the offence committed by that person, to the lapse of time between the naturalisation decision and the withdrawal decision and to whether it is possible for that person to recover his original nationality'. While EU law did not ban the withdrawal of nationality before the person concerned obtained again his original nationality, the national court had to consider whether 'the principle of proportionality requires the person concerned to be afforded a reasonable period of time in order to try to recover the nationality of his Member State of origin'.[22] Finally, the Court made clear that 'the principles stemming from this judgment' as regards the effect of EU law on national powers in the area of nationality law 'apply both to the Member State of naturalisation and to the Member State of the original nationality'.[23]

What is the impact of the *Rottmann* judgment? First of all, as for the scope of the judgment, it did not seem to be relevant in this case that Mr Rottmann had previously exercised free movement rights; the Court referred to the loss of EU citizenship status in principle, not to the particular impact upon people who had moved within the EU pursuant to Article 3(1) of the citizens' Directive or other provisions of EU law.

---

[21] Paras 39–48 of the judgment.
[22] Paras 50–59 of the judgment.
[23] Paras 60–63 of the judgment.

However, the wide scope of the judgment was narrowed by the Court's finding that the initial acquisition of national citizenship fell outside the scope of EU law, distinguishing *Rottmann* from *Kaur* because Mr Rottmann had enjoyed EU citizenship rights, whereas Ms Kaur had never done so because she had never met the criteria for holding a Member State's nationality.[24] But it is clear from the judgment that EU law *can* apply to the *re*-acquisition of nationality in circumstances like those in the *Rottmann* case.[25] Also, while it seems prima facie that EU law would not be triggered unless the person concerned was being left stateless, logically it must also follow that EU law would apply where a person lost the citizenship of a Member State but still retained the nationality of a third State, because he or she would still be losing the status of EU citizenship in that case. While it might seem, conversely, that EU law would *not* be triggered if a person lost the citizenship of a Member State but still retained the nationality of *another Member State*, that conclusion may need to be reconsidered in light of the Court's case law on dual citizens of two Member States (see the commentary on Article 3(1) below).

Where EU law does apply to the loss or reacquisition of citizenship, what substantive and procedural rules apply? Substantively, the Court accepts that the loss of citizenship can be justified on 'public interest' grounds such as deception, subject to the application of the principle of proportionality. The Court did not indicate how the public interest should be weighted as compared to the individual interest in retaining EU citizenship in this particular case. While the Court confirmed its analysis in *Rottmann* by reference to the Council of Europe Convention on Nationality and the 1961 Convention on the Reduction of Statelessness, it should be noted that the former Convention has been ratified by fewer than half of the Member States,[26] and only a slim majority of Member States have ratified the latter.[27] In fact, twelve Member States have not ratified either treaty.[28] So the reliance upon the text of these treaties will in some cases be problematic, except to the extent that they reflect customary international law. Furthermore, there are

---

[24] Para 49 of the judgment.

[25] This would mean that EU law would impose obligations beyond those set out in Art 9 of the Council of Europe Convention on Nationality, which requires State parties to 'facilitate, in the cases and under the conditions provided for by its internal law, the recovery of its nationality by former nationals who are lawfully and habitually resident on its territory'. For one thing, this residence requirement is highly suspect from the perspective of EU free movement law.

[26] Twelve Member States have ratified this Convention: Austria, Bulgaria, the Czech Republic, Denmark, Finland, Germany, Hungary, the Netherlands, Portugal, Romania, Slovakia, and Sweden. Eight Member States have signed the Convention: Croatia, France, Greece, Italy, Latvia, Luxembourg, Malta, and Poland.

[27] Sixteen Member States have ratified this Convention: Austria, Bulgaria, Croatia, the Czech Republic, Denmark, Finland, Germany, Hungary, Ireland, Latvia, the Netherlands, Portugal, Romania, Slovakia, Sweden, and the UK. One Member State has signed the Convention (France).

[28] These are: Belgium, Cyprus, Estonia, France, Greece, Italy, Lithuania, Luxembourg, Malta, Poland, Slovenia, and Spain.

differences between the text of the two treaties as regards loss of nationality (the 1961 Convention makes it easier to deprive a person of nationality as a result of periods abroad, and easier to make a person stateless), which could be relevant as regards the four Member States which have ratified the 1961 Convention but not the Council of Europe Convention.[29] It might also be questionable whether some of the other provisions of these Conventions on the loss of nationality are compatible with EU law, in particular the provisions for the loss of nationality as a result of periods abroad.[30]

Finally, procedurally, there is an obligation to ensure the possibility of judicial review of decisions which withdraw the nationality of a Member State which had been acquired by an EU citizen, in proceedings like those in the *Rottmann* case, but the Court did not elaborate on any of the specific procedural rights that this would entail. Since the decision falls within the scope of EU law, then Article 47 of the EU Charter of Fundamental Rights would apply, and logically Article 41 of the Charter would require Member States to apply minimum standards as regards the administrative procedure concerned.[31] In any event, the Council of Europe Convention on Nationality provides for some procedural rights.[32]

Mutual recognition

As we have seen, EU law has made some modest inroads into the principle that Member States can define their own nationals. As for the obligation to recognize the nationality granted by other Member States, international law requires that in principle such recognition should be granted, but admits for exceptions.[33] But the effect of EU law on this issue is more sweeping, for EU law requires absolute mutual recognition, with no exceptions whatsoever.

Again the starting point is the *Micheletti* judgment.[34] Having referred to the general competence of Member States to define their nationality laws, the Court stated that 'it is not permissible for the legislation of a Member State to restrict the effects of the grant of the nationality of another Member State by imposing an additional condition for recognition of that nationality with a view to the exercise of the fundamental freedoms provided for in the Treaty'. For instance, they could not impose,

---

[29] These Member States are Croatia, Ireland, Latvia, and the UK.

[30] See also the 'mutual recognition' section below.

[31] While Art 41 of the Charter appears to apply to EU institutions only, the Court of Justice has ruled that it also applies to national administrations when they apply EU law: Case C-277/11 *MM*, judgment of 22 November 2012, not yet reported.

[32] Arts 10–13 of that Convention.

[33] See Art 3(2) of the Council of Europe Convention on Nationality: the citizenship of each State 'shall be accepted by other States in so far as it is consistent with applicable international conventions, customary international law and the principles of law generally recognised with regard to nationality'.

[34] Case C-369/90 [1992] ECR I-4239, paras 10–14.

for the purpose of recognizing another Member State's nationality, 'a condition such as the habitual residence of the person concerned in the territory of the first Member State'. If such conditions were permitted, 'the consequence... would be that the class of persons to whom' EU free movement law 'applied might vary from one Member State to another'. Once the person concerned has produced the documents referred to in EU legislation to establish the nationality of a Member State, 'the other Member States are not entitled to challenge that status on the ground that the persons concerned might also have the nationality of a non-member country which, under the legislation of the host Member State, overrides that of the Member State'. Although the issue in *Micheletti* was Mr Micheletti's intention to carry out self-employed activities in a Member State, logically this reasoning must apply by analogy to the position of family members of dual citizens under the citizens' Directive.

Although this case concerned a dual citizen of a Member State and a non-Member State, it is clear from the subsequent *Chen* judgment that the absolute obligation to recognize another Member State's grant of nationality arises also as regards persons with the nationality of a single Member State. In this case, the Court expressly concluded that the UK was not 'entitled to refuse nationals of other Member States... the benefit of a fundamental freedom upheld by Community law merely because their nationality of a Member State was in fact acquired solely in order to secure a right of residence under Community law for a national of a non-member country'.[35]

It can be deduced from these judgments that the EU law rule relating to mutual recognition of nationality of Member States is surprisingly simple, since there are no exceptions from this obligation whatsoever.[36] Unfortunately, the same cannot be said of our next subject—dual citizens—where the case law is rather more complex.

Dual citizens

As noted already, there are two separate categories of dual citizens:[37] those with the nationality of two Member States, and those with the nationality of a Member State and a third State. The former category is discussed as part of the commentary on Article 3(1), because of its close connection with the rule that the Directive only applies where people have moved between Member States, although it should

---

[35] Case C-200/02 [2004] ECR I-9925, para 40.

[36] The opinion in the *Chen* case, at para 37, raised (but did not answer) the question of whether EU law would accept the principle of international law that nationality does not have to be recognized in the absence of a 'real and effective link' with the State of nationality. With great respect, the *Micheletti* judgment indisputably ruled out any such condition.

[37] As regards persons with more than two nationalities, the following analysis applies *mutatis mutandis*.

be pointed out at this stage that, in accordance with the *Micheletti* judgment, the absolute obligation of mutual recognition applies and Member States cannot simply disregard one of the two nationalities held by the person concerned.[38]

Regarding the latter category, it follows from the Court's approach to mutual recognition of Member States' nationality in the *Micheletti* case that the legal position is straightforward—if, as in that case, the person concerned seeks to rely on the nationality of a Member State to invoke his or her EU citizenship rights.[39] This will normally arise where the person concerned has the nationality of a third State and of the *host* Member State, where the host Member State treats its own nationals worse than citizens of other Member States (known in practice as 'reverse discrimination') *or* nationals of third States.[40] In the judgment in *Mesbah*, the Court ruled that a dual citizen of Belgium and Morocco who was resident in Belgium could not rely on his Moroccan nationality to claim benefits that would derive from the EU–Morocco association agreement.[41] The Court distinguished *Micheletti* on the ground that in this case, the person concerned was a national of the host Member State, not another Member State, and sought to rely on his third-country nationality. Also, the person concerned was not seeking to exercise a free movement right, but rather, to obtain social security benefits. However, in the later *Kahveci* judgment,[42] the Court drew a distinction between the EU–Morocco agreement and the EU–Turkey agreement, which aimed 'to improve, in the social field, the treatment accorded to Turkish workers and members of their families with a view to achieving gradually freedom of movement'. So as regards that agreement, dual citizens of Turkey and the host Member State could rely on their Turkish nationality if they chose. Therefore it appears that the dual citizens concerned must have the choice to rely on their third-country nationality when the agreement concerned aims to establish a free movement regime like that in the Treaties (the EEA and the EU–Swiss treaty on free movement of persons would also meet this condition). However, the Court of Justice has not yet ruled on whether dual citizens could rely upon EU immigration and asylum law, or whether there would be some limit on the possibility of the persons concerned to 'cut and paste' the benefits relating from their two nationalities. It should follow that to facilitate accomplishing the Union's objective of creating an area of freedom, security, and justice, dual citizens should be able to rely on their third-country nationality if that would confer more benefits pursuant to EU immigration and asylum law; and that a 'cut and paste' should be permitted where such a practice would facilitate the achievement of one or both of the objectives of the different legal rules concerned.

---

[38] See Case C-148/02 *Garcia Avello* [2003] ECR I-11613, para 28.
[39] See, for instance, Case C-122/96 *Saldanha* [1997] ECR I-5325,
[40] For fuller analysis, see the commentary on Art 3(1) below.
[41] Case C-179/98 [1999] ECR I-7955.
[42] Joined Cases C-7/10 and C-9/10, judgment of 29 March 2012, not yet reported.

(2) 'Family member' means:

    (a) the spouse;

    (b) the partner with whom the Union citizen has contracted a registered partnership, on the basis of the legislation of a Member State, if the legislation of the host Member State treats registered partnerships as equivalent to marriage and in accordance with the conditions laid down in the relevant legislation of the host Member State;

    (c) the direct descendants who are under the age of 21 or are dependants and those of the spouse or partner as defined in point (b);

    (d) the dependent direct relatives in the ascending line and those of the spouse or partner as defined in point (b);

Article 2(2) is explained further by recital 5 in the preamble, which states that '[t]he right of all Union citizens to move and reside freely within the territory of the Member States should, if it is to be exercised under objective conditions of freedom and dignity, be also granted to their family members, irrespective of nationality. For the purposes of this Directive, the definition of "family member" should also include the registered partner if the legislation of the host Member State treats registered partnership as equivalent to marriage.'

First of all, it should be noted that the family members listed in Article 2(2) ('core family members') are not the only family members falling within the scope of the Directive. Article 3(2), discussed below, lists other categories of family members ('extended family members'). But the key distinction between the family members listed in Article 2(2) and those listed in Article 3(2) is that Member States must admit to their territory those family members falling within the scope of Article 2(2), but have a degree of discretion over whether to admit those listed in Article 3(2).[43] Furthermore, Article 7(4) provides that in the case of students, as defined in Article 7(1)(c), only the spouse, the registered partner provided for in Article 2(2)(b), and dependent children shall have the right of residence. For students, the admission of the dependent direct relatives in the ascending lines of the student and his or her spouse of partner is subject instead to Article 3(2).[44]

As noted already, there were precursors to Article 2(2) in the previous free movement legislation. In particular, the Regulation on free movement of workers provided that 'irrespective of their nationality', the worker's spouse, their descendants who were dependants or under 21, and the 'dependent relatives in the ascending line of the worker and his spouse' had 'the right to install themselves with a worker'.[45] The admission of these persons was subject to an accommodation requirement: the worker had to 'have available for his family housing considered normal for

---

[43] See particularly Case C-83/11 *Rahman*, judgment of 5 September 2012, not yet reported, discussed in the commentary on Art 3(2) below.

[44] As pointed out in the commentary on Art 7(3) and (4) in Chapter 3, this distinction does not apply if a student becomes a worker, or has retained the status of worker.

[45] Art 10(1), Reg 1612/68, [1968] OJ L 257/2.

national workers in the region where he is employed', although this rule was subject to a non-discrimination requirement.[46] The legislation on workers who had ceased their employment applied to the same categories of family members.[47] As for nationals of Member States who were self-employed or providing or receiving services in another Member State, Member States had to 'abolish restrictions on the movement and residence of' the same family members, but the relevant legislation did *not* impose an accommodation requirement.[48] Again, the legislation on self-employed persons who had ceased their economic activities applied to the same categories of family members.[49]

Next, the later legislation governing the free movement rights of other categories of EU citizens applied to a narrower category of family members. For pensioners and self-sufficient persons, spouses, dependent descendants, and dependent ascendants had 'the right to install themselves' with the person holding the right of residence.[50] So there was no such right as regards children under twenty-one who were *not* dependants. For students, the family was defined even more narrowly, to include only the spouse and dependent children.[51] But none of the legislation concerned imposed an accommodation requirement.

As compared to the prior legislation, the citizens' Directive has a single definition of family members applicable to all EU citizens—subject to the distinction for students made in Article 7(4), mentioned above. The accommodation requirement applicable to workers' family members has been abolished, while the category of registered partner has been added (even for students); all EU citizens can bring children under twenty-one, even if they are not dependent (except for students); and dependent family members can include those of either the EU citizen or the spouse or partner (there were variations on the precise wording of this rule in the prior legislation). However, it is now specified that the dependent family members must be in the 'direct' line. Some of these changes must be understood in light of the case law on the prior legislation, discussed further below.

In the legislative process that led up to the adoption of the citizens' Directive, the Commission originally proposed to include a category of 'unmarried partner', subject to some of the conditions (equivalence to marriage, and national conditions) that are set out in the final text of Article 2(2)(b). The Commission also proposed to remove the age and dependency criteria as regards family members in the ascending or descending line, and to admit the family members of students on the same

---

[46] Art 10(3), Reg 1612/68. On the interpretation of this provision, see Case 249/86 *Commission v Germany* [1989] ECR 1263, as well as Case 267/83 *Diatta* [1985] ECR 567, discussed further below.
[47] Art 1, Reg 1251/70, [1970] OJ L 142/24.
[48] Art 1(1)(c) and (d), Directive 73/148, [1973] OJ L 172/14.
[49] Art 1, Directive 75/34, [1975] OJ L 14/10.
[50] Art 1(2), Directives 90/364 and 90/365, [1990] OJ L 180/26 and 28.
[51] Art 1, Directive 93/96, [1993] OJ L 317/59.

basis as the family members of other EU citizens. In favour of these changes, the Commission argued that '[t]he "family group" has been recently undergoing rapid change and more and more people, often with children, are forming "de facto" couples', and some Member States have introduced a 'special status' for 'cohabiting unmarried couples'. Since EU law 'could not ignore this development' as regards the right of residence, unmarried partners should be treated the same as spouses where national law 'provides for unmarried partner status and on the terms of any such legislation'.[52]

In its amended proposal,[53] the Commission clarified that the concept of a partner included persons 'linked by registered partnership or with whom [the EU citizen] has duly attested durable relationship'. But it refused to accept amendments from the European Parliament which would have specified expressly that same-sex marriages were covered on the same basis as opposite-sex marriages, on the grounds that the Directive 'should not result in the imposition on certain Member States of amendments to family law legislation, an area which does not fall within the Community's legislative jurisdiction'. It believed that its proposed amended proposal was an 'equitable solution', since 'it complies with the principle of non-discrimination inasmuch as it requires Member States to treat couples from other Member States in the same way as its own nationals' and 'it allows for a possible change in interpretation in the light of developments in family law in the Member States'.

The Council's common position then restricted Article 2(2)(b) to registered partners (as defined further) only, with the category of duly attested partnerships moved to Article 3(2)(b); it also 'maintained the existing *acquis*' as regards the conditions of age and dependency for ascending and descending relatives, and limited the right to family reunion for students in Article 7(4), 'as in the existing *acquis*' (in fact Directive 2004/38 changed the position for students, as the prior legislation did not expressly include their partners).[54] The Council stated that it could not accept the European Parliament's amendments as regards spouses, on the grounds that it was 'reluctant to opt for a definition of the term "spouse" which makes a specific reference to spouses of the same sex', as 'only two Member States' then had legal provisions for such marriages, and, in the Council's view, the CJEU 'has made it clear that, according to the definition generally accepted by the Member States, the term "marriage" means a union between two persons of the opposite sex'. As regards partners, the Council explained that for either registered or unmarried partners, 'recognition of such situations must be based exclusively on the legislation of the host Member State', and recognition based on other Member States'

---

[52] COM(2001) 257.

[53] COM(2003) 199. The condition in the final Directive relating to those with 'serious health grounds' did not appear at this point.

[54] Common Position 6/2004, [2004] OJ C 54 E/12; see the statement of reasons.

legislation 'could pose problems for the host Member State if its family law does not recognise this possibility'; indeed it could 'create reverse discrimination'.

The definition of family members in Article 2(2) is not the only provision of the Directive relevant to them. There is also the requirement, set out in Article 3(1), and so discussed below, that they have accompanied or joined an EU citizen who has moved to or resided in a Member State other than that of which he or she is a national. Furthermore, Article 7(1)(d) and (2) set out rules relating to the right of residence of family members for more than three months; Articles 8(5) and 9–11 govern the administrative formalities relating to their residence; and Articles 12 and 13 set out rules which apply in the event that the family relationship ends (see Chapter 3). Finally, Articles 16(2), 17(3) and (4), and 18 regulate family members' access to permanent residence status (see Chapter 4). The focus below is on the core definition of family members in Article 2(2), rather than the rules in the rest of the Directive relating to those family members' subsequent residence, although the most significant links with those other rules are discussed where relevant.

The definition of each category of family members will be considered in turn. As a general point, though, it should be noted that Article 2(2) does not impose any condition relating to the family member's link with the EU citizen's free movement rights (besides mere residence), or any condition that the absence of the family member would deter the exercise of free movement rights. So any consideration of these issues is irrelevant in the context of Article 2(2),[55] although it might be relevant for the application of Article 3(2), or as regards the admission of family members pursuant to EU rules which fall outside the scope of the Directive (see the commentary on Article 3(1) below).

Spouse

The first question as regards the definition of 'spouse' is the precise nature of the legal relationship which it describes. The Court of Justice made clear as regards the prior legislation that the concept refers to marriage, and so unmarried couples cannot be regarded as spouses, 'in the absence of any indication of a general social development which would justify a broad construction, and in the absence of any indication to the contrary in the Regulation' on free movement of workers.[56] The issue is now addressed by the specific wording of the citizens' Directive, which refers to 'spouse' on the one hand in Article 2(2)(a), and 'registered partner' and 'partner' in Articles 2(2)(b) and 3(2)(b). So the CJEU has simply followed the wording of the Directive to rule that a partner cannot be regarded as a spouse

---

[55] For the contrary view, see A Tryfonidou, 'Family Reunification Rights of (Migrant) Union Citizens: Towards a More Liberal Approach', (2009) 15 ELJ 634 at 639 and 645.

[56] Case 59/85 *Reed* [1986] ECR 1283, para 15.

pursuant to the Directive.[57] Having said that, the Directive treats registered partners essentially the same as spouses—if a person can be defined as a registered partner in the first place (see the discussion of Article 2(2)(b) below).

A key aspect of the case law on this issue is the principle of non-discrimination on grounds of nationality. Before the adoption of the citizens' Directive, the CJEU ruled in the *Reed* case that if a Member State confers a certain benefit on its own nationals as regards the admission of unmarried partners, this falls within the scope of the Treaty, and so such Member States must apply that rule without discrimination on grounds of nationality to the nationals of other Member States.[58] However, in the case of *Singh*,[59] the Court subsequently stated that the Treaty free movement rules 'do not prevent Member States from applying to foreign spouses of their own nationals rules on entry and residence more favourable than those provided for by Community law',[60] without referring to the non-discrimination rule or distinguishing its judgment in *Reed*. Read literally, the two judgments might suggest that the non-discrimination rule applies as regards unmarried partners, but not as regards spouses, but it is hard to imagine what the logical rationale for such a distinction could be. Moreover, while recital 6 of the citizens' Directive (as regards extended family members, including informal partners) refers to the non-discrimination principle, recital 5 of the preamble (referring to core family members) does not—although of course, secondary legislation cannot amend rules set out in EU primary law.

The practical importance of the non-discrimination principle as regards spouses relates not only to conditions for the admission and residence of spouses (discussed below), but also to cases where a Member State might refuse to recognize the existence of a marriage between the citizen of another EU Member State and another person, even though its own nationals in the same situation would be recognized as married. Surely the discrimination permitted in *Singh*—to the extent that this aspect of that judgment is still good law at all—cannot apply to the question of the *existence* of a spousal relationship (as distinct from the conditions related to entry and residence), since this goes to the heart of the effectiveness of the right of

---

[57] Case C-45/12 *Hadj Ahmed*, judgment of 13 June 2013, para 37. Technically the Court was interpreting Art 13, but it necessarily assumed an interpretation of Art 2(2) as well. The same judgment (at para 51) also repeated the prior ruling that a partner could not be considered a spouse pursuant to Reg 1612/68.

[58] Case 59/85 [1986] ECR 1283, paras 21–29. The Court's judgment focused specifically on the question of whether admission of an unmarried partner constituted a 'social advantage' for a worker, pursuant to Art 7(2) of Reg 1612/68, which is still in force (see further the commentary on Art 24, in Chapter 5). However, the Court's reference to the non-discrimination rule in the Treaty must mean, following the development of EU citizenship, that any EU citizens in another Member State could rely on this rule, whether they are a worker or not.

[59] Case C-370/90 *Singh* [1992] ECR I-4265.

[60] Case C-370/90 *Singh* [1992] ECR I-4265, para 23.

free movement. This point is particularly relevant to those Member States which permit same-sex marriages,[61] for the non-discrimination rule must mean that *as between those Member States*, a citizen of another Member State who has contracted a same-sex marriage under the law of another Member State must be able to insist that the person regarded as his or her spouse under the law of the Member State where that marriage took place must also be regarded as a spouse in any other Member State which recognizes same-sex marriage. It should not matter whether the persons concerned are nationals of the Member State where they were married; and in any event, any restrictions which discriminate on grounds of nationality against other EU citizens as regards *whether* they can get married surely infringe the non-discrimination rules in the Treaties also. As for persons who have celebrated a same-sex marriage in a third State, the Treaties' prohibition of discrimination on grounds of nationality would require the host Member State to recognize such marriages involving citizens of other Member States to the extent that it would recognize such marriages if they involved citizens of their own State.

It might be argued that the negotiation history of the Directive contradicts this interpretation. It is true that, during the negotiation of the citizens' Directive, the Commission stated that persons with 'same-sex marriages' should be treated as partners subject to Article 3(2). But the Commission also indicated that (as noted above), its amended proposal 'complies with the principle of non-discrimination inasmuch as it requires Member States to treat couples from other Member States *in the same way as its own nationals*' (emphasis added). For its part, as noted above, the Council referred to CJEU case law which stated that 'according to the definition generally accepted by the Member States, the term "marriage" means a union between two persons of the opposite sex'.[62] However, this judgment was handed down in 2001, before a number of additional Member States decided to provide for same-sex marriages in their national law, and concerned the interpretation of the EU's Staff Regulations, not the question of whether persons who had celebrated a same-sex marriage in one Member State should be regarded as spouses pursuant to free movement law in another Member State which also provides for such marriages.

The non-discrimination rule also means that Member States cannot apply national rules defining marriage based on the age of the spouses, consanguinity, or any other basis in a more restrictive way to nationals of other Member States as compared to their own citizens.[63]

---

[61] At time of writing, those Member States were Belgium, Denmark, France, the Netherlands, Portugal, Spain, Sweden, and the UK.

[62] Joined Cases C-122/99 and C-125/00 *D and Sweden v Council* [2001] ECR I-4319, para 34.

[63] As regards the age of the spouse, there is no equivalent to Art 4(5) of Directive 2003/86, [2003] OJ L 251/12, which permits Member States to set an age limit of up to twenty-one before they admit spouses.

This brings us to cases of *differences* in national law as regards marriages. Most obviously, what about cases involving persons who have celebrated a same-sex marriage and then seek to move to a Member State which does not recognize the existence of such marriages? It was clearly the intention of the EU legislature, as discussed above, not to require the latter Member States to recognize the existence of same-sex marriages if they did not wish to do so. Given the lack of EU competence over substantive family law (other than the cross-border aspects of such law, pursuant to Article 81 TFEU), this intention must be respected. So in that case, the persons concerned are not 'spouses' in the host Member State; but are they merely 'partners' pursuant to Article 3(2), as the Commission suggests? On this point, a distinction must be drawn between Member States which recognize a concept of registered partnership, pursuant to Article 2(2)(b), and those which do not. As regards the former group of Member States, it best respects the underlying logic of the legislation, and the objective of encouraging free movement, to equate persons who have celebrated a same-sex marriage in one Member State to 'registered partners' in a Member State which recognizes the latter concept, subject to the conditions in Article 2(2)(b), discussed below. For the latter group of Member States, it is only possible to recognize the persons concerned as partners—although the principle of proportionality applicable to Article 3(2) (see the commentary below) will point particularly strongly towards their admission.

As for other differences as regards national laws on marriage, the interpretation of the Directive must respect the distinction between Article 2(2)(a), which refers to spouses without qualification, and Article 2(2)(b), which refers to recognition of registered partnerships pursuant only to the law of the host Member State. While on the one hand, the EU has no competence to harmonize substantive family law, on the other hand the application of different national laws on marriage could obviously constitute a barrier to free movement. To reconcile these different principles, the non-discriminatory application of the host State's laws on marriage should be acceptable in the context of the Directive only if such rules have a legitimate aim, the measures by those laws taken are necessary to achieve that aim, and those laws affect the free movement right as little as possible, provided also that they are compatible with human rights obligations.[64] For instance, it would hardly be proportionate to refuse to consider a person as a 'spouse' because the marriage in question was not celebrated at a place of worship or a registry office, if the host Member State's law insisted upon this but the law of the State where the marriage was celebrated did not.[65] Similarly, established customs such as marriage by

---

[64] See Art 12 ECHR and Art 9 of the EU Charter of Fundamental Rights. On the latter provision, see the analysis by S Choudhury, in S Peers, T Hervey, J Kenner, and A Ward, eds, *Commentary on the EU Charter of Fundamental Rights* (Hart, forthcoming).

[65] If there are genuine doubts as to whether a marriage is legally valid, Art 35 might be relevant: see the analysis in Chapter 7.

telephone should be respected.[66] On the other hand, there is a stronger case on public policy grounds for the application of national laws on consanguinity, at least where the persons concerned are blood relatives. In any event, in such cases of 'kissing cousins', a close relative of an EU citizen is obviously likely to be an EU citizen also, and so is likely to be able to claim a personal right under the Directive. As regards the age of the spouse, this problem will solve itself in time, as there would no longer be a legitimate reason to refuse admission once the spouse concerned reaches the minimum age for marriage in the law of the host State.[67] Indeed, it might be questionable to refuse admission once the spouse has reached the age of sexual consent, although it would certainly be acceptable to refuse admission before that point.[68] Differences in national laws on divorce should certainly not result in the refusal to recognize the status of spouse following a person's remarriage in another State, even if the person concerned could not have been remarried under the laws of the host Member State.

Finally, for the reasons set out in its 2009 guidance on the Directive,[69] the Commission has rightly pointed out that a person cannot be regarded as a spouse pursuant to a forced marriage, and that no Member State recognizes polygamy. In the latter situation, it must follow that only one of the spouses (at a time) can be regarded as a spouse for the purposes of the Directive.[70] The question of what happens when an EU citizen has a spouse and a partner at the same time is discussed below, in the context of Article 3(2),[71] and the issue of sham marriages and marriages of convenience is the subject matter of Article 35, discussed in Chapter 7.

---

[66] The leading British text by D Pearl and W F Menski, *Muslim Family Law*, 3rd edn (Sweet and Maxwell, London, 1998) provides (at p 140) that telephone marriages are accepted in Islamic law, subject to formalities such as the presence of witnesses and the promise of dower (*mahr*).

[67] It should not matter that in some Member States (as in parts of the UK) the persons reaching the minimum age would initially need the consent of their parents to get married. Compare with Art 4(5) of Directive 2003/86, which permits Member States to set a minimum age of up to 21 as regards admission of third-country national spouses, without a requirement that such a rule be non-discriminatory as compared to nationals.

[68] See Directive 2011/93 on sexual offences against children ([2011] OJ L 335/1), relied upon by the CJEU in Case C-348/09 *PI*, judgment of 22 May 2012, not yet reported, discussed further in Chapter 6.

[69] COM(2009) 313.

[70] See expressly Art 4(4) of Directive 2003/86. It might be argued by *a contrario* reasoning that the absence of an equivalent provision in the citizens' Directive means that no limit on admission of multiple spouses in the case of polygamy by EU citizens can be enforced. However, the more likely reason for the distinction between the two Directives on this point is that some third countries permit polygamy, while no Member States do, so it was considered that there was no need to regulate the position of EU citizens who have entered into polygamous marriages expressly. For the opposing point of view, see N Rogers, R Scannell, and J Walsh, *Free Movement of Persons in the Enlarged European Union*, 2nd edn (Sweet and Maxwell, London, 2012), para 9-30.

[71] It is assumed that the national law of all relevant Member States precludes simultaneously being married and having a registered partner.

As regards the end of the marriage relationship, the Court of Justice made clear in its *Diatta* judgment that a marriage 'cannot be regarded as dissolved as long as it has not been terminated by the competent authority'; it must be regarded as continuing where the spouses live separately, even if they intend to divorce.[72] Subsequently the Court assumed that a marriage subsisted until it was fully dissolved by a decree absolute (not merely a decree nisi) of divorce,[73] and that a divorce would in principle terminate the status of spouse.[74] As regards the citizens' Directive, the Court of Justice has confirmed that the *Diatta* judgment continues to apply.[75] The position of (former) spouses following a divorce or annulment is now regulated specifically by Article 13, and the position if the marriage terminates due to the death of the EU citizen is governed by Article 12 (see Chapter 3).[76]

This brings us to the question of whether any conditions can be attached to the definition of 'spouse' in the Directive. While the Court has stated simply that Article 2(2)(a) 'does not require the person concerned to satisfy any conditions other than that of being a spouse',[77] this statement needs to be examined further. The foremost question is whether the spouse may or must be required to live with the EU citizen he or she is accompanying or joining in order to enjoy the right of residence. In the *Diatta* judgment, concerning the prior legislation, the Court of Justice ruled that they did not.[78] Such a requirement could not be implied from the obligation in the prior legislation on free movement of workers (since removed) that the worker needed to have accommodation that was normal for his family.[79] The right of family members to take up work anywhere in the territory also suggested that no residence requirement applied.[80] In its *Iida* judgment, the Court of Justice confirmed that this interpretation applied '*a fortiori*' to the interpretation of 'spouse' pursuant to the citizens' Directive, given that the accommodation requirement for workers' family members had now been rescinded.[81] However, there is a requirement, pursuant to Article 3(1) of the Directive (discussed further below), that the spouse must be resident *in the same Member State as the EU citizen*, otherwise the spouse

---

[72] Case 267/83 [1985] ECR 567, para 20.

[73] Case C-370/90 *Singh* [1992] ECR I-4265, para 12. It should be noted that an EU law applicable to almost all Member States, known as the 'Brussels II Regulation', determines which court has jurisdiction over divorce proceedings (Reg 2201/2003, [2003] OJ L 338/1); and another EU law applicable to a number of Member States, known as the 'Rome III' Regulation (Reg 1259/2010, [2010] OJ L 343/10), defines which law applies to divorce.

[74] Case C-413/99 *Baumbast* [2002] ECR I-7091, para 21.

[75] Case C-40/11 *Iida*, judgment of 8 November 2012, not yet reported, para 58.

[76] See also the discussion of the position of former spouses pursuant to Art 12 of Reg 1612/68 (now Art 10 of Reg 492/2011), in the commentary on Art 12(3) in Chapter 3.

[77] Case C-40/11 *Iida*, judgment of 8 November 2012, not yet reported, para 57. This interpretation can be justified by *a contrario* comparison with the 'conditions' referred to in Art 2(2)(b).

[78] Case 267/83 [1985] ECR 567, para 18.

[79] Art 10(3), Reg 1612/68; see also Case 249/86 *Commission v Germany* [1989] ECR 1263.

[80] Art 11, Reg 1612/68; see now Art 23, discussed in Chapter 5.

[81] Case C-40/11, judgment of 8 November 2012, not yet reported, paras 58 and 59.

could not be regarded as accompanying or joining that citizen.[82] Again, the position of the spouse in the event of the EU citizen's departure from the host State is specifically regulated by the Directive, namely, in Article 12(1) and (3).[83] It follows from the case law that the status of 'spouse' pursuant to the Directive could be regained in relation to the same EU citizen, either if the relevant EU citizen returns to the host Member State or if the relevant spouse moves to the (new) host Member State of the EU citizen.[84]

Next, it is obvious, by *a contrario* comparison with Article 2(2)(c) and (d), that a spouse does not have to be dependent on the EU citizen in order to fall within the scope of Article 2(2)(a). This is confirmed by the right of spouses to take up employment or self-employment.[85] Thirdly, the controversial question of whether spouses had to have resided legally in a Member State before they can rely on the Directive is examined below, in the context of Article 3(1). Fourthly, the Court of Justice has expressly stated that the place where the marriage was celebrated is not relevant.[86]

Registered partner

The starting point for the analysis of the concept of 'registered partner' is the similarities and differences with the concept of 'spouse'. Throughout the Directive, the two concepts are essentially placed on the same footing, as regards 'core' family members of students, the dissolution of relationships, and acquisition of permanent residence.[87] However, the definition of the two concepts is different, reflecting the universal nature of the concept of marriage, on the one hand, and the more selective existence of the concept of registered partnership, on the

---

[82] Case C-40/11, judgment of 8 November 2012, not yet reported, paras 61–65. While that case concerned an EU citizen who left her third-country national husband behind in her *home* Member State, the Court's reasoning is clearly equally applicable to cases where a third-country national spouse is left behind in the (previous) *host* Member State of the EU citizen.

[83] Again, see also the discussion of the position of spouses in this situation pursuant to Art 12 of Reg 1612/68 (now Art 10 of Reg 492/2011), in the commentary on Art 12(3) in Chapter 3.

[84] In the event of death, divorce, or annulment, that status can of course also be regained by marrying another EU citizen, or indeed remarrying the *same* EU citizen (if he or she is still alive!). On the facts of *Iida*, the move by the spouse to the EU citizen's host Member State would trigger the *initial* application of the Directive as regards that spouse, since the spouse had previously been resident in the EU citizen's home State, so the Directive did not apply at all (see the discussion of Art 3(1) below). Equally, on the facts of that case, the return of the EU citizen to her Member State of nationality would *not* trigger the application of the Directive in respect of her third-country national husband, unless he had moved to her host Member State in the meantime (see the discussion of 'returnees', in Art 3(1) below). Arguably the position might be different if the EU citizen had acquired the nationality of another Member State in the meantime, as she would then be exercising free movement pursuant to Art 3(1).

[85] Art 23, discussed in Chapter 5; see Case 131/85 *Gul* [1986] ECR 1573.

[86] Case C-127/08 *Metock* [2008] ECR I-6241, para 98. This may be relevant to the discussion above concerning differences in national law as regards the definition of 'spouse'.

[87] Arts 7(4), 13, and 17(2).

other. In place of the lack of conditionality attached to the concept of 'spouse', the concept of 'registered partner' is subject to three separate conditions: (a) the registered partnership must be 'on the basis of the legislation of a Member State'; (b) the legislation of the host Member State must treat 'registered partnerships as equivalent to marriage'; and (c) 'in accordance with the conditions laid down' in that Member State's relevant legislation. If one or more of these criteria is not satisfied, the relationship concerned could still be regarded as a partnership pursuant to Article 3(2) (see the commentary on that provision below); although as with same-sex marriages, the application of the principle of proportionality which applies to Article 3(2) would point strongly towards admission of the persons concerned.

Taking these conditions in turn, the first condition would certainly be satisfied where a registered partnership has been entered into pursuant to a Member State's national law. As with marriage, it should not matter whether the persons concerned are nationals of the Member State where they obtained a registered partnership; and in any event, any restrictions which discriminate on grounds of nationality against other EU citizens as regards *whether* they can enter into a registered partnership surely infringe the non-discrimination rules in the Treaties also. Arguably, the first condition would also be satisfied where 'the legislation of a Member State' gives recognition to a registered partnership concluded in a *third* State, or treats a same-sex marriage concluded in a third State as if it were a registered partnership.[88] Furthermore, as argued above in the commentary on Article 2(2)(a), a same-sex marriage concluded under the law of a Member State must be treated as if it were a registered partnership in Member States which recognize that concept, if the other conditions set out in Article 2(2)(b) are satisfied.

As for the second condition—the host State must treat registered partnerships as equivalent to marriages—some guidance might be distilled from the CJEU's judgments relating to the EU framework legislation on equality in employment, which includes a ban on discrimination on grounds of sexual orientation.[89] Initially, in the first relevant case, the Court of Justice left it to national courts to determine whether a life partnership under national law was equivalent to marriage; if it was, then not granting an equivalent pension to life partners amounted to discrimination on grounds of sexual orientation.[90] The Court subsequently summarized this

---

[88] Under either interpretation, the State where the registered partnership was entered into would have some relevance, unlike the position as regards marriages: see the discussion of Art 2(2)(a) above.

[89] Directive 2000/78, [2000] OJ L 303/16. For a summary of the relevant case law, see H Graubner, 'Comparing People or Institutions? Sexual Orientation Discrimination and the Court of Justice of the European Union', in K Boele-Woelki and A Fuchs, eds, *Legal Recognition of Same-Sex Relationships in Europe: National, Cross-Border and European Perspectives*, 2nd edn (Intersentia, Cambridge, 2012) 271.

[90] Case C-267/06 *Maruko* [2008] ECR I-1757.

judgment in a way which appears to be directly relevant to the interpretation of Article 2(2)(b) of the citizens' Directive, as follows:[91]

> ...first, it is required not that the situations [of marriage and registered partnerships] be identical, but only that they be comparable and, second, the assessment of that comparability must be carried out not in a global and abstract manner, but in a specific and concrete manner in the light of the benefit concerned. In that judgment, concerning the refusal to grant a survivor's pension to the life partner of a deceased member of an occupational pension scheme, the Court did not carry out an overall comparison between marriage and registered life partnership under German law, but, on the basis of the analysis of German law carried out by the court which made the reference for a preliminary ruling, according to which there was a gradual harmonisation in German law of the regime put in place for registered life partnerships with that applicable to marriage, it made it clear that registered life partnership is to be treated as equivalent to marriage as regards the widow's or widower's pension.
>
> Thus, the comparison of the situations must be based on an analysis focusing on the rights and obligations of the spouses and registered life partners as they result from the applicable domestic provisions, which are relevant taking account of the purpose and the conditions for granting the benefit at issue in the main proceedings, and must not consist in examining whether national law generally and comprehensively treats registered life partnership as legally equivalent to marriage.

Applying this analysis by analogy, for the purposes of Article 2(2)(b) of the citizens' Directive, it is sufficient that in the relevant national law, marriage and registered partnerships are comparable, not necessarily identical, and the comparability should relate specifically to the issue of admission of registered partners pursuant to immigration law, not to issues such as (for instance) whether adoption is permitted for registered partners (if at all) on the same basis as married couples. However, unlike the framework employment equality Directive, Article 2(2)(b) of the citizens' Directive is not, as such, a ban on sexual orientation discrimination, and so if a Member State provides for a form of registered partnership also (or even only) for opposite-sex couples, then such partnerships also fall within the scope of this provision if all of the relevant conditions are satisfied.[92]

Finally, as for the third condition—the recognition must be in accordance with the conditions laid down in national law—it is strongly arguable, in light of the legislative history of Article 2(2)(b) and by analogy with the *Reed* judgment regarding unmarried partners (see the discussion of that judgment in the commentary on Article 2(2)(a)), that the reference to the conditions set by national law is a particular

---

[91] Case C-147/08 *Römer* [2011] ECR I-3591, paras 42 and 43. In the subsequent relevant litigation relating to Directive 2000/78, it has not proved necessary to address this point again (Joined Cases C-124/11, C-125/11, and C-143/11 *Dittrich*, judgment of 6 December 2012, not yet reported; see also C-610/12 *Peter*, pending); but the Court has been asked to address comparability issues again in Case C-267/12 *Hay*, pending.

[92] See also the analysis by H Toner, 'Migration Rights and Same-Sex Couples in EU Law: A Case Study', in K Boele-Woelki and A Fuchs, eds, *Legal Recognition of Same-Sex Relationships in Europe: National, Cross-Border and European Perspectives*, 2nd edn (Intersentia, Cambridge, 2012) 285.

expression of the principle of non-discrimination. This means that host Member States must treat citizens of other Member States, who have a registered partnership pursuant to the national law of other Member States, the same as nationals of their own State who have a registered partnership pursuant to the national law of that State, as regards issues within the scope of the citizens' Directive. Also, Member States must treat their *own* citizens who have registered partnerships pursuant to the law of another Member State the same as they would do if those citizens had entered into a registered partnership pursuant to the laws of their State of nationality—otherwise they would be deterring free movement of the persons concerned, since they would be worse off as a result of moving than they would be if they stayed at home.[93]

In light of this interpretation of Article 2(2)(b), to what extent does the analysis relating to spouses (see section entitled 'Spouse') relate to registered partnerships? On the assumption that no Member State permits a person to have two registered partners simultaneously, or a spouse and a registered partner simultaneously, the analysis regarding polygamy apply *mutatis mutandis*—so there can be only one registered partner at a time for the purposes of the Directive. The position if an EU citizen has a registered partner and an informal partner at the same time is discussed below, in the context of Article 3(2), and the prospect of sham registered partnerships and registered partnerships of convenience is the subject matter of Article 35, discussed in Chapter 7.

As for the end of a registered partnership, this is necessarily defined by each Member State's national law. The deference to national law on this point is reinforced by the absence of EU measures determining which law applies, and which court rules, on the termination of registered partnerships, and by the Commission's distinct proposals on the choice of law and court jurisdiction as regards matrimonial property regimes on the one hand,[94] and the property consequences of registered partnerships on the other hand;[95] the latter proposal provides solely for the application of the law relating to the creation of the original partnership. As with marriages, the position of (former) registered partners following the termination of the registered partnership is regulated specifically by Article 13, and the position if the registered partnership terminates due to the death of the EU citizen is governed by Article 12 (see Chapter 3).[96]

The principle that no conditions can be attached to the definition of spouse obviously cannot be extended to Article 2(2)(b), given the reference to national conditions in that provision, although as explained above, no *additional* conditions

---

[93] See by analogy the commentary on Art 3(1) below, as regards returnees.
[94] COM(2001) 126, 16 March 2011.
[95] COM(2001) 127, 16 March 2011.
[96] See also the discussion of the position of former registered partners pursuant to Art 12 of Reg 1612/68 (now Art 10 of Reg 492/2011), in the commentary on Art 12(3) in Chapter 3.

can be applied to nationals of other Member States (or nationals of the same State) who have contracted a registered partnership in another Member State than are applicable to registered partnerships concluded in the host State. So the host Member State may, if it chooses to, impose conditions of living together, of dependence (although like any family member, the registered partners can take up employment pursuant to Article 23), and of prior lawful residence. Finally, as with spouses, the Directive can only apply in any event as long as the registered partners are resident in the same Member State, without prejudice to the application of Articles 12 and 13 in the event of family breakdown, and the personal acquisition by registered partners of permanent residence status or (for third-country nationals) long-term residence status pursuant to the EU's long-term residents' Directive.

Descending or ascending relatives

Due to their close similarity, Article 2(2)(c) and (d) should be analysed together. They raise two issues: the definition of the family relationships within the scope of the rules, and the meaning of the requirement of dependence (keeping in mind that it does not apply to those under the age of twenty-one).[97] Since there is no reference to other conditions or national legislation (*a contrario* Articles 2(2)(b) and 3(2)), it must be assumed that no such measures apply, so for instance, the family members concerned are not obliged to live with the EU citizens (as long as they are resident in the same Member State, pursuant to Article 3(1)),[98] there can be no requirement of prior lawful residence, and it does not matter if the children or grandchildren of the EU citizen have themselves married—as long as they are dependent or under twenty-one. This is equally true of the family members of registered partners—since Article 2(2)(b) only refers to national conditions relating to the *registered partners*, not to their family members, who are the subject of separate provisions of the Directive. In the event of the death or departure of the EU citizen they are joining or accompanying, or a termination of a marriage or registered partnership (which could be relevant if the family members concerned are the stepchildren or in-laws of an EU citizen), then Articles 12 and 13 apply. The provisions of Article 12 of Regulation 1612/68 (now Article 10 of Regulation 492/2011) could also be applicable for the children of migrant workers, but not any of the other family members within the scope of Article 2(2)(c) or (d), unless it might be argued that a grandparent carer

---

[97] It should also be recalled that pursuant to Art 7(4), students only have the right to bring with them their dependent children. The direct dependent ascending relatives of the students and the spouse or dependent partner fall within the scope of Art 3(2).

[98] Again, Art 23. which is broader in personal and material scope than its predecessors (permitting all family members to seek employment or self-employment; see the commentary in Chapter 5), reinforces this conclusion. So does the abolition of the accommodation requirement which was previously imposed by Art 10(3) of Reg 1612/68.

of a child in education might be covered by those provisions, in the absence of a parent carer.[99]

First of all, the persons within the scope of Article 2(2)(c) obviously include the children, grandchildren et al of the EU citizen and Article 2(2)(d) in turn applies to the parents, grandparents et al of that citizen. Both provisions also apply to the relatives of the spouse or registered partner, as distinct from the Union citizen. This is an obvious point as regards Article 2(2)(d), since if the spouses or partners had the *same* parents, they would necessarily be siblings—and so would have been banned from getting married or becoming registered partners in the first place. The point is more relevant as regards Article 2(2)(c), as it means that step-children of the EU citizen are covered by the rule. In fact, the Court of Justice had confirmed that the prior legislation applied to stepchildren as well.[100] As the Commission pointed out in its 2009 guidance on the Directive,[101] the concept of children should apply to adopted children,[102] minors in custody of a permanent legal guardian, and foster children, depending on the strength of the ties. It should be noted that there is no obligation under Article 2(2)(c) or (d) to admit persons who are the spouses or partners of the relatives referred to therein (for instance, if an EU citizen's child has got married, or his or her father has remarried), although such persons may have a right to entry and residence in their own name (particularly if they are EU citizens), and otherwise could fall within the scope of Article 3(2). The principle of proportionality built into the latter provision would surely point strongly towards admission of the persons concerned, given their close relationship with a person who has a right of entry and residence pursuant to Article 2(2)(c) or (d). There is no requirement that the parents of an EU citizen or his or her spouse must still be married (or that they had to be married in the first place) in order for Article 2(2)(d) to apply. Indeed, if the parents are estranged, it is just as well that there is no requirement for them to live under the same roof as the EU citizen!

Secondly, as for the issue of dependence, it must be recalled first of all that there is no requirement that direct descendants of the EU citizen or spouse or partner who are under the age of twenty-one have to be dependent at all.[103] For those family members who do have to be dependent in order to fall within the scope of the rules, there appears to be no distinction between the concept as it applies in Article 2(2)

---

[99] See further the commentary on Art 12(3), in Chapter 3.

[100] Case C-413/99 *Baumbast* [2002] ECR I-7091, para 57.

[101] COM(2009) 313.

[102] See also Art 4(1)(b)–(d) of the family reunion Directive. Logically, if the EU citizen and/or his or her spouse or registered partner had been adopted, Art 2(2)(d) would also apply as regards their adoptive parents. As regards surrogacy arrangements, the CJEU's upcoming judgments in the pending Cases C-167/12 *CD* and C-363/12 *Z* might be relevant by analogy.

[103] It is clear from the wording of Art 2(2)(c) that this does not only refer to children, but could apply to grandchildren et al as well.

(c) or (d).[104] According to the Court of Justice's interpretation of the previous measures, the concept of dependence does not depend on whether a person has applied for a social assistance benefit (this would undermine the right to equal treatment), or whether there is a maintenance obligation as regards that family member (this would lead to variation in applicability of the EU rules), but rather, the result of a 'factual situation', without any need to determine the reasons for the support or to examine whether the family member *could* support himself or herself 'by means of taking up paid employment'. It is sufficient that the family member is supported by the EU citizen.[105] Furthermore, the family members must be considered dependent if, 'having regard to their financial and social conditions, they are not in a position to support themselves. The need for material support must exist in the State of origin of those relatives or the State whence they came at the time when they apply to join' an EU citizen.[106] This latter rule appears to suggest that the family member's need for support must be judged in accordance with the standard of living in the country where he or she was resident (as of the time of the application to join the EU citizen).[107] The CJEU has already confirmed that this case law concerning the prior legislation still applies to the interpretation of the citizens' Directive.[108]

In summary, the concept of dependence turns on whether the family member needs the support of the EU citizen at the time of applying to join that citizen. The case law clearly assumes that the family member must be dependent *upon the EU citizen*, not other persons, and this raises some questions. The Court has not been asked to rule on how to apply the concept in cases where the family member *could* be supported (in whole or in part) by other persons (most likely other family members), or where the family member *is* being supported by other persons in addition to the EU citizen. On the first question, since the case law specifies that the possibility of the family member supporting himself or herself by employment does not matter, the possibility that the family member could be supported by someone else should not matter either. On the second question, there are three possible approaches: the family member must be supported *wholly*, *substantially*, or *significantly* by the EU citizen. A requirement that the EU citizen wholly support the family member is untenable, since in the normal

---

[104] Compare Case 316/85 *Lebon* [1987] ECR 2811 and Case C-1/05 *Jia* [2007] ECR I-1. It is not clear if the concept of dependence in Art 3(2) is identical, however: see the commentary on that provision below.

[105] Case 316/85 *Lebon* [1987] ECR 2811, paras 16–24, confirmed in Case C-200/02 *Chen* [2004] ECR I-9925, para 43.

[106] Case C-1/05 *Jia* [2007] ECR I-1, paras 34–43, which also discusses the evidential requirements to this end: see further Chapter 3. For further clarification of the latter points, see Case C-83/11 *Rahman*, judgment of 5 September 2012, not yet reported, discussed in the commentary on Art 3(2) below.

[107] See further the opinion in Case C-1/05 *Jia* [2007] ECR I-1, paras 94–96.

[108] Case C-40/11 *Iida*, judgment of 8 November 2012, not yet reported, para 55.

course of events there might be at least a degree of support from the EU citizen's spouse or partner, or from other family members. Of the remaining possibilities, the best approach is to require a significant contribution from the EU citizen. This reflects the obligation to interpret the free movement rules broadly,[109] and is consistent with the case law to the effect that the exercise of an economic activity need not be full time or supply all the income of a worker, but need only be 'genuine and effective'.[110]

While the situation in the event of termination of the family link is addressed, as noted above, by Articles 12 and 13, there is nothing in the Directive which expressly addresses the loss of *dependence* of the family member concerned, either because that person takes up employment or self-employment or because that person becomes dependent upon someone else. If the family member were an EU citizen, such a change in status should not matter in most (if not all) cases, because the EU citizen would have the right to take up economic activities, or to become dependent upon someone else, in their own name.[111] However, if the dependent family member is not an EU citizen, there is an obvious tension between admitting that person on the basis of their dependence on the one hand, and their right to take up employment or self-employment in the host State pursuant to Article 23 on the other hand, considering that (according to the case law) the question of whether they could take up employment is irrelevant when assessing the existence of their dependency. The Court of Justice has been asked to clarify this issue, and in particular: (a) whether a Member State can require a family member to have tried to obtain employment or support, or to have supported himself or herself, in the country of origin, to be considered dependent; and (b) whether it is relevant that family member is well placed to obtain employment in a Member State and intends to do so.[112] As regards dependent family members admitted pursuant to Article 3(2), the Court of Justice has ruled that Article 10 (concerning the issue of residence cards) does not regulate what happens if the person concerned ceases to be a dependant while the application for a residence card is pending.[113] This judgment might be relevant by analogy to Article 2(2)(c) and (d), but in any event is not very helpful, since the issue of a residence card is only declaratory of rights (see Article 25, discussed in Chapter 5), and the judgment does not address what happens if the family member ceases to be dependent after obtaining the residence card.

---

[109] See, in this context, Case 316/85 *Lebon* [1987] ECR 2811, para 23.
[110] See the discussion of Art 7(1)(a), in Chapter 3.
[111] See the analysis of Art 7(1)(a) and (b), in Chapter 3.
[112] Case C-423/12 *Reyes*, pending.
[113] Case C-83/11 *Rahman*, judgment of 5 September 2012, not yet reported; see the analysis of Art 3(2) below.

Finally, it should be noted that the Court has consistently held that an adult cannot be regarded as dependent upon a child for the purposes of Article 2(2)(c) or (d) or their predecessor provisions, where (as is usually the case) the child is dependent (as interpreted by the Court) on the adult, not the other way around.[114]

(3) 'Host Member State' means the Member State to which a Union citizen moves in order to exercise his/her right of free movement and residence.

Article 2(3) is a straightforward definition which does not call for further comment. It is linked to the important question of the territorial scope of the Directive— which is more directly addressed by Article 3(1), to which we now turn.

Article 3—Beneficiaries

1. This Directive shall apply to all Union citizens who move to or reside in a Member State other than that of which they are a national, and to their family members as defined in point 2 of Article 2 who accompany or join them.

While Article 3(1) refers to EU citizens on the one hand, and family members as defined in Article 2(2) on the other hand, the position of the two groups of persons is closely linked and so needs to be examined together. The following analysis of Article 3(1) addresses in turn: (a) the extent of the exercise of free movement needed for the Directive to apply; (b) the question of whether family members need to have resided lawfully in a Member State before the Directive can apply to them; (c) the position of 'returnees', ie EU citizens who leave their Member State of nationality and then return to it; and (d) the position of persons who cannot qualify under the Directive under other provisions of EU law.

The free movement requirement

The CJEU has consistently interpreted the prior legislation, the Treaty provisions on free movement, and now Article 3(1) of the citizens' Directive, to the effect that an EU citizen must move between Member States to fall within the scope of the provisions of the Directive. Much, but not all, of this case law has concerned the position of family members, because there are some Member States with stricter rules on the admission of third-country national family members of their own citizens than the rules applicable pursuant to EU free movement law. As regards family members, the line of case law began with *Morson and Jhanjan*, in which the Court ruled both that the secondary legislation did not apply to the admission of third-country national family members into the territory of the host State, and that the principle of non-discrimination in the Treaty did not apply, since there was no link to EU law.[115] Despite the Court's approach, as noted above, the advantageous

---

[114] Case C-40/11 *Iida*, judgment of 8 November 2012, not yet reported, para 55, confirming Case C-200/02 *Chen* [2004] ECR I-9925, paras 44 and 45.
[115] Joined Cases 35/82 and 36/82 [1982] ECR 3723.

position of family members of EU citizens who move between Member States, as compared to (in some Member States) the rules on the admission of family members of 'static' EU citizens, is often described in practice as 'reverse discrimination'. However, the Court did rule subsequently that persons who left their home Member State to exercise their free movement rights, and then returned to their home Member State later, were covered by EU free movement law even after their return (see the discussion of 'returnees' below).

Initially, the position did not change with the creation of a formal concept of EU citizenship, in the original TEU, as the Court ruled in the case of *Uecker and Jacquet* that EU citizenship was not 'intended to extend the scope *ratione materiae* of the Treaty also to internal situations which have no link with Community law'.[116] Subsequently, though, the Court ruled that at least some categories of EU citizens who had not exercised free movement rights could rely on their *EU citizenship*, instead of free movement law, to assert certain rights for their third-country national family members (see the discussion of 'persons outside the scope of the Directive' below).

This brings us to the position of persons who are dual citizens of two Member States.[117] Initially, the Court of Justice ruled that persons who were nationals of one Member State could rely on free movement legislation against their home Member State as long as they were established in another Member State;[118] holding the dual nationality of the two Member States concerned was apparently immaterial.[119] Subsequently, in the case of *Garcia Avello*,[120] concerning children who were dual citizens of Spain and Belgium who had never left Belgium, the Court ruled that unlike its earlier finding in *Uecker and Jacquet*, there was a link with EU law, since the children were 'nationals of one Member State lawfully resident in the territory of another Member State', and '[t]hat conclusion cannot be invalidated by the fact that the children involved in the main proceedings also have the nationality of the Member State in which they have been resident since their birth and which, according to the authorities of that State, is by virtue of that fact the only nationality recognised by the latter'. Following *Micheletti* (discussed in the commentary on Article 2(1) above), Member States could not restrict the effects of the grant of the nationality of another Member State by imposing an additional condition before recognizing that nationality 'with a view to the exercise of the fundamental freedoms provided for in the Treaty'. Therefore the children could rely on the Treaty rule on non-discrimination on grounds of nationality, as regards discrimination relating to their surname. Applying that rule, there was discrimination because the Belgian law failed to recognize the different situation of dual citizens

---

[116] Joined Cases C-64/96 and C-65/96 [1997] ECR I-3171.
[117] On other issues relating to dual citizens, see the commentary on Art 2(1) above.
[118] Case 115/78 *Knoors* [1979] ECR 399.
[119] Case 292/86 *Gullung* [1988] ECR 111.
[120] Case C-148/02 [2003] ECR I-11613.

of Spain and Belgium, and refusing to allow Spanish citizens to apply the Spanish rules relating to surnames would 'cause serious inconvenience for those concerned at both professional and private levels'.

While the *Garcia Avello* judgment gives the clear impression that dual citizens can rely on their EU citizenship in order to invoke EU free movement law in *either* of the Member States of their nationality (as well as, obviously and incontestably, any *other* Member State), the Court of Justice later took a more restrictive approach. In the *McCarthy* case, concerning a dual citizen of the UK and Ireland who had never left the UK, but sought to rely upon the rules on admission of family members in the citizens' Directive to obtain the admission of her third-country national spouse to the UK,[121] the Court emphasized that the Directive only applies to EU citizens who move from one Member State to another. So, 'so far as the Union citizen concerned has never exercised his right of free movement and has always resided in a Member State of which he is a national, that citizen is not' within the scope of Article 3(1), 'so that that directive is not applicable to him'. Unlike in *Garcia Avello*, this interpretation 'cannot be influenced by the fact that the citizen concerned is also a national of a Member State other than that where [s]he resides', as 'the fact that a Union citizen is a national of more than one Member State does not mean that [s]he has made use of [her] right of freedom of movement'. Since Mrs McCarthy was not within the scope of Article 3(1) (and therefore the Directive), her husband was not either, since 'the rights conferred by that directive on the family members of a beneficiary of that directive are not autonomous rights of those family members, but derived rights, acquired through their status as members of the beneficiary's family' (confirming case law relating to the prior legislation).[122] The Court then went on to assess whether Mrs McCarthy could alternatively derive a right of entry for her husband based on her status as a 'static' EU citizen (see the discussion below), and in this discussion it distinguished the prior *Garcia Avello* judgment, on the grounds that in that case the discrimination in question impeded the exercise of free movement rights, whereas Mrs McCarthy was free to move to another Member State.[123]

Assessing the *McCarthy* judgment, first of all it is necessary to stress that it does not exclude *all* dual citizens of two Member States from the scope of the Directive. Obviously, as noted already, such persons would be within the scope of the Directive if they moved to a *third* Member State, and would remain within it by analogy if they then returned to either of their States of nationality (see the discussion of 'returnees' below). More significantly, perhaps, such dual citizens could bring themselves within the scope of the Directive if they exercised their right of free movement to move to the other Member State of which they hold the nationality,

---

[121] Case C-434/09 [2011] ECR I-3375.
[122] Paras 41–50 of the judgment.
[123] Paras 51–54 of the judgment.

and would remain within it (by analogy) if they returned to their 'original' State of nationality. Although the Court stated that merely holding dual citizenship of two Member States 'does not mean that' the person concerned 'has made use of' his or her free movement rights, the judgment does not expressly state that such persons would *never* fall within the scope of the Directive *even if* they moved to the Member State of their other nationality. This interpretation is confirmed by the prior statement that the Directive does not apply to an EU citizen who 'has never exercised his right of free movement and has always resided in a Member State of which he is a national'. It is only where these *two* criteria are *both* satisfied that the Directive does not apply.[124] The importance of this rule can be seen in the earlier judgment in *Chen*—concerning an Irish baby girl who had always resided in the United Kingdom.[125] The Court held that she was covered by the precursor legislation even though she had never moved between Member States, simply because her only nationality was Irish. So for the purpose of EU law, the baby was exercising free movement rights even before she could crawl.

The distinction drawn by the Court between *McCarthy* and *Garcia Avello* is also, with great respect, utterly unconvincing. As is clear from the summary above, in the latter judgment the Court first of all assessed whether a dual citizen of two Member States who had never moved was within the scope of free movement law—and only then assessed whether the national law in question was a discriminatory impediment to those free movement rights.[126] Indeed, this is logically the only approach

---

[124] This is clear from paras 25 and 26 of the judgment, where the Court specifically referred to the absence of any exercise of free movement rights as regards the Directive or EU citizenship rights; paras 30, 36, 38, and 43, where the Court makes the same point specifically as regards the Directive; and paras 44, 46, and 56, where it makes the point specifically as regards Art 21 TFEU. The operative part of the judgment also refers to the absence of any exercise of free movement rights. While paras 34 and 37 of the judgment make no reference to free movement, referring only to the position of an EU citizen with the nationality of his or her host Member State, the correct interpretation of the judgment is clear if it is read as a whole. It might be argued that the Court implicitly considered that free movement can only be regarded as taking place where the individual is not a national of either State concerned, but this should be rejected in light of paras 26 and 30 of the judgment, where the Court refers to Mrs McCarthy's absence of movement and citizenship of the UK as separate factors. Any attempt to read the judgment more broadly—so that dual citizens of two Member States could *never* exercise free movement rights in either of those States, even if those dual citizens *had* moved between those two States—would not only be inconsistent with the wording of the judgment, but also contradict the Treaty, free movement legislation, and prior case law, creating even more anomalies and reasons for denunciation of nationality than those discussed below. Just because an EU citizen has 'an unconditional right of residence' in the State(s) of his her nationality (para 34 of the judgment), it does not follow that free movement law should not apply where such a person has moved between those Member States—since free movement law also regulates important issues such as recognition of qualifications, admission of family members, and equal treatment for such persons. See by analogy Case C-419/92 *Scholz* [1994] ECR I-505, where a person who had acquired Italian nationality and lost her prior nationality could rely on free movement law against Italy, because she had moved between Member States.

[125] Case C-200/02 [2004] ECR I-9925.

[126] For a contemporary view, see B Hofstotter, 'A Cascade of Rights, or Who Shall Care for Little Catherine? Some Reflections on the *Chen* Case' (2005) 30 ELRev 548 at 542: 'it amounts to

that could be taken: how could a person suffer an impediment to free movement rights unless he or she was exercising (or entitled to exercise) such rights in the first place? The Court's 'recasting' of the *Garcia Avello* case in *McCarthy* as a case about the content of EU citizenship ignores the structure and content of that prior decision, in particular the reference to 'the exercise of the fundamental freedoms provided for in the Treaty' as regards dual citizenship.[127] In an event, the Court's attempt to disguise the subject matter of its prior judgment is soon 'rumbled', since the analysis in *McCarthy* classifies the *Garcia Avello* judgment as a case concerning citizenship rights as regards 'impeding the exercise of her right to move and reside freely within the territory of the Member States', rather than a case of 'depriving [an EU citizen] of the genuine enjoyment of the substance of the rights associated with…status as a Union citizen' (the latter category of case is discussed further below). But this leads us back to the same question, merely with the addition of the word 'citizen': how can a citizen's right to move and reside freely be impeded, unless that citizen is exercising free movement rights, or has the right to exercise them? In short, why must a dual citizen of Spain and Belgium who has never left Belgium be regarded as exercising free movement rights, while a dual citizen of the UK and Ireland who has never left the UK is not?

Even if the focus of the distinction is on the effect of the different measures concerned—which, as explained already, is conceptually flawed—the inability to live with a spouse is surely no less of an impediment than the requirement to hold documents with different names in them. Indeed, Mrs McCarthy might well have been willing to change her name to (say) Mrs Oliver Cromwell, in return for her husband being admitted! And the Garcia Avello family was no more prevented by such measures from moving to other Member States than Mrs McCarthy was prevented from leaving the UK by the restriction on her husband's entry there. In any event, the latter finding is inconsistent with the Court's ruling in the *Carpenter* judgment (discussed below) that the failure to admit the spouse of a British national resident in the UK, and providing services to other Member States, *was* an impediment to his free movement rights.

The result of the *McCarthy* judgment is also hard to defend by way of comparison with the *Chen* judgment. Both the persons concerned are Irish nationals resident in the UK, and neither of them has ever left that State. Why should free movement law still apply to the Irish national who does not have UK citizenship, but not apply to the Irish national who does?

---

a sufficient link with Community [law] if children of a migrant worker, who themselves have never moved between Member States, have the nationalities of two Member States and are resident in one of them'.

[127] See also A Tryfonidou, 'Redefining the Outer Boundaries of EU Law: The *Zambrano*, *McCarthy* and *Dereci* Trilogy' (2012) 18 EPL 493 at 516–517.

This particular comparison implicitly raises a further question. Would a person in the position of Mrs McCarthy be able to trigger the application of the Directive simply by denouncing her British nationality—putting her in exactly the same position as baby Chen? Since it is possible to bring oneself within the scope of EU free movement law by acquiring the nationality of a Member State (cf *Micheletti*), it is hard to see why one should not be able to bring oneself within the scope of EU law by denouncing one's nationality. After all, it is sometimes necessary to renounce a *third* State's nationality when acquiring a Member State's nationality (and the status of EU citizenship, along with actual or potential free movement rights). Why should the denunciation of a *Member State*'s nationality be different in principle, particularly as the Directive even recognizes that sometimes EU citizens lose one Member State's nationality when they acquire another Member State's nationality?[128] It should not be objected that the person concerned has never left a Member State, since it might also be possible for a third-country national to acquire a Member State's nationality (and therefore free movement rights) without ever moving between Member States,[129] and it is clearly possible for a third-country national to obtain derived free movement rights as a family member of an EU citizen without ever moving between Member States.[130]

Of course, there may be constraints on denouncing one's nationality. Article 8 of the Council of Europe Convention on Nationality, a treaty which the CJEU referred to in the context of *involuntary* loss of nationality (see the commentary on Article 2(1) above), provides that each State party must permit its nationality to be renounced, unless the person concerned becomes stateless—which would obviously not happen in the case of a dual citizen who denounced only one of his or her nationalities. However, State parties may optionally provide that their nationals can only renounce that State's nationality if they are 'habitually resident abroad'. Arguably this is consistent with the logic of *McCarthy*, although the rule in question would also be satisfied if the person concerned were habitually resident in a third State, for instance the State of origin of Mrs McCarthy's husband (Jamaica). This would still confer an advantage in that Mrs McCarthy could return from Jamaica to the UK and exercise free movement rights, whereas a British national returning to the UK from a third State would not usually be able to exercise such rights (see the discussion below). If any Member States which have not signed this Convention allow for wider grounds for their authorities to resist denunciation of their nationality, the relevant national law should be set aside to the extent that it hinders the exercise of free movement rights. Indeed, arguably no limits

---

[128] Art 17(2) and (4)(c), discussed in Chapter 4.

[129] For instance, an American citizen with Irish roots, who is resident in the UK when he or she obtains Irish citizenship. Like baby Chen, it is bizarre that someone in this situation, if he or she has never moved between Member States, would then fall within the scope of the Directive, whereas Mrs McCarthy does not.

[130] See the discussion of Case C-127/08 *Metock* [2008] ECR I-6241, in the next section.

on denunciation of a Member State's nationality should be permitted, where such denunciation is the only possible route to exercise free movement rights.

Assuming that the *McCarthy* judgment remains good law, it also means that if Mrs McCarthy's husband had been resident pursuant to national law, the Directive would not apply as regards (for instance) equal treatment rights and access to permanent residence.[131] If Mrs McCarthy then moved to another Member State with her husband, they would both then be covered by free movement law,[132] although he would not be covered by free movement law if she left him behind in the UK and exercised such rights by herself.[133]

If a dual citizen of two Member States who had (unlike Mrs McCarthy) moved between those two Member States then lost the nationality of one of those States, then he or she should logically still be treated as a 'returnee' (see the discussion below) even if he or she now only held the nationality of the Member State where he or she was currently resident.[134]

Next, while most discussion of Article 3(1) of the citizens' Directive (and of the equivalent provisions of the Treaties and of the predecessor legislation) is the requirement of a move *between two Member States*, it should be noted that Article 3(1) still applies if the national of one Member State moves to another Member State from a *third* (ie non-EU) State. There is no express requirement in Article 3(1) that the EU citizens' movement or residence 'in a Member State other than that of which they are a national' must come 'from a Member State', and no such requirement should be inferred, even if the EU citizen has spent most or all of his or her life resident in one or more third States. There are many EU citizens (or their parents) who, at least at some point in their lives, reside in a third State, for work, study, or other reasons, and there is no reason why this should disqualify them from exercising rights under the citizens' Directive, as long as they are in a Member State other than that of their nationality. The case law of the Court of Justice has assumed and stated as much.[135] However, for a dual citizen of two Member States who has not moved between either of them, a move to a third State and back to the *same*

---

[131] See the discussion of Art 16 of the Directive in Chapter 4, as regards the requirement that family members spend a period of five years' legal residence on the territory *pursuant to the Directive* to obtain permanent residence status.

[132] Or they could move directly to another Member State to exercise free movement rights; as discussed below, there is no requirement for 'prior lawful residence' in a Member State for her husband in that case.

[133] See the discussion below of Case C-40/11 *Iida*, judgment of 8 November 2012, not yet reported.

[134] See by way of comparison the discussion above (in the commentary on Art 2(1)) of the judgment in Case C-135/08 *Rottmann* [2010] ECR I-1449.

[135] See Case C-369/90 *Micheletti* [1992] ECR I-4239 and Case C-138/02 *Collins* [2004] ECR I-2703. In Case C-127/08 *Metock* [2008] ECR I-6241, the Court stated simply (at para 49) that 'as regards family members of a Union citizen, no provision of Directive 2004/38 makes the application of the directive conditional on their having previously resided in a Member State'.

Member State would not be enough to trigger the application of the Directive, following the logic (such as it is) of the *McCarthy* judgment.[136] Also, an EU citizen would not in principle be covered by other relevant EU measures, such as the rules on social security coordination, on the basis of stays in a third State, except where there are treaty arrangements on this issue between the EU and the third state in question.[137]

It should be emphasized that when an EU citizen moves to another Member State for the first time, any family members left behind in that citizen's home State will not be covered by the free movement Directive, for even though the EU citizen has exercised free movement rights, the family member cannot claim to be exercising such rights along with that citizen unless he or she is in the same Member State as that citizen.[138] However, it should be reiterated that the family members need only live in the same *Member State*, not the same *household*.[139] The position if the EU citizen *temporarily* leaves his or her family members behind in a host Member State is discussed in Chapter 3.

Finally, the position of frontier workers (or perhaps 'frontier citizens', as they might be exercising other forms of cross-border activity) is worth considering. The Commission's guidance on the application of the Directive states that frontier workers are covered by the Directive as workers in the host State and as persons with sufficient income in the Member State of residence.[140] But if the person concerned is a national of one of those States, it is arguable that the Directive does not apply to their position in that State. It would only apply, according to the literal wording of Article 3(1), to the Member State in which they are not a national. So since the position of EU citizens' family members is linked to the State of residence of the EU citizen whom they are accompanying or joining,[141] then those family members can only invoke the Directive (as regards the right of entry and residence, access to employment, and other provisions) in that State.[142] In practical terms,

---

[136] See by analogy Case C-40/11 *Iida*, judgment of 8 November 2012, not yet reported, in which it was assumed that the position of a third-country national husband of a German woman who had lived in the United States with him, and then returned with him to Germany, was outside the scope of the Directive.

[137] There might, of course, also be relevant national laws, or treaties between the Member State and the third State(s) in question.

[138] Case C-40/11 *Iida*, judgment of 8 November 2012, not yet reported.

[139] Case 267/83 *Diatta* [1985] ECR 567, para 20, reiterated (as regards the citizens' Directive) in Case C-40/11 *Iida*, judgment of 8 November 2012, not yet reported. See further the commentary on Art 2(2)(a) above. Nor does Art 7, discussed in Chapter 3, require the family members to live together in the same household, because the Directive does not reduce the level of rights set out in the prior legislation and relevant case law (Case C-127/08 *Metock* [2008] ECR I-6241).

[140] COM(2009) 313.

[141] See Case C-10/05 *Mattern and Cikotic* [2006] ECR I-3145 and Case C-40/11 *Iida*, judgment of 8 November 2012, not yet published.

[142] Of course, for those family members who are EU citizens, it may be possible to rely on the Directive as primary right-holders, if they have moved between Member States.

this means that (a) if the EU frontier citizen is resident in a Member State other than that of his or her nationality, his family members can invoke the Directive in that Member State, but *only* in that Member State; or (b) if the EU frontier citizen is resident in the Member State of his or her nationality, the position of his family members is not governed by the Directive directly. However, in the latter case, the position of the family members might be governed by *other* provisions of EU law, or even the Directive by analogy—an issue discussed further below.

The question of prior lawful residence of family members

The early case law of the CJEU on the third-country national family members of EU citizens who moved between Member States paid no attention to the question of whether the family had been formed in the home or the host State. Nor did the Court concern itself with whether those family members were lawfully resident, until 2002, when it appeared to dismiss this issue as entirely irrelevant.[143] However, in the *Akrich* judgment of 2003, concerning a British woman with a Moroccan husband who was not lawfully resident in the UK, who then moved to Ireland with her husband and then sought to return with him to the UK, the Court apparently stated that prior lawful residence in one Member State was a precondition for a third-country national to accompany or join an EU citizen in another Member State, and also that it was a precondition for exercising rights as a 'returnee' to the EU citizen's home Member State.[144] This judgment was both controversial and unclear,[145] and the Court of Justice attempted to clarify and limit it in two further judgments,[146] before finally overturning it entirely in the *Metock* judgment, which concerned a number of third-country nationals who were not lawfully resident in Ireland who had married nationals of other Member States who were living there.[147]

---

[143] Case C-459/99 *MRAX* [2002] ECR I-6591. See also Case C-60/00 *Carpenter* [2002] ECR I-6279, discussed below.

[144] Case C-109/01 [2003] ECR I-9607.

[145] See C Schlitz, '*Akrich*: A Clear Delimitation without Limits' (2005) 12 MJ 241; E Spaventa, case note on *Akrich* (2005) 42 CMLRev 225; A P van der Mei, case note on *Akrich* (2004) 6 EJML (2004) 277; and R White, 'Conflicting Competences: Free Movement Rules and Immigration Laws' (2004) 29 ELRev 385.

[146] Cases C-1/05 *Jia* [2007] ECR I-1 and C-291/05 *Eind* [2007] ECR I-10719. On these cases, see B Olivier and J H Reestman, case note on *Jia* (2007) 3 EUConst 463; D. Martin, case note on *Jia* (2007) 9 EJML 457; A Tryfonidou, '*Jia* or "Carpenter II": The Edge of Reason' (2007) 32 ELRev 908; and M Elsmore and P Starup, case note on *Jia* (2007) 44 CMLRev 787;

[147] Case C-127/08 [2008] ECR I-6241; see also Case C-551/07 *Sahin* [2008] ECR I-10453. On the *Metock* judgment, see E Fahey, 'Going Back to Basics: Re-embracing the Fundamentals of the Free Movement of Persons in *Metock*' (2009) 36 LIEI 83; S Currie, 'Accelerated Justice or a Step Too Far? Residence Rights of Non-EU Family Members and the Court's Ruling in *Metock v Minister for Justice, Equality and Law Reform*' (2009) 34 ELRev 310; and C Costello, '*Metock*: Free Movement and "Normal Family Life" in the Union' (2009) 46 CMLRev 587.

In *Metock*, primarily the Court took a literal approach to the Directive, noting first of all that it did not require family members to have lived previously in a Member State, and then pointing out that the definition of 'family members' in Article 2(2) 'does not distinguish according to whether or not they have already resided lawfully in another Member State'. The provisions on entry and residence of family members in Articles 5–7 of the Directive (see Chapters 2 and 3) did not make 'any reference to the place or conditions of residence they had before arriving in that Member State'. In particular, since Article 5(2) made provision for those third-country national family members who did not already have a 'residence card' provided for in Article 10, this showed that the Directive is 'capable of applying also to family members who were not already lawfully resident in another Member State'. Furthermore, the 'exhaustive' list of documents needed to prove family member status, set out in Article 10, 'does not provide for the possibility of the host Member State asking for documents to demonstrate any prior lawful residence in another Member State'. This finding was confirmed by the prior legislation, the citizens' Directive, and case law, and so the 'conclusion [in *Akrich*] must be reconsidered' as '[t]he benefit of such [free movement] rights cannot depend on the prior lawful residence of such a spouse in another Member State'. This interpretation applies *a fortiori* to the citizens' Directive; since recital 3 in the preamble indicates that it aims to 'simplify and strengthen' the relevant legislation, 'Union citizens cannot derive less rights from that directive than from the instruments of secondary legislation which it amends or repeals'.

The CJEU then rejected arguments based on the division of competence between the EU and its Member States,[148] because if EU citizens 'were not allowed to lead a normal family life in the host Member State, the exercise of the freedoms they are guaranteed by the Treaty would be seriously obstructed'. So the free movement provisions of the Treaty could be used to adopt measures on third-country national family members' entry and residence, 'where the fact that it is impossible for the Union citizen to be accompanied or joined by his family in the host Member State would be such as to interfere with his freedom of movement by discouraging him from exercising his' free movement rights in that Member State. If Member States had 'exclusive competence' to control the admission of third-country national family members of EU citizens who have not already resided lawfully in another Member State, then 'freedom of movement of Union citizens in a Member State whose nationality they do not possess would vary from one Member State to another, according to the provisions of national law concerning immigration, with some Member States permitting entry and residence of family members of a Union citizen and other Member States refusing them'. This would infringe the concept of

---

[148] As the Court suggested in para 66 of the judgment, for most Member States (other than the UK, Ireland, and Denmark, due to their opt-outs), the question is rather *which EU competence* applies, since the EU can adopt measures on immigration and asylum pursuant to Arts 77–79 TFEU.

an 'internal market' set out in the Treaties, which implied that the immigration rules for EU citizens moving between Member States 'are the same in all the Member States'. It would be 'paradoxical' if third-country national sponsors could bring in their family members pursuant to the EU's family reunion Directive without being subject to a requirement of prior lawful residence, while such a rule was applicable to EU citizens exercising free movement rights. As to the argument that the absence of a 'prior lawful residence' requirement would undermine immigration control, the Court pointed out that the only third-country nationals who would benefit from the ruling would be those who were family members of EU citizens who exercised free movement rights, and Member States retained the power to reject entry on grounds of public policy, public security, or public health (see Chapter 6) or to control abuses of free movement rights pursuant to Article 35 (see Chapter 7). As to the impact of the judgment on 'reverse discrimination', ie treating 'static' EU citizens worse than those who exercised free movement rights, the Court observed that this issue fell outside the scope of EU law.

Secondly, the Court clarified that spouses of EU citizens could benefit from the Directive 'irrespective of when and where the marriage took place and of the circumstances in which he [or she] entered the host Member State'. Again, none of the relevant provisions of the Directive 'requires that the Union citizen must already have founded a family at the time when he moves to the host Member State in order for his family members who are nationals of non-member countries to be able to enjoy the rights established by that directive'. Also, by referring to family members who 'join' an EU citizen, the EU legislature 'accepted the possibility of the Union citizen not founding a family until after exercising' his or her free movement rights. This was consistent with the purpose of the Directive, since a refusal to admit the EU citizen's family members into the host Member State 'discourage him from continuing to reside there and encourage him to leave in order to be able to lead a family life in another Member State or in a non-member country'. This even applied if the third-country national was resident in the host Member State *before* becoming the family member of an EU citizen, because '[i]t makes no difference' whether the third-country national family members of an EU citizen 'have entered the host Member State before or after becoming family members of that Union citizen, since the refusal of the host Member State to grant them a right of residence is equally liable to discourage that Union citizen from continuing to reside in that Member State'. So the reference in Article 3(1) to family members who 'accompany' the EU citizen 'must be interpreted as referring both to the family members of a Union citizen who entered the host Member State with him and to those who reside with him in that Member State, without it being necessary, in the latter case, to distinguish according to whether the nationals of non-member countries entered that Member State before or after the Union citizen or before or after becoming his family members'. It was still possible for Member States to 'penalise' the third-country nationals concerned for breaching national immigration law before becoming an EU citizen's family member, but this would have to be in compliance with the rules in Article 27 of the Directive on public policy et al (see Chapter 6), or alternatively Member States could impose penalties 'which do not interfere with freedom of movement and residence, such as a fine, provided that they are proportionate'.

The impact of *Metock* is to lift any doubt or ambiguity relating to the effect of the immigration position of third-country nationals upon their status as family members of EU citizens who have exercised free movement rights. In principle, it seems that their previous immigration position is totally irrelevant to their subsequent status, although it has been argued that at least in some cases, the 'abuse of rights' provision in Article 35 could be relevant (see Chapter 7). It should also follow from *Metock* that if an EU citizen leaves his family behind for a short period after moving to another Member State, because, for instance, the EU citizen's job has started there already and he or she is looking for appropriate housing before the family comes, and/or the citizen's children are finishing their school year before moving, the citizen's family members are still covered by the Directive when they move to join him or her in the host Member State. However, the family members' position in the previous country of the EU citizen's residence in the meantime will be subject either to that Member State's national law (if the citizen had not previously exercised free movement rights),[149] to a third State's national law (if the family remains behind in a third State), or to Article 12 of the Directive, on the departure of the EU citizen from the host State (if the citizen *had* previously exercised free movement rights).[150]

The position of returnees

The CJEU has long held that EU free movement law can be relied upon by nationals of a Member State who exercise free movement rights and then return to their Member State of nationality.[151] This also applies to the citizens' Directive, as confirmed first of all (as regards its precursor legislation) in the Court's *Surinder Singh* judgment.[152] In this case, a British citizen with an Indian national husband moved to Germany with her husband to exercise employed activities, then moved back to Britain with him to exercise self-employment. The spouses then separated, with a view to divorce,[153] and the question was whether the third-country national family

---

[149] See Case C-40/11 *Iida*, judgment of 8 November 2012, not yet reported.

[150] See the commentary on Art 12 in Chapter 3. In the first and third scenarios, EU law must surely implicitly require that the citizen be given a reasonable period to move his family members before their immigration status in that Member State is challenged, as otherwise the citizen's free movement rights would be impeded.

[151] See Case 136/78 *Auer I* [1979] ECR 437.

[152] Case C-370/90 [1992] ECR I-4265.

[153] The husband had to be regarded as her 'spouse' until the divorce was completely final: see the commentary on Art 2(2)(a) above.

member could still invoke rights pursuant to EU free movement law, in the EU citizen's home State, given that the citizen concerned had exercised free movement rights (with her family member) and then returned to that State. The CJEU ruled that 'a national of a Member State might be deterred from leaving his country of origin in order to pursue an activity as an employed or self-employed person as envisaged by the Treaty in the territory of another Member State if, on returning to the Member State of which he is a national in order to pursue an activity there as an employed or self-employed person, the conditions of his entry and residence were not at least equivalent to those which he would enjoy under the Treaty or secondary law in the territory of another Member State'. He would be deterred 'in particular ... if his spouse and children were not also permitted to enter and reside in the territory of his Member State of origin under conditions at least equivalent to those granted them by Community law in the territory of another Member State'. So it followed that an EU citizen 'has the right, under' the free movement provisions of the Treaties, 'to be accompanied in the territory' of his or her home State by his or her third-country national family member 'under the same conditions as are laid down by' the free movement legislation which applied at the time. Even though the UK citizen resided in the UK as a matter of national law, the free movement rights granted to EU citizens by Treaty 'cannot be fully effective if such a person may be deterred from exercising them by obstacles raised in his or her country of origin to the entry and residence of his or her spouse', so the third-country national family members of a returnee 'must enjoy at least the same rights of entry and residence as would be granted to him or her under Community law if his or her spouse chose to enter and reside in another Member State', although (as noted above) Member States could always extend to 'foreign spouses of their own nationals rules on entry and residence more favourable than those provided for by Community law'.

The *Surinder Singh* judgment was confirmed in *Akrich*.[154] As regards the position of returnees, *Akrich* first of all confirmed (unsurprisingly) that the *Singh* judgment also applied to persons who had moved to another Member State in order to take up employment, and who now planned to return to their Member State of origin. Secondly, answering the argument that the persons concerned planned to abuse EU law rights, the CJEU stated that the motives which led an EU citizen to obtain work in another Member State were irrelevant,[155] as long as the work carried out there was 'genuine and effective'.[156] However, the impact of this judgment was limited because, as discussed above, it also developed the 'prior lawful residence' rule, which was liable to affect returnees in particular, until it was overturned in *Metock*.

---

[154] Case C-109/01 [2003] ECR I-9607.

[155] In this case, the couple admitted that they had moved to Ireland with a view to moving back to the UK later to regularize Mr Akrich's immigration status.

[156] On that concept, see the commentary on Art 7(1)(a), in Chapter 3; on the concept of 'abuse of rights', see the commentary on Art 35, in Chapter 7.

The most recent judgment on the position of returnees is *Eind*,[157] concerning a Dutch national who had obtained work in the UK, been joined there by his third-country national daughter, and then returned to the Netherlands with his daughter, although he did not obtain work back in the Netherlands. In its judgment, the CJEU extended its prior rulings to cover such a case, on the grounds that an EU citizen might be deterred from going to another Member State to work, if, upon return to his or her home Member State, he or she could not bring family members also, even if he or she were not employed in the latter State. Also, the Court stated more precisely that in this case, the legislation governing the free movement of workers applied 'by analogy', so that the daughter only had rights pursuant to this legislation until she turned twenty-one or for as long as she remained dependent on her father.

Presumably, since the citizens' Directive cannot be interpreted in a more restrictive manner than the prior legislation,[158] the case law on the position of returnees pursuant to that legislation continues to be relevant. So, at the very least, the rights of entry and residence (as set out in Article 3(1)) apply to the family members (as defined in Article 2(2)), but the EU citizen concerned does not have to satisfy the conditions set out in Article 7 upon return to the home Member State. While the cases to date have all concerned EU citizens who exercised economic activities in another Member State before they returned home, there seems no reason, in light of the development of the concept of citizenship of the Union, why the same rule would not apply to any EU citizen who has exercised the right of residence in another Member State pursuant to any of the grounds set out in Article 7.[159]

This brings us to two key questions: the extent of stay in another Member State which would trigger the acquisition of returnee status,[160] and the status of the returnees' family members in the home Member State. On the first point, the answer must surely take account of the case law, which states that it is necessary to avoid deterring EU citizens from exercising free movement rights because of the risk that their family members would not be able to join them in their home State. The best approach, which also reflects the structure of the Directive, is therefore to require that EU citizens must have exercised the right of residence in another

---

[157] Case C-291/05 [2007] ECR I-10719.

[158] See Case C-127/08 *Metock* [2008] ECR I-6241.

[159] See the Opinion in Case C-10/05 *Mattern and Cikotic* [2006] ECR I-3145, para 57, which applies the 'returnee' rule equally to EU citizens who have exercised free movement rights to study in another Member State and then returned to their home State with their family member. Similarly, the CJEU has confirmed that EU citizens who study in another Member State and then return to their home Member State can rely on the principle of equal treatment as citizens of the Union: Case C-224/98 *D'Hoop* [2002] ECR I-6191.

[160] These issues have been raised before the Court of Justice in Case C-456/12 *O*, pending. See also the analysis by G Barrett, 'Family Matters: European Community Law and Third-Country Family Members' (2003) 40 CMLRev 369 at 380–381.

Member State pursuant to Article 7 before they can claim the status of returnees in their home Member State as regards their family members.

On the second point, it should follow from the logic of the Court's previous rulings on the status of returnees that EU citizens would be deterred from exercising free movement rights if their family members could not, upon their return to their home Member State, have access to the benefits of the citizens' Directive as regards equal treatment, access to employment, protection against expulsion, and permanent residence status. This is confirmed by an Advocate-General's opinion on the issue of access to employment for returnees' family members, which argued that 'in order best to guarantee the mobility of a migrant worker—including his right to return to the labour market in his home Member State—and in particular to enable him to maintain his family life, it is necessary to confer on the migrant worker's spouse and children not only rights of entry and residence but also a right to work in the same Member State in which the migrant worker works. Therefore, where the migrant worker returns to the labour market of his home Member State the members of his family must have a right to work there too, under Article 11 of Regulation No 1612/68.'[161]

Finally, it should be noted that presumably an EU citizen who has exercised free movement rights and then returned to his or her home Member State could not then rely on the Directive as regards the admission of his or her family members into the home Member State unless those family members had previously been residing as family members with that citizen during the exercise of his or her free movement rights in the other Member State.

The position of persons outside the scope of the Directive

The first category of persons who are obviously wholly outside the scope of the Directive are those third-country nationals who have no EU citizens in their family at all. Their position might be covered by EU immigration or asylum law,[162] and does not need to be examined further here.

For persons who have EU citizens in their family, the Directive might be inapplicable to them either: (i) more frequently, because they have not exercised free movement rights at all; or (ii) less often, because even though there is a cross-border element to their circumstances, those circumstances still do not fit within the definition of free movement set out in Article 3(1), as discussed above. These two categories will be discussed in turn.

---

[161] Opinion in Case C-10/05 *Mattern and Cikotic* [2006] ECR I-3145, para 48.
[162] See further Peers et al, *EU Immigration and Asylum Law: Text and Commentary*, 2nd edn (3 volumes: Brill 2012–2013).

(i) No exercise of free movement rights

While the majority of such cases will fall wholly within the scope of national law, the Court of Justice has indicated that some of them are affected by the provisions of the Treaties on EU citizenship. This case law calls for some consideration here, even though it does not concern the Directive as such, due to its close link with the interpretation of Article 3(1). The key judgment is *Ruiz Zambrano*, concerning two Colombian nationals in Belgium, two of whose children have Belgian nationality (an older child has Colombian nationality).[163] Both Colombian national parents were failed asylum-seekers, but nevertheless they were not returned due to concerns about the situation in that country. Mr Ruiz Zambrano completed some employment in Belgium, but his subsequent application for unemployment benefit was refused on the grounds that his employment had not been authorized, due to his irregular immigration status. The CJEU's judgment pointed out first of all that the position of this family did not fall within the scope of the citizens' Directive, since the EU citizens in the family were resident in the Member State of their nationality and had not moved outside it. Nevertheless, two of the children in the family were EU citizens, and 'Article 20 TFEU precludes national measures which have the effect of depriving citizens of the Union of the genuine enjoyment of the substance of the rights conferred by virtue of their status as citizens of the Union', referring to a judgment on the loss of nationality of a Member State.[164] A refusal to grant a work permit and a residence permit to 'a third country national with dependent minor children in the Member State where those children are nationals and reside...has such an effect', because:

> It must be assumed that such a refusal would lead to a situation where those children, citizens of the Union, would have to leave the territory of the Union in order to accompany their parents. Similarly, if a work permit were not granted to such a person, he would risk not having sufficient resources to provide for himself and his family, which would also result in the children, citizens of the Union, having to leave the territory of the Union. In those circumstances, those citizens of the Union would, in fact, be unable to exercise the substance of the rights conferred on them by virtue of their status as citizens of the Union.

The scope of the Court's judgment in *Ruiz Zambrano* was shortly clarified in *McCarthy*,[165] which (as noted above), concerned a dual citizen of the UK and Ireland who had never left Ireland, who sought to rely on the citizens' Directive as regards the admission of her husband. As discussed above, the CJEU took the view that she could not rely on the Directive. It then moved on to examine whether she could rely on the Treaty provisions on EU citizenship, as a 'static' EU citizen. In the

---

[163] Case C-34/09 [2011] ECR I-1177. See: P van Elsuwege, 'Shifting the Boundaries? European Union Citizenship and the Scope of Application of EU Law' (2011) 38 LIEI 262.

[164] Case C-135/08 *Rottmann* [2010] ECR I-1449, discussed above in the commentary on Art 2(1).

[165] Case C-434/09 [2011] ECR I-3375.

Court's view, she could not, on the grounds that the refusal to admit her husband did not have 'the effect of depriving her of the genuine enjoyment of the substance of the rights associated with her status as a Union citizen, or of impeding the exercise of her right to move and reside freely within the territory of the Member States'. Unlike the situation in *Ruiz Zambrano*, the national measure did 'not have the effect of obliging Mrs McCarthy to leave the territory of the European Union', since she had the right to reside in the UK as a British citizen. As discussed above, the CJEU then distinguished her case from previous judgments which had ruled that dual citizens of two Member States who faced complications using their names in one of the Member States of their nationality would face 'serious inconvenience for the Union citizens concerned that constituted an obstacle to freedom of movement', thereby 'impeding the exercise of their right of free movement and residence within the territory of the Member States'.[166]

Next, the judgment in *Dereci*, concerning a number of third-country national family members of Austrian nationals who had not exercised free movement rights, offered more clarification of the *Ruiz Zambrano* judgment.[167] Unsurprisingly, the Court reiterated that the persons concerned could not derive rights from the citizens' Directive, even though (as spouses and direct descendants, if they were dependent) they satisfied the definition of 'family member' in Article 2(2), since there had been no movement of the EU citizen to another Member State as required by Article 3(1). As to the relevance of EU citizenship, 'the criterion relating to the denial of the genuine enjoyment of the substance of the rights conferred by virtue of' EU citizenship, referred to in *Ruiz Zambrano*, 'refers to situations in which the Union citizen has, in fact, to leave not only the territory of the Member State of which he is a national but also the territory of the Union as a whole'. This test is 'specific in character' because it only applies to cases where 'although subordinate legislation on the right of residence of third country nationals is not applicable, a right of residence may not, exceptionally, be refused' to a third-country national family member of an EU citizen, 'as the effectiveness of Union citizenship enjoyed by that [EU citizen] would otherwise be undermined'. So 'the mere fact that it might appear desirable to' an EU citizen, 'for economic reasons or in order to keep his family together in the territory of the Union, for the members of his family who do not have the nationality of a Member State to be able to reside with him in the territory of the Union, is not sufficient in itself to support the view that the Union citizen will be forced to leave Union territory if such a right is not granted'. As to the relevance of human rights, the EU's Charter of Fundamental Rights was only applicable if the situation fell within the scope of EU law in the first place.

---

[166] The Court referred to Case C-148/02 *García Avello* [2003] ECR I-11613 and Case C-353/06 *Grunkin and Paul* [2008] ECR I-7639.

[167] Case C-256/11, judgment of 15 November 2011, not yet reported.

Subsequent judgments have clarified the case law a little further. In *Iida*,[168] the third-country national husband stayed in Germany when his German wife moved to Austria, and so the citizens' Directive did not apply to him, although it did apply to his wife and their daughter, who had moved to Austria with her mother. As for the impact of EU citizenship, referring to the *Ruiz Zambrano* line of cases, along with the case law on returnees (see section entitled 'The position of returnees') and the *Chen* case (see section (ii) 'Different forms of free movement'), the Court stated that '[t]he common element' in these situations 'is that, although they are governed by legislation which falls a priori within the competence of the Member States, namely legislation on the right of entry and stay of third-country nationals outside the scope' of the citizens' Directive and EU immigration legislation, 'they none the less have an intrinsic connection with the freedom of movement of a Union citizen which prevents the right of entry and residence from being refused to those nationals in the Member State of residence of that citizen, in order not to interfere with that freedom'. However, Mr Iida's lack of EU law status in Germany had not 'discouraged his daughter or his spouse from exercising their right of freedom of movement by moving to Austria', he had a renewable right of residence under German law, and he could qualify for long-term residence status under the relevant EU immigration legislation. So the refusal to grant him a residence card pursuant to Article 10 of the citizens' Directive was not 'liable to deny Mr Iida's spouse or daughter the genuine enjoyment of the substance of the rights associated with their status of Union citizen or to impede the exercise of their right to move and reside freely within the territory of the Member States'. The purely hypothetical prospect of obstructing that right was not relevant. It should be noted that the Court did not rule (since it did not need to do so) on whether the removal of Mr Iida from Germany *altogether* would have impacted upon his wife's and daughter's citizenship rights, considering that he had joint parental responsibility for his daughter.

Next, in *O and S*,[169] the CJEU ruled on the position of two third-country national women who had each married Finnish men and lived in Finland, had children (of Finnish nationality) with their Finnish husbands, obtained divorces from those husbands (obtaining sole custody of their Finnish children), married third-country national husbands and had a third-country national child with their second husbands, and then applied for the admission of those second husbands. The Court's judgment first of all pointed out that the EU citizen children had not moved within the EU, so the citizens' Directive did not apply. As for EU citizenship, the Court noted that the third-country national mothers of the EU citizen children each had permanent resident permits, so there was no legal obligation for them or their children to leave Finland or the EU as a whole. But the Court did not end its analysis there; it ruled that 'the question of the custody of the sponsors' children and the

---

[168] Case C-40/11, judgment of 8 November 2012, not yet reported.
[169] Joined Cases C-356/11 and C-357/11, judgment of 6 December 2012, not yet reported.

fact that the children are part of reconstituted families are also relevant', because a decision by the mothers to leave the EU 'in order to preserve the family unit, would have the effect of depriving those Union citizens of all contact with their biological fathers, should such contact have been maintained up to the present'. But alternatively, staying in the EU to preserve those citizens' relationships with their biological fathers would harm the relationship of the third-country national children with *their* biological fathers. However, the Court reiterated its ruling in *Dereci* that the mere desirability of third-country national family members living with an EU citizen in the Member State of that citizen's nationality was not enough to demonstrate that the EU citizen would be forced to leave the territory if those family members were not admitted. It was not a decisive factor that the person concerned already lived together with the sponsor and other family members, as it was always possible that some family members would arrive separately from the rest of the family. Importantly, the Court also stated that the *Ruiz Zambrano* case law was not confined to cases of a 'blood relationship' between the EU citizen and the third-country national concerned. The national court had to take account of both the mothers' permanent right of residence and the EU citizen children's lack of legal, financial, or emotional dependence on their step-parents, because it was the existence of dependency between the EU citizen and the third-country national who was refused a right of residence that was crucial, since only that dependency could lead to the EU citizen being obliged to leave the EU as a whole.

Most recently, in *Ymeraga*,[170] concerning a naturalized adult citizen of Luxembourg who had not exercised free movement rights and sought the admission of his third-country national parents and siblings, the CJEU first of all pointed out that the citizens' Directive was not applicable, and then observed that applying its prior case law on citizenship of the Union, there was no basis to conclude that refusing to admit Mr Ymeraga's family members would deprive him of the substance of EU citizenship.

Finally, in the pending case of *Alokpa*,[171] concerning French national twins resident in Luxembourg with their third-country national mother, the Advocate-General's opinion argues that their mother's expulsion from Luxembourg would not infringe the principles set out in *Ruiz Zambrano*, since the twins have the right to reside in their State of nationality, which would also have to accept their mother's residence as a consequence.

This complex and important case law raises two key issues: the personal scope and the material scope of the obligation to protect the substance of EU citizenship, as regards immigration law. As for the personal scope, the key requirement is that the EU citizen must be emotionally, legally, or financially dependent on the

---

[170] Case C-87/12, judgment of 8 May 2013.
[171] Case C-86/12, opinion of 21 March 2013.

third-country national who seeks to enter or remain upon the territory of that citizen's State of nationality. The judgment in *O and S* makes it clear that an indirect link (ie the citizens' dependence upon their mothers, who seek the entry of a third-country national spouse) is not sufficient. While a relationship of dependence is more likely to be found as between EU citizen children and third-country national parents, it is at least conceivable that an EU citizen adult could be dependent upon a third-country national. Moreover, the CJEU has expressly made clear that the EU citizen and the third-country national concerned need not be blood relations: the key issue is the existence of a dependent relationship.

According to the case law, the concept of *dependency* has to be distinguished from *desirability*. To paraphrase the Rolling Stones, EU citizens cannot always get what they want—but if they try real hard, national authorities must give them what they need. The case law points to a test of whether it would be *impossible in practice* for the EU citizens to remain on the territory of their home Member State, and therefore the entire EU, unless the third-country national relative is allowed to enter or stay.[172] In fact, it would always be possible for EU citizen children to go into care in their home Member State if their third-country national parents leave the EU, but the CJEU has implicitly ruled out this drastic solution, presumably because it would mean breaking the legal relationship between the children and their parents. It has also implicitly ruled out the possibility of the EU citizen children moving to another Member State—presumably because since their parents could not claim rights as those childrens' dependants (see the commentary on Article 2(2)(c) and (d) above), this would not be practical. However, the position is probably different where, as in *Alopka*, the children are citizens of another Member State; in that event, according to the Opinion in that case, the Member State of nationality must admit the third-country national parent concerned along with the children. With great respect, the case law is hard to reconcile to the extent that financial dependence falls within the scope of the *Ruiz Zambrano* criteria, but economic desirability does not. More broadly, the 'impossible in practice' test probably significantly understates the likelihood that EU citizens will end up leaving the Union because of a third-country national parent's understandable desire to live with his or her spouse or other family member.[173]

The application of the criteria developed by the Court is undoubtedly more complicated when, unlike the case of *Ruiz Zambrano*, the parents' relationship has ended. In both *Iida* and *O and S*, the CJEU appeared to assume that the

---

[172] In the words of S Adam and P van Elsuwege, the 'reasoning only applies when "static" Union citizens would have no choice but to follow their third-country national family member(s) out of the territory of the Union when the latter would not be granted a right of residence' in the EU citizen's State of nationality: 'Citizenship rights and the Federal Balance between the European Union and its Member States: Comment on *Dereci*' (2012) 37 ELRev 176 at 181.

[173] See A Tryfonidou, 'Redefining the Outer Boundaries of EU Law: The *Zambrano, McCarthy* and *Dereci* Trilogy' (2012) 18 EPL 493 at 515.

third-country national parent had to retain some sort of continuing residence in the Member State of nationality of the EU citizen, in order for the latter's citizenship rights not to be deprived of substance. In these cases, however, the third-country national parents respectively had joint custody and sole custody of the child concerned. Implicitly, while it would always be possible for the EU citizen to stay in his or her home Member State with his or her EU citizen parent even if the third-country national parent was compelled to leave the EU, this would be unacceptable, because again it would mean breaking the legal relationship between the child and the parent with joint or sole custody. This applies a fortiori when the parents' relationship is still ongoing, whether the parents are both third-country nationals or a combination of an EU citizen and a third-country national. Arguably, however, the position might be different where the third-country national parent does not have custody, although there is a prima facie case that a parent with the right of access to a child also should be allowed to remain, by analogy with Article 13(1)(d). In any event, it is implicit from *Ruiz Zambrano* that the parents of the EU citizen child do not both have to be carers of that child, unlike some other categories of EU law, in order to obtain or retain a right of residence. After all, it was Mr Ruiz Zambrano's need to earn income to support his family that formed the main subject matter of that judgment.

Finally, it would surely be necessary, in cases like *Ruiz Zambrano*, to extend the right of residence to the minor or dependent third-country national siblings of the EU citizens concerned, for otherwise it would be effectively impossible for the EU citizens to remain on the territory given the likelihood that their parents would keep the family intact by moving all the family members to the sibling's State of nationality.

The latter point brings us neatly to the second issue: the material scope of the obligation to protect the substance of EU citizenship. In *Ruiz Zambrano*, the CJEU requires specifically that the person concerned receive a right of residence, so the children do not have to leave the territory with their parents, as well as a work permit, so the parent has sufficient resources to provide for the family. It is implicit that the de facto tolerance of the family members is not enough, so some form of renewable residence permit must be issued, and the need for sufficient resources suggests that the work permit needs to confer broad access to the labour market, including the prospects of self-employment if necessary. Moreover, the vicissitudes of the labour market point to the need for both parents to have a work permit, as well as access to social security and social assistance if they are out of work. The importance for the EU citizens of their parents remaining on the territory suggests that they must be protected against expulsion pursuant to substantive and procedural rules at least broadly similar to those in chapter VI of the citizens' Directive. However, it does not seem necessary that the parents must receive permanent residence status pursuant to the Directive, since a right of residence for them is sufficient in order to prevent the EU citizen from being deprived of his or her rights, although in most Member States, it is arguable that the 'right of residence' must necessarily entail the prospects of qualifying for status under the EU's long-term residence Directive.[174] It is striking that the Court places so much stress on ensuring sufficient resources by means of labour market access in *Ruiz Zambrano*, whereas in *Dereci* and subsequent case law it dismissed the idea that family members ought to be reunited for economic reasons. What if the only (or the easiest) means of ensuring sufficient resources for the family of an EU citizen is to admit a particular third-country national family member?

As noted already, in its judgment in *Iida*, the Court stated that there were links between persons protected pursuant to the *Ruiz Zambrano* line of case law, and those protected pursuant to the *Chen* line of case law (see section (ii) 'Different forms of free movement') and returnees (see section entitled 'The position of returnees'). But it does not necessarily follow that the rights of all of the persons concerned must be the same. In particular, since returnees have already been subject to the Directive in another Member State, there is a strong case to continue applying the Directive back in the EU citizen's home State so as to avoid deterrents to free movement; but such considerations do not apply in cases like *Ruiz Zambrano* and *Chen*. However, in the case of *Alokpa*,[175] discussed above, if the French children are returned to France with their third-country national parent, then the *Ruiz Zambrano* case law would be applicable as such, and it must follow that the parent has access to employment in France. While the Advocate-General's Opinion in this case suggests that the parent would also be entitled to obtain cross-border access into the Luxembourg labour market, it should be noted that this would give her better rights than third-country national family members pursuant to the citizens' Directive.[176]

(ii) Different forms of free movement

This brings us to the second category of persons who are outside the scope of the Directive—those whose legal position does have a specific cross-border element, but whose circumstances do not fit precisely within the definition of free movement set out in Article 3(1). This category of persons includes two subcategories which are discussed elsewhere in this book: returnees (discussed above) and the children of migrant workers exercising access to education, along with their parent carers, who are within the scope of Regulation 1612/68 (now Regulation 492/2011).[177] Two further subcategories of persons have been identified by the Court to date: those whose status is linked to the exercise of free movement rights by an EU citizen resident in his or her Member State of nationality (referred to here as '*Carpenter* cases'), and those whose status is linked to an EU citizen child who

---

[174] Directive 2003/109, [2004] OJ L 16/44. See Case C-40/11 *Iida*, judgment of 8 November 2012, not yet reported.
[175] Case C-86/12, Opinion of 21 March 2013.
[176] See Case C-10/05 *Mattern and Cikotic* [2006] ECR I-3145.
[177] On this subcategory, see the commentary on Art 12(3), in Chapter 3.

is exercising rights pursuant to the Directive in a different Member State (referred to here as '*Chen* cases').

In *Carpenter*, a British national resident in the UK was providing services to other Member States, and his third-country national spouse, who was present without authorization, sought to resist her expulsion.[178] In the Court's view, the prior legislation did not apply, since Mr Carpenter was not resident in a different Member State; this finding would obviously be equally applicable to the citizens' Directive. However, the Court examined whether other rules of EU law might be applicable, and decided that '[i]t is clear that the separation of Mr and Mrs Carpenter would be detrimental to their family life and, therefore, to the conditions under which Mr Carpenter exercises a fundamental freedom. That freedom could not be fully effective if Mr Carpenter were to be deterred from exercising it by obstacles raised in his country of origin to the entry and residence of his spouse', referring to the *Singh* judgment on the position of returnees. The Court of Justice has been asked to elaborate on the position of third-country national family members in similar positions, namely, the family members of frontier workers who are resident in their Member State of nationality and the family members of other workers resident in their State of nationality who must travel to other Member States as part of their employment.[179] The *Carpenter* line of reasoning must also logically be applicable to these family members, as well as to the family members of EU citizens who are 'posted' to another Member State. As to the personal scope of the rule, it should follow from the case law on returnees that family members should be admitted as long as the exercise of free movement rights towards another Member State is genuine and effective.[180]

In the *Chen* case,[181] as noted already, an Irish national baby resident in the UK fell within the scope of the prior legislation as the national of one Member State resident in the territory of another Member State. The CJEU also ruled that the baby met the 'sufficient resources' requirement to reside (see now Article 7(1)(b) of the citizens' Directive, discussed in Chapter 3), as such resources were provided by her third-country national mother, who was residing with her. While the baby therefore fell within the scope of the prior legislation (and now the Directive), her mother did not, since she could not be regarded as dependent upon her child

---

[178] Case C-60/00 [2002] ECR I-6279.

[179] Case C-457/12 *S*, pending. On the other hand, as noted above, the position of family members of frontier workers who reside in a Member State other than that of their nationality falls within the scope of the Directive.

[180] For discussion of this issue, see G Barrett, 'Family Matters: European Community Law and Third-Country Family Members' (2003) 40 CMLRev 369 at 406–407. In the view of S Acierno, in 'The *Carpenter* judgment: fundamental rights and the limits of the Community legal order' (2003) 28 CMLRev 393 at 403, the threshold is a 'significant proportion' of services provided to recipients in other Member States.

[181] Case C-200/02 [2004] ECR I-9925.

(see the discussion of Article 2(2)(c) and (d) above). However, the mother was still entitled to a right to reside, since the baby's exercise of free movement rights would be ineffective without the mother's presence on the territory. As noted above, in *Iida* the Court bracketed *Chen* with the subsequent *Ruiz Zambrano* line of case law, as another case where the substance of EU citizenship could only be exercised by permitting a third-country national family member to exercise a residence right. Similarly, in the pending case of *Alokpa*,[182] EU citizen babies present on the territory of another Member State have a third-country national carer, who in this case is blocked from taking up employment. In the Advocate-General's view, the Member State of residence should take account of her prospects of obtaining employment when assessing whether her children have 'sufficient resources' pursuant to the Directive. Of course, this raises the question as to whether she has a right to take up employment—which brings us to the issue of the material scope of the rights of these categories of persons.

While the CJEU did not address the material scope of the status of the persons concerned in detail in the *Carpenter* or *Chen* cases, it was at least clear from the *Carpenter* judgment that Mrs Carpenter could not be expelled unless that expulsion could be justified pursuant to Article 8(2) ECHR, as an exception from the right to respect for private and family life. For the sake of consistency, this must be the minimum standard applicable to persons in the *Chen* line of case law also. As for access to employment, in the *Chen* line of case law, there is an obvious analogy with the *Ruiz Zambrano* judgment, in which the Court ruled that the parent of EU citizen children who had not moved within the EU was entitled not only to a right of residence but also to a work permit. From one point of view (cf the pending *Alokpa* case), it could be argued that the substance of the right of EU citizenship could be secured in the home State of nationality of the children concerned, without needing to grant the parents of those children a right of employment in any other Member State. But the better view is that it would be odd to grant a work permit to the third-country national parents of EU citizen children who are resident in their Member State of nationality—a situation which only exceptionally falls within the scope of EU law—but to deny the same right to such parents of EU citizen children who have actually in principle exercised rights pursuant to the Directive. Finally, as for the termination of status, in the *Carpenter* cases it should follow that the family member would lose the EU law rights once the provision of services et al to another Member State ceases.[183] In the *Chen* cases, it should follow by analogy with the case law on Article 10 of Regulation 492/2011 that the parent's right will cease once the children no longer need his or her care.[184]

---

[182] For discussion, see N Reich and S Harbacevica, 'Citizenship and Family on Trial: A Fairly Optimistic Overview of Recent Court Practice with Regard to Free Movement of Persons' (2003) 40 CMLRev 615 at 629.

[183] Case C-86/12, Opinion of 21 March 2013.

[184] See the commentary on Art 12(3) in Chapter 3.

2. Without prejudice to any right to free movement and residence the persons concerned may have in their own right, the host Member State shall, in accordance with its national legislation, facilitate entry and residence for the following persons:

    (a) any other family members, irrespective of their nationality, not falling under the definition in point 2 of Article 2 who, in the country from which they have come, are dependants or members of the household of the Union citizen having the primary right of residence, or where serious health grounds strictly require the personal care of the family member by the Union citizen;

    (b) the partner with whom the Union citizen has a durable relationship, duly attested.

    The host Member State shall undertake an extensive examination of the personal circumstances and shall justify any denial of entry or residence to these people.

Article 3(2) is explained further by recital 6 in the preamble to the Directive, which states that '[i]n order to maintain the unity of the family in a broader sense and without prejudice to the prohibition of discrimination on grounds of nationality, the situation of those persons who are not included in the definition of family members under this Directive, and who therefore do not enjoy an automatic right of entry and residence in the host Member State, should be examined by the host Member State on the basis of its own national legislation, in order to decide whether entry and residence could be granted to such persons, taking into consideration their relationship with the Union citizen or any other circumstances, such as their financial or physical dependence on the Union citizen'.

Moreover, Article 3(2) applies to the dependent ascending relatives of students, according to Article 7(4) of the Directive, and so the following analysis of Article 3(2) applies mutatis mutandis to such persons.[185] Presumably, students can also rely on Article 3(2) as regards the categories of extended family members listed in that provision, in the absence of any provision to the contrary.[186] For all extended family members, the Directive includes specific rules on proving that the relevant criteria are satisfied.[187]

The purpose of Article 3(2) is to specify which extended family members falling outside the scope of the core family members listed in Article 2(2) can fall within the scope of the Directive, at least to the extent that Member States must 'facilitate' their 'entry and residence'. This provision of the Directive is in part a successor to prior legislation, which was (surprisingly) never interpreted by the CJEU. In particular, the Regulation on free movement of workers provided that 'Member States shall facilitate the admission' of those family members, other than the core family

---

[185] In particular, such persons should logically be regarded as another category of 'dependants' of EU citizens.

[186] Art 7(4) is only a derogation from Art 7(1)(d) and (2) of that Directive, not from Art 3(2).

[187] Arts 8(5)(e) and (f) and 10(2)(e) and (f), discussed in Chapter 3.

members as defined in that Regulation, who were 'dependent' on the worker or 'living under his roof in the country whence he comes'.[188] The accommodation requirement referred to above also applied to this category of family members.[189] The same rule applied to family members of the self-employed, except that there was no accommodation requirement.[190] These provisions were extended to those workers or self-employed persons who ceased their economic activities.[191] However, there were no such rules as regards the extended family members of other EU citizens.

As compared to the prior legislation, Article 3(2) applies to the extended family members of all EU citizens, a reference to national legislation has been added, the list of family members covered is longer (now including partners and persons with 'serious health grounds'), and the subparagraph on the extent of Member States' obligations is new.[192] The inclusion of the dependent direct relatives of students is also new, and the accommodation requirement for workers' extended family members has been dropped.

During the legislative process, the Commission originally proposed a simple extension of the prior rules to the extended family members of all EU citizens.[193] In its amended proposal, the Commission accepted a European Parliament suggestion to add to Article 3(2) family members 'where there are serious health or humanitarian grounds', on the grounds that 'this is justifiable for family members who, for compelling reasons, need to be near the Union citizen'.[194] However, the Council then deleted the reference to 'humanitarian grounds', on the basis that 'they already constitute part of the commitments undertaken by Member States in the field of fundamental rights'.[195] It also shifted the category of partner to Article 3(2)(b) (leaving registered partners covered by Article 2(2)(b); see the commentary above), and added the condition related to the family members with 'serious health' issues, the second subparagraph on the nature of Member States' obligations, and recital 6, the latter 'in order to clarify the notion of facilitation provided for in Article 3'. In the Commission's view, a 'durable relationship' with a partner 'may cover different situations: same-sex marriage, registered partnership, legal cohabitation and common-law marriage'.[196]

---

[188] Art 10(2), Reg 1612/68.

[189] Art 10(3), Reg 1612/68; see the commentary on Art 2(2) above.

[190] Art 1(2), Directive 73/148.

[191] Art 1 of each of Directive 75/34 and Reg. 1251/70.

[192] The reference to the possible right of personal free movement of the individuals concerned is also new, but this presumably confirms the prior status quo.

[193] COM(2001) 257.

[194] COM(2003) 199. The condition in the final Directive relating to those with 'serious health grounds' did not appear at this point.

[195] Common Position 6/2004, [2004] OJ C 54E/12; see the statement of reasons.

[196] Communication on the Common Position (SEC(2003) 1293, 30 December 2003).

According to the Commission's report on the application of the Directive, thirteen Member States 'failed to transpose Article 3(2) correctly', while ten applied it more favourably by giving extended family members an automatic right to reside.[197] Such higher standards are compatible with the Directive.[198] It would be open to Member States, if they chose, to provide for automatic admission only to some of the categories of persons referred to in Article 3(2), rather than all of them.[199]

Article 3(2) raises three fundamental issues, which will be considered in turn: (a) the extent of the obligation it imposes upon Member States; (b) the definition of the persons within its scope (ie the personal scope); and (c) the extent to which the persons within the scope of Article 3(2) can benefit from the other provisions of the Directive (the material scope).

Extent of the obligations

The wording of Article 3(2) was interpreted for the first time by the Court of Justice in its *Rahman* judgment.[200] According to the Court, first of all there was a fundamental distinction between the family members defined in Article 2(2) and those defined in Article 3(2). In particular, it followed from the wording of Article 3(2) and from the 'general system of the directive' that the family members defined in Article 2(2) had 'a right of entry and residence in that citizen's host member state', whereas for those defined in Article 3(2), their 'entry and residence has only to be facilitated by that Member State'. This interpretation was confirmed by recital 6 in the preamble. So the Directive 'does not oblige the Member States to grant every application for entry and residence submitted by persons who show' that they fall within the scope of Article 3(2).

Having said that, the Court emphasized that Article 3(2) still had some practical relevance for EU citizens' extended family members. More specifically, it was 'clear from the use of the words "shall facilitate" that that provision imposes an obligation on the Member States to confer a certain advantage, compared with applications for entry and residence' by other third-country nationals, on applications by extended family members. This obligation meant that Member States had to 'make it possible' for the extended family members to 'obtain a decision on their application that is founded on an extensive examination of their personal circumstances and, in the event of refusal, is justified by reasons'. When examining such an application, the authority concerned had to 'take into account of the various

---

[197] COM(2008) 840.
[198] See Art 37, discussed in Chapter 7, although for the reasons set out below in the discussion of material scope, persons within the scope of Art 3(2) cannot be considered to have been admitted pursuant to national law, even where a Member State set such higher standards.
[199] See by analogy Case C-123/08 *Wolzenburg* [2009] ECR I-9621.
[200] Case C-83/11, judgment of 5 September 2012, not yet reported.

factors that may be relevant in the particular case, such as' the factors specifically listed in recital 6 in the preamble.

Moreover, in light of the reference to national legislation in Article 3(2), and in the absence of more specific rules in the Directive, the Court ruled that each Member State 'has a wide discretion as regards the selection of factors to be taken into account'. But there is a core substantive obligation for Member States: their legislation must 'contain criteria which are consistent with the normal meaning of the term "facilitate" '—presumably as defined by the Court—'and of the words relating to dependence used in Article 3(2), and which do not deprive that provision of its effectiveness'. Finally, the Court conceded that Article 3(2) was not directly effective, although 'an applicant is entitled to a judicial review of whether the national legislation and its application have remained within the limits set by that Directive'.[201]

It is evident that the degree of obligation established by Article 3(2) occupies a middle ground between an obligation to admit the persons concerned and full discretion as to whether to admit them.[202] The obligations for the Member States are both substantive and procedural. Substantively, they must ensure a margin of preference for the extended family members of EU citizens, as compared to other third-country nationals.[203] They must also ensure that the relevant national rules are consistent with the correct interpretation (discussed further below) of the categories of persons referred to in Article 3(2). Finally, they cannot 'deprive' that interpretation of its 'effectiveness'—another obligation discussed further below.

Procedurally, there are two sets of obligations. At the administrative stage, Member States must make a reasoned decision on the application.[204] Presumably the reasons which they must give in the event of refusal must relate to the interpretation of the criteria set out in Article 3(2), so they must assess not only whether the family member falls within one (or more) of the categories referred to in Article 3(2), and satisfies the conditions attached to those categories, but also whether the refusal of the application can be justified in light of the personal circumstances (considering also the factors referred to in recital 6). Subsequently, the applicant is entitled to a judicial review of the exercise of the discretion. The question obviously arises

---

[201] *Rahman* judgment, paras 18–26.

[202] On this point, see further paras 47–58 of the Advocate-General's opinion.

[203] As the Advocate-General pointed out in para 57 of his Opinion, the words 'shall facilitate' in Art 3(2) can be compared with the words 'may authorise' (as regards extended family members) in Art 4(2) and (3) of Directive 2003/86 ([2003] OJ L 251/12) on family reunion for third-country nationals. Presumably, however, this preference must be guaranteed as compared to a *category* of third-country nationals in the same position, not to third-country nationals *generally*. After all, Art 4(1) of Directive 2003/86 contains an obligation to admit the *core* family members of third-country nationals (see Case C-540/03 *EP v Council* [2006] ECR I-5769), which is a stronger obligation than Art 3(2) of the citizens' Directive sets out as regards the *extended* family members of EU citizens.

[204] In its guidance on the Directive (COM(2009) 313), the Commission states that the decision on denial of entry must be in writing.

whether, at each stage, the applicant is entitled to rely on the relevant provisions of the Directive as regards standards of administrative procedure and judicial review; this point is considered further below.

Finally, it should be noted that although the *Rahman* judgment only concerned the dependent family members of EU citizens, the Court's interpretation of the degree of obligation imposed by Article 3(2) logically applies to all of the other categories of extended family members referred to in that provision (and, for students, in Article 7(4)),[205] in the absence of any wording in the Directive differentiating between the various categories of extended family member.

Personal scope

First of all, there are five general points which apply to all four categories of persons referred to in Article 3(2). Firstly, the nationality of the extended family members is not relevant.[206] While the words 'irrespective of their nationality' appear in Article 3(2)(a), but not Article 3(2)(b), this cannot mean that only extended family members who are EU citizens fall within the scope of the latter provision. After all, Article 2(2) does not include the words 'irrespective of their nationality' either, but its application to third-country nationals as such has not been questioned.[207] This interpretation is confirmed by other provisions of the Directive.[208] In fact, it is likely that the extended family members referred to in Article 3(2) will usually be third-country nationals, although it is possible that EU citizens could also fall within the scope of the provision.[209]

Next, recital 6 in the preamble expressly confirms that Article 3(2) is '[w]ithout prejudice to the prohibition of discrimination on grounds of nationality'. This suggests that the authors of the Directive acknowledged that the principle set out in the *Reed* judgment (discussed above in the commentary on Article 2(2)) is applicable also to Article 3(2). Most obviously, in light of the *Reed* judgment, the principle applies to the admission of partners, but the wording of recital 6 makes no express distinction between the different categories of extended family members referred to in Article 3(2).

---

[205] See para 44 of the Advocate-General's Opinion in *Rahman*.

[206] See para 76 of the Advocate-General's Opinion in *Rahman*.

[207] See, for instance, Case C-127/08 *Metock* [2008] ECR I-6241. Recital 5 in the preamble confirms that family members should be admitted 'irrespective of nationality'.

[208] Art 10(2)(f) applies solely to third-country nationals within the scope of Art 3(2)(b).

[209] See para 44 of the Opinion in *Rahman*, and Art 8(5)(e) and (f). However, it should be kept in mind that EU citizens who are being fully supported by others will satisfy the 'sufficient resources' criterion of Art 7(1)(b) or (c) in their own name (see Chapter 3), so they would not fall within the scope of Art 3(2). See, for instance, Joined Cases C-147/11 and C-148/11 *Czop and Punakova*, judgment of 6 September 2012, not yet reported, where one of the EU citizens fell within the scope of Art 7(1)(b) and subsequently Art 16, and the other fell within the scope of Reg 1612/68 (see the discussion of Art 12(3) in Chapter 3).

Thirdly, as noted already, in the *Rahman* judgment, the Court of Justice stated that the national application of Article 3(2) could not deprive that provision of its effectiveness. The Court did not elaborate any further on the meaning of the principle of effectiveness in the particular context of Article 3(2), although some of the analysis in the Advocate-General's Opinion in *Rahman* may be relevant.[210] In his view, Member States could not simply exclude from consideration categories of person covered by Article 3(2), in whole or in part. So they could not limit themselves to examining the application of registered partners only, or refuse to examine applications regarding collateral family members, or those in the direct line beyond a certain degree of relationship.[211] Furthermore, Member States' discretion was also limited by free movement and human rights considerations. As regards free movement, a national decision pursuant to Article 3(2) 'must not have the effect of unjustifiably impeding the exercise' of free movement rights by an EU citizen. Such a 'serious impediment' would exist if the EU citizen were 'forced to leave the territory of the home Member State' or the EU altogether, referring to *Dereci* (see the commentary on Article 3(1) above), since 'the genuine enjoyment of the right of residence of the Union citizen effectively confers a right of residence on the members of his family'. As for human rights considerations, at least the jurisprudence of the ECHR on the protection of family life had to be applied. While that case law did not oblige the admission of family members in most cases, the 'combination' of free movement and human rights rules 'may therefore effectively establish a right of residence for members of the family of the Union citizen', which was not limited to 'core' family members.

Fourthly, as the Commission pointed out in its 2009 guidance on the Directive, the Directive must be interpreted in accordance with the 'best interests of the child'.[212] This could obviously be relevant to any of the four categories of persons listed in Article 3(2). Any of the persons mentioned in Article 3(2)(a) could *be* a child, and the Union citizen and his or her partner mentioned in Article 3(2)(b) could have (a) joint child(ren)—or the Union citizen could be, in effect, a step-parent to his or her partner's child(ren).

Finally, is it possible for Member States to lay down additional criteria relating to the categories of persons listed in Article 3(2)? In the *Rahman* judgment, the Court ruled that it was indeed possible for Member States, when exercising their discretion pursuant to Article 3(2), to 'lay down in their legislation particular requirements as to the nature and duration of dependence, in order in particular to satisfy themselves that the situation of dependence is genuine and stable and has not been

---

[210] Paras 65–78 of the opinion. However, this part of the analysis was not expressly linked to the principle of effectiveness.

[211] Similarly, the Commission's 2009 guidance on the Directive rightly points out that Art 3(2) 'does not lay down any restrictions as to the degree of relatedness'.

[212] COM(2009) 313. See by analogy Case C-540/03 *EP v Council* [2006] ECR I-5769.

brought about with the sole objective of obtaining entry and residence into the host Member State'. However, such rules would still have to be consistent with the normal meaning of 'dependence' (discussed below) and could not deprive Article 3(2) of its effectiveness (see discussion above).[213] On this point, the Advocate-General discussed specifically the application of the principle of effectiveness in this context. In his view, the conditions which a Member State might impose could not render the exercise of the free movement right 'practically impossible', by depriving the persons concerned 'of all possibility of obtaining a right of entry and residence'. For instance, a requirement of twenty years' dependency would be 'unacceptable'. Any such rules would have to 'pursue a legitimate objective' and be 'appropriate for securing the attainment of the objective and not go beyond what is necessary to attain it'.[214] Applying these criteria, arguably a condition relating to social assistance would be acceptable. Furthermore, any rule relating to the duration of dependence or serious health grounds could at most take the form of a rebuttable presumption, since it is always possible that a serious health condition is recent, or that an extended family member recently became dependent due to (for example) the death of a spouse. By analogy with *Metock*, no 'prior lawful residence' requirement would be permissible.[215]

Next, as for the specific categories of persons referred to in Article 3(2), first of all the *Rahman* judgment has provided a useful clarification of the interpretation of 'dependants'.[216] In particular, the Court of Justice examined national rules related to the place and time of dependence. As regards the place of dependence, the Court ruled that the words 'in the country from which they have come' did not refer to the country where the *EU citizen* resided before settling in the host Member State, but to the State where the *extended family member* was resident when he or she applied to accompany or join the EU citizen.[217] As regards the time of dependence, the Court interpreted recital 6 in the preamble to mean that the persons covered by Article 3(2) 'maintain close and stable family ties with [an EU citizen] on account of specific factual circumstances, such as' those listed in Article 3(2)(a). The Court pointed out that such ties could exist even if the extended family member had not lived in the same country as the citizen or been a dependant of the citizen when the latter person settled in the host Member State. Rather, the situation of dependence must exist at the time when the family member applies to join the EU citizen.[218] The Court did not give any other indication as to the meaning of dependence, but the Advocate-General argued that the term had the same meaning that it did in

---

[213] Paras 36–40, *Rahman* judgment.
[214] Paras 102–108, *Rahman* Opinion.
[215] See the commentary on Art 3(1) above.
[216] On the position if the person ceases to become dependent after applying for a residence card, see the commentary on Art 2(2)(c) and (d) above.
[217] Paras 27–31, *Rahman* judgment.
[218] Paras 32–33, *Rahman* judgment.

Article 2(2)(c) and (d).[219] This interpretation is logical in the absence of any wording suggesting a contrary interpretation, subject to the possibility (discussed above) of some national rules relating to the duration and nature of the dependency.[220] It is also consistent with the application of Article 3(2) to certain family members of students, who, if they were family members of EU citizens who were exercising rights under the Directive in any other capacity, would have fallen within the scope of Article 2(2)(c) or (d).[221] Moreover, *a contrario* the 'serious health grounds' category, there is no reason why the EU citizen needs to show that he or she is the *only* person who can look after the extended family member concerned.

As for the members of the household, it does make sense that this category of person had to live with the EU citizen in the same country which he or she came from and at the same time that he or she entered the host Member State.[222] But by analogy with Article 3(1), some limited time gap must be permissible to take account of practical issues such as accommodation needs and school years.[223]

Next, for the persons who need personal care on 'serious health grounds', the words 'strictly require' do suggest that the EU citizen needs to show that he or she is the only person who can look after the extended family member, or at least that the person concerned will receive substantially better care with the Union citizen than with anyone else. However, it would be unreasonable to apply too strictly the rule that the Union citizen must provide the personal care directly; surely it would be possible for other family members or some outside assistance to contribute to that care, for instance in light of the EU citizen's need to earn money and/or look after other family members. Also, the Court's judgment in *Rahman* expressly ruled out any requirement that the extended family member concerned had to come from the same country as the EU citizen, or enter the host Member State at the same time as that citizen. In any event, the words 'in the country from which they have come' do not even apply to this category of extended family member.

Finally, as regards partners, the word 'durable' in Article 3(2)(b) suggests that a condition relating to the duration of the relationship is particularly acceptable,[224] although again a requirement of a very lengthy prior relationship would be disproportionate. The nature of this category of family member also suggests that a requirement that the partner resided in the same place and the same time as the EU citizen would be acceptable. But again by analogy with Article 3(1), some

---

[219] Paras 94–100, *Rahman* Opinion. See the commentary on Art 2(2) above.

[220] At the very least, logically (as with Art 2(2)(c) and (d): see the commentary above) if an EU citizen is being supported by an extended family member, the latter cannot be considered a dependant of the former.

[221] See Art 7(4).

[222] Paras 89–90, *Rahman* Opinion.

[223] See the commentary on Art 3(1) above.

[224] See the Commission guidance (COM(2009) 313): national rules on a 'minimum amount of time' are acceptable.

limited time gap must be permissible to take account of practical issues such as accommodation needs and school years.[225] The Commission has rightly pointed out that a joint mortgage would be highly probative as evidence that a partnership existed.[226]

As for the definition of 'partner', the Commission's indication during the negotiation of the Directive that the concept could cover all of those partnerships which do not fall within the scope of 'spouse' or 'registered partner' in Article 2(2) is in principle sound, subject of course to the interpretation of that other provision of the Directive.[227] In particular, as noted above,[228] a partner would include registered partners and same-sex spouses, in cases where the host Member State does not recognize such concepts or where the conditions set out as regards registered partners in Article 2(2)(b) are not met.

As noted in the analysis of Article 2(2)(a), there is no requirement that an EU citizen live under the same roof as his or her spouse, and the status of 'spouse' is not lost even if the couple concerned is estranged. Since Member States do not permit polygamy, it is not possible for a second spouse to benefit from the Directive until the couple is divorced. But would it be possible for an EU citizen to ask for a right of residence as regards a partner pursuant to Article 3(2), while he or she still has an estranged spouse pursuant to Article 2(2)(a), or an estranged registered partner pursuant to Article 2(2)(b)? In principle, if the relationship in question is genuine, there seems no reason why not, in the absence of any wording to the contrary in the Directive. Similarly if an estranged spouse starts a relationship with a partner who was already resident in the host Member State, there is no reason why the person concerned should lose the status of spouse, and the relevant benefits pursuant to the Directive.[229]

Material scope

The final question regarding Article 3(2) is whether the persons within its scope can benefit from the provisions of the remainder of the Directive, and if so, to what extent. Of course, it is possible that after their entry their circumstances could change in such a way that they became covered by the scope of Article 2(2)—most obviously, an EU citizen could marry his or her partner—and in that case, by analogy with *Metock*,[230] Article 2(2) would then apply to their situation. But what if their status is not 'upgraded' in that way?

---

[225] See the commentary on Art 3(1) above.

[226] Commission guidance (COM(2009) 313).

[227] The Court has decided several cases involving partners, without defining the term: Joined Cases C-147/11 and C-148/11 *Czop and Punakova*, judgment of 6 September 2012, not yet reported, and Case C-45/12 *Hadj Ahmed*, judgment of 13 June 2013.

[228] See the commentary on Art 2(2)(a) and (b).

[229] See Case C-244/12 *Ogieriakhi*, pending.

[230] See the commentary on Art 3(1) above.

First of all, since the citizens' Directive makes many general references to 'family members', it is necessary to examine whether this term can apply, at least in some cases, to the extended family members falling within the scope of Article 3(2). At first sight, it might seem not, because the Directive contains a definition of 'family member' in Article 2(2), which applies only to core family members. However, Article 3(2)(a) refers to *'any other* family members'* (emphasis added), and Article 8(5) also expressly refers to 'family members' as including both persons within the scope of Article 3(2)(a) and (b). Third-country nationals within the scope of Article 3(2) can obtain the 'Residence card of a *family member* of a Union citizen' referred to in Article 10(1).[231] Moreover, the *Rahman* judgment refers to persons within the scope of Article 3(2) as 'family members'; recital 6 in the preamble refers to 'the unity of the family in the broader sense'; and the prior legislation referred to the persons concerned as family members.[232] So it follows that references to 'family members' in the citizens' Directive cannot be considered to refer only to the core family members listed in Article 2(2) in all cases.

This brings us to the question of *which* provisions of the Directive apply to extended family members. Article 11, on the validity of the residence card, must do, since it refers back to Article 10. So must Article 5(2) and (3), on visas and passport stamps, since these provisions refer back to Article 10 also. Article 9 appears to be referring to the same 'residence card' as Article 10. Otherwise the Directive does not contain any provisions which either expressly apply to extended family members, or which expressly exempt extended family members from their application. Faced with this silence, there are four possible rules of interpretation: *presumed inclusion* (ie the Directive applies to extended family members except where it excludes them implicitly); *presumed exclusion* (ie the Directive does *not* apply to extended family members except where it includes them implicitly or expressly); *case-by-case* interpretation of the individual provisions of the Directive, to see whether they are apt to apply to extended family members; and *national discretion* (in light of the silence of the Directive, Member States can do what they like).

In its judgment in *Rahman*, the Court appeared to endorse a 'national discretion' approach, ruling that the Directive 'did not settle' the question of whether to issue the residence card referred to in Article 10 if an extended family member ceased to be dependent after arrival in the host Member State.[233] Notwithstanding this, the Court did not suggest that its ruling had broader implications beyond this specific issue. It is submitted that the best approach would be the 'presumed inclusion'

---

[231] Art 10(2)(e) and (f) expressly provide for the persons referred to in Art 3(2)(a) and (b) to obtain this card, and the *Rahman* judgment interpreted these provisions in this context (see further below).

[232] In particular, Art 10(2) of Reg 1612/68 referred to 'any member of the family not coming within the provisions of paragraph 1', and Art 1(2) of Directive 73/148 referred to 'any other member of the family'.

[233] Paras 41–45 of the judgment.

approach, since this approach would be the most consistent with the Directive's intention to 'strengthen the right of free movement and residence of all Union citizens' (recital 3 in the preamble). For example, the expulsion of an extended family member from a host Member State is bound to affect the likelihood of the EU citizen remaining in that Member State in practice. If Member States had wanted to exclude such extended family members from the entirety of the Directive (besides the provisions expressly referring to such persons), they would surely have done so expressly.

However, the 'presumed inclusion' approach does not mean that *every* provision of the Directive applies to extended family members in full. The key to this analysis is the wording of recital 6, which states that there is no '*automatic right* of entry and residence' for extended family members, but rather each Member State decides, in accordance with the criteria set out in the recital, whether 'entry and residence could be granted to such persons'. It must follow that *if* a Member State grants 'entry and residence' to extended family members, *then* the relevant rules in the Directive apply to those individuals. This is best demonstrated by Article 5. While Article 3(2) does not confer a 'right of entry' as set out in Article 5, the express reference to Article 10 in Article 5(2) and (3) must mean that *if* an extended family member has been admitted to a host Member State and obtained a residence card pursuant to Article 10, *then* he or she does not need an entry visa and his or her passport cannot be stamped. By analogy, *if* an extended family member is admitted to reside in a Member State pursuant to Article 3(2), *then* either Article 7(1)(d) or (2) (depending on the family member's nationality) applies to that person.[234] This interpretation is consistent with the structure of Article 10, which provides in its first paragraph for the issue of a residence card to evidence 'the right of residence' of third-country national family members of EU citizens, but then sets out rules in its second paragraph for extended family members to obtain such cards, even though such persons do not have 'the right of residence' as such. Therefore extended family members retain their residence pursuant to Article 14(1) and (2) so long as, like EU citizens and core family members, they continue to satisfy the criteria set out in Articles 7, 12, and 13;[235] and the protections set out in Article 14(3) and (4) must equally apply to them.

It follows from this that extended family members can then obtain the right of permanent residence, pursuant to chapter IV of the Directive, since their previous

---

[234] Given that Art 8(3) refers expressly to the conditions in Art 7(1), it would be odd if extended family members, expressly referred to in Art 8(5), were entirely outside the scope of Art 7.

[235] See Case C-45/12 *Hadj Ahmed*, judgment of 13 June 2013, para 37 of the judgment, in which the Court ruled that the former partner of an EU citizen could not retain residence pursuant to Art 14, since she did not satisfy the conditions set out in Art 13. If extended family members could not qualify to retain residence pursuant to Art 14 *at all*, then it would have been unnecessary for the Court to examine whether Ms Hadj Ahmed met the conditions set out in Art 13.

residence will have fallen within the scope of Article 7.[236] Even if the 'presumed inclusion' approach is rejected in whole or part (ie as regards the right of permanent residence), at the very least the family members of EU citizens who have ended their work or self-employment pursuant to the rules in Article 17 have a right to permanent residence—since the prior legislation provided for this.[237] This means that the general rules in chapter V of the Directive are also applicable to extended family members.[238]

As for the remaining provisions of the Directive, the procedural safeguards in Article 15(2) expressly apply to persons with residence cards, and the 'presumed inclusion' approach would mean that the rest of Article 15 also applies to extended family members, with the result that the procedural standards set out in Articles 30 and 31 apply to any decision to refuse their entry and residence.[239] As regards the rest of chapter VI of the Directive, since that chapter applies to persons who are not legally resident at all,[240] it would be odd if it did not also apply to extended family members.[241]

Finally, as regards the issue of family breakdown, it is necessary to distinguish between the different reasons for the end of family life and the nationality of the persons concerned. In the event of the death or departure of the EU citizen whom the extended family members were joining, Article 12 does not suggest any distinction based on the type of family members who remain. So, following the 'presumed inclusion' approach, the rules in Article 12 apply equally to core family members and extended family members. However, Article 13 does draw such a distinction between some categories of family members, since it only applies in the event of divorce or annulment of a marriage, or the termination of a registered partnership as defined in Article 2(2)(b). The necessary implication is that it does not apply to the end of a partnership relationship as referred to in Article 3(2)(b), and the Court

---

[236] See the commentary on Art 16(1) and (2), in Chapter 4. This interpretation is reinforced by the identical wording of Arts 11(2) and 16(3), given that the former provision indisputably applies to extended family members.

[237] In particular, Art 1 of Reg 1251/70 referred to 'family members' as defined in Art 10 (not just Art 10(1)) of Reg 1612/68, and Art 1 of Directive 75/34 referred to 'members of their families' as defined in Art 1 (not just Art 1(1)) of Directive 73/148. In accordance with the *Metock* judgment, recital 3 of the preamble, by referring to the objective to 'simplify and strengthen' the prior rules, confirms that the citizens' Directive does not lower standards compared to the prior rules.

[238] In any event, Arts 25 and 26 must apply to extended family members, since they refer expressly to residence cards.

[239] See Art 15(1), and the discussion above regarding the procedural rights built in to Art 3(2).

[240] See Cases C-459/99 *MRAX* [2002] ECR I-6591 and C-50/06 *Commission v Netherlands* [2007] ECR I-4383, discussed in Chapter 6.

[241] Therefore Art 29 restricts the reasons related to public health which a Member State might invoke to refuse entry of a family member who seeks to reside with the EU citizen on 'serious health grounds'. By analogy with Art 32, it should be possible to make a repeat application for entry and residence of an extended family member.

of Justice has confirmed this in *Hadj Ahmed*.[242] It might be thought that Article 13 could equally not apply to the end of the other forms of relationship referred to in Article 3(2), and the Court's approach to Article 10 as regards the termination of dependency in the *Rahman* judgment is consistent with this analysis. However, the *Hadj Ahmed* judgment casts some doubt on this, since the Court made a point of observing that Ms Hadj Ahmed was not dependent on her former partner.[243] Where the extended family members left behind after a partnership ends are EU citizens, they might be able to rely upon the Directive in their own name;[244] and even if the former partner is not an EU citizen, he or she might derive rights from being the parent of a child of that EU citizen who is undertaking education.[245] If a family relationship is still extant, but a dependant is no longer dependent, then the issue should be resolved the same way as it would be if the dependent family members referred to in Article 2(2)(c) and (d) ceased to be dependent (see the commentary above).

It might be argued that the more restrictive 'presumed exclusion' approach would be justified, in whole or part by the Court's interpretation in *Ziolkowski*, which stated that if a Member State was more generous to an EU citizen (and presumably also a citizen's family member) than the Directive provided for, pursuant to Article 37, the person concerned could not qualify for permanent residence.[246] But this judgment should be distinguished, because a Member State which applies Article 3(2), even if it admits all extended family members automatically, is exercising an option provided for expressly in the Directive, and its actions therefore remain within the scope of the system established by the Directive[247]—as distinct from allowing entry and residence of persons who are solely reliant on social assistance, which is outside the scope of the Directive but permitted pursuant to Article 37.

F. Evaluation

Articles 2 and 3 are at the heart of EU free movement law in general and of the citizens' Directive in particular. The three issues addressed here—the definition

---

[242] Case C-45/12, judgment of 13 June 2013, para 37 of the judgment. It was presumed in this case that Ms Hadj Ahmed's former partner had not left the territory of the host State, since the national court's questions concerned only Art 13, not Art 12.

[243] Case C-45/12, judgment of 13 June 2013, para 14.

[244] See Joined Cases C-147/11 and C-148/11 *Czop and Punakova*, judgment of 6 September 2012, not yet reported.

[245] *Hadj Ahmed*, paras 43–54 of the judgment. The same might apply to former partners who are EU citizens, in the same circumstances: see Joined Cases C-147/11 and C-148/11 *Czop and Punakova*, judgment of 6 September 2012, not yet reported.

[246] Joined Cases C-424/10 and C-425/10, judgment of 21 December 2011, not yet reported.

[247] See by analogy Joined Cases C-411/10 and C-493/10, *NS and ME*, judgment of 21 December 2011, not yet reported.

of EU citizens, the requirement of movement between Member States, and the position of family members—determine the application of the rest of the Directive, and so delineate exactly which persons have the right to enter and reside, enter the labour market, resist expulsion, claim social benefits, and obtain permanent residence status. While the basic tenets of the Directive can be described quite simply—EU citizens have the right to move to another Member State and to bring their family members with them—the detailed interpretation of the key rules defining the scope of that simple tenet has proven increasingly complex and controversial. It is striking that liberal judgments of the Court of Justice (*Carpenter*, *MRAX*, and *Baumbast* in 2002, and *Ruiz Zambrano* in 2011) are often soon followed by a conservative counter-reaction (*Akrich*, *Kaba*, and *Givane* in 2003,[248] and *McCarthy* and *Dereci* in 2011), leading (with respect) to an overall lack of direction, which manifests itself in incoherent and conceptually flawed judgments, most notably *Akrich* and *McCarthy*. The latter judgment in particular is inconsistent with prior case law, and creates many anomalies by comparison with essentially identical situations. It appears that at least some judgments turn on whether the plight of the particular wives or children involved strikes a sympathetic chord with the Court's judges or not, in place of any attempt to create a logical and systematic doctrine that can easily be understood and applied by the relevant national administrators and courts. While the key judgments of the CJEU in this field (most notably *Diatta*, *Baumbast*, and *Metock*) have built a solid foundation, one can only hope that the overall standard and consistency of the case law will improve in future.

On the specific issue of discrimination, while there might be a perception that this is caused solely by the CJEU's case law,[249] or that EU law 'is only protecting a privileged minority of its citizens',[250] the reality is that as with every type of discrimination, the position of two groups has to be compared, and in the absence of EU legislation on the admission of family members of one of these groups (static EU citizens), it is up to Member States to regulate the position of such persons.[251] It must be concluded that when Member States complain about 'reverse discrimination', their aspiration is to *lower* the standard for migrant EU citizens—since they can *raise* the standard for their own static citizens at any time, if they really want to ensure that no reverse discrimination occurs.

---

[248] On *Kaba II* (Case C-466/00 [2003] ECR I-2219), see Chapter 5; on *Givane* (Case C-257/00 [2003] ECR I-345), see Chapter 4.

[249] See N Nic Shiubhne, 'Free Movement of Persons and the Wholly Internal Rule: Time to Move On?' (2002) 39 CMLRev 763.

[250] C Dautricourt and S Thomas, 'Reverse Discrimination and Free Movement of Persons Under Community Law: All for Ulysses, Nothing for Penelope?' (2009) 34 ELRev 433 at 436.

[251] Note also that the Commission's original proposal for the family reunion Directive would have extended the EC free movement family reunion rules to the admission of family members of home State national sponsors (see COM(1999) 638, 1 December 1999, Art 4), but the Council (ie the Member States) deleted this provision from the Directive.

Even if the prior lawful residence rule, abolished in *Metock*, still applied, there would still be some reverse discrimination (as between mobile EU citizens whose family members could satisfy that rule, and static EU citizens), as well as discrimination *between categories of mobile EU citizens* (as between those who had family members who could not satisfy that rule, and those who did not face such an impediment). In any event, any national law which seeks to limit the admission of third-country national family members of that Member State's static citizens is liable to have a disproportionate impact on racial and religious minorities, since persons in such minority groups are more likely to have historical links with third countries (for instance, former colonies of the UK and the Netherlands). So the argument for curtailing EU free movement law in order to prevent 'reverse discrimination' is fatally flawed—as it would lower standards for migrant EU citizens (creating impediments to free movement) and facilitate a more pernicious form of discrimination.

The best way to solve the reverse discrimination problem without lowering standards for anyone is to call upon the European Court of Human Rights to rethink its case law on Article 8 ECHR, as regards the application of the right to family and private life in family reunion cases.[252] This case law states that subject to limited exceptions, there is no right to insist on the initial admission of family members, since they could move to another country to enjoy family life there. Such reasoning ignores the absolute right of citizens to reside in their own country, and the qualified right of established residents to continue to live there also, by allowing States to impose an obligation to leave if those persons also wish to enjoy the right to family life with a foreign national. This position is untenable on its own terms, and reversing it would have the added advantage of significantly reducing the gap between static and migrant EU citizens in this field.

---

[252] For detailed criticism of the case law, see S Peers, 'Family Reunion and Community Law', in N Walker, ed, *Towards an Area of Freedom, Security and Justice* (OUP, Oxford, 2004), 143 at 190–197.

2

RIGHT OF EXIT AND ENTRY

A. Function

Articles 4 and 5 of Directive 2004/38 affirm the right of Union citizens and members of their family to leave their Member State of origin and to enter any other Member State of their choosing. As such, these Articles constitute 'gateway' provisions permitting the exercise of rights of residence and rights of permanent residence provided for in the Directive.

In addition to affirming the right of free movement, Articles 4 and 5 specify the administrative documentation and procedures governing travel between Member States. In so doing they provide the necessary detail to enable EU citizens and their family members to exercise free movement rights conferred upon them by Union law.

Union citizens may wish to travel to other Member States for a number of different reasons, in a variety of different circumstances, at different stages of their lives, and for different periods of time. They may wish to move as tourists, students, jobseekers, workers, self-employed persons, pensioners, or indeed, without any specific or declared purpose. A significant feature of the Directive is that it creates a single overarching framework that is capable of applying to a diversity of factual and legal contexts.

B. Historical development

As discussed in the introductory chapter, the right of Union citizens to travel between Member States developed from rights that had initially been conferred on economically active Member State nationals. Given that the Treaties establishing the European Communities were intended to further economic cooperation and the creation of a single market, they sought to facilitate movement connected with economic pursuits. The right of Member States' nationals to move between

Member States for the purposes laid down in the Treaties has been considered to form part of the very foundations of what is now the European Union.[1] Article 48 of the EEC Treaty affirmed that freedom of movement for workers entailed the right, subject to limitations, 'to move freely within the territory of the Member States'.[2] Similarly, freedom of establishment, provided for in Article 52 EEC, included 'the right to take up and pursue activities as self-employed persons and to set up and manage undertakings'.[3]

Successive legislative measures dating from the early 1960s were introduced to facilitate the movement of economically active Member State nationals between Member States. The first such measures included Regulation No 15/1961[4] laying down key principles governing freedom of movement for workers and an associated Directive setting out procedures on entry, employment, and residence.[5] The right to free movement as provided for in the 1961 Directive was limited to facilitating travel for the purposes of taking up jobs that had already been offered. From the outset free movement and residence rights were also conferred on family members of migrant Member State nationals.[6] Initially, the definition of family member was limited to the worker's spouse and children under the age of twenty-one.[7]

Every Member State of origin was required to provide its nationals with a passport or an identity card in order to permit them to exercise their right to move to take up employment in another Member State.[8] Passports granted were to be valid for all Member States as well as for 'transit' non-Member States through which it was necessary to pass when travelling between Member States. Article 2(2) of the 1961 Directive stipulated that where a passport is the only document authorizing the lawful departure from a Member State, its period of validity could not be less than five years. Every host Member State was required to admit such nationals on the

---

[1] Case 139/85 *Kempf* [1986] ECR 1741, para 13, and Case C-215/03 *Oulane* [2005] ECR I-1215, para 16.

[2] Following the Treaty of Amsterdam, freedom of movement for workers was provided for in Art 39 EC and the right of establishment appeared under Art 43 EC. Since the entry into force of the Lisbon Treaty on 1 December 2009, the relevant provisions appear in Arts 45 TFEU (workers) and 49 TFEU (establishment).

[3] The Council and the Commission were entrusted with adopting measures to ensure that migrant workers may remain in the host Member State for the purposes of taking up activities therein as self-employed persons.

[4] Reg 15 of 16 August 1961 on initial measures to bring about free movement of workers within the Community ([1961] OJ 57/1073, hereinafter 'Regulation 15').

[5] Council Directive of 16 August 1961 on administrative procedures and practices governing the entry into and employment and residence in a Member State of workers and their families from other Member States of the Community ([1961] OJ 80/1513, hereinafter 'the 1961 Directive').

[6] Arts 2 and 3 of the 1961 Directive.

[7] Art 1(b) of the 1961 Directive incorporates the definition of family member provided for in Art 11 of Reg 15.

[8] Art 2 of the 1961 Directive.

simple presentation of such documentation.[9] The imposition of entry visas was expressly prohibited.[10]

The obligation that the 1961 Directive imposed on Member States to issue travel documentation was supplemented by an express right of exit from the State of origin and a right of entry into the host Member State. The right of exit was set out in Article 5 of Regulation No 15/1961 while the right of entry was provided for in Article 3 of the 1961 Directive. These provisions were subsequently re-enacted in Articles 2 and 3 of Directive 64/240 of 25 March 1964.[11] Article 2(1) of Directive 64/240 required Member States to ensure Member State nationals and their family members were free to leave the territory of such States for the purposes of taking up employment in another Member State and that such nationals would subsequently be permitted to return to their Member State of origin. Article 2(4) of the Directive expressly prohibited Member States from imposing a requirement for exit visas or any equivalent obligation. Pursuant to Article 3, migrant Member State workers were required to be admitted to the territory of the host Member State in order to engage in an employed activity.

Directive 64/240 further extended the circumstances in which individuals could exercise free movement rights. It ensured that the right of entry and residence in a host Member State was no longer conditional on a job having been actually offered, but was granted generally for the purposes of taking up employment.[12] It also contained certain measures detailing entry requirements for third-country national family members of workers. While the 1961 Directive had generally exempted Member State nationals and their family members from entry visas or equivalent requirements, Directive 64/240 specified that such documentation could still be requested from third country national family members. Nevertheless, family members subject to visa requirements were to be facilitated in obtaining the necessary documentation.[13]

In addition to revising legislation on workers, the Community legislature also adopted a specific Directive regulating the right of movement for the purposes of conducting a self-employed activity in a host Member State or for providing and receiving services.[14] Directive 64/220 required any restrictions on such movement to be abolished.[15] The Community legislature also adopted measures regulating

---

[9] Art 3(1) of the 1961 Directive.

[10] Art 3(2) of the 1961 Directive.

[11] Directive 64/240 of 25 March 1964 on the abolition of restrictions on the movement and residence of Member States' workers and their families within the Community ([1964] OJ 64/981).

[12] Arts 2(1) and 3(1) of Directive 64/240.

[13] Art 3(2) of Directive 64/240.

[14] Directive 64/220/EEC of 25 February 1964 on the abolition of restrictions on movement and residence within the Community for nationals of Member States with regard to establishment and the provision of services ([1964] OJ 64/845).

[15] Art 1 of Directive 64/220.

and circumscribing Member States' entitlement to restrict entry or residence on grounds of public policy, public security, and public health.[16]

The legislation adopted in 1964 broadened the definition of family members entitled to benefit from free movement rights to include ascendants and descendants of the migrant Member State nationals as well as of their spouses.[17] In addition, Member States were required to facilitate the admission of any other family member for whom the Member State national was responsible and who formed part of his or her household.[18] The entitlement of family members to join a migrant Community worker in the host Member State was conditional on the worker possessing suitable accommodation for his or her family. The Directive specified that such accommodation should be considered normal by the standards of nationals of the host State working in the same region as the migrant Member State national.[19]

The provisions on exit and entry as expressed in Directive 64/240 (as regards workers) and Directive 64/220 (as regards self-employed persons and providers or recipients of services) were essentially reproduced in subsequent free movement legislation[20] and have largely remained unchanged in the citizens' Directive. Essentially, Member States of origin continue to be obliged to issue travel documentation to their nationals and remain prohibited from restricting their departure to another Member State. Similarly, host Member States continue to be obliged to grant Union citizens entry upon their territory once they are in possession of the required documentation. Nevertheless, the beneficiaries of free movement rights, and in particular, the purposes for which such rights may be relied upon, have expanded progressively and significantly over time. Through successive legislative measures, rights of movement and residence have been extended to various categories of economically inactive Member State nationals including

---

[16] Directive 64/221/EEC of 25 February 1964 on the co-ordination of special measures concerning the movement and residence of foreign nationals which are justified on grounds of public policy, public security or public health ([1964] OJ 56/850).

[17] See Art 17 of Reg 38/64/EEC of 25 March 1964 on the freedom of movement for workers within the Community ([1964] OJ 64/965). See also Art 1 of Directive 64/240 (which extends rights to workers' family members on the basis of their definition in Regulation 38/64) and Art 1 of Directive 64/220.

[18] See Art 17(2) of Reg 38/64 (which was incorporated into Directive 64/240 by Art 1 of that Directive) and Art 1(2) of Directive 64/220.

[19] Art 17(3) of Reg 38/64. This requirement also featured subsequently in Art 10(3) of Reg 1612/68 of 15 October 1968 on freedom of movement for workers ([1968] OJ L 257/2) and was considered by the Court of Justice in Case 249/86 *Commission v Germany* [1989] ECR 1263.

[20] Regarding workers, see for example, Directive 68/360/EEC on the abolition of restrictions on movement and residence within the Community for workers of Member States and their families ([1968] OJ L 257/13). Regarding establishment and the provision of services, see Arts 2–4 of Directive 73/148/EEC of 21 May 1973 on the abolition of restrictions on movement and residence within the Community for workers and their families. The exit and entry provisions contained in Directive 68/360 were in turn applied *mutatis mutandis* to former workers, students, and all other classes of Member State national in the three residence Directives adopted in 1990 (see nn 21 to 24 below).

former workers,[21] students,[22] and jobseekers.[23] Free movement rights were also conferred on Member State nationals who did not belong to any of those categories but who merely wished to visit or spend time in another Member State without any specific or stated purpose.[24] Following the establishment of Union citizenship by the Maastricht Treaty, an automatic, general, and freestanding primary law right of free movement, detached from any requirement for economic activity, was conferred on all Union citizens and their family members. Crucially, such rights derived directly from their status as Union citizens, rather than from the economic function that they performed.

C. Interrelationship of Articles 4 and 5 with other provisions of the Directive

The right of Union citizens and their family members to travel between Member States in accordance with Articles 4 and 5 constitutes the necessary condition for the exercise of other rights provided for in the Directive, in particular, the right of residence and the right of permanent residence, provided for in chapters III and IV of the Directive.

As a matter of practice, the provisions governing the right of exit and entry are typically invoked in opposition to decisions of national authorities seeking to limit or restrict such a right. Consequently, the provisions of chapter VI of the Directive (Articles 27–33), which permit restrictions on freedom of movement on grounds of public policy, public security, or public health, are of particular relevance to the rights affirmed in Articles 4 and 5.

In addition, it is implicit from the wording of Article 15 that the right of free movement may additionally be restricted on grounds other than policy, security, or health. Such restrictions may arise in circumstances provided for in Article 14, namely, where Union citizens and their family members fail to comply with conditions attaching to their right of residence, such as the possession of sufficient resources and comprehensive sickness insurance. Pursuant to Article 15(3),

---

[21] Council Directive 90/365/EEC of 28 June 1990 on the right of residence for employees and self-employed persons who have ceased their occupational activity ([1990] OJ L 180/28).

[22] Council Directive 93/96/EEC of 29 October 1993 on the right of residence for students ([1993] OJ L 317/59).

[23] The process by which residence rights were progressively extended to various categories of economically inactive Member State national is considered in greater detail in 'Historical development', Section B of Chapter 3. For examination of the right to equal treatment of economically inactive Union citizens, see 'Historical development', Section B, and 'Analysis', Section E, of the commentary relating to Art 24 in Chapter 5.

[24] See Council Directive 90/364/EEC of 28 June 1990 on the right of residence ([1990] OJ L 180/26).

expulsion measures imposed on grounds other than public policy, public security, or public health may not be accompanied by a ban on entry.

D. Other relevant norms

The citizens' Directive gives effect to free movement rights that are enshrined in the EU Treaties, notably in Articles 20(2)(a) and 21 of the TFEU. In particular, these provisions declare that citizens of the Union shall have the right to move and reside freely within the territory of the Member States. Article 21 TFEU specifies, however, that such rights are subject to the limitations and conditions laid down in the Treaties and by the measures adopted to give them effect. More recently, the right to move and reside freely has also been recognized as a fundamental right enshrined in Article 45 of the EU Charter of Fundamental Rights. The explanations to Article 45 observe that the right of free movement provided for in the Charter is to be applied in accordance with conditions and within the limits defined by the Treaties.[25] The right of an individual to leave his or her country is also enshrined in Article 2(2) of Protocol 4 to the European Convention on Human Rights.[26]

The Schengen *acquis* is of particular relevance to the practical exercise of the right of exit and entry provided for in Articles 4 and 5. Initially developed through intergovernmental agreement outside the framework of the EEC (now EU), the Schengen *acquis* constitutes a body of law that is intended to permit the progressive abolition of internal borders between participating States ('the Schengen States'), in conjunction with rules on freedom to travel, a common short-term visa policy, standard rules on external border controls, and flanking measures such as the Schengen Information System, which inter alia contains a list of persons who should be refused entry into any of the Schengen States.[27]

The Schengen *acquis* comprises: (a) the initial Schengen Agreement, which was signed on 14 June 1985 and originally applied as between Belgium, France, Germany, Luxembourg, and the Netherlands; (b) the Convention Implementing the Schengen Agreement, which was signed on 19 June 1990 and entered into force

---

[25] Explanations to the Charter ([2007] OJ C 303/17).

[26] Art 2 of Protocol 4 of the ECHR is entitled 'Freedom of movement'. Art 2(1) enshrines the right of free movement within the territory of a State. Art 2(2) states that: 'Everyone shall be free to leave any country, including his own.' In Case C-249/11 *Hristo Byankov*, judgment of 4 October 2012, not yet reported, the Court of Justice, at para 47, refers expressly to the case law of the European Court of Human Rights (ECtHR) concerning a person's right to leave his country. In particular, the Court refers to *Ignatov v Bulgaria*, judgment of 2 July 2009, Application No 50/02 (§ 37), and *Gochev v Bulgaria*, judgment of 26 November 2009, Application No 34383/03 (§§ 55–57). See also Case C-434/10 *Aladzhov*, judgment of 17 November 2011, not yet reported, para 37, where the Court of Justice refers expressly to the ECtHR judgment in *Riener v Bulgaria* (judgment of 23 May 2006).

[27] See generally S Peers, E Guild, and J Tomkin, *EU Immigration and Asylum Law: Text and Commentary*, vol 1 (Martinus Nijhoff, Leiden, 2012).

on 1 September 1993, and which gives more detailed expression to the objectives enshrined in the Agreement; and (c) the measures implementing those treaties.[28] The Schengen *acquis* was integrated into the Union legal order following the entry into force of the Treaty of Amsterdam on 1 May 1999.[29] Since then the application of the Schengen *acquis* has gradually been extended to an increasing number of States.[30] At the time of writing the core provisions of the Schengen *acquis* apply to every EU Member State except Ireland, the UK, Romania, Bulgaria, Cyprus, and Croatia. In addition, these core provisions apply to certain associated non-EU Member States, namely, Iceland, Liechtenstein, Norway, and Switzerland. All the remaining Member States except Ireland and the UK are obliged to apply the Schengen *acquis* in full eventually, and from the date of accession to the EU they must apply the rules relating to the external borders and a common visa list. Their eventual application of all the Schengen *acquis* is subject to a decision of the Council, acting unanimously. As for the UK and Ireland, they essentially participate only in the criminal law aspects of the Schengen *acquis*, but in none of the measures most directly related to the abolition of internal border controls.[31]

The main components of the relevant provisions of the Schengen *acquis* concern rules on the abolition of internal border controls, strengthening external border controls, freedom to travel, and a common short-term visa policy.[32] First of all, as regards border controls, the main rules are set out in the Schengen Borders Code,[33] which sets out detailed rules on the abolition of internal border controls,[34] as well

---

[28] [2000] OJ L 239. In 1990 Italy acceded to the Agreement and Convention, followed by Spain and Portugal in 1991. Greece followed in 1992, then Austria in 1995. Denmark, Finland, and Sweden acceded in 1996, and Norway and Iceland also signed an association treaty.

[29] See the 'Protocol integrating the Schengen *acquis* into the framework of the European Union', which was annexed by the Treaty of Amsterdam to the Treaty on European Union and the Treaty establishing the European Community, and the Council Decisions in [1999] OJ L 176.

[30] Since the integration of the Schengen *acquis* into the EU legal order in May 1999, the Council extended its application on 21 December 2007 to the Czech Republic, Estonia, Latvia, Lithuania, Hungary, Malta, Poland, Slovenia, and Slovakia. Switzerland joined in 2008, and Liechtenstein joined in 2011.

[31] See Council Decision 2002/192/EC concerning Ireland's request to take part in some of the provisions of the Schengen *acquis* ([2002] OJ L 64/20) and Council Decision 2012/764/EU concerning Ireland's participation in Schengen provisions relating to the establishment of a European Agency for the operational management of large-scale IT systems in the area of freedom, security and justice ([2012] OJ L 337/48). For the equivalent Decisions for the UK, see [2000] OJ L 131/43 and [2010] OJ L 333/58.

[32] Long-term visas are primarily a matter for Member States, although EU immigration legislation has impacted upon their issue, and there are provisions of the Schengen *acquis* which harmonize their format and validity: see Art 18 of the Schengen Convention, as amended by Reg 265/2010 ([2010] OJ L 85/1).

[33] Reg 562/2006, [2006] OJ L 105/1. See Peers, Guild, and Tomkin (n 27 above), ch 5.

[34] Arts 20–22 of the Borders Code. However, Arts 23–31 of the Code provide for the temporary reintroduction of internal border controls in certain cases. The European Parliament and Council have agreed changes to the latter rules, which will be formally adopted in the second half of 2013 (for the text, see Council doc 10687/13, 19 June 2013).

as the controls at the external borders of the Schengen States.[35] Crucially, the recitals to the Borders Code, along with Article 3(a) of the Code, make it clear that its provisions are subordinate to rights of free movement which derive from the Treaty and in particular from Directive 2004/38. For instance, the rules on external border checks in the Borders Code are expressly subordinate to the rules in the citizens' Directive.[36] Indeed, the CJEU has referred to Recital 5 in the preamble to the Borders Code, and Article 3(a) of the Code, to confirm that the Code is not designed to restrict free movement rights.[37] It is settled case law that provisions of the Schengen *acquis* incorporated into the Union legal order are applicable only in so far as they are compatible with EU law.[38]

Secondly, as regards freedom to travel, the relevant rules are still set out in the Schengen Convention. In principle, any third-country nationals with residence permits or long-stay visas issued by a Schengen State, or who do not need a visa to cross the external borders, or who have been issued with a short-stay visa by one of the Schengen States (a 'Schengen visa') can travel freely across the territory of the Schengen States for a period of 90 days in every 180 days.[39]

Finally, as for visas, there are two main issues: the list of States whose nationals do or do not need short-term visas (applicable to all Member States except the UK and Ireland, and also applicable to the Schengen associates), and the common rules on the processing of short-term visa applications (applicable to all the States fully applying the Schengen *acquis*). On the former issue, the lists in question are set out in Regulation No 539/2001, as amended, which is of particular relevance to Article 5 of the Directive.[40] Pursuant to Article 5, short-term entry visas may only be imposed on family members who are nationals of third countries listed in Annex I of the Regulation (and only if such persons do not hold the residence card referred to in Article 10 of the Directive). As Ireland and the UK have opted out of this Regulation, they may still apply national law in designating third countries whose nationals must be in possession of short-term visas.[41] On the latter issue, the rules on short-term visa applications (which primarily govern the issue of Schengen visas) are set out in a visa code, which was adopted in 2009.[42] The provisions of this code are important in the context of EU free movement law because they are

---

[35] Art 7 of the Borders Code.

[36] Art 7(6) of the Borders Code, as amended by Reg 610/2013, [2013] OJ L 182/1.

[37] Case C-430/10 *Hristo Gaydarov*, judgment of 17 November 2011, not yet reported, para 28.

[38] Case C-503/03 *Commission v Spain* [2006] ECR I-1097, para 34, and Case C-430/10 *Hristo Gaydarov*, judgment of 17 November 2011, not yet reported, para 35.

[39] See Arts 18–22 of the Convention, as amended by Regs 265/2010 ([2010] OJ L 85/1) and 610/2013 ([2013] OJ L 182/1).

[40] Council Reg 539/2001 listing the third countries whose nationals must be in possession of visas when crossing the external borders and those whose nationals are exempt from the requirement [2001] OJ L 81/1.

[41] Art 5 permits the use of domestic law 'where appropriate'; see the 'Analysis' section below.

[42] Reg 810/2009, [2009] OJ L 243/1.

in principle applicable to visa applications made by third-country national family members of EU citizens exercising free movement rights—although Article 5 of the citizens' Directive provides for certain exceptions from the rules in the code.

Taken as a whole, the intersection between the EU free movement rules and the Schengen *acquis* means that in practice there are three different sets of rules applying to EU citizens and their third-country national family members who cross borders between Member States. The first of these regimes is the Schengen system. In this system, if migrant EU citizens or their family members who are beneficiaries of free movement rights under the Directive cross the internal borders between the twenty-two Member States which are fully applying the Schengen *acquis* (or the borders between any of those States and the Schengen associates), then in principle they should not be checked at all, unless one of the States concerned has exceptionally and temporarily reintroduced internal border controls.[43] Similarly, family members of Union citizens who have not taken up residence in another Member State (and who therefore do not possess a residence card under Article 10 of the citizens' Directive, discussed in Chapter 3) may also enjoy the freedom to travel between those Member States, if they have a residence permit or long-stay visa issued by any of those States in accordance with their domestic law (which EU law has partly harmonized). Union citizens and their family members (whether migrant or otherwise) that cross between a Schengen State and any of the six Member States not (or not fully) applying the Schengen rules, will be subject to Schengen rules on external borders and visas, as modified by this Directive.[44]

The second regime applies between the two Member States[45] which do not apply the Schengen regime at all. These Member States have full freedom to determine the rules on visa requirements, on the conditions for issuing visas, and on external border control, as regards movements to or from any other Member State (including each other), although they must still comply with the basic rules of the Directive.[46]

The third regime applies between the four Member States[47] which partly apply the Schengen regime. As regards movements between those States, or movements to and from those States to the other Member States, they must apply the Schengen rules on external borders and visa lists, as modified by the citizens' Directive, but not the other Schengen rules.

The specific consequences of the interaction between these various regimes and the citizens' Directive is explored in the detailed analysis of Articles 4 and 5 below.

---

[43] Title III, Schengen Borders Code.

[44] The application of the Schengen rules on external borders and visas to persons exercising free movement rights is considered in detail in the analysis of Arts 4 and 5 below.

[45] UK and Ireland.

[46] See the discussion of Case C-202/13 *McCarthy*, pending, in the commentary on Art 5 below.

[47] Romania, Bulgaria, Cyprus, and Croatia.

E. Analysis

Article 4—Right of exit

1. Without prejudice to the provisions on travel documents applicable to national border controls, all Union citizens with a valid identity card or passport and their family members who are not nationals of a Member State and who hold a valid passport shall have the right to leave the territory of a Member State to travel to another Member State.
2. No exit visa or equivalent formality may be imposed on the persons to whom paragraph 1 applies.
3. Member States shall, acting in accordance with their laws, issue to their own nationals, and renew, an identity card or passport stating their nationality.
4. The passport shall be valid at least for all Member States and for countries through which the holder must pass when travelling between Member States. Where the law of a Member State does not provide for identity cards to be issued, the period of validity of any passport on being issued or renewed shall be not less than five years.

The right of free movement conferred by Union law on EU citizens and their family members entails not merely the right to enter and reside in the territory of another Member State, but also to leave one's Member State of origin.[48] Article 4(1), entitled 'Right of exit', expressly recognizes the right of Union citizens, in possession of a valid identity card or passport, and their third-country national family members, in possession of a passport, to leave the territory of a Member State for the purposes of travelling to another Member State. The Directive does not regulate travel from Member States to third countries, but such travel would fall within the scope of the Fourth Protocol to the ECHR, discussed above. In legislation preceding the Directive, the entitlement to leave a Member State was exercised simply 'on production of a valid identity card or passport'.[49] However, with the abolition of internal borders between Schengen States, it was sufficient for beneficiaries of free movement rights to be in possession of the relevant document and the wording was changed accordingly.[50] Pursuant to Article 4(2), exit visas or equivalent formalities

---

[48] Case C-33/07 *Jipa* [2008] ECR I-5157, para 18. See also Case C-430/10 *Hristo Gaydarov*, judgment of 17 November 2011, not yet reported, para 25; Case C-434/10 *Aladzhov*, judgment of 17 November 2011, not yet reported, para 25; and Case C-249/11 *Hristo Byankov*, judgment of 4 October 2012, not yet reported, para 31. For analogous case law concerning the freedom of establishment and free movement of workers, see, Case 81/87 *Daily Mail and General Trust* [1988] ECR 5483, para 16; Case C-379/92 *Peralta* [1994] ECR I-3453, para 31; and Case C-415/93 *Bosman* [1995] ECR I-4921, para 97. On the *Jipa* judgment in particular, see D-M Sandru, C-M Banu, and D A Calin, 'The Preliminary Reference in the *Jipa* case and the Case Law of the Romanian Courts on the Restriction on the Free Movement of Persons' (2012) 18 EPL 623.

[49] See Art 2(1) of Directive 68/360.

[50] See the 2001 Proposal, p 9. Otherwise Art 4 of the Directive is essentially identical to Art 2 of Directive 68/360 and Art 2 of Directive 73/148.

may not be imposed on Union citizens moving between Member States and their family members.

Member States are required, in accordance with national law, to issue and upon expiry renew an identity card or passport to their own nationals stating their nationality.[51] Passports are required to be valid for all Member States and transit countries through which the holder must pass when travelling between Member States. If the national law of a Member State does not provide for the issuing of identity cards, the period of validity of any passport that is first issued or subsequently renewed, must not be less than five years.[52] There is separate EU legislation (not applicable to the UK or Ireland) which regulates the security features of EU passports.[53]

In a number of references, the Court has been asked to consider possible limits on citizens' entitlement to leave their Member State of origin for the purposes of travelling to another Member State. In its replies, the Court of Justice has consistently recalled that the right of free movement includes the right to leave one's State of origin and that every Union citizen with a valid identity card or passport has the right to leave the territory of a Member State to travel to another Member State.[54] The Court has specified that the right enshrined in Article 4 is not made subject to the prior exercise of free movement rights.[55]

The right of free movement is not absolute and may be limited on grounds of public policy, public security, and public health provided for in Article 27.[56] Each Member State is afforded a measure of discretion to determine its own policy and security requirements.[57] Nevertheless, as derogations to a fundamental freedom, restrictions may be subject to review by the Union institutions.[58] Restrictions on policy grounds in particular will only be permitted where, in addition to the perturbation of the social order which any infringement of the law involves, a person's conduct constitutes a genuine, present, and sufficiently serious threat to one of the fundamental interests of society.[59]

Member States have sought to justify the imposition of exit restrictions on Union citizens in a variety of different grounds, including: prior unlawful residence

---

[51] Art 4(3) of the Directive.

[52] Art 4(4) of the Directive.

[53] Reg 2252/2004 ([2004] OJ L 385/1), as amended by Reg 444/2009 ([2009] OJ L 142/1).

[54] Case C-33/07 *Jipa* [2008] ECR I-5157, paras 18 and 19; Case C-430/10 *Hristo Gaydarov*, judgment of 17 November 2011, not yet reported, paras 25 and 26; Case C-434/10 *Aladzhov*, judgment of 17 November 2011, not yet reported, paras 24 and 25; and Case C-249/11 *Hristo Byankov*, judgment of 4 October 2012, not yet reported, paras 31 and 32.

[55] Case C-249/11 *Hristo Byankov*, judgment of 4 October 2012, not yet reported, para 32.

[56] The nature and extent of Member States' entitlement to restrict free movement is considered further in Chapter 6.

[57] Case C-33/07 *Jipa* [2008] ECR I-5157, para 23.

[58] Case C-33/07 *Jipa* [2008] ECR I-5157, para 23.

[59] Case C-33/07 *Jipa* [2008] ECR I-5157, paras 23–26.

abroad;[60] prior conviction and imprisonment in a third State;[61] a tax debt to the Member State which they wished to leave;[62] and the existence of considerable debt to a private legal person in the Member Sate of origin.[63] In each case, the Court has expressed doubts as to whether the facts underlying the travel restriction constituted a genuine, present, and sufficiently serious threat that would justify the restriction of free movement rights. In particular, as regards preventing free movement on the grounds of debt to private persons, the Court observed that the objective of protecting creditors did not feature among the limitations on free movement rights listed in Article 27.[64] The Court further observed that even if a restriction could be regarded as a matter of public policy, such a justification could not be invoked for economic objectives. Typically, it is a matter for the national courts to apply the principles to the facts of the particular case before them.[65]

Article 5—Right of entry

1. Without prejudice to the provisions on travel documents applicable to national border controls, Member States shall grant Union citizens leave to enter their territory with a valid identity card or passport and shall grant family members who are not nationals of a Member State leave to enter their territory with a valid passport.

    No entry visa or equivalent formality may be imposed on Union citizens.

Article 5(1) provides for a right of entry into a Member State that is corollary to the right of exit set out in Article 4(1), and precludes Member States from imposing entry visa requirements or equivalent formalities on Union citizens who exercise free movement rights. Unlike the right of exit, Article 5(1) implicitly applies also to entry from third countries.[66] It is essentially identical to prior legislation.[67]

The Court has consistently held that the right of Union citizens to move to the territory of another Member State for the purposes intended by the Treaty is a right conferred directly by the Treaty or, as the case may be, by the provisions of secondary law adopted for its implementation.[68] As a consequence, national administrative procedures do not create, but only give effect to existing rights. Member States

---

[60] Case C-33/07 *Jipa* [2008] ECR I-5157.

[61] Case C-430/10 *Hristo Gaydarov*, judgment of 17 November 2011, not yet reported.

[62] Case C-434/10 *Aladzhov*, judgment of 17 November 2011, not yet reported,

[63] Case C-249/11 *Hristo Byankov*, judgment of 4 October 2012, not yet reported.

[64] Case C-249/11 *Hristo Byankov*, judgment of 4 October 2012, not yet reported, paras 35–37.

[65] See the operative provision of Case C-33/07 *Jipa* [2008] ECR I-5157. See also Case C-430/10 *Hristo Gaydarov*, judgment of 17 November 2011, not yet reported, para 39 (although the Court did indicate at para 36 that the situation giving rise to the proceedings did not appear to meet the prescribed requirements).

[66] See the commentary on Art 3(1), in Chapter 1.

[67] Art 3(1) of Directive 68/360 and Art 3(1) of Directive 73/148. On the concept of an entry visa under the prior legislation, see Case 157/79 *Pieck* [1980] ECR 2171.

[68] Case 48/75 *Royer* [1976] ECR 497, paras 31–33; Case C-357/89 *Raulin* [1992] ECR I-1027, paras 36 and 42; Case C-459/99 *MRAX* [2002] ECR I-6591, para 74, and Case C-215/03 *Oulane* [2005] ECR I-1215, paras 17 and 18.

must therefore not make the exercise of free movement rights subject to any additional conditions that are not provided for in Union law.[69]

Union citizens are entitled to be admitted onto the territory of another Member State once they are in possession of a valid identity card or passport, and their third-country national family members must be admitted if they have possession of a passport. As mentioned in the context of Article 4, prior residence Directives had made the exercise of free movement rights subject to the 'production of' relevant documentation.[70] However, following the abolition of internal borders in accordance with the Schengen *acquis*, it was sufficient for beneficiaries of free movement rights to be in possession of such documentation (without necessarily having to present the relevant documents) and this development is reflected in the wording of Article 5(1) and (2).[71]

Notwithstanding the abolition of border checks within the Schengen States, Union citizens and their family members may still be requested to provide evidence of identity and nationality upon their entry into the territory of Member States, where those States do not apply the Schengen *acquis*, or upon crossing the external borders of a Schengen State, or if a Schengen State temporarily reintroduces border controls.[72] In the case of *Wijsenbeek*,[73] the Court observed that since not every traveller will be a beneficiary of free movement rights, a Member State must be able to require presentation of a valid identity card or passport in order to ascertain whether the person concerned is in fact such a beneficiary.[74] The Court has held, however, that any penalties for the breach of the obligation to present a valid identity card or passport must be comparable to those which apply to similar infringements under national law. In addition, any penalty must not be disproportionate such that it would create an obstacle to the free movement of persons, such as detention with a view to deportation.[75] Article 5(1) makes it clear that the right of entry does not displace provisions concerning travel documents applicable to national border controls.

2. Family members who are not nationals of a Member State shall only be required to have an entry visa in accordance with Regulation (EC) No 539/2001 or, where appropriate, with national law. For the purposes of this Directive, possession of the valid residence card referred to in Article 10 shall exempt such family members from the visa requirement. Member States shall grant such persons

---

[69] Case C-157/03 *Commission v Spain* [2005] ECR I-2911, paras 29 and 30.

[70] See Art 3(1) of Directive 68/360.

[71] See the 2001 Proposal, p 9.

[72] See Art 21 of the Borders Code. Moreover, as regards States to which the Code does not apply, see Case C-378/97 *Wijsenbeek* [1999] ECR I-6207.

[73] Case C-378/97 *Wijsenbeek* [1999] ECR I-6207.

[74] Case C-378/97 *Wijsenbeek* [1999] ECR I-6207, para 43. See also Case C-215/03 *Oulane* [2005] ECR I-1215, para 21.

[75] Case C-378/97 *Wijsenbeek* [1999] ECR I-6207, para 44 and Case C-215/03 *Oulane* [2005] ECR I-1215, para 21.

every facility to obtain the necessary visas. Such visas shall be issued free of charge as soon as possible and on the basis of an accelerated procedure.

3. The host Member State shall not place an entry or exit stamp in the passport of family members who are not nationals of a Member State provided that they present the residence card provided for in Article 10.

Article 5(2) extends the right of entry to the family members of a Union citizen, regardless of nationality.[76] It is based on prior legislation,[77] with the addition of the reference to other EU legislation in the first sentence, the exemption from the visa requirement for some persons in the second sentence, and the requirement to issue visas on an accelerated basis in the fourth sentence. The Commission has reported that the transposition of Article 5(2) 'is often incorrect and/or incomplete, and the legislative shortcomings often result in frequent violations of the rights of family members, notably those who are third-country nationals'. Only seven Member States provided for facilitation of the issue of visas, and five Member States refused to waive the visa requirement for persons with a residence card. Some Member States still required third-country national family members to show proof of accommodation, sufficient resources, and an entry letter, or a return ticket, ie they imposed the general conditions which apply to the issue of a visa for third country nationals who are required to obtain one.[78]

Recital 5 in the preamble to the Directive observes that the extension of free movement rights to family members is a prerequisite for the exercise of such rights under objective conditions of freedom and dignity. Moreover, the CJEU has explained that in conferring family members with the right to move and reside freely, the Union legislature has recognized the importance 'from a human point of view' for Union citizens to be surrounded by their family in the host Member State.[79] Furthermore, the Court has held that this right gives expression to the principle of respect for family life as provided for under Article 8 of the European Convention on Human Rights.[80] The Court has also recognized that refusing entry to family members of Union citizens would deter the exercise of free movement rights and constitute an obstacle to the exercise of fundamental freedoms guaranteed by the Treaty.[81] The right of family members who are third-country nationals to enter an EU Member State arises by virtue of the family relationship[82] and derives from

---

[76] On the application of this provision to extended family members, see the commentary on Art 3(2), in Chapter 1.

[77] Arts 3(2) and 9(2) of Directive 68/360 and Arts 3(2) and 7(2) of Directive 73/148.

[78] COM(2008) 840.

[79] Case C-413/99 *Baumbast and R* [2002] ECR I-7091, para 68.

[80] Case C-413/99 *Baumbast and R* [2002] ECR I-7091, para 72; Case C-503/03 *Commission v Spain* [2006] ECR I-1097, para 47.

[81] Case C-60/00 *Carpenter* [2002] ECR I-6279, para 38; Case C-459/99 *MRAX* [2002] ECR I-6591, para 53; Case C-441/02 *Commission v Germany* [2006] ECR I-3449, para 109; Case C-291/05 *Eind* [2007] ECR I-10719, para 44; and Case C-127/08 *Metock and others* [2008] ECR I-6241, para 56.

[82] Case C-157/03 *Commission v Spain* [2005] ECR I-2911, para 28 Case C-40/11 *Iida v Stadt Ulm*, judgment of 8 November 2012, not yet reported.

Union law. Therefore, just as with Union nationals, the issuing of residence cards to family members who are third-country nationals simply attests the right to reside and does not create or establish that right.[83]

Pursuant to Article 5(2), Member States which participate in Union measures harmonizing short-stay visa requirements (namely, all Member States except the UK and Ireland)[84] may only impose such visa requirements on third-country nationals in accordance with Regulation No 539/2001. That Regulation lists third countries whose nationals are required to possess and who are exempted from possessing short-term entry visas.[85] Member States which do not participate in this EU legislation (ie the UK and Ireland) may impose short-term visa requirements on third-country nationals in accordance with their domestic law. Article 5(2) further provides that family members subject to short-stay visa requirements must be afforded every facility to obtain the necessary visas, which are to be issued free of charge, as soon as possible, and on the basis of an accelerated procedure.

The second sentence of Article 5(2) provides that third-country national family members must be exempted from short-term visa requirements where they are already in possession of a residence card issued by another Member State pursuant to Article 10 (see Chapter 3). The Commission had initially proposed abolishing the visa requirement for *all* third-country national family members who held residence documents from a Member State. As such, it had been proposed to exempt not only family members of *migrant Union citizens* (issued with residence cards on the basis of Article 10), but also the family members of *nationals residing in their own Member State* who had not exercised free movement rights and who held residence permits only under national law. It was observed that such a provision would represent a significant development as it would essentially provide for the recognition of visas and residence documents as between Member States.[86] However, the Council only accepted the Commission's proposal insofar as it applied to family members of migrant Union citizens holding residence cards under Article 10.

The requirement to grant third-country national family members 'every facility to obtain the necessary visas' was interpreted by the CJEU in its judgment in *MRAX*.[87] The Court observed that previous EU legislation at issue in those proceedings,[88] which is identical to the third sentence of Article 5(2), required Member States to issue a visa without delay and as insofar as possible at the place of entry into

---

[83] Case C-459/99 *MRAX* [2002] ECR I-6591, para 74, and Case C-157/03 *Commission v Spain* [2005] ECR I-2911, para 28.

[84] The Union has been conferred with competence to adopt such measures by virtue of Art 77 TFEU.

[85] [2001] OJ L 81/1.

[86] See the 2001 Proposal, p 9.

[87] Case C-459/99 [2002] ECR I-6591. See also Case C-157/03 *Commission v Spain* [2005] ECR I-2911, which was considered above in relation to Art 5(2).

[88] Art 3(2) of Directive 68/360 and Art 3(2) of Directive 73/148.

national territory. It is therefore clear from this judgment that the issue of a visa is obligatory where the person concerned is a family member of an EU citizen, within the scope of Article 2(2).[89]

In accordance with established case law,[90] Article 5(2) applies both to short stays by third-country national family members in another Member State, and to the admission of such family members to accompany or join an EU citizen who is exercising or intends to exercise a longer-term right of residence in another Member State. In the latter case, the question arises whether a Member State can impose a long-stay visa requirement on the third-country national family members wishing to accompany or join a Union citizen. This issue was considered by the Court in *Commission v Spain*.[91] The Commission had issued infringement proceedings against Spain on the ground that its national law imposed a long-stay visa requirement which essentially conflated the entry visa with the separate and subsequent procedure for obtaining a residence permit. In particular, under national law, the granting of a visa was made conditional on third-country national family members demonstrating, prior to entry on Spanish territory, compliance with the substantive conditions necessary for long-term residence. Moreover, the possession of such an entry visa was a pre-condition to obtaining a residence permit.[92] In its judgment, the Court observed that by making the granting of residence documentation dependent on such an entry visa, the Member State was essentially imposing conditions for residence that were not provided for in Union law, when the conditions governing the issuing of residence documentation were already regulated exhaustively in the applicable legislation.[93] The Court recalled that while third-country nationals could be made subject to an entry visa, they must be issued without delay and, as far as possible, at the place of entry onto the national territory.[94] The Court concluded that the national measures at issue were incompatible with Union law. Clearly the adoption of the Directive reinforces the prohibition on imposing a long-stay visa requirement on third-country national family members of EU citizens, since Article 5(2) refers only to legislation regarding a short-stay visa requirement.[95]

---

[89] The wording of the third sentence of Art 5(2) must therefore be distinguished from the 'facilitation' obligation as regards extended family members in Art 3(2), which is not as binding: see Case C-83/11 *Rahman*, judgment of 5 September 2012, not yet reported, and the commentary on Art 3(2) in Chapter 1. See also Case C-503/03 *Commission v Spain* [2006] ECR I-1097, para 42, and the Commission's guidance on the application of the Directive (COM(2009) 313), which refers to 'a right to obtain an entry visa'.

[90] Case C-459/99 *MRAX* [2002] ECR I-6591 and Case C-157/03 *Commission v Spain* [2005] ECR I-2911.

[91] Case C-157/03 [2005] ECR I-2911.

[92] Case C-157/03 [2005] ECR I-2911, para 12.

[93] Case C-157/03 [2005] ECR I-2911, paras 29 and 30.

[94] Case C-157/03 [2005] ECR I-2911, para 33. See also Case C-459/99 *MRAX* [2002] ECR I-6591, para 60.

[95] See also the Commission's guidance on the application of the Directive (COM(2009) 313), which rules out requiring an application for a long-term, residence, or family reunion visa.

As noted already, Union citizens or their family members travelling between Schengen States benefit from the abolition of internal border controls between those States. Third-country national family members can enjoy the freedom to travel for 90 days in every 180 days not only if they have a residence card pursuant to Article 10, but also if they have a residence permit issued by a Member State under national law (this would be the case if they are residing with a Union citizen who has remained in his or her Member State of nationality and therefore does not fall within the scope of the Directive). When Union citizens or their family members cross the external borders of the Schengen States to or from non-Schengen States, they are subject to the rules in the Schengen Borders Code on external border checks.[96] These rules provide that Union citizens and their family members are usually subject only to a 'minimum check' on entry or exit, to establish their identity and nationality and to verify the validity of their travel documents. There may be further consultation of databases, on a non-systematic basis, but this cannot jeopardize the right of free movement set out in the citizens' Directive.[97] Such checks are much less stringent than those applicable to third-country nationals generally.[98] Union citizens and their family members can also use the 'fast track' crossing lanes at Schengen external borders.[99]

As regards visas, the exemption from the visa requirement for those third-country national family members of Union citizens who have a residence card takes priority over the EU legislation which obliges all Member States except the UK and Ireland to insist upon visas for the nationals of a long list of third countries.[100] The obligation to waive the fee saves the persons concerned up to €60, which they would otherwise have to pay for a Schengen visa application,[101] and the requirement (in the case law) to issue visas at the border is an 'exceptional' case, according to the visa code.[102]

---

[96] Reg 562/2006, [2006] OJ L 105/1. As noted already, the external borders provisions of the Code also apply to persons crossing the borders of Romania, Cyprus, Bulgaria, and Croatia to or from any other Member State. For those crossing the borders between the UK and Ireland and any other Member State, national rules apply on the British and Irish side, while the Schengen borders rules apply on the side of the Schengen States.

[97] Art 7(2) of the Code; on the scope of this provision, see the definition in Art 2(5) of the Code. Art 7(6) of the Code guarantees that all checks must be carried out in compliance with the citizens' Directive. Each of these provisions was amended by Reg 610/2013, [2013] OJ L 182/1. As regards the use of databases, any use of the Schengen Information System to deny entry to EU citizens or their family members must also be in compliance with EU free movement law: see Case C-503/03 *Commission v Spain* [2006] ECR I-1097, and now Art 25 of Reg 1987/2006 establishing the second-generation Schengen Information System ([2006] OJ L 381/4), which began operations on 9 April 2013.

[98] See Art 7(3) of the Code, as amended by Reg 81/2009 ([2009] OJ L 35/56) to provide for checks in the Visa Information System, which establishes a database concerning visa applications by third-country nationals (including, where relevant, family members of EU citizens).

[99] Art 9(2) of the Borders Code, as amended by Reg 610/2013, [2013] OJ L 182/1.

[100] Reg 539/2001, [2001] OJ L 81/1.

[101] See Art 16 of the Visa Code (Reg 810/2009, [2009] OJ L 243/1). For Member States not subject to the Schengen visa system, the national fee for visa applications must be waived.

[102] See Art 35 of the Visa Code, and the discussion of the *MRAX* judgment above.

The issue of a visa at the border obviates the normal waiting period of fifteen days for a decision, which can be extended,[103] and due to the precedence of EU free movement law over the Schengen *acquis*, the substantive and procedural rules in the citizens' Directive must take priority over the relevant provisions of the visa code, to the extent that the rules in the Directive are more favourable to the persons concerned.[104]

As for the UK and Ireland, the Court of Justice has been asked whether they have the power, pursuant to their special Protocols to the Treaties, not to apply some aspects of Article 5(2).[105] The best answer to these questions is that while these Protocols allow those Member States to maintain their national border controls and opt out of the Schengen provisions if they wish, they do not exempt those Member States from the requirements relating to visas for third-country national family members of EU citizens set out in the citizens' Directive. In particular, they do not exempt the UK and Ireland from the obligation to waive the visa requirement for those persons holding a residence card pursuant to Article 10. Each Member State must exercise mutual trust in this regard. Nor would a blanket measure refusing such a waiver be justified by (generalized reliance on) the 'abuse of rights' clause set out in Article 35.

Article 5(3) restricts the placing of an entry or exit stamp on passports of third-country national family members who are in possession of and present a residence card issued pursuant to Article 10. This provision did not appear in prior legislation. As with Article 5(2), the Council limited the scope of this exemption as compared to the Commission's proposal. In its proposal, the Commission noted that once a third-country national family member has been issued with a residence card, they are entitled to enter or leave freely for the duration of its validity. Consequently the stamping of their passports serves no purpose.[106] This provision of the Directive is matched by a corresponding clause in the Schengen Borders Code,[107] although it should be recalled that Article 5(3) also applies to the UK and Ireland. The relevant provisions of the Borders Code would be repealed and replaced by an entry–exit system instead, according to proposals now under discussion.[108]

---

[103] Art 23 of the Visa Code. The Commission's guidance on the application of the Directive (COM(2009) 313) states that by way of comparison with the Code, a delay of more than four weeks to issue the visa is not reasonable.

[104] See by analogy Case C-503/03 *Commission v Spain* [2006] ECR I-1097. For instance, the Commission's guidance on the application of the Directive (COM(2009) 313), points out (as regards third-country nationals) that a Member State can only require the evidence or documents referred to in Art 10(2), so cannot require proof of accommodation, sufficient resources, an invitation letter, or a return ticket.

[105] See Case C-202/13 *McCarthy*, pending.

[106] See the 2001 proposal, p 9.

[107] Art 10(2) of the Borders Code, as amended by Reg 610/2013, [2013] OJ L 182/1.

[108] COM(2013) 96, 28 February 2013. See also the proposals to establish the entry–exit system and a registered travellers programme (COM(2013) 95 and 98, 28 February 2013). Third-country national family members of EU citizens who hold a residence card pursuant to Art 10 of the Directive will not be subject to the entry–exit system: see Art 3(2)(a), COM(2013) 95.

As with the right of exit, the right of entry into another Member State is not absolute and may be limited on grounds of public policy, public security, and public health set out in Article 27.[109] As derogations to a fundamental freedom, the right to restrict admission of Union citizens or their family members on grounds of public policy and public security has been interpreted narrowly by the CJEU. Restrictions on policy or security grounds will only be permitted where a person's conduct constitutes a genuine, present, and sufficiently serious threat to one of the fundamental interests of society.[110]

The Court has, however, recognized that in addition to grounds set out in the Directive, overriding principles of international law may also be capable of justifying a restriction on free movement rights enshrined in the Treaty and the Directive. In *Hungary v Slovak Republic*,[111] the applicant Member State instituted infringement proceedings against the respondent State after it had denied the President of Hungary access to its territory for the purposes of participating in a ceremony on Hungary's national day in the Slovak town of Komárno.[112] The refusal had initially been justified inter alia on the basis of restrictions provided for in the Directive. Hungary contested the justification advanced and considered that the denial of entry constituted an interference with the President's free movement rights in breach of the Directive. Before the Court, the Slovak Republic varied the basis upon which it considered it had been entitled to refuse entry to the Hungarian President. The Slovak Republic essentially argued that the dispute fell within the sphere of diplomatic relations governed by customary international law and did not fall within the scope of EU law, as the Treaties themselves excluded the application of Union law to Heads of State.[113]

In its judgment, the Court essentially agreed with the Slovak Republic. The Court considered that even if, in principle, the Hungarian President enjoys the status of a Union citizen and may benefit from the right of free movement conferred by the Union Treaties, his special status, as Head of State, places him within the scope of international law and the law governing diplomatic relations.[114] The Court held that having regard to the specific character attaching to the status of Head of State,

---

[109] The nature and extent of Member States' entitlement to restrict free movement is considered further in Chapter 6.

[110] Case 30/77 *Bouchereau* [1977] ECR 1999, para 35; Case C-348/96 *Calfa* [1999] ECR I-11, para 25; Joined Cases C-482/01 and C-493/01 *Orfanopoulos and Oliveri* [2004] ECR I-5257, para 66; Case C-503/03 *Commission v Spain* [2006] ECR I-1097, para 46, and Case C-50/06 *Commission v Netherlands* [2007] ECR I-4383, para 43.

[111] Case C-364/10 *Hungary v Slovak Republic*, judgment of 16 October 2012, not yet reported.

[112] Case C-364/10 *Hungary v Slovak Republic*, judgment of 16 October 2012, not yet reported, para 5.

[113] Case C-364/10 *Hungary v Slovak Republic*, judgment of 16 October 2012, not yet reported, para 36.

[114] Case C-364/10 *Hungary v Slovak Republic*, judgment of 16 October 2012, not yet reported, paras 40–49.

it was permissible for special conditions to apply as regards such a person's exercise of free movement rights.[115] In particular, a citizen performing the duties of a Head of State could have rights of free movement limited on grounds based in international law and that the refusal of entry on such grounds was not incompatible with Union law.[116] The Court considered, however, that the Slovak Republic had erred in initially referring to that Directive as grounds for justifying its refusal of entry and found that the facts of the case did not fall within the material scope of the citizens' Directive.[117]

4. Where a Union citizen, or a family member who is not a national of a Member State, does not have the necessary travel documents or, if required, the necessary visas, the Member State concerned shall, before turning them back, give such persons every reasonable opportunity to obtain the necessary documents or have them brought to them within a reasonable period of time or to corroborate or prove by other means that they are covered by the right of free movement and residence.
5. The Member State may require the person concerned to report his/her presence within its territory within a reasonable and non-discriminatory period of time. Failure to comply with this requirement may make the person concerned liable to proportionate and non-discriminatory sanctions.

Article 5(4) applies in circumstances where a Union citizen, or a third-country national family member, is not able to produce the necessary travel documents or visas. In such cases, prior to being turned back, such persons must be afforded every reasonable opportunity to obtain the necessary documents or have them brought to them within a reasonable period of time or to corroborate or prove by other means that they are covered by the right of free movement and residence. The Commission has reported that the transposition of Article 5(2) 'is often transposed and applied incorrectly'.[118]

The obligation contained in Article 5(4) is consistent with the judgment of the Court of Justice in the case of *MRAX*.[119] Here, a non-governmental organization contested national measures authorizing a State to send back at the border third-country national family members who did not possess the required entry visas. As noted above,[120] the Court in its judgment acknowledged that Member States were entitled to impose visa requirements on third-country national family members and that Union law did not expressly regulate the action that could be taken where

---

[115] Case C-364/10 *Hungary v Slovak Republic*, judgment of 16 October 2012, not yet reported, paras 59 and 50.
[116] Case C-364/10 *Hungary v Slovak Republic*, judgment of 16 October 2012, not yet reported, paras 50 and 51.
[117] Case C-364/10 *Hungary v Slovak Republic*, judgment of 16 October 2012, not yet reported, paras 56 and 60.
[118] COM(2008) 840.
[119] Case C-459/99 [2002] ECR I-6591. See also Case C-157/03 *Commission v Spain* [2005] ECR I-2911, which was considered above in relation to Art 5(2).
[120] See the commentary on Art 5(1).

such visa requirements were not met.[121] The Court found that in any event, having regard to the importance that the Union legislature has attached to family life, it would be disproportionate and prohibited to return a third-country national married to a Union citizen where the spouse is able to prove his or her identity and the relevant conjugal ties and there is no evidence to establish that he or she represents a risk to the requirements of public policy, public security, or public health.[122]

Pursuant to Article 5(5), a person may be required to report his or her presence within the territory within a reasonable and non-discriminatory period of time. The failure to comply with any such requirement may expose the person concerned to proportionate and non-discriminatory sanctions. Although the Commission had proposed a minimum fifteen-day period for any reporting requirements, the Council preferred not to specify a time limit. While the possibility of a reporting requirement had already featured in prior legislation,[123] the requirement that the relevant period be reasonable and the limitation on possible sanctions reflect the case law of the CJEU.[124] This jurisprudence specified that deportation for breach of such rules was 'certainly incompatible' with the Treaties, since it 'negates' the free movement right. As for fines and detention, while national authorities could penalize EU citizens and their family members for a failure to notify their presence 'which are comparable to those attaching to infringements of provisions of equal importance by nationals, they are not justified in imposing a penalty so disproportionate to the gravity of the infringement that it becomes an obstacle to the free movement of persons'. Presumably, by analogy with the case law relating to Article 5(1), Member States cannot subject the person concerned to detention with a view to deportation for breach of the reporting obligation.[125]

This provision can be compared to the Schengen Convention, which permits Schengen States to require third-country nationals to report their presence on the territory, either on entry or within three days of entry.[126] There is no specific rule on sanctions. Since the Directive takes precedence over the Schengen *acquis*, it must follow that for third-country national family members of EU citizens, the limit on sanctions set out in Article 5(5) applies to any national rules which implement the Convention; and arguably, the requirement that the reporting obligation must be reasonable would rule out an obligation to report within one or three days.[127]

---

[121] Case C-459/99 *MRAX* [2002] ECR I-6591, paras 57 and 59.

[122] Case C-459/99 *MRAX* [2002] ECR I-6591, para 61. See also by analogy Case C-215/03 *Oulane* [2005] ECR I-1215, para 25. The latter judgment also makes clear (at paras 28–35) that Member States cannot impose more stringent identity requirements upon nationals of other Member States than they impose on their own nationals, when making checks on their territory; this rule must also apply by analogy as regards border crossings.

[123] Art 8(2) of Directive 68/360 and Art 4(2) of Directive 73/148.

[124] Case 118/75 *Watson and Belmann* [1976] ECR 1185, paras 18–23.

[125] For instance, see, by analogy, Case C-215/03 *Oulane* [2005] ECR I-1215, paras 36–44.

[126] Art 22 of the Convention, as amended by Art 2(4) of Reg 610/2013, [2013] OJ L 182/1.

[127] See, however, para 6 of the Opinion in *Watson and Belmann*, which argues that one-day or three-day reporting periods are acceptable.

Finally, it is arguable that the words 'the persons concerned' in Article 5(5) limit its scope to the persons referred to in Article 5(4), ie the persons without documentation.

F. Evaluation

As stated at the outset, Articles 4 and 5 are a gateway to the rest of the rights in the Directive, since free movement rights cannot be enjoyed at all if an EU citizen or his or her family members cannot leave one Member State or enter another one. So it is particularly troubling that the Commission reports significant failures to transpose these provisions correctly, that some Member States impose exit controls on their own citizens, and that some Member States quite blatantly ignore the clear legal requirements of the Directive (cf the pending *McCarthy* case). Perhaps a possible solution would be the use of a harmonized format for the residence cards issued to third-country national family members of EU citizens,[128] which could be agreed informally if (arguably) there are no legal bases which would permit EU legislation on this issue, and could apply only to some Member States if not all of them are willing to agree to it. Given the diversity of national practice today, which in some cases entails issuing a residence card without the correct title indicated upon it, this would likely lead in practice to at least some improvements in the treatment of third-country national family members of EU citizens at consulates and border posts.

---

[128] There would be no need to gather as much data as required for the standard residence permits for third-country nationals (Reg 1030/2002, [2002] OJ L 157/1, as amended by Reg 380/2008, [2008] OJ L 115/1), since for family members of EU citizens, it is only permissible to gather as much data as is needed to apply the free movement rules: see Case C-524/06 *Huber* [2008] ECR I-9705.

3

RIGHT OF RESIDENCE

A. Function

The citizens' Directive regulates and gives detailed expression to the right of free movement and residence conferred by the Treaties on Union citizens. At its simplest, the Directive regulates residence on the basis of the intended duration of a stay in another Member State. Short-term residence for a period of up to three months is permitted without conditions or limitations other than presentation of an identity card or passport. A right of residence in excess of three months is conditional upon migrant Union citizens engaging in economic activity in the host Member State or possessing sufficient resources and health insurance to support themselves as well as family members accompanying or joining them. Union citizens and their family members who have resided lawfully for at least five years in the host Member State and obtained permanent residence status are exempt from such conditions and are entitled to be treated equally to host Member State nationals. The right of permanent residence is considered in detail in Chapter 4.

It is notable that the Directive does not contain an express definition of 'residence' for the purposes of the Directive. However, given that the term is used without reference to the individual laws of the Member States, it must be interpreted uniformly and autonomously in accordance with the provisions of the Directive, and may not be subject to divergent interpretations by the Member States.[1] The CJEU has confirmed that in calculating periods of 'lawful residence' for the purposes of assessing eligibility for permanent residence, only periods of residence which complied with conditions defined in the Directive may be taken into account.[2]

---

[1] See, by analogy, Case C-66/08 *Kozłowski* [2008] ECR I-6041, para 42. See also Joined Cases C-424/10 and C-425/10 *Ziolkowski and Szeja v Land Berlin*, judgment of 21 December 2011, not yet reported, para 32.

[2] See Joined Cases C-424/10 and C-425/10 *Ziolkowski and Szeja v Land Berlin*, judgment of 21 December 2011, not yet reported and Case C-529/11 *Alarape and Tijani*, judgment of 8 May 2013.

Notwithstanding its autonomy, the citizens' Directive forms part of a continuum of measures adopted over time to facilitate and enhance the exercise of free movement rights. Residence spent lawfully in a host Member State on the basis of prior residence Directives which have since been codified by the citizens' Directive or on the basis of prior national legislation with conditions equivalent to those imposed by that Directive has thus been found to be reckonable for the purposes of calculating lawful residence.[3] The Court observed that the Directive sought to build on existing legislation and strengthen free movement rights and that excluding individuals who have resided for five years on the basis of the relevant previous legislation prior to the date of adoption of Directive 2004/38 from obtaining permanent residence status would be contrary to its purpose.[4]

The definition of 'residence' as it applies for the purpose of the Directive will not necessarily coincide with the term as used in other EU law contexts.[5] Thus, for example, in the context of the Framework Decision establishing the European Arrest Warrant (EAW),[6] a distinction is drawn between individuals who *'reside'* in an executing Member State and those that are merely *'staying in'* the relevant Member State. Individuals *resident* in a Member State are recognized as having a greater entitlement to remain and serve a sentence in its territory compared with individuals who are merely *staying in* that Member State, unless the latter can demonstrate links comparable to those of residents.[7] Similarly, Union legislation concerning the coordination of social security systems, distinguishes between the term *'residence'* (defined as habitual) and *'stays'* (considered as temporary).[8] By contrast, the citizens' Directive makes no such terminological distinction and the term 'resident' is used to refer to all individuals who have moved to another Member State, whether for a

---

[3] Case C-162/09 *Taous Lassal* [2010] ECR I-9217 as clarified in Case C-529/11 *Alarape and Tijani*, judgment of 8 May 2013. See also Joined Cases C-424/10 and C-425/10 *Ziolkowski and Szeja v Land Berlin*, judgment of 21 December 2011, not yet reported, and Joined Cases C-147/11 and C-148/11 *Czop and Punakova*, judgment of 6 September 2012, not yet reported.

[4] Case C-162/09 *Taous Lassal* [2010] ECR I-9217 .

[5] The definition of 'habitual' or 'normal residence' arises in a variety of different Union law contexts, for example, in the application of EU conflicts of law legislation, the function of which is to establish the Member State responsible for the provision of social assistance or the State which has jurisdiction to hear civil, commercial, and family law disputes. The concept of 'residence' also arises in the context of applying Directives in the field of taxation, see for example, Directive 83/182/EEC of 28 March 1983 on tax exemptions within the Community for certain means of transport temporarily imported into one Member State from another ([1983] OJ L 105/59).

[6] Council Framework Decision 2002/584/JHA of 13 June 2002 on the European arrest warrant and the surrender procedures between Member States ([2002] OJ L 190/1, hereinafter 'the EAW Framework Decision').

[7] Case C-66/08 *Kozłowski* [2008] ECR I-6041, paras 32–54. This is subject to Member States' decision to exercise the option provided for in Art 4(6) of the EAW Framework Decision.

[8] See Reg 883/2004 on the coordination of social security systems ([2004] OJ L 166/1). For an examination of the concept of 'residence' in the context of social security coordination see, for example, Case C-90/97 *Swaddling* [1999] ECR I-1075 (and cases cited) and Case C-589/10 *Wencel*, judgment of 16 May 2013. See also Case C-255/13 *Peter Flood*, pending.

short stay or for long-term residence. While the citizens' Directive distinguishes between different categories of residents depending on the duration of the time spent in the Member State, the conditions and rights attaching to each category are self-contained within the Directive and may be ascertained by reference to its provisions.

The rights of residence provided for by the Directive are not limited to Union citizens, but extend to their family members. Nevertheless, the rights conferred on family members may be considered secondary in character, since they are indirect beneficiaries of EU citizens' rights, and their rights are obtained through Union citizens as a result of those citizens' exercise of free movement rights.[9] The Court of Justice has consistently recognized that extending free movement rights to family members of Union citizens facilitates the exercise of free movement rights,[10] and ensures respect of the right to family life as guaranteed in the Union legal order.[11]

The Directive further requires Member States to facilitate the entry and residence of certain categories of persons who do not fall within the scope of the definition of 'family member' as provided for in Article 2(2).[12] Such persons may include other relatives who are dependants or were members of the migrant Union citizen's household in the country from which they have come. The entry and residence of relatives must equally be facilitated where serious health grounds strictly require them to be cared for by the Union citizen. Member States are further required to facilitate entry and residence of the partner of a Union citizen with whom he or she has a durable relationship.

B. Historical development

As discussed in the introductory chapter, by virtue of the Union's economic origins, free movement rights initially provided for in the founding Treaties were essentially confined to movement connected with an economic activity. Successive

---

[9] The secondary or 'derived' nature of rights accorded to third-country national family members is considered at length in Case C-40/11 *Iida v Stadt Ulm*, judgment of 8 November 2012, not yet reported. See also Case C-127/08 *Metock and Others* [2008] ECR I-6241, para 73 and Case C-256/11 *Dereci and Others*, judgment of 15 November 2011, not yet reported, para 56. See further the commentary on Art 3(1) in Chapter 1.

[10] Case C-370/90 *Singh* [1992] ECR I-4265, para 20; Case C-60/00 *Carpenter* [2002] ECR I-6279, para 38; Case C-459/99 *MRAX* [2002] ECR I-6591, para 53; Case C-441/02 *Commission v Germany* [2006] ECR I-3449, para 109; and Case C-291/05 *Eind* [2007] ECR I-10719, paras 35–37 and 44.

[11] Case 249/86 *Commission v Germany* [1989] ECR 1263, para 10; Case C-413/99 *Baumbast and R* [2002] ECR I-7091, para 72; Case C-60/00 *Carpenter* [2002] ECR I-6279, paras 41 and 42; and Case C-503/03 *Commission v Spain* [2006] ECR I-1097, para 47.

[12] The nature of Member States' obligation to facilitate entry and residence is considered in detail by the Court in Case C-83/11 *Rahman and Others*, judgment of 5 September 2012, not yet reported. See the commentary on Art 3(2) in Chapter 1.

legislative measures dating from the early 1960s sought to facilitate the movement of Member State nationals in order to take up employment or establish a business in other Member States.

An important first step was the adoption in 1961 of Regulation No 15/1961[13] setting out key principles governing freedom of movement for workers and an associated Directive detailing procedures on entry, employment, and residence.[14] Although affirming the right of workers to enter and reside in a host Member State, these initial measures were expressed in relatively restrictive terms. Migrant workers were, as a rule, only afforded free movement rights where there was an absence of suitable candidates from among the regular workforce of the host Member State.[15] They could only move and reside in another Member State for the purposes of accepting employment actually offered.[16] Furthermore, migrant workers could be restricted both in terms of the geographical location in which they were permitted to work and the professional activities they were entitled to pursue.[17] Indeed, it was only after a minimum of four years' regular work that migrant Member State nationals were afforded unrestricted access to the labour market.[18] From the outset, free movement and residence rights were extended to family members of migrant Member State nationals.[19] However, the definition of family member was limited to the worker's spouse and children under the age of twenty-one.[20]

Regulation 15/61 and the 1961 Directive were subsequently replaced by Regulation 38/64 and Directive 64/240[21] which sought to enhance the free movement rights of Member State national workers. The Community legislature (as it was then) further adopted a specific Directive to facilitate movement for the purposes of exercising the right to establishment and the right to provide and receive services.[22]

---

[13] Regulation 15 of 16 August 1961 on initial measures to bring about free movement of workers within the Community (1961 OJ 57/1073, hereinafter 'Regulation 15').

[14] Council Directive of 16 August 1961 on administrative procedures and practices governing the entry into and employment and residence in a Member State of workers and their families from other Member States of the Community (1961 OJ 80/1513, hereinafter 'the 1961 Directive').

[15] Art 1 of Regulation 15.

[16] Arts 2 and 3 of the 1961 Directive.

[17] Art 4 of the 1961 Directive and Arts 3 and 6 of Regulation 15.

[18] Art 6 of Regulation 15. The relevant period was five years for seasonal workers spending between eight and twelve months a year in employment in the host Member State.

[19] Arts 2 and 3 of the 1961 Directive.

[20] Art 1(b) of the 1961 Directive incorporates the definition of family member provided for in Art 11 of Regulation 15.

[21] Reg 38/64/EEC of 25 March 1964 on the freedom of movement for workers within the Community ([1964] OJ 64/965) and Directive 64/240 of 25 March 1964 on the abolition of restrictions on the movement and residence of Member States' workers and their families within the Community ([1964] OJ 64/981).

[22] Directive 64/220/EEC of 25 February 1964 on the abolition of restrictions on movement and residence within the Community for nationals of Member States with regard to establishment and the provision of services ([1964] OJ 64/845).

It also adopted a Directive regulating and circumscribing Member States' entitlement to restrict free movement on grounds of public policy, public security, and public health.[23]

With respect to workers, Regulation 38/64 required migrant workers who were Member State nationals to be conferred with an equal entitlement to apply for vacancies arising in another Member State. Member States could no longer therefore, as a general rule, maintain in force measures favouring their own nationals.[24] However, by derogation from this rule, free movement provisions could be suspended in respect of defined categories of migrant worker where there was an over-supply of labour available as regards a particular professional activity or a particular geographical territory. Directive 64/240 ensured that the right of entry and residence in a host Member State was no longer conditional on a job having been actually offered, but was granted generally for the purposes of taking up employment.[25] Moreover, it introduced a distinction between short- and long-term residence in a host Member State, which continues to feature in the present citizens' Directive. Member State nationals taking up employment for a period of three months or less were exempted from the requirement of possessing residence permits.[26] Similar derogations were extended to frontier workers and seasonal workers.[27] Directive 64/240 additionally required Member States to take measures necessary to simplify as much as possible the delivery of relevant travel and residence documentation.[28]

As regards the right of establishment and the provision of services, Directive 64/220 required Member States to abolish any restriction on movement and residence in connection with such activities.[29] Member States were under a positive obligation to recognize a permanent right of residence of Member State nationals establishing themselves within their territory, duly attested by the issuing of a residence permit.[30] Providers and recipients of services were only required to be issued with a residence card if the duration of such services exceeded three months.[31] The right of residence of providers and recipients of services was limited to the period during which they were providing or receiving the relevant services.

---

[23] Directive 64/221/EEC of 25 February 1964 on the co-ordination of special measures concerning the movement and residence of foreign nationals which are justified on grounds of public policy, public security or public health ([1964] OJ 56/850).

[24] Art 8 of Reg 38/64.

[25] Arts 2(1) and 3(1) of Directive 64/240.

[26] Art 6(1)(a) of Directive 64/240.

[27] Art 6(1)(b) and (c) of Directive 64/240.

[28] Art 7(3) of Directive 64/240.

[29] Art 1 of Directive 64/220/EEC.

[30] Art 3(1) of Directive 64/220/EEC.

[31] Nevertheless, such individuals may still be obliged to notify their presence in the host Member State. See Art 3(2) of Directive 64/220/EEC.

The measures adopted in 1964 broadened the definition of family members to include ascendants and descendants of the migrant Member State nationals as well as of their spouses.[32] Member States were further required to facilitate the admission of any other family member for whom the Member State national was responsible and who formed part of his or her household. Notably, for Community workers, the entitlement to be accompanied by family members was conditional on the availability of suitable accommodation. The Directive specified that such accommodation should be considered normal by the standards of nationals of the host State working in the same region as the migrant Member State national.[33]

The legal framework governing free movement of workers was subsequently amended in 1968 with the adoption of Regulation 1612/68 on the freedom of movement for workers[34] and Directive 68/360/EEC on the abolition of restrictions on movement and residence within the Community for workers of Member States and their families.[35] Regulation 1612/68 did not retain provisions authorizing the suspension of free movement rights in the light of national circumstances. It prohibited any discrimination against migrant Member State national workers in respect of conditions of employment and work.[36] Regulation 1612/68 remained in force for over forty years, until its codification and repeal by Regulation 492/2011 on 5 April 2011.[37]

While such measures contributed significantly to enhancing the free movement and residence rights of Member State nationals, they were only intended to facilitate movement that took place in connection with economic activity. This was because prior to the entry into force of the Maastricht Treaty, the scope of free movement provisions in the Treaties was limited to furthering economic objectives, primarily the establishment of a functioning common market. The scope of secondary Union legislation could not extend beyond the scope of primary law on which such legislation was based.

The founding Treaties did, however, confer an autonomous residence entitlement on one category of migrant Member State national, whose link to economic activity, though by no means non-existent, may be regarded as indirect. In particular, Article 48(3)(d) of the EC Treaty recognized residence rights for Member State

---

[32] See Art 17 of Reg 38/64. See also Art 1 of Directive 64/240 (extending rights to 'family members' falling within the scope of the Regulation) and Art 1 of Directive 64/220.

[33] Art 17(3) of the Reg. This requirement continued to feature in subsequent legislation and was considered by the Court of Justice in Case 249/86 *Commission v Germany* [1989] ECR 1263.

[34] Reg 1612/68 on freedom of movement for workers ([1968] OJ L 257/2).

[35] Directive 68/360/EEC on the abolition of restrictions on movement and residence within the Community for workers of Member States and their families ([1968] OJ L 257/13).

[36] Art 7 of Reg 1612/68.

[37] [2011] OJ L 141/1.

nationals who had previously spent time working in the host Member State but who were not now economically active.[38] Regulation 1251/70, adopted on that basis, set out the conditions in which Member State nationals and their family members could remain in the host Member State where they had ceased working because they reached retirement age or where they had become permanently incapacitated.[39] The Regulation further extended residence rights to former workers who had subsequently taken up employment in another Member State, but wished to retain their residence in their previous State of employment. An analogous measure was subsequently adopted in 1975 in relation to self-employed persons who, following the cessation of their occupation in the relevant Member State, wished to retain their residence in that State.[40]

By the mid-1970s, consideration was given to conferring upon Member State nationals a free-standing right of residence detached from the exercise of an economic activity. Such initiatives were developed in the context of a growing recognition that the activities of the European Communities were not merely of concern to Member States in facilitating economic integration, but also impacted directly upon the lives of Member State nationals. It was considered that the European project's continuing legitimacy required a more direct—and visible—connection between the Community and the nationals of its constituent Member States.[41] Successive European Councils, Parliamentary committees, and working groups under the chairmanship of prominent statesmen[42] were entrusted with developing

---

[38] Art 48(3)(d) of the EEC Treaty.

[39] Reg (EEC) No 1251/70 of the Commission of 29 June 1970 on the right of workers to remain in the territory of a Member State after having been employed in that State ([1970] OJ L 142/24). The Regulation was repealed by Reg 635/2006 of 25 April 2006 ([2006] OJ L 112/9). As the recital to the repealing Regulation observes, the provisions of Reg 1251/70 were substantially incorporated into Art 17 of the citizens' Directive.

[40] Directive 75/34/EEC ([1975] OJ L 14/10). Additionally, the Community legislature adopted a Directive extending the scope of legislation restricting free movement rights (on public policy, public security, and public health grounds) to include Member State nationals who have remained in a host Member State after having pursued self-employed activities there: Directive 75/35 extending the scope of Directive No 64/221 to include nationals of a Member State who exercise the right to remain in the territory of another Member State after having pursued therein an activity in a self-employed capacity ([1975] OJ L 14/14).

[41] See S O'Leary, 'The Options for the Reform of EU Citizenship', in *Citizenship and Nationality Status in the New Europe*, S O'Leary and T Tiilikainen, eds (Sweet & Maxwell, London, 1998), 83–86. See also, J Shaw, 'The Interpretation of EU citizenship' (1998) 6(3) *The Modern Law Review* 295. See also K Neunreither, 'Citizens and the Exercise of Power in the European Union' in *A Citizens' Europe: In search of a New Order*, Alan Rosas and Esko Antola, eds (Sage Publications, London, 1995), 6.

[42] In 1975, Belgian Prime Minister, Mr Leo Tindemans, published a report *Towards a Europe for Citizens*, which included a chapter about civil and political rights to be granted to nationals of Member States. A 1978 report by the European Parliament's Political Affairs Committee, under the chairmanship of Mr Mario Scelba emphasized the importance of strengthening the ties of solidarity among 'citizens of the Community' by granting special rights falling within the category of civil and political rights. Mr Pietro Adonnino chaired an '*Ad hoc* Committee on a People's Europe' established by the European Council which published two reports, entitled 'A People's Europe',

initiatives for strengthening ties of solidarity and bringing 'Europe' closer to citizens through the direct conferral of rights on nationals of the Member States.[43] Among such initiatives featured a proposal for the conferral of a free-standing right of residence that was not dependent on economic occupation. In 1979 the Commission submitted a proposal for a Directive to this effect.[44]

According to the recitals of the 1979 Proposal, the removal of obstacles to the free movement of persons served the objectives of laying the foundations of an ever closer union among the peoples of Europe.[45] It was observed that while the Treaty had provided powers to take action to ensure freedom of movement for workers and self-employed persons, no provision had been made for movement independent of the pursuit of an occupational activity.[46] However, it was considered that freedom of movement of persons, a founding freedom of the Community, could only be fully attained if a right of permanent residence were granted to those 'Community nationals' in whom such right did not already vest.[47] Despite being the subject of protracted debate for almost a decade, agreement could not be reached and the proposal was eventually withdrawn in 1989. Negotiations floundered on the issue of identifying an appropriate legal basis as well as the conditions that were to be imposed as a precondition to the exercise of a general free-standing right of residence. In its place, it was proposed to introduce three separate Directives, each of which would contain specific provisions intended to regulate distinct categories of migrant Member State national.[48]

In the meantime, while the legislative process stalled, the Court of Justice continued to deliver a series of rulings on questions concerning the personal and material scope of the Treaty's provisions on the freedom of movement for persons. In its case law, the Court interpreted the scope of treaty rights broadly, applying them to a variety of different categories of economically inactive Member State national,

---

which sought to 'propose arrangements of direct relevance to Community citizens and which would visibly offer tangible benefits in their everyday lives'.

[43] For detailed consideration of the context and negotiations leading to the introduction of Union citizenship and free-standing residence rights, see S O'Leary, *The Evolving Concept of Community Citizenship—from the Free Movement of Persons to Union Citizenship* (Kluwer Law International, The Hague, 1996), 111–118.

[44] Proposal for a Council Directive on the right of residence for nationals of Member States in the territory of another Member State submitted to the Council on 31 July 1979 ([1979] OJ C 207/14, hereinafter 'the 1979 Proposal').

[45] First recital of the 1979 Proposal.

[46] Second recital of the 1979 Proposal.

[47] Third recital of the 1979 Proposal.

[48] For detailed consideration of the context and negotiations leading to the adoption of the residence Directives, see S O'Leary, *The Evolving Concept of Community Citizenship—from the Free Movement of Persons to Union Citizenship* (Kluwer Law International, The Hague, 1996), 111–118.

including job-seekers,[49] former workers,[50] and even vocational students[51] within parameters laid down in such case law.

In 1990, the Union legislature proceeded to adopt three separate residence Directives, Directive 90/364,[52] Directive 90/365,[53] and Directive 90/366,[54] in respect of specific categories of economically inactive migrant. Directive 90/365 governed the residence rights of former workers or self-employed persons no longer pursuing an occupational activity. Directive 90/366, (subsequently annulled and replaced by Directive 93/36) regulated the residence rights of vocational students.[55] Directive 90/364 provided a general right of residence to Member State nationals who did not fall within the scope of any other provision of Community law. Although these Directives extended free movement rights to economically inactive individuals, such rights were nevertheless made subject to a requirement of adequate health insurance and sufficient financial resources. Moreover, the students' residence Directive contained an express provision excluding students' entitlement to the payment of maintenance grants by the host Member State.[56]

The conferral of a free-standing right of residence on economically inactive Member State nationals resided, at least initially, in something of a primary law vacuum, since the free movement rights contemplated by the Treaties related solely to travel and residence connected with economic pursuits. Indeed, the absence of a primary law legal basis was reflected in the decision to adopt the 1990 Residence Directives on the basis of Article 235 EEC, which conferred the Community with a general power to act where no specific legal basis existed in the Treaties.[57] This primary law

---

[49] Case 316/85 *Lebon* [1987] ECR 2811, para 26 (where the Court acknowledged job-seekers' entitlement to equal access to employment—though not to social or tax advantages); Case 53/81 *Levin* [1982] ECR 1035, para 21; Case 48/75 *Royer* [1976] ECR 497, para 31; and Case 66/85 *Lawrie-Blum* [1986] ECR 2121. See, especially, Case C-292/91 *Antonissen* [1991] ECR I-745. In *Antonissen*, the Court observed that the freedom of movement for workers forms one of the foundations of the Community and, consequently, the provisions laying down that freedom must be interpreted broadly. The Court further noted that a strict interpretation of the Treaty provision at issue would jeopardize the chances of a job-seeker finding employment and that what is now Art 45(3) TFEU must entail freedom of movement for the purposes of seeking employment.

[50] Case 39/86 *Lair* [1988] ECR 3161, paras 29–36. See also, subsequent to the entry into force of the Maastricht Treaty, Case C-57/96 *Meints* [1997] ECR I-6689 and Case C-35/97 *Commission v France* [1998] ECR I-5325.

[51] Case 293/83 *Gravier* [1985] ECR 593.

[52] [1990] OJ L 180/26.

[53] [1990] OJ L 180/28.

[54] [1990] OJ L 180/30.

[55] [1993] OJ L 317/59. Directive 90/366 had been annulled by the Court in Case C-295/90 *Parliament v Council* [1992] ECR I-4193 on the ground that it had been adopted on an incorrect legal basis.

[56] The third Recital to Directive 90/366 refers expressly to the case law of the Court of Justice.

[57] Art 235 EEC also required that the Community's action had to be considered necessary to attain an objective relating to the effective functioning of the common market. Nevertheless, in Case C-295/90, the Court considered that insofar as the students' residence Directive was concerned, recourse to a general legal basis was unnecessary and unjustified. The Court considered that Art 7 EEC (now Art 18 TFEU), applying the principle of non-discrimination with respect to access

gap was, however, soon filled following the introduction of Union citizenship in the EC Treaty by the 1992 Maastricht Treaty. In addition to establishing the status of Union citizenship, the newly inserted provisions conferred on Union citizens an express right of free movement detached from the performance of any economic activity and which could thus be exercised regardless of the grounds or economic nature of such movement.

Although the new provisions' extension of free movement and residence rights to economically inactive Union citizens was made subject to conditions and limitations, it nevertheless represented a fundamental paradigm shift as regards the status of Member State nationals within the Union legal order. Prior to the introduction of Union citizenship, Member State nationals were conferred with free movement rights essentially on the basis of the economic function they performed. Following the introduction of Union citizenship, however, movement in connection with an economic activity was relegated to constituting merely the 'specific expression' of a personal and overarching right of free movement enshrined in Article 21 TFEU.[58] The retrospective requalification of economic free movement rights as a subset of more fundamental citizenship rights reflected the fact that Member State nationals were no longer afforded rights on the basis of their constituting economic means serving economic ends, but more fundamentally, by virtue of their citizenship of the Union.

The establishment of Union citizenship and accompanying rights of free movement as provisions of primary law paved the way for the adoption of the citizens' Directive as a single legislative act that would govern and regulate the exercise of free movement by Union citizens regardless of economic activity. It was considered that consolidation of different categories of free movement and residence rights within a single legislative document would facilitate the exercise of free movement rights.[59] In 2001 the Commission adopted a Proposal for a European Parliament and Council Directive on the right of citizens of the Union and their family members to move and reside freely within the territory of the Member States, subsequently amended on 15 April 2003.[60] The Directive, the subject of this book, was adopted on 29 April 2004.

---

to vocational training (which was an area which fell within the scope of Union activity by virtue of Art 128 EEC (now Art 166 TFEU)) could imply a right of residence and provided an appropriate legal basis for such a directive.

[58] See, for example, Case C-212/06 *Government of the French Community and Walloon Government* [2008] ECR I-1683, para 59.

[59] Recitals 3 and 4 in the preamble to the Directive. See also Joined Cases C-424/10 and C-425/10 *Ziolkowski and Szeja v Land Berlin*, judgment of 21 December 2011, not yet reported, para 37.

[60] COM(2001) 257, 23 May 2001 ([2001] OJ C 270 E/150), hereinafter 'the 2001 Proposal'. The Commission subsequently adopted an amended Proposal on 15 April 2003 (COM(2003) 199), hereinafter 'the 2003 Proposal'.

C. Interrelationship of Articles 6–15 with other provisions

Given that the right of Union citizens to move for the purposes of taking up residence in other Member States lies at the very core of the Directive, the provisions governing the right of residence set out in chapter III, Articles 6 to 15, interacts in some way with a number, if not a majority, of the Directive's provisions.

Nevertheless, Articles 22 to 26, appearing in chapter V, may be considered to be of particular relevance as these provisions contain overarching principles applicable to the exercise of residence rights generally, including permanent residence as provided for in Article 16. Such provisions define the territorial scope of residence rights (Article 22) and confirm the entitlement of family members to engage in economic activity (Article 23). They further elaborate on the application of the principle of equal treatment to migrant Union citizens and their family members (Article 24), clarify the status of residence documents issued by national authorities (Article 25), and regulate the entitlement of Member States to carry out checks on non-nationals (Article 26).

The right to equal treatment as expressed in Article 24 informs the way in which a number of conditions and administrative formalities set out in Articles 6 to 15 are to be applied in practice. Moreover, there is a clear connection and even tension between the prohibition of discrimination and the possible exclusion of economically inactive migrant Union citizens (and their family members) from social benefits that are available to nationals of the host Member State. While such a difference in treatment may be implicit in the Directive's requirement for migrants to possess sufficient resources, Article 24 may, in appropriate circumstances, serve as a counterweight to an excessively rigid application of that requirement as grounds for refusing access to a particular benefit.[61]

The issuing of registration certificates and other equivalent documents provided for in Article 8 and Article 9, and the status accorded to such documents, falls to be interpreted in the light of Article 25. That provision clarifies that possession of national residence documents may not, under any circumstances, be made a precondition for the exercise of a right or the completion of an administrative formality, since entitlement to such rights may be attested by any other means of proof. This provision reinforces the Court's case law according to which residence documentation issued by national authorities are declaratory rather than constitutive. They do not confer or create rights but merely serve to attest existing rights conferred directly under Union law.[62]

---

[61] This is considered in greater detail in the commentary on Art 24 in Chapter 5.
[62] Case 48/75 *Royer* [1976] ECR 497, paras 31–33; Case C-357/89 *Raulin* [1992] ECR I-1027, paras 36 and 42; Case C-459/99 *MRAX* [2002] ECR I-6591, para 74; and Case C-215/03 *Oulane* [2005] ECR I-1215, paras 17 and 18.

Articles 27 to 33 (in chapter VI), which set out the grounds for exclusion from a host Member State, are also relevant, since these provisions circumscribe the rights of residence enshrined in Articles 6 to 15. Article 15 incorporates by reference Articles 30 and 31, which set out procedural safeguards applicable in dealings with administrative authorities, particularly in the context of decisions restricting free movement and residence rights.

Articles 35 to 37 (in chapter VII) are also capable of impacting upon the inter-pretation and application of Articles 6 to 15. In the first instance, the rights of residence provided for under the Directive are subject to their being exercised in good faith. Pursuant to Article 35, Member States are authorized to refuse, terminate, and withdraw any right conferred by the Directive in the event of abuse of rights or fraud, such as the contraction of marriages of convenience. Sanctions that may be imposed pursuant to Articles 8 and 9 in particular will be subject to compliance with requirements set out in Article 36, which provides that Member States are required to lay down provisions on the sanctions applicable to breaches of national rules adopted for the implementation of the Directive and to take the measures required for their application. Any sanctions imposed must be effective and proportionate. Finally, it is noteworthy that pursuant to Article 37, the provisions of the Directive do not affect national legislative or administrative provisions that provide more favourable rights to the persons falling within the scope of the Directive.

D. Other relevant norms

Articles 6 to 15 affirm and give detailed expression to the Union citizens' right of free movement conferred directly in Articles 20(2)(a) and 21 TFEU. The right of free movement enshrined in Article 21 TFEU has been recognized as having direct effect.[63] The Court has frequently had recourse to interpreting and applying the Treaty's citizenship provisions in circumstances where the situation of a Union citizen or his family members, does not fall within the scope of the Directive.[64]

Migrant Union citizens who are workers in another Member State will, in addition to rights conferred by the citizens' Directive, benefit from rights and protections conferred by Regulation 492/2011 on the freedom of movement for workers, which replaced and recast Regulation 1612/68. In particular, such citizens are afforded more extensive equal treatment rights that concern specifically conditions

---

[63] Case C-413/99 *Baumbast and R* [2002] ECR I-7091.

[64] See, for example, Case C-34/09 *Ruiz Zambrano* [2011] ECR I-1177, Case C-434/09 *Shirley McCarthy* [2011] ECR I-3375, and Case C-364/10 *Hungary v Slovak Republic*, judgment of 16 October 2012, not yet reported, and more generally the commentary on Art 3(1) in Chapter 1.

of employment, but which also concern the entitlement to access social and tax advantages for themselves and their family members.[65] Article 10 of Regulation 492/2011 is of particular importance, as it has been interpreted as conferring an autonomous right of residence on the children of workers or former workers, as well as those children's primary carers, distinct from and additional to the provisions of the citizens' Directive,[66] for the purposes of enabling such children to complete their studies in the host Member State in circumstances where the worker from whom they had initially derived free movement rights has left the household or ceased working in the host Member State.[67] Crucially, in such circumstances, the right of residence conferred by Article 10 of Regulation 492/2011 will not be subject to the requirement for compliance with the conditions that would apply to the family members of other categories of Union citizen pursuant to the citizens' Directive.[68] It is therefore apparent that by falling within the scope of Regulation 492/2011, children of workers and their primary carers may, in principle, benefit from enhanced rights of residence and equal treatment.[69] Nevertheless, the conceptual boundaries between the rights of workers, on the one hand, and economically inactive citizens, on the other, have not always been clearly respected. In certain instances, the Court has analysed the situation of workers or their families from a general citizenship perspective, rather than through the prism of their status as workers.[70] Such an approach has been to the detriment of economically active Union citizens.[71]

---

[65] For detailed consideration of the right of equal treatment of migrant Union citizen workers, see Chapter 5 of this commentary.

[66] Case C-310/08 *Ibrahim* [2010] ECR I-1065 and Case C-480/08 *Maria Teixeira* [2010] ECR I-1107. See further the commentary on Art 12(3) below.

[67] Case C-310/08 *Ibrahim* [2010] ECR I-1065; Case C-480/08 *Maria Teixeira* [2010] ECR I-1107; Joined Cases C-147/11 and 148/11 *Czop and Punakova*, judgment of 6 September 2012, not yet reported; and Case C-529/11 *Alarape and Tijani*, judgment of 8 May 2013.

[68] See the commentary on Arts 12 and 13 below. Although, as discussed below, Art 12(3) also waives the usual requirements for the residence of children in education and their carers, this provision only applies in the event of the death or departure of the EU citizen, whereas Art 10 of Reg 492/2011 applies also where the EU citizen *remains in the host Member State*, but is either no longer employed there or the family relationship has broken down. See the Opinion in Case C-480/08 *Maria Teixeira* [2010] ECR I-1107, paras 52–55.

[69] The special rights accorded to children of workers are considered in further detail in the commentary on Art 12(3) below. See also Case C-20/12 *Giersch and others*, judgment of 20 June 2013, as regards Art 7(2) of Reg 492/2011.

[70] For a comparison between the Court's approach to analysing the rights of Union citizen workers on the one hand, and economically inactive citizens on the other, see Section B of Chapter 5.

[71] See Case C-213/05 *Geven* [2008] ECR I-6347. See also Case C-20/12 *Giersch and others*, judgment of 20 June 2013. For further discussion on this point see S O'Leary, 'Developing an Ever Closer Union between the People's of Europe? A reappraisal of the case-law of the Court of Justice on the free movement of persons and EU citizenship' (2008) 27 YEL 167–194 and D Martin, 'La libre circulation des personnes: au-delà de l'évolution et des revolutions, la perpétuelle quête de sens' (2012) 1 Rev Aff Eur 85.

E. Analysis

Article 6—Right of residence for up to three months

1. Union citizens shall have the right of residence on the territory of another Member State for a period of up to three months without any conditions or any formalities other than the requirement to hold a valid identity card or passport.
2. The provisions of paragraph 1 shall also apply to family members in possession of a valid passport who are not nationals of a Member State, accompanying or joining the Union citizen.

Pursuant to Article 6, Union citizens and their family members may reside in any Member State of their choosing for a period of up to three months without any conditions or formalities other than travelling with a valid identity card or passport.[72] The provision reflects the terms of recital 11, which recalls that the fundamental and personal right of residence in another Member State is conferred directly on Union citizens by the Treaty and is not dependent upon their having fulfilled administrative procedures. The right of residence covers the whole territory of the Member States and restrictions may only be placed to the extent that equivalent restrictions apply to nationals of the host Member State.[73] The Commission had initially proposed that the period of unconditional free movement would be six months long, but the Council rejected this idea and the subsequent review of this issue did not result in a proposal to extend this time period.[74]

Although Article 6 does not impose any minimum financial resource requirement on migrant Union citizens, the right of residence conferred by this Article is only retained as long as Union citizens and family members do not become an unreasonable burden on the social system of the host Member State.[75] Equally, Member States are expressly authorized to limit access to social assistance during the first three months of residence.[76]

During their stay, Union citizens and third-country national family members may be required to provide evidence of their identity and nationality.[77] However, any such requirement must apply equally to nationals of the Member State concerned.[78]

---

[72] Art 6(2) makes clear that third-country national family members who are accompanying or joining the EU citizen need only possess a valid passport.

[73] Art 22.

[74] See the discussion of Art 39 in Chapter 7.

[75] Art 14(1).

[76] See recital 21 and Art 24(2).

[77] Case C-215/03 *Oulane* [2005] ECR I-1215, para 21. While this case concerned a Union citizen, the reasoning underpinning the judgment would apply equally to third-country national family members. Moreover, pursuant to the second sentence of Art 24(1), the benefit of the right to equal treatment extends to family members who are not nationals of a Member State and who have a right of residence or permanent residence.

[78] Case 321/87 *Commission v Belgium* [1989] ECR 997, para 12, and Case C-215/03 *Oulane* [2005] ECR I-1215, paras 32–35.

Controls carried out in a systematic, arbitrary, or unnecessarily restrictive manner are liable to be incompatible with Article 6.[79] The Court has acknowledged that ascertaining the identity and nationality of persons exercising free movement rights could be necessary to resolve any questions relating to evidence of a person's right of residence.[80] Moreover it may assist national authorities in ensuring they respect the applicable limits regarding the information they are entitled to seek from the persons concerned.[81] However, for the purpose of ascertaining an individual's nationality, the competent authorities cannot insist on the presentation of a valid identity card or passport, but must accept any form of unequivocal proof.[82] Any sanctions imposed on nationals of EU Member States who fail to produce identification as required, must be comparable to sanctions imposed under national law for similar infringements and must respect the principle of proportionality.[83]

While Member States may require migrant Union citizens and their family members to register with the competent authorities for periods of residence exceeding three months' duration, the deadline for such registration cannot fall within the initial three-month period of residence.[84] Conversely, the Directive is silent on the question of whether an application for registration could be made within the three-month period, if the EU citizen wishes to make one. Since some EU citizens will be certain from the outset that they wish to reside for longer than three months, and registration as soon as possible could simplify their daily life, this ought to be permitted.[85] The right of residence provided for by Article 6 may be restricted on grounds of public policy, public security, or public health in accordance with the provisions laid down in Articles 27 to 33,[86] and this initial three-month period of residence on the territory counts toward the acquisition of permanent residence status pursuant to chapter IV.[87]

Article 7—Right of residence for more than three months

1. All Union citizens shall have the right of residence on the territory of another Member State for a period of longer than three months if they:

---

[79] See, by analogy, Case 321/87 *Commission v Belgium* [1989] ECR 997, para 15. While that case refers specifically to checks upon entry into the Member State, it is submitted that the Court's reasoning would apply equally to checks carried out subsequently on individuals residing on the basis of Art 6.

[80] Case C-215/03 *Oulane* [2005] ECR I-1215.

[81] Case C-215/03 *Oulane* [2005] ECR I-1215, para 22.

[82] Case C-215/03 *Oulane* [2005] ECR I-1215, para 23.

[83] Case C-378/97 *Wijsenbeek* [1999] ECR I-6207, para 44; Case C-215/03 *Oulane* [2005] ECR I-1215, para 38.

[84] Art 8(2). The same rule applies to applications for residence cards for third-country national family members: see Art 9(2).

[85] The same argument applies a fortiori to applications for residence cards for third-country national family members, given that Art 9(1) refers to a '*planned* period of residence' of more than three months, and Art 5(2) confers the tangible benefit of requiring other Member States to waive any visa requirement for persons holding such cards.

[86] These restrictions on rights of movement and residence are considered further in Chapter 6.

[87] See the commentary on Art 16, in Chapter 4.

(a) are workers or self-employed persons in the host Member State; or

(b) have sufficient resources for themselves and their family members not to become a burden on the social assistance system of the host Member State during their period of residence and have comprehensive sickness insurance cover in the host Member State; or

(c) – are enrolled at a private or public establishment, accredited or financed by the host Member State on the basis of its legislation or administrative practice, for the principal purpose of following a course of study, including vocational training; and
– have comprehensive sickness insurance cover in the host Member State and assure the relevant national authority, by means of a declaration or by such equivalent means as they may choose, that they have sufficient resources for themselves and their family members not to become a burden on the social assistance system of the host Member State during their period of residence; or

(d) are family members accompanying or joining a Union citizen who satisfies the conditions referred to in points (a), (b) or (c).

Article 7 affirms the right of Union citizens and their family members to reside in the territory of another Member State for periods exceeding three months' duration. In affirming such rights, Article 7 differentiates between three categories of residents, namely: (1) residents that are economically active (workers and self-employed persons); (2) residents that are economically inactive but are able to support themselves and their families and possess requisite health insurance cover; and (3) residents whose primary purpose is to follow a course of study in the host Member State. Article 7(1)(d) confirms that the right of residence extends to family members who are EU citizens accompanying or joining Union citizens, provided that the latter Union citizens satisfy the conditions applicable to them pursuant to Article 7(1)(a) to (c).[88] Significantly, the conditions attaching to each category of Union citizen and their family members are set out exhaustively in Article 7. As a consequence, Member States may not make the right of residence subject to conditions other than those provided for in that Article.[89] For example, as the Commission has observed, EU citizens and their family members cannot be required to satisfy 'integration conditions' before

---

[88] In addition, Art 7(2) (see the commentary below) expressly provides that the right of residence conferred on family members includes third-country national family members.

[89] In its Report to the European Parliament and the Council on the application of Directive 2004/38/EC, COM(2008) 840 ('the 2008 Report'), the Commission observes that certain Member States have sought to introduce additional conditions not provided for in the Directive which, having regard to the exhaustive nature of Art 7, are incompatible with the Directive. In particular, the Commission noted that the Czech Republic made the right of residence conditional on the family possessing satisfactory accommodation and Malta required Union citizens to obtain a work licence in order to reside as workers. Although Member States may not impose conditions additional to those provided for in the Directive, they are not precluded from granting more extensive free movement rights (see Art 37, discussed in Chapter 7). Thus for example, in the same 2008 Report, the Commission observes that Estonia and Spain do not require Union citizens to meet any of the conditions set out in Art 7(1) and the right of residence is given solely on the basis of having citizenship of the Union.

exercising the rights set out in Article 7 (or, in fact, any of the other rights in the Directive).[90]

Economically active EU citizens

Workers or self-employed Union citizens, constituting the first category of resident, are conferred with the most expansive free movement and residence rights under the Directive. Such citizens derive a right of residence directly by virtue of the economic activity they pursue in a host Member State. They are not therefore subject to the sufficient resources and comprehensive sickness insurance requirements applicable to the categories of migrant Union citizen referred to in Article 7(1)(b) and (c).

Insofar as Article 7(1)(a) affirms the right of workers to move and reside in another Member State, the Directive essentially gives effect to the free movement of workers, as set out in Article 45 TFEU. It follows that the autonomous Union law definition of 'worker' as developed in case law interpreting Article 45 TFEU applies equally to the interpretation and application of Article 7(1). According to that case law, Member State nationals will be regarded as workers where, for a certain period of time, they have been performing services for and under the direction of another person, in return for remuneration. The activities must further be genuine and effective and cannot be on such a small scale as to be regarded as purely marginal or ancillary.[91] Article 7(1)(a) equally incorporates a reference to the Treaty right of establishment, as regards natural persons (ie self-employed persons).[92] As for frontier workers, the Directive applies to them if they have moved their residence to another Member State, but not if they still reside in their host Member State. In the latter case, other provisions of EU law will apply.[93]

Individuals who have previously worked or engaged in self-employed activities and have since ceased exercising economic activity in another Member State will retain the status of 'worker' or 'self-employed person' for the purposes of enjoying a right of residence in accordance with Article 7(1)(a) once they comply with conditions laid down in Article 7(3), paragraphs (a) to (d).[94] As a rule, the status of

---

[90] See the Commission's guidance on the application of the Directive, COM(2009) 313. Compare with Art 7(2) of Directive 2003/86 on family reunion of third-country nationals ([2003] OJ L 251/12).

[91] Case 66/85 *Lawrie-Blum* [1986] ECR 2121, paras 16 and 17; Case C-337/97 *Meeusen* [1999] ECR I-3289, para 13; Case C-138/02 *Collins* [2004] ECR I-2703, para 26; Case C-456/02 *Trojani* [2004] ECR I-7573, para 15; Case C-208/07 *von Chamier-Glisczinski* [2009] ECR I-6095, para 69; Joined Cases C-22/08 and C-23/08 *Vatsouras and Koupatantze* [2009] ECR I-4585, para 26; and Case C-46/12 *LN*, judgment of 21 February 2013, paras 40–43.

[92] See Case C-268/99 *Jany* [2001] ECR I-8615, para 34: 'any activity which a person performs outside a relationship of subordination must be classified as an activity pursued in a self-employed capacity for the purposes of' the freedom of establishment conferred by the Treaty.

[93] See the commentary on Art 3(1) in Chapter 1.

[94] The conditions governing the retention of the status of 'worker' and 'self-employed person' is considered further in the commentary on Art 7(3) below.

worker or self-employed person will be retained where the persons concerned are either temporarily unable to work as a result of illness or accident or have registered as job-seekers after having become involuntarily unemployed. The status of 'worker' or 'self-employed person' will further be maintained where a Union citizen ceases economic activity in order to embark on vocational training courses. Where cessation of employment is voluntary, the subject matter of the training course must relate to that of the previous employment. Former workers or self-employed persons who have reached retirement age or have become permanently incapacitated are conferred with privileged access to obtaining a right of permanent residence.[95]

Possessing the status of 'worker' or 'self-employed person' brings with it a number of advantages. In addition to being exempt from the requirement to possess sufficient resources and health insurance applicable to other categories of migrant Union citizen, such individuals are entitled to access social advantages and benefits under the same conditions as nationals of the host Member State.[96] Economically active Union citizens who embark on vocational studies will have more extensive rights concerning the entitlement to be accompanied or joined by their family members, as they will not be subject to the limitations applicable to other migrant Union students set out in Article 7(4).[97] Such individuals will further retain reinforced protection against expulsion in accordance with Article 14(4)(a). Union citizens who possess 'worker' status, in particular, also benefit from specific and extensive rights to equal treatment provided for in Regulation 492/2011.[98]

Economically inactive EU citizens

The second category of resident comprises economically inactive Union citizens. While such persons are also conferred with the right to reside in any Member State of their choosing, that entitlement is conditional on Union citizens possessing sufficient resources to support themselves and their families, so as not to become a burden on the social assistance system of the host Member State.[99] In addition, such migrant Union citizens are required to possess comprehensive sickness insurance cover in the host State.

Although Member States are afforded discretion in determining the level of resources that may be considered 'sufficient', the exercise of such discretion is closely

---

[95] See the commentary on Art 17, in Chapter 4.

[96] The right to equal treatment, particularly as regards the entitlement to access social benefits, is considered in the commentary on Art 24, in Chapter 5.

[97] On the position of students who are also workers, see Case C-46/12 *LN*, judgment of 21 February 2013.

[98] See the commentary on Art 24, in Chapter 5.

[99] See also recital 10 in the preamble.

circumscribed by the Directive. In the first instance, it is clear from the wording of Article 7(1)(b) that the concept of 'sufficient resources' is not open-ended, but refers to a minimum level of resources capable of sustaining migrant Union citizens so as to prevent them from becoming a burden on the budgetary resources of the host Member State.[100] Moreover, the parameters governing the determination and evaluation of sufficient resources are further specified in Article 8(4).

As the objective of the citizens' Directive is to facilitate the exercise of a fundamental freedom, the requirement for sufficient resources must not be interpreted in a manner that would undermine the objective and effectiveness of the Directive.[101] In the context of interpreting equivalent conditions in legislation preceding the citizens' Directive, the Court has emphasized that it is not necessary for a Union citizen to prove he or she personally has sufficient resources, if such resources are put at his or her disposal by a carer[102] or another third party.[103] The Court has further held that the requirement regarding the possession of health insurance is complied with even if the insurance policy is contracted in another State, once cover extends fully to the host State.[104] As regards the reference to 'social assistance' in Article 7(1)(b), the Court of Justice has clarified that this concept 'must be defined by reference to the objective pursued by that provision...and not by reference to formal criteria'. In particular, this provision should not be interpreted in light of the concept of 'special non-contributory benefits' as set out in Regulation 883/2004 on coordination of social security, since that Regulation 'pursues different objectives' than the citizens' Directive. Rather, the concept of 'social assistance' in Article 7(1)(b) of the Directive must 'be given an autonomous and uniform interpretation throughout the European Union, which must take into account the context of that provision and the purpose pursued'. More specifically, 'social assistance' refers to 'all assistance introduced by the public authorities, whether at national, regional or local level, that can be claimed by an individual who does not have resources sufficient to meet his own basic needs and the needs of his family and who, by reason of that fact, may become a burden on the public finances of the host Member State during his period of residence which could have consequences for the overall level of assistance which may be granted by that State'. The concept includes a compensatory supplement for pensioners 'which is intended to ensure a minimum means of subsistence for its recipient where his pension is insufficient, is funded in full by the public authorities, without any contribution being made by insured persons'. Furthermore, meeting the conditions of eligibility for social assistance 'could be

---

[100] See, by analogy, Case C-578/08 *Chakroun* [2010] ECR I-1839, para 46 concerning the interpretation of a substantially equivalent obligation provided for in Directive 2003/86 on the right to family reunification ([2003] OJ L 251/12).

[101] See, by analogy, Case C-578/08 *Chakroun* [2010] ECR I-1839, para 43.

[102] Case C-200/02 *Zhu and Chen* [2004] ECR I-9925, paras 29–33.

[103] Case C-408/03 *Commission v Belgium* [2006] ECR I-2647, paras 40–42.

[104] Case C-413/99 *Baumbast and R* [2002] ECR I-7091, para 92.

an indication that that national does not have sufficient resources to avoid becoming an unreasonable burden on the social assistance system of the host Member State for the purposes of Article 7(1)(b)'. However, an automatic refusal to grant residence to a person eligible for such a benefit is a breach of Article 8(4) (on which, see the commentary below).[105]

Students

The third category of resident contemplated by Article 7(1) comprises Union citizens who have relocated primarily for the purposes of undertaking a course of studies, including vocational studies, in the host Member State. Although students are also required to be self-supporting and have comprehensive health insurance cover,[106] less stringent rules (as compared to the second category) apply to proving possession of sufficient resources. Students may demonstrate they have such resources by way of a declaration or by such equivalent means as they choose. In this context, the Court has held national measures which did not accept such a declaration but required specific documentation attesting resources of a specific amount to be incompatible with Union law.[107] The provisions on students apply to studies undertaken at either a private or public establishment, once they are accredited or financed by the host Member State, either on the basis of national legislation or administrative practice.

Vocational training has been defined in the case law of the Court as including any form of education which prepares for a qualification for a particular profession, trade, or employment or which provides the necessary skills for such a profession, trade, or employment.[108] The Court has confirmed that a course of training may be regarded as vocational regardless of the age or the level of training of the pupils or students and even if the training programme includes an element of general education.[109]

Furthermore, the Court has confirmed that a Union citizen's status is not static and may change during the period of residence in the host Member State.[110] Thus, for example, a Union citizen who initially entered the territory of a State in order to pursue studies is not prevented from taking up employed activity contemporaneously.

---

[105] Judgment of 19 September 2013 in Case C-140/12 *Brey*, paras 46–80.

[106] The entitlement of students to be accompanied by family members is subject to limitations laid down in Art 7(4). In particular, family members who may accompany a Union citizen are limited to the spouse, the registered partner, and dependent children. In addition, Member States are required to facilitate the entry and residence of dependent direct relatives in the ascending line of the Union citizen or his or her spouse in accordance with Art 3(2) (on which, see the commentary in Chapter 1).

[107] Case C-424/98 *Commission v Italy* [2000] ECR I-4001.

[108] Case law beginning with Case 293/83 *Gravier* [1985] ECR 593, para 30.

[109] Case 293/83 *Gravier* [1985] ECR 593, para 30.

[110] Case C-46/12 *LN*, judgment of 21 February 2013.

Once such activity is genuine and effective in accordance with the Union law definition of worker, then that citizen may be regarded as a worker residing on the basis of Article 7(1)(a).[111] In that case, the limitations which apply to students residing in accordance with Article 7(1)(c) shall not apply.[112] Presumably the limitation on the admission of students' family members set out in Article 7(4) will also cease to apply. Finally, it should also be recalled that some students who are former workers or self-employed persons will retain the status of worker or self-employed person pursuant to Article 7(3)(d), discussed below. For such persons also, the limitations of Article 7(1)(c) and (4) will not apply.

The sufficient resources requirement

It follows from the sufficient resource requirement imposed on economically inactive migrant Union citizens that the right of such citizens to equal treatment is qualified insofar as access to social benefits is concerned. Recourse to social assistance may indicate an inability to comply with the sufficient resource requirement which could in turn result in the termination of residence rights. Moreover, the Directive provides for an express derogation from the principle of equal treatment insofar as it applies to the right of economically inactive citizens' to access specific forms of social benefit, before they obtain the status of permanent resident.[113]

One question which is liable to emerge in practice is whether an economically inactive Union citizen may be regarded as possessing sufficient resources if such resources are derived from his or her third-country national spouse.[114] The approach to considering this question will depend upon whether it is claimed that sufficient resources exist prior to the move or whether it is argued that the citizen would possess sufficient resources if his or her third-country national spouse were permitted to access the labour market of the host Member State as contemplated by Article 23.[115]

It is submitted that if prior to relocating, a Union citizen can show that the family unit has sufficient resources, it is immaterial whether such resources derive from the Union citizen or another person, including a third-country national family

---

[111] Case C-46/12 *LN*, judgment of 21 February 2013, paras 39–43.

[112] Case C-46/12 *LN*, judgment of 21 February 2013, para 48.

[113] See Case C-75/11 *Commission v Austria*, judgment of 4 October 2012, not yet reported, para 53 onwards. The tension between the right of Union citizens to equal treatment, on the one hand, and the limitations of their right to access social benefits, on the other, is considered in further detail in the commentary on Art 24, in Chapter 5.

[114] In any event, Union citizens who reside as a family member of a citizen who satisfies the conditions laid down in Art 7(1), (b), and (c) will not have to provide independent proof of compliance with those conditions, since it will be up to the primary right-holder to demonstrate that those conditions are satisfied.

[115] Art 23 expressly authorizes family members of Union citizens to engage in economic activity in the host Member State. See further Chapter 5.

member.[116] Thus, for example, in the case of *Zhu and Chen*, a Union citizen was considered to satisfy the sufficient resources requirement on the basis of resources placed at the disposal of a Union citizen by a third-country national, and the Court of Justice has consistently confirmed that for the purposes of obtaining residence rights, it is 'having' sufficient resources and not their origin which is decisive.[117]

The situation is less clear-cut where an economically inactive Union citizen claims that he or she would have sufficient resources if his or her third-country national spouse were permitted to take up employment in the host Member State. It is evident from the scheme of the Directive that rights accorded to third-country national family members to reside and work in a host Member State are derived from the Union citizen's right of residence (and not vice versa).[118] Consequently, on a strict interpretation, third-country nationals would only be able to derive a right to reside and work after the Union citizen has established his or her right of residence which, in turn, is conditional on that citizen having first met the conditions laid down in Article 7(1). If, however, a Union citizen sought to demonstrate sufficient resources on the basis of the future activities of the third-country national in the host Member State (who did not have an independent right of residence or a right to work in that State), it would imply that the third-country national was exercising rights prior to having formally obtained them from the Union citizen he or she is accompanying or joining. It would therefore be conceptually challenging to permit an economically inactive Union citizen to derive residence rights on the basis of work carried out by his or her third-country national spouse in the host Member State. This interpretation is further reinforced by the wording of Article 7(1)(b), (c), and (d) which provides that it is Union citizens that must meet the sufficient resources requirement 'for themselves and for their family members'.[119]

Nevertheless, it is submitted that a teleological approach to interpreting the Directive would lead to the opposite conclusion. The Directive's primary objective is to facilitate free movement and the sufficient resources requirement is a restriction designed to prevent excessive pressure being placed on the social assistance systems of the host Member State. However, once a family unit is self-sufficient, the social assistance system is not burdened and therefore it should be immaterial whether

---

[116] The CJEU appears to have implicitly accepted that an EU citizen can qualify for residence pursuant to Art 7(1)(b), and eventually permanent residence, if he or she is receiving support from an EU citizen partner: see the judgment in Joined Cases C-147/11 and C-148/11 *Czop and Punakova*, judgment of 6 September 2012, not yet reported.

[117] Case C-200/02 [2004] ECR I-9925, which concerned Directive 90/364 (preceding the citizens' Directive). At paras 29–33, the Court observed that, according to the very wording of the relevant provision 'it is sufficient for the nationals of Member States to "have" the necessary resources, and that provision lays down no requirement whatsoever as to their origin'. See also Case C-408/03 *Commission v Belgium* [2006] ECR I-2647.

[118] See Art 23.

[119] Also, Art 23 specifies that the right to take up employment or self-employment concerns the family members of citizens who 'have the right of residence or the right of permanent residence'.

the source of income derives from the Union citizen or from the third-country national family member.[120] Indeed, the Court has consistently held that it is not necessary for a Union citizen to prove he or she personally has sufficient resources, if such resources are put at his or her disposal by a carer[121] or other third party.[122] Moreover, as a restriction upon a fundamental freedom, the requirement for sufficient resources falls to be interpreted narrowly.[123] The wording of the Directive reflects a concern to limit claims upon Member States' social assistance budgets, rather than a concern to limit access by third-country national family members to the labour market; and such labour market access will in fact reduce the number of claims for social assistance. Additionally, the requirement that the Union citizen be economically active would restrict the useful effect of Article 7(1)(b), since it could force Union citizens to engage in work or self-employed activities, when its purpose is precisely to facilitate the residence of economically inactive Union citizens. Furthermore, in *Ruiz Zambrano*,[124] the Court expressly confirmed that a third-country national father of a Union citizen must be permitted to reside and work so as to ensure that a Union citizen is in a position to continue residing within the territory of a Member State. It would seem to follow from the logic underpinning that judgment that the same principle should apply to family members who have accompanied or joined Union citizens exercising free movement rights as provided for by the Directive and who therefore fall within its scope of application. Finally, requiring one particular party in a couple to work may potentially be discriminatory and interfere unduly with the right to family life and the autonomy of the family unit.

Therefore, it is submitted that subject to the particular facts of any individual case, there is scope to interpret Article 7(1)(b) as permitting Union citizens to establish sufficient resources on the basis of the third-country national's income, obtained through the exercise of a derived right to pursue employed or self-employed activities in accordance with Article 23. However, for the time being it remains a matter to be determined by the Court of Justice.

---

[120] See, by analogy, Case C-200/02 *Zhu and Chen* [2004] ECR I-9925, paras 32 and 33.

[121] In Case C-200/02 *Zhu and Chen* [2004] ECR I-9925, the Court held that a Union citizen child could rely on the resources of the third-country national family member, in that case the Union citizen's mother.

[122] Case C-408/03 *Commission v Belgium* [2006] ECR I-2647, paras 38–51.

[123] See, for example: Case 66/85 *Lawrie-Blum* [1986] ECR 2121, para 26; Case C-200/02 *Zhu and Chen* [2004] ECR I-9925; and Case C-208/09 *Ilonka Sayn-Wittgenstein* [2010] ECR I-13693. In a variety of areas, the Court has held that derogations, insofar as they constitute exceptions to objectives laid down in Union law, are to be interpreted restrictively. See, for example, Joined Cases C-267/95 and C-268/95 *Merck and Beecham* [1996] ECR I-6285, para 23 (in relation to Acts of Accession); Case C-481/99 *Heininger* [2001] ECR I-9945, para 31 (consumer protection); Case C-337/06 *Bayerischer Rundfunk and Others* [2007] ECR I-11173, para 64 (public procurement); and Case C-554/09 *Seeger* [2011] ECR I-7131, para 33 (regulation in the road transport industry).

[124] Case C-34/09 [2011] ECR I-1177. See further the commentary on Art 3(1) in Chapter 1.

Family members

Article 7(1)(d) confers a right of residence on family members, who are EU citizens, who wish to accompany or join a Union citizen who satisfies the applicable conditions of residence set out in Article 7(1)(a) to (c). Given that, as discussed already, EU citizens can satisfy the requirements of Article 7(1)(b) if they are being supported by a family member, and that all EU citizens have the right to carry out economic activities which would satisfy the requirements of Article 7(1)(a), Article 7(1)(d) has little independent scope of application. It could be relevant, however, in the case of family break-up (in conjunction with Articles 12 or 13), or in the event that the family member concerned is the national of a newly acceded Member State who does not yet have an independent right to work. The Commission's 2008 report on the application of the Directive therefore rightly criticizes those Member States which have not made express provision for the rights of these categories of persons.[125] According to the EFTA Court, an EU citizen who has acquired permanent residence status pursuant to chapter IV no longer needs to meet the requirement of minimum resources as regards the admission of his or her family members.[126]

> 2. The right of residence provided for in paragraph 1 shall extend to family members who are not nationals of a Member State, accompanying or joining the Union citizen in the host Member State, provided that such Union citizen satisfies the conditions referred to in paragraph 1(a), (b) or (c).

Article 7(2) expressly confirms that a right of residence also extends to third-country national family members of Union citizens. The definition of family member for the purposes of the Directive is set out in Article 2(2) and includes the spouse, registered partner as referred to in Article 2(2)(b), direct descendants of either the Union citizen or his or her spouse or registered partner, under the age of twenty-one, and dependent direct relatives in the ascending line of either the Union citizen or of his or her spouse or registered partner.[127] A more restricted group of family members may accompany or join a Union citizen who is exercising free movement rights in order to pursue studies in another Member State.[128] The family members are not obliged to live under the same roof as the EU citizen.[129]

---

[125] COM(2008) 840.

[126] Case E-4/11 *Clauder*, judgment of the EFTA Court of 26 July 2011; presumably the same finding applies to Art 7(2). The CJEU was implicitly asked to address a similar issue in Case C-434/09 *McCarthy* [2011] ECR I-3375, but did not answer the relevant questions due to its approach to the scope of the Directive in this case (see the commentary on Art 3(1), in Chapter 1).

[127] For detailed consideration of the definition of 'family members', see the commentary on Art 2, in Chapter 1.

[128] Pursuant to Art 7(4), a student Union citizen may be accompanied by his or her spouse or registered partner and dependent children. In addition, Member States are required to facilitate the entry and residence of the dependent direct relatives in the ascending line of a student Union citizen or his or her spouse or registered partner. See the commentary on Art 7(4) below.

[129] See Case 267/83 *Diatta* [1985] ECR 567 and Case C-40/11 *Iida v Stadt Ulm*, judgment of 8 November 2012, not yet reported. Also, the citizens' Directive dropped an accommodation

The entitlement of Member State nationals to the company of their family members, regardless of nationality, has been recognized long before the introduction of Union citizenship and the Directive. It has featured in a number of different instruments adopted to give effect to free movement rights enshrined in the Treaty.[130] Aside from considerations relating to the respect for family life enshrined in Article 8 of the European Convention on Human Rights,[131] the Court has consistently recognized that measures restricting family members of Member State nationals from accompanying or joining such nationals in a host Member State would be liable to discourage the exercise of free movement rights.[132]

Of course, as noted above, family members accompanying or joining a Union citizen may be Union citizens in their own right. In this case, they may also be direct beneficiaries of free movement and residence rights under the Union Treaties and the Directive. However, as 'family members', such individuals will not be obliged to prove that they satisfy conditions for residence, namely sufficient resources or sickness insurance, independently of the Union citizen that they are accompanying or joining. By contrast, family members who are not Union citizens, but third-country nationals, will not necessarily enjoy an independent right of residence in a Member State. In such cases, their entitlement to stay in a host Member State may depend entirely on their relationship to the migrant Union citizen, until they obtain permanent residence status pursuant to the Directive, or unless they qualify for long-term residence status in their own name pursuant to EU immigration legislation.[133] Nevertheless, the Union legislature has been careful to adopt safeguard measures to ensure that family members (regardless of their nationality) who have settled in a host Member State do not automatically lose their right of residence in that State if their Union citizen family member either dies or leaves the Member State or there is otherwise a change in the family relationship.[134]

In the case of *Metock*,[135] the Court confirmed that family members of Union citizens who are third-country nationals are entitled to accompany, join, and reside with a Union citizen in the host Member State regardless of whether they had

---

requirement that used to apply to workers' families. These points apply equally to EU citizen family members covered by Art 7(1)(d). See further the discussion of Art 2(2) in Chapter 1.

[130] See the various measures referred to in Section B of this chapter. See, for example, recital 5 and Arts 10–12 of Reg 1612/68.

[131] Case C-413/99 *Baumbast and R* [2002] ECR I-7091, para 72; Case C-60/00 *Carpenter* [2002] ECR I-6279, paras 41 and 42; and Case C-503/03 *Commission v Spain* [2006] ECR I-1097, para 47.

[132] Case C-370/90 *Singh* [1992] ECR I-4265, para 20; Case C-60/00 *Carpenter* [2002] ECR I-6279, para 38; Case C-459/99 *MRAX* [2002] ECR I-6591, para 53; Case C-441/02 *Commission v Germany* [2006] ECR I-3449, para 109; and Case C-291/05 *Eind* [2007] ECR I-10719, paras 35–37 and para 44.

[133] Case C-40/11 *Iida v Stadt Ulm*, judgment of 8 November 2012, not yet reported.

[134] See the commentary on Arts 12 and 13 below.

[135] Case C-127/08 *Metock and Others* [2008] ECR I-6241.

previously been lawfully resident in another Member State.[136] The Court emphasized that third-country nationals are entitled to reside in the host Member State regardless of whether they were already family members at the time the Union citizen moved to the host Member State or whether they only became family members after the Union citizen moved to the host Member State. Equally, it was confirmed that the right of residence of third-country national family members does not depend on the circumstances of entry into the host Member State and whether or not they were already resident in the host Member State when the Union citizen moved there.[137] The CJEU has emphasized that a restrictive approach to interpreting Union citizens' entitlement to the company of their family members would deter the exercise of free movement rights and thus constitute an obstacle to the exercise of fundamental freedoms guaranteed by the Treaty.[138]

In addition, pursuant to Article 3(2), Member States are required to facilitate the entry and residence of other categories of persons, even if they do not fall within the scope of the definition of 'family member' in Article 2(2). Such persons may include extended family members who are dependants or were members of the migrant Union citizen's household in the country from which they have come. The entry and residence of relatives must equally be facilitated where serious health grounds strictly require them to be cared for by the Union citizen. Member States are further required to facilitate entry and residence of the partner of a Union citizen with whom he or she has a durable relationship (an 'informal partner').[139]

3. For the purposes of paragraph 1(a), a Union citizen who is no longer a worker or self-employed person shall retain the status of worker or self-employed person in the following circumstances:

(a) he/she is temporarily unable to work as the result of an illness or accident;

(b) he/she is in duly recorded involuntary unemployment after having been employed for more than one year and has registered as a job-seeker with the relevant employment office;

(c) he/she is in duly recorded involuntary unemployment after completing a fixed-term employment contract of less than a year or after having become involuntarily unemployed during the first twelve months and

---

[136] Case C-127/08 *Metock and Others* [2008] ECR I-6241, paras 48–80.

[137] Case C-127/08 *Metock and Others* [2008] ECR I-6241, paras 85–93, 97, and 99. See also Case C-459/99 *MRAX* [2002] ECR I-6591, paras 77–79; and Case C-551/07 *Sahin* [2008] ECR I-10453, paras 27, 28, 32, and 33. For detailed consideration of the free movement rights of family members, see the commentary on Art 3(1) in Chapter 1.

[138] Case C-60/00 *Carpenter* [2002] ECR I-6279, para 38; Case C-459/99 *MRAX* [2002] ECR I-6591, para 53; Case C-441/02 *Commission v Germany* [2006] ECR I-3449, para 109; Case C-291/05 *Eind* [2007] ECR I-10719, para 44; and Case C-127/08 *Metock and Others* [2008] ECR I-6241, para 56.

[139] Case C-83/11 *Rahman*, judgment of 5 September 2012, not yet reported. See the commentary on Art 3(2) in Chapter 1.

has registered as a job-seeker with the relevant employment office. In this case, the status of worker shall be retained for no less than six months;

(d) he/she embarks on vocational training. Unless he/she is involuntarily unemployed, the retention of the status of worker shall require the training to be related to the previous employment.

Pursuant to Article 7(3), certain specific categories of migrant Union citizen, who were previously workers or self-employed may retain their 'worker' or 'self-employed' status and thereby continue to rely on the advantages that possession of such status entails.[140] In particular, they are not subject to the resources and sickness insurance conditions referred to in Article 7(1)(b) and (c); expulsions on economic grounds are ruled out, pursuant to Article 14(4)(a); the restriction on obtaining mainte-nance aid for studies expressly does not apply to them (see Article 24(2), discussed in Chapter 5); and, as noted already, students who are former workers are not subject to the limitation on admission of family members set out in Article 7(4).[141] Because it is easier for the former workers and self-employed persons to retain a right of residence, it is indirectly easier for their family members to do so also, pursuant to Article 7(1)(d) and (2). Moreover, Article 7(3) is without prejudice to the separate and privileged right that Article 17 confers on former workers and self-employed persons to obtain permanent residence status (see Chapter 4).[142]

The retention of rights of former workers or self-employed persons has long been recognized in the Union legal order.[143] In particular, the Treaty establishing the European Economic Community, in its Article 48(3)(d), expressly provided for the granting of residence rights to persons who had previously been in employment in the host Member State, subject to conditions that were to be developed by the Commission in secondary legislation. Such rights were provided for in Regulation 1251/70,[144] which authorized Union citizens who ceased working in another Member State, either as a consequence of having reached the age of retirement or because of having suffered permanent incapacity, to retain a right of residence in that Member State. The Union legislature also introduced additional meas-ures to safeguard the status of migrant Union citizens who became economically inactive temporarily. Article 7 of Directive 68/360 prohibited the withdrawal of residence permits from migrant workers on the sole ground that the cessation of

---

[140] The special rights attaching to the status of 'worker' or 'self-employed person' are considered in the commentary on Art 7(1)(a) above.

[141] The Commission is therefore right to criticize those Member States who only provide for a right to residence for such persons, not the retention of worker status (see the 2008 report).

[142] Even if Art 17 does not apply, residence pursuant to Art 7(3) counts towards the acquisition of permanent residence pursuant to chapter IV of the Directive for former workers or self-employed persons and (indirectly) their family members.

[143] See Section B of this chapter. For discussion on the rights of former workers to equal treat-ment, see Section B and Section E of the commentary on Art 24, in Chapter 5.

[144] Reg 1251/70 was adopted precisely to provide for the right of residence of workers who wished to remain in the territory of a Member State in which they had worked. See now Art 17, discussed in Chapter 4.

such activities resulted from temporary incapacity arising from illness or accident or because of involuntary unemployment, although it also permitted residence to be restricted to a period of not less than twelve months when a residence permit was renewed for the first time,[145] if the worker had been involuntarily unemployed for more than twelve months. The citizens' Directive has therefore improved the position of such persons.

The rights of former workers were further supplemented by the case law of the Court of Justice. In particular, the Court has consistently held that Union citizen workers are guaranteed certain rights linked to the status of worker even when they are no longer in an employment relationship, in the context of their eligibility for certain tax or social advantages that had been linked to their status as worker.[146] Thus, for example, even after the cessation of employed activities, migrant Union citizens have been held to be entitled to rely on their worker status to benefit from a right to equal treatment in respect of a compensation scheme offered to agricultural workers[147] or to access maintenance grants for vocational studies.[148]

Interestingly, unlike the provisions of Regulation 1251/70, Article 7(3) does not specify that the right of Union citizens to retain their 'worker' or 'self-employed' status in a host Member State is conditional on their having previously exercised such activities in that same host Member State. Such a condition may, however, be regarded as implicit. An interpretation according to which Article 7(3) provides for the recognition of the 'worker' or 'self-employed' status of citizens who had never worked in the host Member State (but had previously engaged in economic activity in other Member States) would be inconsistent with the wording, scheme, and spirit of the Directive. In the first instance, it would conflict with the express terms of Article 7(1)(a), according to which the intended beneficiaries of that provision are citizens who are workers or self-employed persons *in the host Member State*. Moreover, it has been held that the rights afforded to Union citizens who are economically active in a host Member State are granted in recognition of their participation in and contribution to the economic life of a Member State, particularly through the payment of taxes and the consequent financing of the social policies of that State.[149] It would thus be inconsistent with that rationale if Union citizens were to be conferred with rights reserved to workers or self-employed persons in circumstances where they have not in fact pursued economic activities in the host

---

[145] The residence permit had to be valid for at least five years (Art 6(1)(b), Directive 68/360), although Art 6(3) of that Directive also provided for the issue of temporary residence permits for work lasting between three months and one year. See also Art 4(1) of Directive 73/148.

[146] Case 39/86 *Lair* [1988] ECR 3161, paras 29–36; Case C-57/96 *Meints* [1997] ECR I-6689; and Case C-35/97 *Commission v France* [1998] ECR I-5325.

[147] Case C-57/96 *Meints* [1997] ECR I-6689.

[148] Case 39/86 *Lair* [1988] ECR 3161.

[149] Case C-542/09 *Commission v Netherlands*, judgment of 14 June 2012, not yet reported, paras 63–66.

Member State. It is therefore submitted that to retain the status of a 'worker' or 'self-employed person' in a host Member State it is necessary for the citizens concerned to have previously exercised economic activities in that same Member State.

The categories of migrant Union citizen entitled to retain their worker or self-employed status following cessation of economic activities is enumerated in Article 7(3), paragraphs (a) to (d). Such categories include former workers or self-employed persons who are temporarily unable to work due to illness or accident; persons who have become involuntarily unemployed and have registered as job-seekers; and persons who have embarked upon vocational training. If an individual ceases employment by choice to pursue such training, then the subject matter of the training must be related to that of the previous employment.

Article 7(3)(a) provides for the retention of the 'worker' or 'self-employed' status of individuals who are temporarily unable to work due to illness or having suffered an accident. In the absence of a reference to the laws of Member States, the concept of temporary inability will be subject to an autonomous definition in Union law.[150] The Directive does not set any time limit regarding periods that are to be qualified as 'temporary'. However, having regard to the approach adopted by the Court in other areas of Union law, it is suggested that an inability to work may be regarded as temporary where it is anticipated that the individual will resume his occupational activity in the future.[151]

The Court of Justice has assumed that a person on maternity leave retains the status of worker during that period.[152] However, in the pending case of *Saint Prix v Secretary of State for Work and Pensions*,[153] the question has arisen as to whether a migrant Union citizen who temporarily gives up work[154] during the late stages of pregnancy and in the immediate aftermath of childbirth may be regarded as retaining the status of 'worker' pursuant to Article 7(3). This question did not arise in connection with a claim for a right of residence per se, but in the context of an application for income support in the United Kingdom. Pursuant to national law, only United Kingdom nationals, economically active migrant Union citizens, and Union citizens with permanent residence status were entitled to such income support, but any other 'person from abroad' was excluded. Therefore the applicant sought to rely on her status as a worker in order to qualify for the benefit in question.

---

[150] See Joined Cases C-424/10 and C-425/10 *Ziolkowski and Szeja v Land Berlin*, judgment of 21 December 2011, not yet reported, para 32.

[151] In the context of interpreting the Union's Staff Regulations, see the opinion and the judgment of the Court in Case C-198/07 P *Donal Gordon* [2008] ECR I-10701. See also, by analogy, the case law on the EU's framework equality Directive (Directive 2000/78, [2000] OJ L 303/16), which defines disability (as distinct from illness) as a 'long-term' condition: Joined Cases C-335/11 and C-337/11, *HK Danmark*, judgment of 11 April 2013.

[152] Case C-325/09 *Dias* [2011] ECR I-6387.

[153] Case C-507/12, *Jessy Saint Prix v Secretary of State for Work and Pensions*, pending before the Court of Justice.

[154] The applicant was not, however, formally on maternity leave.

In the context of domestic proceedings, it was apparent that the particular situation of the applicant did not readily fall within any of the specific cases contemplated by Article 7(3). Indeed, it seems unlikely that pregnancy could be considered either an illness or accident within the meaning of subparagraph (a) of Article 7(3).[155] However, as indicated above, although the Directive sets out certain categories of individual who may retain the status of 'worker', that term is not in fact defined by the Directive and as such falls to be considered in light of the definition developed in the case law of the Court of Justice on what is now Article 45 TFEU.[156] According to that case law, the concept of worker must not be interpreted narrowly.[157] Moreover, as recalled above, the Court has consistently held that Union citizen workers may continue to benefit from certain rights linked to the status of worker even when they are no longer in an employment relationship.[158]

It is submitted that the exclusion of pregnant women from income support is not reconcilable with the principle of equality and non-discrimination recognized as a general principle of Union law, guaranteed in Article 23 of the EU Charter of Fundamental Rights and afforded specific expression in (inter alia) EU legislation on pregnant workers.[159] It is further submitted that the Union law concept of 'worker' falls to be interpreted in a manner that is consistent with fundamental rights protected in the Union legal order. As regards the interpretation of Article 7(1)(a), the Court has consistently held that respect for fundamental rights and the general principles of Union law is a condition for the lawfulness of Union secondary legislation[160] and that Union legislation must be capable of being interpreted and applied in a manner consistent with fundamental rights.[161] Member States are precluded from relying on an interpretation of an instrument of secondary legislation which would be in conflict with general principles of European Union law.[162]

---

[155] In a number of cases, the CJEU has ruled out the possibility of comparing pregnancy with illness: see, for instance, Case C-32/93 *Webb* [1994] ECR I-3567. In light of the context of Art 7(3), it would be untenable to interpret an 'accident' as including an unplanned pregnancy (if indeed it was unplanned in this case).

[156] See the commentary on Art 7(1) above.

[157] Case C-357/89 *Raulin* [1992] ECR I-1027, para 10; Case C-94/07 *Raccanelli* [2008] ECR I-5939, para 33; and Joined Cases C-22/08 and C-23/08 *Vatsouras and Koupatantze* [2009] ECR I-4585, para 26.

[158] Case 39/86 *Lair* [1988] ECR 3161, paras 29–36; Case C-57/96 *Meints* [1997] ECR I-6689; and Case C-35/97 *Commission v France* [1998] ECR I-5325.

[159] Council Directive 92/85/EEC of 19 October 1992 on the introduction of measures to encourage improvements in the safety and health at work of pregnant workers and workers who have recently given birth or are breastfeeding ([1992] OJ L 348/1). On Art 23 of the Charter, see for instance Case C-236/09 *Test-Achats* [2011] ECR I-773, where the Court ruled that a permitted exception from the principle of equal treatment set out in EU legislation was invalid.

[160] Joined Cases C-402/07 and C-432/07 *Sturgeon and Others* [2009] ECR I-10923, paras 47 and 48.

[161] See, to that effect, Case C-101/01 *Lindqvist* [2003] ECR I-12971, para 87 and Case C-305/05 *Ordre des barreaux francophones et germanophone and Others* [2007] ECR I-5305, para 28.

[162] Case C-101/01 *Lindqvist* [2003] ECR I-12971, para 87; Case C-305/05 *Ordre des barreaux francophones et germanophone and Others* [2007] ECR I-5305, para 28; and Joined Cases C-411/10 and C-493/10 *NS and ME*, judgment of 21 December 2011, not yet reported, at para 77.

Having regard to such considerations, it is suggested that certain categories of former workers, though not referred to in Article 7(3), may still rely on that status under Union law. More particularly, it is submitted that the concept of 'worker' within the meaning of Article 45 TFEU and for the purposes of Article 7(1)(a) must include women who have temporarily had to cease economic activity due to pregnancy, given that (in accordance with established case law) lack of equal treatment due to pregnancy is directly discriminatory on grounds of sex.[163]

Subparagraphs (b) and (c) of Article 7(3) provide for the retention of the status of 'worker' or 'self-employed person' of Union citizens who have become unemployed involuntarily and have registered as job-seekers with the relevant employment office. Pursuant to Article 7(3)(b) a Union citizen job-seeker will retain his worker or self-employed status if prior to having been made redundant, the individual had been employed for more than one year. Arguably this time period should be calculated in accordance with Article 16(3), which concerns the acquisition of permanent residence status.[164] Job-seekers who have worked for less than one year may also be able to retain their worker status under Article 7(3)(c), where they have completed a fixed term contract of less than one year's duration or where they have become involuntarily unemployed during the first twelve months in the host Member State. In this case the status of worker shall be retained for no less than six months.

The Directive thus draws a distinction between Union citizen job-seekers who have previously engaged in economic activities and those who are seeking work for the first time. It is apparent from Article 7(3)(b) and (c) that the entitlement to continue to benefit from 'worker' or 'self-employed' status for the purposes of Article 7(1)(a) is confined to job-seekers who have previously been economically active. By contrast, first time job-seekers and their families will not be regarded as workers but as economically inactive Union citizens who may reside on the basis of Article 7(1)(b) subject to possession of sufficient resources and comprehensive health insurance. This differentiation reflects the case law of the Court of Justice according to which it is legitimate for host Member States to distinguish between job-seekers on the basis of their connection with the job market of a host Member State.[165] Nevertheless, even first time job-seekers and their families are afforded some additional protection by the Directive. Pursuant to Article 14(4)(b), Union citizens who enter for the purposes of seeking employment may not in any event be the subject of an expulsion decision where they can provide evidence that they are continuing to seek employment and have a genuine chance of being engaged.[166]

---

[163] See, for instance, Case C-32/93 *Webb* [1994] ECR I-3567. Also, this interpretation would best reflect the Court's concern in the *Webb* judgment (among others) to avoid the risk of encouraging abortions (para 21 of the judgment).

[164] See the commentary on this provision in Chapter 4.

[165] Case C-138/02 *Brian Francis Collins* [2004] ECR I-2703.

[166] See the commentary on Art 14(4)(b) below.

Pursuant to Article 7(3)(d), enrolment on a course of vocational training constitutes an additional ground on which migrant Union citizens may retain their 'worker' or 'self-employed' status. The inclusion of such a provision reflects the priority attached by the Union legislature to facilitating access to such training.[167] Indeed, the Court has observed that provision for the development of vocational training policy, included in the EEC Treaty,[168] was to be regarded as constituting an indispensable element of the Community's activities, the objectives of which included the free movement of persons, the mobility of labour, and the improvement of the living standards of workers.[169]

The retention by vocational students of their 'worker' or 'self-employed' status provided for in Article 7(3)(d) is consistent with the approach adopted by the Court of Justice in its judgment in *Lair v University of Hannover*.[170] Here, the Court held that a migrant Member State national who ceased an occupational activity in a host Member State in order to pursue a course of vocational studies must be regarded as having retained her worker status for the purpose of accessing and maintaining a training grant, provided that in the event of voluntary unemployment, there is continuity between the purpose of the studies and the previous occupational activity. The Court further ruled out the entitlement of Member States to make the provision of the maintenance and training grant conditional on having fulfilled a minimum period of occupational activity. In line with this judgment—and in contrast to Articles 7(1)(b) and (c)—Article 7(1)(d) does not provide for any minimum period before which an individual is entitled to engage in vocational training for the purposes of retaining his or her status as an economically active migrant Union citizen. In his Opinion in the case of *Förster*, Advocate-General Mazák argued that any requirement for a continuity as regards the nature of previous employment and vocational studies undertaken should be interpreted broadly because in the current working environment a continuous career path in a single field of activity is less

---

[167] This priority is also reflected in the terms of Reg 492/2011. Recital 9 in the preamble to that Regulation emphasizes the proximity and interdependence between the freedom of movement for workers, employment, and vocational training.

[168] Art 128 of the EEC Treaty, which now appears in somewhat reinforced terms in Art 166 TFEU. Art 128 EEC had initially required the Council, acting on a proposal from the Commission, to lay down general principles for implementing a common vocational training policy capable of contributing to the harmonious development both of the national economies and of the common market. Art 166 TFEU now confers the Union with competence to implement a vocational training policy which shall support and supplement the action of the Member States who continue to be responsible for the content and organization of vocational training.

[169] Case 293/83 *Gravier* [1985] ECR 593. Moreover, since that judgment the place of vocational training has been further reinforced, through the insertion by the Maastricht Treaty of 'Education and Vocational Training' as a separate chapter into what was then Title VIII of the Treaty establishing the European Community. Following the entry into force of the Treaty of Amsterdam, Title VIII became Title XI. Since the entry into force of the Lisbon Treaty, the provision now appears in Title XII of the TFEU, entitled 'Education, vocational training, youth and sport'.

[170] Case 39/86 *Lair* [1988] ECR 3161.

typical and members of the workforce are frequently expected to show flexibility as regards their education and training.[171]

A notable feature of the drafting of Article 7(3) is that although its *chapeau* refers to the retention of both 'worker' and 'self-employed person' status, the specific circumstances contemplated by subparagraphs (a) to (d) appear essentially to concern former workers only. In particular Article 7(3)(a) refers to individuals who are unable to 'work'—without making any reference to individuals who no longer engage in self-employed activity. Similarly, subparagraphs (b) to (d) of Article 7(3) each make express reference to individuals who have suffered involuntary unemployment without making any reference to individuals who have been compelled to cease self-employed activity as a result of external circumstances. Subject to guidance by the Court of Justice on this issue, it is submitted that insofar as possible, Article 7(3) must be interpreted as applying to both Union citizens who have been economically active, whether as workers or as self-employed persons. Such an approach is suggested not only by the wording of the *chapeau* but would be consistent with the equivalence afforded to these two forms of economic activity in the case law of the Court of Justice.[172]

> 4. By way of derogation from paragraphs 1(d) and 2 above, only the spouse, the registered partner provided for in Article 2(2)(b) and dependent children shall have the right of residence as family members of a Union citizen meeting the conditions under 1(c) above. Article 3(2) shall apply to his/her dependent direct relatives in the ascending lines and those of his/her spouse or registered partner.

Article 7(4) largely re-enacts a provision contained in the students' residence Directive[173] limiting the family members that may accompany or join migrant Union citizens who move to pursue a course of studies in another Member State. In particular, such migrant citizens may only be accompanied or joined by their spouse or registered partner and any dependent children. The inclusion of a 'registered partner' is new as compared to the prior legislation.

Although the dependent direct relatives in the ascending line of the Union citizen or his or her spouse or registered partner are not granted an automatic right of residence, their entry and residence must be facilitated in accordance with Article 3(2).[174] In its 2008 Report on the application of the Directive,[175] the Commission observes

---

[171] Opinion of AG Mazák in Case C-158/07 *Förster* [2008] ECR I-8507, para 83. See also S O'Leary, *The Evolving Concept of Community Citizenship—from the Free Movement of Persons to Union Citizenship* (Kluwer Law International, The Hague, 1996), 87. The Court's case law relating to former workers has not so much been concerned with the right of residence as the right to access particular benefits or social advantages. This aspect of the case law is considered further in the commentary on Art 24 and the right to equal treatment (see Chapter 5).

[172] Case C-337/97 *Meeusen* [1999] ECR I-3289.

[173] Art 2(2) of Directive 93/96/EEC.

[174] See the commentary on Art 3(2), in Chapter 1.

[175] COM(2008) 840.

that twelve Member States did not make use of the option to restrict the right of residence of family members in accordance with Article 7(4).[176] On the other hand, eight Member States had failed to transpose the obligation to facilitate the entry and residence of such family members. As noted above, the limitations set out in Article 7(4) will cease to apply if the student takes up economic activities, and will not apply if the student is a former worker or self-employed person who retains such status pursuant to Article 7(3)(d).

Article 8—Administrative formalities for Union citizens

1. Without prejudice to Article 5(5), for periods of residence longer than three months, the host Member State may require Union citizens to register with the relevant authorities.
2. The deadline for registration may not be less than three months from the date of arrival. A registration certificate shall be issued immediately, stating the name and address of the person registering and the date of the registration. Failure to comply with the registration requirement may render the person concerned liable to proportionate and non-discriminatory sanctions.
3. For the registration certificate to be issued, Member States may only require that

   – Union citizens to whom point (a) of Article 7(1) applies present a valid identity card or passport, a confirmation of engagement from the employer or a certificate of employment, or proof that they are self-employed persons;
   – Union citizens to whom point (b) of Article 7(1) applies present a valid identity card or passport and provide proof that they satisfy the conditions laid down therein;
   – Union citizens to whom point (c) of Article 7(1) applies present a valid identity card or passport, provide proof of enrolment at an accredited establishment and of comprehensive sickness insurance cover and the declaration or equivalent means referred to in point (c) of Article 7(1). Member States may not require this declaration to refer to any specific amount of resources.

Article 8 sets out the administrative formalities applicable to Union citizens wishing to reside in a host State for a period exceeding three months. Article 8(1) authorizes Member States to require Union citizens to register with the relevant authorities. This is without prejudice to Member States' entitlement to require a Union citizen and his or her family members to report their presence to competent authorities in accordance with Article 5(5).

Article 8 simplifies the administrative procedures that may be imposed on migrant Union citizens compared with equivalent provisions contained in legislation preceding the entry into force of the Directive. Previous residence Directives had required Member States to issue migrant Union citizens with residence permits valid for defined periods of time.[177] Although the permits of workers and self-employed

---

[176] Austria, Bulgaria, Denmark, Estonia, Spain, Ireland, Italy, Lithuania, Latvia, Portugal, Slovenia, and the Slovak Republic.

[177] See, for example, Art 4(2) of Directive 68/360, Art 2 of Directive 90/364, Art 2 of Directive 90/365, and Art 2 of Directive 93/36.

persons were automatically renewable,[178] other categories of migrant Union citizen could be made subject to more burdensome renewal procedures. Former employees and self-employed persons could, for example, be required to 'revalidate' their permit at the end of the first two years of residence.[179] For students, the validity of a residence permit could be limited to the duration of the course of studies or to a maximum of one year, renewable annually.[180] By contrast, Article 8 merely requires Union citizens to comply with an obligation to register. Moreover, after having registered with the competent authorities of a host Member State, Union citizens must be provided immediately with a registration certificate, stating the name and address of the person registering and the date of registration.[181] Member States are not obliged to establish a registration system. In its 2008 Report, the Commission observes that Ireland is the only Member State without a registration system, while the Czech Republic, Slovakia, and the United Kingdom provide for an optional registration scheme.[182]

Article 8(2) prohibits Member States from imposing a registration obligation for Union citizens within three months of their arrival. This serves to reinforce the clear distinction between residence for periods of up to three months governed by Article 6 and residence exceeding that duration provided for in Article 7.[183] It ensures that stays for three months can indeed be free of administrative formalities and that Union citizens visiting another Member State have a clear minimum period within which to decide future intentions without incurring the risk that administrative inaction would expose them to sanction for failure to comply with any applicable registration requirements.[184] Following registration, Union citizens must be issued with a registration certificate immediately, stating the name and address of the person registering and the date of registration. Member States may make the failure to comply with a registration requirement subject to sanctions, provided always that they are proportionate and are not discriminatory. With respect to comparable provisions in legislation preceding the Directive, the Court has provided guidance on the manner in which breaches of registration formalities may be sanctioned.[185] In particular, the Court has confirmed that the expulsion of individuals protected by Union law would certainly be incompatible with Member States' obligations, since it would amount to negating the very right of free movement conferred and guaranteed by the Treaty.[186] The Court further specified that

---

[178] Art 6(1) of Directive 68/360 and Art 4(1) of Directive 73/148/EEC.

[179] Art 2(1) of Directive 90/365.

[180] Art 2 of Directive 93/36.

[181] Art 8(2).

[182] 2008 Report, p 6.

[183] This distinction is further reflected in the wording of Art 24(2), which limits the entitlement of migrant Union citizens to access social benefits within the first three months of residence.

[184] See Art 6. As noted in the commentary on Art 6, Member States must permit EU citizens to make applications for registration within the initial three-month period if they wish.

[185] Case 118/75 *Watson and Belmann* [1976] ECR 1185.

[186] Case 118/75 *Watson and Belmann* [1976] ECR 1185, para 21.

while national authorities are entitled to impose penalties in respect of a breach that is comparable to those attaching to infringements of equal importance in national law, such penalties must not in any event be so disproportionate to the gravity of the infringement that they become an obstacle to the free movement of persons.[187]

Article 8(3) sets out exhaustively ('may *only* require') the documentation that Member States may require from Union citizens as part of the registration process.[188] In particular, Union citizens may be asked to present a valid identity card or passport,[189] together with documents necessary to demonstrate the specific legal basis upon which the right of residence is claimed or compliance with any applicable conditions. Migrant Union citizen workers may be required to produce confirmation of engagement from the employer or a certificate of employment. Self-employed migrant citizens must present evidence that they are self-employed.[190] Economically inactive citizens are required to provide proof of sufficient resources and comprehensive health insurance.[191] Migrant students may be asked to provide proof of enrolment at an accredited establishment, comprehensive sickness insurance cover, and the declaration (or equivalent means) of resources; Member States may not require this declaration to refer to any specific amount of resources.[192]

Although Member States may be entitled to require Union citizens to register with competent authorities, the Court has repeatedly affirmed that registration certificates do not create rights of residence, but simply serve to attest existing rights conferred directly by Union law.[193] Article 25 emphasizes that possession of a registration certificate may under no circumstances be made a precondition for the exercise of a right or the completion of an administrative formality.

As the right of residence derives directly from Union law, Member States must not make the exercise of free movement rights, including the issuing of residence

---

[187] Case 118/75 *Watson and Belmann* [1976] ECR 1185, para 22.

[188] In the context of interpreting equivalent provisions in legislation preceding the citizens' Directive, the Court has consistently held that the conditions which may be required by a Member State for the issuing of residence documentation, as set out in such legislation, are exhaustive in nature. See: Case 48/75 *Royer* [1976] ECR 497, para 37; Case C-363/89 *Roux* [1991] ECR I-273, paras 14 and 15; Case C-376/89 *Giagounidis* [1991] ECR I-1069, para 21; and Case C-157/03 *Commission v Spain* [2005] ECR I-2911, paras 29 and 30. See also, by analogy, Case C-127/08 *Metock* [2008] ECR I-6241, para 53, as regards Art 10(2).

[189] Art 8(3).

[190] Art 8(3), first indent.

[191] Art 8(3), second indent. The persons concerned may use any means of proof: see Case C-424/98 *Commission v Italy* [2000] ECR I-4001.

[192] Art 8(3), third indent.

[193] Case 48/75 *Royer* [1976] ECR 497, paras 31–33; Case C-357/89 *Raulin* [1992] ECR I-1027, paras 36 and 42; Case C-376/89 *Giagounidis* [1991] ECR I-1069, para 12; Case C-370/90 *Singh* [1992] ECR I-4265, para 17; Case C-344/95 *Commission v Belgium* [1997] ECR I-1035, para 22; Case C-459/99 *MRAX* [2002] ECR I-6591, para 74; and Case C-215/03 *Oulane* [2005] ECR I-1215, paras 17 and 18.

documentation, subject to additional conditions[194] not provided for in Article 8(3) or to excessively burdensome administrative procedures.[195] In *Commission v Belgium*,[196] the Commission brought infringement proceedings against Belgium on the grounds that the administrative procedure necessary to obtain a residence permit in Belgium was excessively burdensome and costly. The Court noted that migrant Union citizen workers had to register in the 'Foreigners' Register' and obtain a 'Registration-Certificate' initially valid for three months. They subsequently were required to reapply for its renewal for a further three months at the expiry of which the residence permit would be issued. In order to obtain the relevant documentation, the workers had to go through several administrative stages and at each stage were required to pay a fee. The Court found that the procedure constituted an obstacle to the free movement of workers contrary to what is now Article 45 TFEU.[197] In its proposal for the adoption of the Directive, the Commission emphasized that the objectives set out in the Directive will not be regarded as having been achieved if the administrative practicalities and procedures were so unwieldy and disproportionate that they constituted an additional obstacle standing in the way of the exercise of free movement rights. The Commission thus emphasized that the purpose underlying the proposal was to ensure that the safeguards and formalities for Union citizens and their family members are equivalent to those enjoyed by nationals.[198]

4. Member States may not lay down a fixed amount which they regard as 'sufficient resources', but they must take into account the personal situation of the person concerned. In all cases this amount shall not be higher than the threshold below which nationals of the host Member State become eligible for social assistance, or, where this criterion is not applicable, higher than the minimum social security pension paid by the host Member State.

5. For the registration certificate to be issued to family members of Union citizens, who are themselves Union citizens, Member States may require the following documents to be presented:

   (a) a valid identity card or passport;
   (b) a document attesting to the existence of a family relationship or of a registered partnership;
   (c) where appropriate, the registration certificate of the Union citizen whom they are accompanying or joining;
   (d) in cases falling under points (c) and (d) of Article 2(2), documentary evidence that the conditions laid down therein are met;
   (e) in cases falling under Article 3(2)(a), a document issued by the relevant authority in the country of origin or country from which they are arriving certifying that they are dependants or members of the household of the

---

[194] Case C-157/03 *Commission v Spain* [2005] ECR I-2911, paras 29 and 30.
[195] Case C-344/95 *Commission v Belgium* [1997] ECR I-1035. See also Case C-215/03 *Oulane* [2005] ECR I-1215.
[196] Case C-344/95 *Commission v Belgium* [1997] ECR I-1035.
[197] Case C-344/95 *Commission v Belgium* [1997] ECR I-1035, paras 23–27.
[198] 2001 Proposal, para 2.3, p 3.

Union citizen, or proof of the existence of serious health grounds which strictly require the personal care of the family member by the Union citizen;

(f)   in cases falling under Article 3(2)(b), proof of the existence of a durable relationship with the Union citizen.

Article 8(4) lays down parameters concerning the approach to determining what constitutes 'sufficient resources' for the purposes of entitling an economically inactive Union citizen to be recognized with residence rights in a host Member State. In particular, Member States may not lay down a fixed amount which they regard as sufficient resources and instead must take into account the personal situation of the person concerned. The amount shall not in any event exceed the minimum amount that would permit an individual to exist without recourse to social assistance. Alternatively, where this criterion is not applicable, the level of sufficient resources required cannot exceed the minimum social security pension paid by the host State. The Commission's 2008 Report on the application of the Directive criticized a number of Member States for applying the 'sufficient resources' requirement 'incorrectly or ambiguously', for instance setting a minimum amount or not requiring consideration of the particular circumstances of the individual.[199]

As the objective of the citizens' Directive is to facilitate the exercise of a fundamental freedom, the requirement for sufficient resources must not be interpreted in a manner that would undermine the objective and effectiveness of the Directive.[200] In the context of interpreting equivalent conditions in legislation preceding the citizens' Directive, the Court has emphasized that it is not necessary for a Union citizen to prove he or she personally has sufficient resources, if such resources are put at his or her disposal by a carer[201] or another third party.[202] The Court has further held that the requirement regarding the possession of health insurance is complied with even if the insurance policy is contracted in another State, once cover extends fully to the host State.[203]

Member States' requirement for sufficient resources must respect the principle of proportionality. Thus, legislation in the Netherlands requiring evidence of sufficient resources to cover a period of at least one year's residence, regardless of the intended duration of the stay, was held to be disproportionate to the objective of safeguarding public finances and incompatible with Union law.[204] Furthermore, again applying

---

[199]   COM(2008) 840.

[200]   See, by analogy, Case C-578/08 *Chakroun* [2010] ECR I-1839, para 43.

[201]   Case C-200/02 *Zhu and Chen* [2004] ECR I-9925, paras 29–33.

[202]   Case C-408/03 *Commission v Belgium* [2006] ECR I-2647, paras 40–42.

[203]   Case C-413/99 *Baumbast and R* [2002] ECR I-7091, para 92.

[204]   Case C-398/06 *Commission v Netherlands* [2008] ECR I-56, para 29. As the case pre-dated the entry into force of the citizens' Directive, the Court was applying equivalent 'sufficient resources' provisions contained in previous residence Directives, in particular Directives 68/360, 90/364, and 90/365.

the principle of proportionality, the right of residence of an economically inactive EU citizen cannot be refused automatically merely because he or she has applied for a 'social assistance' benefit within the meaning of Article 7(1)(b). While 'Member States may indicate a certain sum as a reference amount, they may not impose a minimum income level below which it will be presumed that the person concerned does not have sufficient resources, irrespective of a specific examination of the situation of each person concerned'. In accordance with recital 16 in the preamble, 'in order to determine whether a person receiving social assistance has become an unreasonable burden on its social assistance system, the host Member State should, before adopting an expulsion measure, examine whether the person concerned is experiencing temporary difficulties and take into account the duration of residence of the person concerned, his personal circumstances, and the amount of aid which has been granted to him [or her]'. An automatic refusal to grant a particular benefit could not be justified, without 'an overall assessment of the specific burden which granting that benefit would place on the social assistance system as a whole by reference to the personal circumstances characterising the individual situation of the person concerned'. In making such an assessment, the national authorities have 'to take into account, inter alia, the following: the amount and the regularity of the income which he receives; the fact that those factors have led those authorities to issue him with a certificate of residence; and the period during which the benefit applied for is likely to be granted to him'. Also, 'in order to ascertain more precisely the extent of the burden which that grant would place on the national social assistance system, it may be relevant . . . to determine the proportion of the beneficiaries of that benefit who are Union citizens in receipt of a retirement pension in another Member State'.[205]

Article 8(5) enumerates the documents and proofs that family members of Union citizens, who are Union citizens themselves, may be required to produce. Essentially, such family members must be able to prove that they are Member State nationals and that they are the Union citizen's family members. The nature of the evidence required to be submitted will depend on the nature of the relationship with the Union citizen. In light of the objective of the Directive of simplifying and strengthening the right of residence, the list of documents which a Member State may request from EU citizens, set out in Article 8(5), is exhaustive.[206]

Article 9—Administrative formalities for family members who are not nationals of a Member State

1. Member States shall issue a residence card to family members of a Union citizen who are not nationals of a Member State, where the planned period of residence is for more than three months.

---

[205] Case C-140/12 *Brey*, judgment of 19 September 2013, paras 67–78.
[206] See, by analogy, Case C-127/08 *Metock* [2008] ECR I-6241, para 53, as regards Art 10(2).

2. The deadline for submitting the residence card application may not be less than three months from the date of arrival.

3. Failure to comply with the requirement to apply for a residence card may make the person concerned liable to proportionate and non-discriminatory sanctions.

Pursuant to Article 9(1), third-country national family members of a Union citizen must be issued with a residence card in the event that they plan to reside in the host Member State for a period exceeding three months. The administrative burden is notably more onerous than that which applies to Union citizens pursuant to Article 8. Firstly, third-country national family members are obliged not merely to register with the competent authorities of the host Member State, but to apply for a residence card. Secondly, this provision is not optional for Member States, but mandatory.

Despite this obligation, the Court has repeatedly affirmed that such documents do not create rights of residence, but simply serve to attest existing rights conferred directly—and regulated exhaustively—by Union law.[207] Member States may not therefore make the issuing of residence documentation subject to additional conditions not provided for in Union law.[208] Article 25 emphasizes that possession of residence documentation, including certificates attesting submission of an application for a family member residence card, or the residence card itself, may under no circumstances be made a precondition for the exercise of a right or the completion of a formality. Similarly, Member States may not make the application procedure subject to excessively burdensome administrative procedures such that it would essentially undermine the effectiveness of the rights guaranteed in Union law.[209]

States may not require the deadline for applications for a residence card to fall within the first three months of arrival.[210] This provision preserves a clear conceptual delineation between short stays governed by Article 6 and longer-term stays falling within the scope of Article 7. It ensures that stays for three months can indeed be free of administrative formalities and that Union citizens and their

---

[207] Case 48/75 *Royer* [1976] ECR 497, paras 31–33; Case C-357/89 *Raulin* [1992] ECR I-1027, paras 36 and 42; Case C-370/90 *Singh* [1992] ECR I-4265, para 17; Case C-344/95 *Commission v Belgium* [1997] ECR I-1035, para 22; Case C-459/99 *MRAX* [2002] ECR I-6591, para 74; and Case C-215/03 *Oulane* [2005] ECR I-1215, paras 17 and 18.

[208] In the context of interpreting equivalent provisions in legislation preceding the citizens' Directive, the Court has consistently held that the conditions which may be required by a Member State for the issuing of residence documentation, as set out in such legislation, are exhaustive in nature. See Case 48/75 *Royer* [1976] ECR 497, para 37; Case C-363/89 *Roux* [1991] ECR I-273, paras 14 and 15; Case C-376/89 *Giagounidis* [1991] ECR I-1069, para 21, and Case C-157/03 *Commission v Spain* [2005] ECR I-2911, paras 29 and 30.

[209] See, by analogy, Case C-344/95 *Commission v Belgium* [1997] ECR I-1035. See also Case C-215/03 *Oulane* [2005] ECR I-1215.

[210] However, as noted above (see the commentary on Art 6), Member States must permit third-country national family members of EU citizens to make applications for residence cards within the initial three-month period if they wish.

families visiting another Member State have a clear minimum period within which to decide future intentions without incurring the risk that administrative inaction would expose them to sanction for failure to comply with any applicable registration requirements.

Indeed, it is noteworthy that Article 9(1) emphasizes that residence cards must be granted where '*the planned period of residence*' is liable to exceed three months. The use of the term '*planned*' suggests that the requirement to apply for a residence card will depend on the *intended* duration of the stay. Reading Article 9(1) in conjunction with Article 9(2), it is apparent that Union citizens and their family members are entitled to enter another Member State for a short stay of up to three months without being subject to an obligation to register and if they intend to remain longer then they are required to apply for an application card at a date specified by the host Member State which cannot fall within the initial three-month period.

It is submitted that any national measure which would require third-country national family members of Union citizens to declare, in advance of their visit, the intended duration of the stay and be bound by such a declaration, would be incompatible with both the scheme and purpose of the Directive. Such a measure would prevent a migrant citizen from converting a short stay to a long stay, such that the exercise of rights under Article 6 would actually restrict future residence entitlements under Article 7. It is suggested such an interpretation of the Directive would contravene the Directive's primary objective of facilitating the freedom of movement of Union citizens. In addition, any such measure would undermine the effect of Article 9(2). It would effectively require individuals who express an intention of long-term residence, not merely within three months of arrival (which itself is prohibited by the Directive), but actually prior to their arrival. Indeed, in the context of residence Directives preceding the entry into force of the citizens' Directive, the Court has found that the imposition of entry visa requirements which were required to be completed at the Spanish consulate in the last country of domicile, and which essentially pre-empted the subsequent application procedure for residence permits, added conditions for residence that were not provided for in such Directives and were prohibited.[211]

Where a Member State prescribes a deadline for applications for a residence card in accordance with the Directive, it may impose a sanction where there is a failure to comply with that requirement. However, any sanction must be proportionate and must not be discriminatory. In the context of considering comparable provisions in legislation preceding the Directive, the Court has provided guidance on the manner in which breaches of registration formalities may be sanctioned.[212] In particular, the Court has confirmed that the expulsion of individuals protected by

---

[211] Case C-157/03 *Commission v Spain* [2005] ECR I-2911.
[212] Case 118/75 *Watson and Belmann* [1976] ECR 1185.

Union law would certainly be incompatible with Member States' obligations, since it would amount to negating the very right of free movement conferred and guaranteed by the Treaty.[213] The Court further specified that while national authorities are entitled to impose penalties in respect of a breach that is comparable to those attaching to infringements of equal importance in national law, such penalties must not in any event be so disproportionate to the gravity of the infringement that they become an obstacle to the free movement of persons.[214]

Article 10—Issue of residence cards

1. The right of residence of family members of a Union citizen who are not nationals of a Member State shall be evidenced by the issuing of a document called 'Residence card of a family member of a Union citizen' no later than six months from the date on which they submit the application. A certificate of application for the residence card shall be issued immediately.

2. For the residence card to be issued, Member States shall require presentation of the following documents:

   (a) a valid passport;
   (b) a document attesting to the existence of a family relationship or of a registered partnership;
   (c) the registration certificate or, in the absence of a registration system, any other proof of residence in the host Member State of the Union citizen whom they are accompanying or joining;
   (d) in cases falling under points (c) and (d) of Article 2(2), documentary evidence that the conditions laid down therein are met;
   (e) in cases falling under Article 3(2)(a), a document issued by the relevant authority in the country of origin or country from which they are arriving certifying that they are dependants or members of the household of the Union citizen, or proof of the existence of serious health grounds which strictly require the personal care of the family member by the Union citizen;
   (f) in cases falling under Article 3(2)(b), proof of the existence of a durable relationship with the Union citizen.

Pursuant to Article 10, the right of third-country national family members to reside in a host Member State is evidenced by the issuing of a residence card. In accordance with Article 5(2), Member States must waive any visa requirement for the persons holding such cards.[215] Following the submission of an application for a residence card, third-country family members must immediately be issued with a certificate attesting that the application has been submitted. Article 10(1) further specifies that Member States must issue the residence card within six months of the date of application. Essentially, applicants must submit documents providing evidence of their identity and nationality and of their relationship with the Union

---

[213] Case 118/75 *Watson and Belmann* [1976] ECR 1185, para 21.
[214] Case 118/75 *Watson and Belmann* [1976] ECR 1185, para 22.
[215] For details, see the commentary on Art 5(2), in Chapter 2.

citizen from whom their right of residence derives. The Commission has criticized a number of Member States for not issuing residence cards with the official title referred to in Article 10(1), since this makes it more difficult for the persons concerned to show that their position falls within the scope of the Directive, rather than national immigration law.[216] Also, in the Commission's view, the residence card can be issued in different formats, as long as it is in the form of a self-standing document, not a sticker in a passport.[217]

Aside from specifying the relevant time period within which the competent authorities must process applications for residence cards, the Directive does not regulate the administrative procedures that national competent authorities must follow. In accordance with settled case law, Member States may apply their own national administrative law, subject to compliance with the principles of effectiveness and equivalence.[218] According to the principle of effectiveness, national rules must not render practically impossible or excessively difficult the exercise of rights conferred by Union law.[219] Equally, pursuant to the principle of equivalence, rules giving effect to Union rights must also be equivalent to comparable rules in other areas of national procedural law. In addition, measures implementing rights under Union law must respect general principles of Union law, for example, the principle of proportionality.

Applying these principles to Article 10, it is apparent that national procedures must operate in a manner that does not impede the exercise of free movement rights. Given that the conditions for the right of a residence card are regulated exhaustively by Articles 9 and 10, Member States may not make the issuing of such a card conditional on any additional requirements or criteria not provided for in those articles.[220] In the Commission's view, Member States may require a translation, notarization, or legalization of the documents concerned, if the national authority does not understand the language of the document or doubts its authenticity.[221] However, the Court of Justice has ruled that Article 10 does not regulate the legal position if a person applies for a residence card pursuant to Article 3(2), and then

---

[216] COM(2008) 840, the 2008 report on application of the Directive.

[217] COM(2009) 313, the guidance on application of the Directive.

[218] Case C-456/08 *Commission v Ireland* [2010] ECR I-859 and Joined Cases C-317/08 to C-320/08 *Alassini and Others* [2010] ECR I-2213.

[219] On the use of evidence to demonstrate the existence of an informal partnership, see the commentary on Art 3(2), in Chapter 1.

[220] The CJEU expressly confirmed that the list in Art 10(2) is exhaustive in Case C-127/08 *Metock* [2008] ECR I-6241, para 53. As regards Art 10(2)(e) in particular, see the Opinion in Case C-83/11 *Rahman*, judgment of 5 September 2012, not yet reported, para 92. See also, in the context of equivalent provisions in legislation preceding the entry into force of the Directive, Case 48/75 *Royer* [1976] ECR 497, para 37; Case C-363/89 *Roux* [1991] ECR I-273, paras 14 and 15; Case C-376/89 *Giagounidis* [1991] ECR I-1069, para 21; and Case C-157/03 *Commission v Spain* [2005] ECR I-2911, para 30.

[221] COM(2009) 313.

ceases to be a dependent family member of the EU citizen concerned before the residence card is issued.[222]

It is submitted that where an application appears substantially well founded but an error of a formal or technical nature arises, the outright refusal to grant a residence card in such cases would be inconsistent with the principle of proportionality. In such cases, applicants ought to be afforded an opportunity to rectify the error identified. If national administrative procedures provide for internal appeals in comparable procedures, then such procedures must also be available to citizens applying for residence cards. Although the Directive does not specify a time frame for appeals, it is submitted that any such period must be reasonable and in any event not exceed the six-month period imposed for processing the initial application.

Given that the issuing of a residence card by national authorities does not create rights of residence but merely serves to attest existing rights conferred directly by Union law, third-country nationals awaiting receipt of a residence card must not be prevented from enjoying or exercising residence rights, or the right to engage in economic activity.[223] Nevertheless, the possession of a residence card by third-country national family members may be of considerable practical importance, particularly for the purposes of seeking or maintaining employment (as evidence of legal status) or for the purposes of travel as between Member States, since it will exempt some family members from a visa requirement that would otherwise apply.[224]

Consequently, there may be some urgency in obtaining a residence card, reflected in the imposition of a six-month time limit within which such cards must be issued.[225] This rule reflects obligations set out in prior legislation,[226] and enhances legal certainty and facilitates enforceability. In the Commission's view, the maximum six-month period is only justified if there is a public policy issue as regards examination of the application.[227] Indeed, the failure to issue a residence card within the period fixed by the Directive may potentially expose a Member State to liability for the infringement of EU law in accordance with the Court's judgment in *Francovich*.[228] Article 10(1) confers a defined right on individuals.

---

[222] Case C-83/11 *Rahman*, judgment of 5 September 2012, not yet reported, paras 41–45. See further the commentary on Art 3(2), in Chapter 1.

[223] See Art 25 and Case C-459/99 *MRAX* [2002] ECR I-6591, para 74.

[224] See the commentary on Art 5 (Chapter 2), and Case C-202/13 *McCarthy*, pending.

[225] Although a three-month period had initially been envisaged by the Commission in the 2001 Proposal.

[226] Previously, there was a six-month deadline to decide on whether to issue a residence permit to EU citizens or their family members, set out in Art 5(1) of Directive 64/221. The Court criticized a failure to comply with this deadline in a particular case in Case C-157/03 *Commission v Spain* [2005] ECR I-2911, paras 40–49.

[227] COM(2009) 313.

[228] Joined Cases C-6/90 and C-9/90 *Francovich and Others* [1991] ECR I-5357, para 35. This analysis applies *mutatis mutandis* to Art 20 (see Chapter 4).

That right entails a corresponding and foreseeable obligation in respect of which Member States have no discretion.[229] Finally, it cannot be excluded that the delay in issuing a residence card could result in loss suffered by a third-country national family member of the Union citizen. Consequently, in appropriate cases a delay in the processing of a residence card could give rise to a claim in damages.

It is submitted that the period of residence recognized by a residence card must cover the entire duration of the period of actual residence in that Member State on the basis of the relevant EU Treaty right and, where applicable, date back to the third-country national's first entry onto the host Member State as a family member of a Union citizen. An alternative interpretation according to which the period of recognition afforded by a residence card would be limited by reference to the date of application or the date of issue of such cards would be incompatible with the purely declaratory character of residence cards. In any event, it must follow from the declaratory nature of the residence cards that any period of lawful residence spent on the territory without holding such a card still counts toward the acquisition of permanent residence provided for in chapter IV, and also toward the satisfaction of any other time limit referred to in the Directive.

While Article 10(2) is in principle mandatory, Article 37 provides that Member States may provide more favourable standards for the persons concerned. In the event that Member States do not do so, it is arguable that the requirement set out in Article 10(2) that the person concerned have a valid passport cannot be applied in cases of *force majeure*, in particular as regards those persons in need of international protection, given that the EU's asylum legislation (and the Geneva Convention on refugee status) expressly provides that Member States must issue such persons with travel documents in place of a passport from their country of origin.[230] This should apply *mutatis mutandis* to asylum-seekers, at least until there has been a final decision rejecting their application. Logically a passport cannot be required from stateless persons either, taking account of their obvious inability to obtain a passport and Member States' obligations to issue travel documents to such persons instead, pursuant to the 1954 United Nations Statelessness Convention.[231]

Article 11—Validity of the residence card

1. The residence card provided for by Article 10(1) shall be valid for five years from the date of issue or for the envisaged period of residence of the Union citizen, if this period is less than five years.

---

[229] The Court has emphasized that where, at the time of a breach of Union law, the Member State had only limited or no discretion, then the mere infringement of Union law in itself may establish the existence of a sufficiently serious breach capable of giving rise to State liability. See: Case C-5/94 *The Queen v MAFF, ex parte Hedley Lomas* [1996] ECR I-2553, para 28; Case C-127/95 *Norbrook Laboratories v MAFF* [1998] ECR I-1531, para 109; and Case C-424/97 *Haim* [2000] ECR I-5123, para 38.

[230] See Art 25 of Directive 2011/95 ([2011] OJ L 337/9).

[231] See Art 27 of that Convention. All Member States are party to the Convention except Estonia, Poland, Malta, and Cyprus.

2. The validity of the residence card shall not be affected by temporary absences not exceeding six months a year, or by absences of a longer duration for compulsory military service or by one absence of a maximum of twelve consecutive months for important reasons such as pregnancy and childbirth, serious illness, study or vocational training, or a posting in another Member State or a third country.

Article 11 governs the validity of residence cards issued to third-country national family members of a Union citizen. Pursuant to Article 11(1), residence cards are to be valid for a period of five years from the date of issue or for the period of residence envisaged, if that period is less than five years.

It is apparent from Article 11(2) that absences, beyond temporary absences for periods less than six months, may affect the validity of residence cards. However, the Directive provides for a number of exceptions from that general rule. Permitted absences include leaving the host Member State for the purposes of compliance with compulsory military service obligations. In addition, the Directive permits absences up to a maximum period of twelve consecutive months for '*important reasons*', such as pregnancy and childbirth, serious illness, study or vocational training, or posting in another Member State. The wording of Article 11(2)—'such as'– means that this is not an exhaustive list and so further grounds besides those expressly listed can be determined on a case-by-case basis.

The Union legislature was careful to ensure that the wording of Article 11(2) closely follows the wording of Article 16(3), which sets out what may be regarded as continuous residence for the purposes of being eligible for permanent residence status. The correspondence between the two provisions ensures that permitted absences which are not regarded as affecting the validity of residence cards equally do not affect continuous residence required for the acquisition of permanent residence, and logically the two provisions should be interpreted the same way.[232] It follows that the presentation of residence cards which have been valid for five years provides prima facie evidence of continuous residence for the purpose of obtaining permanent residence status.

Article 12—Retention of the right of residence by family members in the event of death or departure of the Union citizen

1. Without prejudice to the second subparagraph, the Union citizen's death or departure from the host Member State shall not affect the right of residence of his/her family members who are nationals of a Member State.

    Before acquiring the right of permanent residence, the persons concerned must meet the conditions laid down in points (a), (b), (c) or (d) of Article 7(1).

Article 12(1) regulates the right of residence of family members of a Union citizen, who are themselves EU citizens, in the event that the Union citizen they have joined

---

[232] See the commentary in Chapter 4.

or accompanied dies or leaves the territory of the host Member State. Pursuant to Article 12(1), the death or departure of a Union citizen will not affect those family members' right of residence.[233] However, if such individuals have not yet acquired permanent residence status, they must satisfy the conditions for residence set out in Article 7(1). In particular, they must either be pursuing an economic activity in accordance with Article 7(1)(a), or they must be self-supporting in accordance with Article 7(1)(b) or (c). Alternatively, family members may retain residence rights if they form part of the family of another Union citizen satisfying applicable conditions in accordance with Article 7(1)(d). If the EU citizen leaves the Member State in question and then comes back and complies with the conditions set out in Article 7(1)(a), (b), or (c), then the family members in question will be able to rely on Article 7(1)(d) again.[234]

It follows from Article 12(1) that Union citizen family members who have not acquired permanent residence status, who were previously supported by a Union citizen and are not independently self-sufficient, may encounter difficulties in retaining residence rights after the Union citizen they were accompanying died or left the host Member State. The requirement for self-sufficiency passes onto the family members of the Union citizen unless they can derive rights from another Union citizen family member who is able to satisfy the conditions laid down in Articles 7(1)(a), (b), or (c) pursuant to Article 7(1)(d).

Where the family members concerned are an EU citizen migrant worker's child who has undertaken a course of education and the parent carer of that child, then Article 10 of Regulation 492/2011 sets out different rules.[235] Article 12(3), discussed below, also sets out a special rule for the children of EU citizens in general (ie, not just workers) and their parent carers, if those children have undertaken a course of education. In the event of a divorce, annulment, or termination of a registered partnership with an EU citizen, then Article 13(1) applies to the family members of that citizen who are also EU citizens. In the case of EU citizen family members, it is not necessary to decide what happens in the event of a divorce et al *and* a departure from the host State, since the rules in Articles 12(1) and 13(1) are identical, although it should be noted that Article 12(1), unlike Article 13(1), protects informal partners.[236] Also, in certain circumstances, the death of an EU citizen will trigger

---

[233] Since Art 12(1) and (3) make no references to the *reasons* for departure of the EU citizen, it follows that those reasons are irrelevant, even if (for instance) the citizen was expelled pursuant to Arts 14 or 28, or was surrendered to another Member State pursuant to a European Arrest Warrant.

[234] See note 7 of the Opinion in Case C-310/98 *Ibrahim* [2010] ECR I-1065. As regards family members who remain in a host Member State temporarily while planning to join the EU citizen in another Member State, see the commentary on Art 3(1) in Chapter 1.

[235] On this category of persons, see the commentary on Art 12(3) below.

[236] Art 12(1) refers to 'family members', which may be regarded as including all family members granted residence whether on the basis of Art 2(2) or Art 3(2). By contrast, Art 13(1) applies only in the event of the end of a marriage or registered partnership, so cannot apply to informal partners: see Case C-45/12 *Hadj Ahmed*, judgment of 13 June 2013.

'fast-track' permanent residence status for his or her family members, without the conditions in Article 7(1), referred to in Article 12(1), having to be satisfied.[237]

In addition, there exists, perhaps unintentionally, a conceptual gap in the protection afforded to Union citizen family members of Union citizens who have died or left the host Member State. Pursuant to Article 12(1), such family members may, in accordance with Article 7(1)(d), derive rights through another family member who is a *Union citizen* and meets the applicable conditions of self-sufficiency. However, it is not inconceivable that the surviving spouse or registered partner of the Union citizen who could meet the sufficient resources requirement is a third-country national. On a strict interpretation, the family members that are Union citizens would not be entitled to derive a right of residence from the third-country national spouse or partner since Article 7(1)(d) permits secondary residence rights through *Union citizens* only. Moreover, such Union citizen family members cannot fall within the scope of Article 12(2), since that provision governs the residence rights of third-country national family members, not EU citizen family members. Nevertheless, such a gap is closed by the Court's settled case law,[238] according to which a Union citizen will be regarded as having 'sufficient resources' within the meaning of Article 7(1)(b) if such resources have been put at his or her disposal by a carer[239] or another third party.[240]

The conditions governing the entitlement of Member States to verify whether migrant Union citizens and their family members satisfy relevant conditions for residence and the circumstances in which the failure to satisfy such conditions may result in the expulsion of the individuals concerned is governed by Article 14, which is considered below.

2. Without prejudice to the second subparagraph, the Union citizen's death shall not entail loss of the right of residence of his/her family members who are not nationals of a Member State and who have been residing in the host Member State as family members for at least one year before the Union citizen's death.

 Before acquiring the right of permanent residence, the right of residence of the persons concerned shall remain subject to the requirement that they are able to show that they are workers or self-employed persons or that they have sufficient resources for themselves and their family members not to become a burden on the social assistance system of the host Member State during their period of residence and have comprehensive sickness insurance cover in the host Member State, or that they are members of the family, already constituted

---

[237] These rules are set out in Art 17(4); see the commentary in Chapter 4.

[238] See the commentary on Art 7 above.

[239] Case C-200/02 *Zhu and Chen* [2004] ECR I-9925, paras 29–33. This case concerned equivalent 'sufficient resource' requirements contained in legislation preceding the citizens' Directive.

[240] Case C-408/03 *Commission v Belgium* [2006] ECR I-2647, paras 40–42, which similarly concerned 'sufficient resource' requirements contained in legislation preceding the entry into force of the citizens' Directive.

in the host Member State, of a person satisfying these requirements. 'Sufficient resources' shall be as defined in Article 8(4).

Such family members shall retain their right of residence exclusively on a personal basis.

Article 12(2) regulates the retention of residence rights by third-country national family members in the event of the death of the Union citizen they were joining or accompanying in the host Member State. Such family members will be entitled to retain their right of residence, provided that they have been residing in the host Member State as family members for at least one year before the Union citizen's death.[241] Arguably, any interruptions of this time period must be calculated by analogy with Article 16(3), which sets out rules on permitted interruptions of residence for the purpose of obtaining permanent residence.[242] If they satisfy the conditions set out in Article 12(2), the family members retain their right of residence exclusively on a personal basis.[243] Thus their right of residence will be regarded as autonomous as opposed to a right derived through the Union citizen they were joining or accompanying.

The right of residence of third-country national family members that have not yet acquired permanent residence status is dependent on their satisfying conditions equivalent to those applicable in Article 7(1). In particular, they must show they are workers or self-employed persons or have sufficient resources for themselves and their family members not to become a burden on the social assistance system of the host Member State during their period of residence as well as having comprehensive sickness insurance cover in the host Member State, or that they are family members of persons satisfying such requirements.[244] It is thus implicit from the wording of Article 12(2), in light of the principle of effectiveness, that the retention of residence rights afforded to third-country national family members includes the retention of the right to engage in economic activity, otherwise Article 12(2) would be entirely nugatory. This interpretation is confirmed by the absence of a relevant derogation from Article 23, which specifically governs family members' access to economic activity. Presumably the drafters of the Directive did not refer to Article 7(1) directly, because only EU citizens can be primary right-holders pursuant to Article 7(1). It would certainly be odd if third-country national family members who had been exercising rights pursuant to the Directive before the EU citizen's death could not retain access to the labour market, whereas the third-country national parents

---

[241] This temporal requirement is an additional condition applicable to third-country nationals which of course does not apply to Union citizen family members (pursuant to Art 12(1)) since they are direct beneficiaries of free movement rights on the basis of their status as Union citizens.

[242] On this provision, see Chapter 4. This interpretation is supported by the fact that Art 12(2), second subparagraph, also addresses the issue of acquiring permanent residence status.

[243] Art 12(2), third subparagraph.

[244] For instance, a remaining third-country national spouse could support his or her dependent third-country national parents. According to the Commission's 2008 Report, six Member States failed to transpose this aspect of the Directive.

of EU citizen children who have *never* moved within the EU have a right to labour market access.[245]

In the event that an EU citizen leaves behind both EU citizen family members *and* third-country national family members, Article 12(3) (discussed below) will likely be applicable, because the persons concerned are likely to be a third-country national spouse and EU citizen children. In the event of a more complicated scenario (such as third-country national parents of the spouse also being left behind), then the family members concerned will have to satisfy the separate provisions of Article 12 independently. It should be noted that Article 12(2), unlike Article 13(2), applies to informal partners of the EU citizen, if they have obtained a right of entry and residence pursuant to Article 3(2).

While the second subparagraph of Article 12(2) provides for a 'sufficient resources' requirement which appears to correspond with the substance of Article 7(1), as noted already, it does not expressly apply Article 7(1) to third-country nationals. Consequently, there is no indication as to whether the slightly less stringent evidentiary requirements applicable to migrant Union citizen students under Article 7(1)(c) are also intended to apply to third-country national students. While Union law does permit Union citizens to be treated differently from third-country national family members, it is difficult to identify any ground that would justify a difference in treatment of third-country national family members as regards the proofs necessary to demonstrate possession of sufficient resources. On the contrary, Article 12(2) specifies that the definition of 'sufficient resources' must be understood in accordance with Article 8(4), which governs administrative formalities for Union citizens. It is submitted that the evidentiary requirements applicable to Union citizen students by virtue of Article 7(1)(c) ought to be read as applying equally to third-country national students falling within the scope of Article 12(2). In any event, such students will usually fall within the separate provisions of Article 12(3). Furthermore, by the same reasoning, as third-country national family members are required only to 'have' sufficient resources (as opposed to needing to be the income-generating source of such resources), the interpretation of Article 7(1)(b) on this point must apply *mutatis mutandis.*

By contrast to Article 12(1), Article 12(2) only applies in the event of a Union citizen's death and does not confer any right of residence on third-country nationals where the Union citizen has merely left the territory of the host Member State. However, in that case, residence rights may be granted on the basis of other provisions of the Directive or other EU legislation. First of all, Article 12(3), discussed below, extends a right of residence to children of EU citizens enrolled at an

---

[245] Case C-34/09 *Ruiz Zambrano* [2011] ECR I-1177. See further the commentary on Art 3(1) in Chapter 1.

educational establishment for the purposes of studying there as well as to the parent having custody of the children, regardless of nationality, in the case of departure *or* death of the EU citizen. Secondly, where the family members concerned are an EU citizen migrant worker's child in education and the parent carer of that child, then Article 10 of Regulation 492/2011 sets out different rules.[246] Thirdly, a further basis for claiming a right of residence is Article 13, which provides for the retention of rights of residence in the event of divorce, annulment of marriage, or termination of registered partnership. Finally, in certain circumstances, the death of an EU citizen will trigger immediate permanent residence status for his or her family members, without having to satisfy the criteria set out in Article 12(2).[247]

The conditions governing the entitlement of Member States to verify whether third-country national family members satisfy the applicable conditions and the circumstances in which the failure to satisfy such conditions may result in the expulsion of the individuals concerned are regulated by Article 14, considered below.

> 3. The Union citizen's departure from the host Member State or his/her death shall not entail loss of the right of residence of his/her children or of the parent who has actual custody of the children, irrespective of nationality, if the children reside in the host Member State and are enrolled at an educational establishment, for the purpose of studying there, until the completion of their studies.

Article 12(3) provides special measures designed to preserve the residence rights of the children of Union citizens residing in a host Member State and enrolled at an educational establishment for the purposes of studying there, until completion of their studies, along with the parent who has custody over them. Neither the death nor the departure of the Union citizen from the territory of the host Member State will deprive such children or the parent having actual custody of the children, of their right of residence for the duration of their studies. The right expressly applies 'irrespective of nationality', presumably of the parent or of the children. As with the other provisions of Article 12, Article 12(3), unlike Article 13, protects informal partners, if they have been admitted pursuant to Article 3(2) and are the carer of the children in question.[248]

This provision was intended to give effect to the CJEU's rulings in *Echternach and Moritz*[249] and *Baumbast*[250] concerning the entitlement of children of an EU migrant worker integrated in the host State's education system to continue their residence and studies where the worker ceased employment in that State. Since the relevant provision of the prior legislation in question remains in force, it is

---

[246] On this category of persons, see the commentary on Art 12(3) below.
[247] These rules are set out in Art 17(4); see the commentary in Chapter 4. Failing that, Art 18 provides that the family members concerned can obtain permanent residence status if they fulfil the criteria set out in Art 12(2).
[248] See, by analogy, Case C-45/12 *Hadj Ahmed*, judgment of 13 June 2013.
[249] Joined Cases 389/87 and 390/87 [1989] ECR 723. See the 2001 Proposal at p 14.
[250] Case C-413/99 [2002] ECR I-7091. See the 2003 Proposal at p 7.

necessary to consider in turn its interpretation, the interpretation of Article 12(3), and then the prospect of overlapping rules in this area.

Prior legislation

The relevant provision is the first sentence of Article 12 of Regulation 1612/68 on the free movement of workers, now Article 10 of Regulation 492/2011, which reads as follows:

> The children of a national of a Member State who is or has been employed in the territory of another Member State shall be admitted to that State's general educational, apprenticeship and vocational training courses under the same conditions as the nationals of that State, if such children are residing in its territory.

In *Echternach and Moritz*, the Court ruled that children retained the right of access to education even if their migrant worker parent left the territory of the host State, and that this entailed a right of residence and equal access to study finance. Moreover, this provision 'refers to any form of education, including university courses . . . and advanced vocational training at a technical college'. The Court also subsequently confirmed that the right to education of migrant workers' children was not subject to the conditions of age and dependence that initially applied to the admission of such children.[251]

In *Baumbast*, the Court held that the fact that the parents of the children concerned have divorced or that the migrant Union worker is no longer economically active in the host Member State cannot affect the children's entitlement to remain for the purpose of continuing their studies in the host Member State.[252] It was further held that a third-country national parent who is the children's carer must also be entitled to reside in that State, as a refusal would otherwise risk depriving the children of a right granted to them by the legislature of the Union.[253] The Court considered that precluding a child of a Union worker from remaining in such circumstances would be liable to dissuade the worker from exercising rights laid down in Article 45 TFEU and would thus create an obstacle to the effective exercise of the freedom of movement of workers.[254]

Notwithstanding the entry into force of the citizens' Directive and the general right of residence that Article 12(3) confers on Union citizen children and their parents (regardless of nationality or economic activity) in the event of the death or departure of the EU citizen, Article 12 of Regulation 1612/68 (now Article 10 of Regulation 492/2011) remains in force, since the citizens' Directive did not repeal or amend that provision. In light of this, the CJEU has held that where

---

251 Case C-7/94 *Gaal* [1995] ECR I-1031.
252 Case C-413/99 [2002] ECR I-7091, para 63.
253 Case C-413/99 [2002] ECR I-7091, para 71.
254 Case C-413/99 [2002] ECR I-7091, para 52.

the parents of children in education are workers or former workers who are EU citizens, the children may continue to derive a right of residence directly from Article 12 of Regulation 1612/68 (now Article 10 of Regulation 492/2011).[255] Consequently, the parents of such children (whether they are EU citizens or third-country nationals) are not subject to the sufficient resource requirements laid down in Article 7(1)(b).[256] It should also be noted that Article 10 of Regulation 492/2011 applies to the former informal partners of EU citizens, if they care for the EU citizen's child who has been admitted to education, unlike Article 13 of the citizens' Directive, which does not apply to such former partners.[257] Arguably, in the absence of a parent, a grandparent or other relative caring for the child could alternatively benefit from Article 10 of the Regulation, if this is necessary to enable the child to continue his or her education in the host State.

In a number of references, national courts have sought guidance on the duration and nature of a parent's right to reside in a host Member State where such residence is based exclusively on that parent's role as a carer of a child of an EU citizen who is a worker or former worker, where that child is undertaking education pursuant to Article 10 of Regulation 492/2011. In particular, questions have arisen as regards (a) the degree of link required between the child and the migrant worker; (b) whether the right of residence of such parents only subsists until Union citizen children reach the age or majority; and (c) the status of the parents and children concerned, as regards access to benefits, and whether the parents (presumably and/or the children) may eventually acquire permanent residence pursuant to the citizens' Directive if they have resided in the host Member State for a period exceeding five years.

On the first point, the CJEU has confirmed that while it is necessary for the child to have lived with the EU citizen migrant worker at some point when that EU citizen was working in the host State,[258] it is not necessary for the worker to have been working in that host State when the child began his or her studies, and a fortiori while those studies continued. Also, the rules protect children who were born in the host State, not just those who moved there with their parents.[259]

On the second point, in the case of *Teixeira*,[260] the Court found that the duration of a parent's right of residence pursuant to what is now Article 10 of Regulation

---

[255] Case C-310/08 *Ibrahim* [2010] ECR I-1065 and Case C-480/08 *Maria Teixeira* [2010] ECR I-1107.

[256] Nor are the children themselves: see Case C-310/08 *Ibrahim* [2010] ECR I-1065, paras 51–59.

[257] Case C-45/12 *Hadj Ahmed*, judgment of 13 June 2013.

[258] Arguably this criterion is also satisfied if the parent retains the status of worker pursuant to Art 7(3) (see the commentary above).

[259] Case C-480/08 *Maria Teixeira* [2010] ECR I-1107, confirmed (as regards the issue of synchronicity between the child starting education and the exercise of the free movement of workers) in Joined Cases C-147/11 and C-148/11 *Czop and Punakova*, judgment of 6 September 2012, not yet reported.

[260] Case C-480/08 *Maria Teixeira* [2010] ECR I-1107.

492/2011 is not so much determined by reference to the particular age of a child as to the nature and level of that child's dependence on his or her parent. The Court considered that while children who have reached the age of majority may be assumed to be capable of meeting their own needs, it could not be excluded that children who attained majority still required the care and presence of their parents in order to be able to continue to complete their education. So it concluded that while, in principle, a parent's right of residence terminates when the child reaches the age of majority, that right may however continue for the period necessary to ensure that a child is able to pursue and complete his or her education in the host Member State.[261] Subsequently, the Court clarified that 'determining whether an adult child does or does not continue to need the presence and care of his parent in order to pursue and complete his education is a question of fact that falls to be resolved by the national courts', which could 'take into account the particular circumstances and features . . . which might indicate that the need was genuine, such as, inter alia, the age of the child, whether the child is residing in the family home or whether the child needs financial or emotional support from the parent in order to be able to continue and to complete his education'.[262]

On the third point, as regards access to benefits, the Court had already ruled that Article 12 of Regulation 1612/68 entails equal treatment as regards study assistance for students, back in *Echternach and Moritz*.[263] This ruling was confirmed in *Ibrahim*.[264] As for social assistance more broadly, the opinion in *Teixeira* advocates that social assistance claims by the children or their parents would not normally constitute an unreasonable burden on national social assistance systems, given that the migrant worker will have paid taxes and contributions into that system.[265]

It should also follow that the persons concerned should have access to employment or self-employment, given that Article 23 would have conferred such a right while the migrant worker was present. Indeed, there is nothing in the Directive to suggest that labour market access is withdrawn, and it would be odd if parents of EU citizen children who have not moved within the EU were afforded labour market access[266] while some of the family members of EU citizens who have exercised free movement rights would not be afforded such access.[267]

As regards access to permanent residence status, in *Alarape and Tijani*,[268] the question arose as to the circumstances in which the period spent by a third-country national parent residing as a carer of a Union citizen child pursuant to Regulation

---

[261] Case C-480/08 *Maria Teixeira* [2010] ECR I-1107, paras 78–79.
[262] Case C-529/11 *Alarape and Tijani*, judgment of 8 May 2013, para 30.
[263] Joined Cases 389/87 and 390/87 [1989] ECR 723, para 35.
[264] Case C-310/08 [2010] ECR I-1065, para 54.
[265] Case C-480/08 [2010] ECR I-1107, para 81 of the Opinion.
[266] Confirmed by the Court in C-34/09 *Ruiz Zambrano* [2011] ECR I-1177.
[267] See by analogy the commentary on Art 12(2) above.
[268] Case C-529/11 *Alarape and Tijani*, judgment of 8 May 2013.

492/2011 may be regarded as reckonable for the purposes of acquiring permanent residence status in the host Member State. In its judgment, the Court observed that pursuant to Article 16(2), the family members of a Union citizen were only entitled to permanent residence where the Union citizen himself or herself satisfied the conditions laid down in Article 16(1) and where the family members resided with the Union citizen for the period in question.[269] The Court further observed that Union citizens could only be considered to satisfy the condition in Article 16(1) where such citizens 'resided legally' in the host Member State, and that such legal residence must be understood as residence in compliance with the conditions laid down by the Directive, and in particular, by its Article 7(1).[270]

In the Court's view, as permanent residence is particular to the citizens' Directive, and as the Directive sought to leave behind a sector-by-sector piecemeal approach to freedom of movement, only residence in compliance with conditions laid down in *that Directive* could give rise to a right of permanent residence.[271] Therefore, lawful residence on the basis of other provisions of Union law, including Article 10 of Regulation 492/2011, could not, in itself, give rise to a right of permanent residence if it did not also comply with the terms imposed by the citizens' Directive.

The Court's ruling in *Alarape and Tijani* is founded on the premise that residence is lawful, for the purposes of being eligible to obtain permanent residence status pursuant to Article 16, only where it complies with the conditions laid down in Article 7(1). As observed above, an essential aspect of this justification appears to be the intention of the citizens' Directive to leave behind the 'piecemeal approach' to establishing rights of residence. However, it is submitted that this reasoning does not sit comfortably with the judgment in *Teixeira*, in which the Court essentially reinforced the sector-by-sector approach to residence by emphasizing how (what is now) Article 10 of Regulation 492/2011 must be regarded as constitutive of an entirely autonomous basis for residence—even though its substance appeared substantially to coincide with Article 12(3). It is of course, accepted that there were good reasons to maintain the distinction, not least in order to ensure that the special protection afforded to workers was not reduced to the slightly lower order of rights conferred on other categories of migrant Union citizens. Nevertheless, after having established and reinforced different legal bases for residence, it seems somewhat arbitrary to suggest that only residence on the basis of the citizens' Directive is to be regarded as 'lawful' for the purposes of acquiring permanent residence under Article 16.

While the parent that will assume responsibility for a child in education and derive residence rights under Article 10 of Regulation 492/2011 may well be the EU

---

[269] Case C-529/11 *Alarape and Tijani*, judgment of 8 May 2013, para 34.
[270] Case C-529/11 *Alarape and Tijani*, judgment of 8 May 2013, para 35.
[271] Case C-529/11 *Alarape and Tijani*, judgment of 8 May 2013, paras 39, 46, and 47.

citizen 'worker' of the family unit and therefore reside on the basis of Article 7(1)(a) of the citizens' Directive, this will not necessarily be the case. Therefore, in order to protect the children of workers enrolled in the educational system of a host Member State, Article 10 of Regulation 492/2011 has been interpreted as conferring the carers of such children with residence rights regardless of nationality and regardless of whether such carers were economically active.[272] The effect of the judgment in *Alarape and Tijani* is that although such persons are living in a host Member State on the basis of Union law they will not be considered as 'lawfully resident' within the meaning of Article 16(1) and therefore will not be eligible to obtain permanent residence status.

It is submitted that if the child who retains a right of residence pursuant to Article 10 of Regulation 492/2011 is an EU citizen, and the child is being supported by a primary carer (of any nationality) who has a derivative right to reside according to the case law, then the child can qualify for permanent residence after five years' residence because he or she has fulfilled the 'sufficient resources' condition laid down in Article 7(1).[273] In that case, it would be odd if the primary carer would be worse off than another family member of the household of the EU citizen referred to in Article 3(2)(a), whose entry and residence merely has to be facilitated, but who can qualify for permanent residence.[274] So it should follow that the primary carer in such a case must be regarded as a family member of a Union citizen who has resided legally with the Union citizen in the host Member State for the requisite period of time in accordance with the requirement set out in Article 16(2).

Article 12(3)

First of all, as compared to Article 10 of Regulation 492/2011,[275] Article 12(3) applies to the children (and their parent carers) of all EU citizens who have exercised free movement rights, not just the children of workers.[276] However, Article 12(3) only applies where the EU citizen has died or left the territory, whereas Article 10 of Regulation 492/2011 also applies if the EU citizen is alive and still resident in the host State, following divorce or the termination of his or her labour market activity.[277] Article 12(3) does not expressly specify that the child had to reside on

---

[272] See for example *Baumbast* and *Teixeira*, where the carer was no longer engaging in economic activity and found not to be subject to the sufficient resource requirement.

[273] Case C-200/02 *Zhu and Chen* [2004] ECR I-9925.

[274] See the commentary on Art 16, in Chapter 4.

[275] See the Opinion in Case C-480/08 *Teixeira* [2010] ECR I-1107, paras 52–55.

[276] In Joined Cases C-147/11 and C-148/11 *Czop and Punakova*, judgment of 6 September 2012, not yet reported, the CJEU ruled that Art 12 of Reg 1612/68 (now Art 10 of Reg 492/2011) did not apply to the children of self-employed persons, as distinct from workers.

[277] However, it has been argued that Art 12(3) should apply by analogy in the case of divorce: see P Starup and M Elsmore, 'Taking a Logical or Giant Step Forward? Comment on *Ibrahim* and *Teixeira*' (2010) 35 ELRev 571 at 583.

the territory or enter education at the same time as the EU citizen was resident there. Logically, given the close connection between Article 12(3) and Regulation 1612/68, it should follow by analogy from the rulings on the latter measure that it is sufficient that the child was resident at the same time that the EU citizen was exercising free movement rights in the host State.

An important question is the status of the children and parents with rights pursuant to Article 12(3), in particular whether they must comply with conditions of sufficient resources et al, and their access to benefits, employment, and permanent residence status. On the first point, the *Ibrahim* and *Teixeira* judgments make clear that there is no sufficient resources requirement in order to retain a right of residence under Article 12(3).[278] This interpretation is confirmed by a comparison of Article 12(3) with the wording of Articles 12(1), 12(2), 13(1), and 13(2). On the second point, it would be logical if the persons concerned had access to benefits and employment by analogy with the position of those subject to Regulation 492/2011 (see the discussion above); and arguably, for the reasons set out in Chapter 4, they can also acquire permanent residence status.[279]

Overlapping provisions

A number of rules could in principle overlap, where the persons concerned could fall within the personal scope of both sets of provisions. First of all, Article 12(3) could overlap with each of Article 12(1) or 12(2).[280] Secondly, Article 10 of Regulation 492/2011 could overlap with Article 12(1), 12(2), 13(1), or 13(2). Thirdly, a situation could fall simultaneously within the scope of *three* provisions: (a) Article 12(1) or 12(2); (b) Article 12(3); and (c) Article 10 of Regulation 492/2011. As noted already, Article 17(4) also provides for 'fast-track' permanent residence to some of the persons affected by some EU citizens' deaths.

In the latter case, it is clear that Article 17(4) takes precedence over Articles 12 or 13, since Article 18 expressly states that obtaining permanent residence pursuant to the latter provisions is 'without prejudice to Article 17',[281] and Article 17(4) will

---

[278] Case C-480/08 *Teixeira* [2010] ECR I-1107, paras 68–69: the absence of a sufficient resources requirement in Reg 1612/68 'is supported by' Art 12(3), which 'illustrates the particular importance' which the citizens' Directive 'attaches to the situation of children who are in education in the host Member State and the parents who care for them'. These comments are repeated in Case C-310/08 *Ibrahim* [2010] ECR I-1065, paras 57–58, and the Court moreover states expressly in para 56 of that judgment that the citizens' Directive 'likewise does not make the right of residence in the host Member State of children who are in education and the parent who is their primary carer depend, in certain circumstances, on their having sufficient resources and comprehensive sickness insurance cover'. See also the Opinion in *Teixeira,* at paras 78–80.

[279] See the commentary on Art 18 in Chapter 4.

[280] Art 12(3) could not overlap with Art 13, on the assumption that if an EU citizen leaves the host Member State *and* becomes divorced (et al) from his or her third-country national family members, then whichever event takes place first should determine which provision of the Directive applies.

[281] See the commentary on Art 18 in Chapter 4.

always be a favourable rule for the persons concerned.[282] However, there is nothing in the legislation or any of the relevant judgments or opinions which discusses the resolution of any overlap. The issue is particularly important as regards the over-lap between Articles 12(1), 12(2), 13(1), and 13(2) on the one hand, where there is a requirement to have sufficient resources, and Article 12(3) and Regulation 492/2011 on the other hand, where no such requirement applies. Surely in such cases the objective of the legislation can only be respected if the rule most favour-able to the persons concerned takes precedence. The same rule applies *mutatis mutandis* if (which is not clear yet) Regulation 492/2011 sets higher standards than Article 12(3), or vice versa.

Since Article 10 of Regulation 492/2011 and Article 12(3) of the Directive only apply while a child is in education, and only for as long as this is the case, they do not apply where a child is too young to start education or once a child has finished taking educational courses. It follows that when a child enters the edu-cation system, the child and his or her parent carer is 'upgraded' from having status pursuant only to Articles 12(1), 12(2), 13(1), or 13(2) from having status pursuant to Article 12(3) or Regulation 492/2011 instead.[283] Conversely, when the child's education is finished, the status of the child and his or her parent carer is 'downgraded' in the opposite direction.[284] But this does not mean that the child and parent now have to leave the host Member State—only that they now have to satisfy the more stringent standards set out in Articles 12(1), 12(2), 13(1), or 13(2) in order to continue exercising the rights of residence. In any event, in the mean-time they may have been able to qualify for permanent residence under national law or the EU's long-term residence Directive (or the citizens' Directive, assuming that Article 12(3) is a route to that end),[285] or to enhance their immigration status in other ways, for instance by finding work or remarrying.

Article 13—Retention of the right of residence by family members in the event of divorce, annulment of marriage or termination of registered partnership

---

[282] See the commentary on Art 17 in Chapter 4. It is also a more favourable rule for the persons within the scope of Art 10 of Reg 492/2011, given that they cannot obtain permanent residence status at all.

[283] If there is more than one child involved, the upgrade occurs as soon as any one of the chil-dren enters the education system: see implicitly Joined Cases C-147/11 and C-148/11 *Czop and Punakova*, judgment of 6 September 2012, not yet reported. Technically, the younger children would not yet benefit from the upgraded status, but continuing to subject them to the more strin-gent requirements of Arts 12(1), 12(2), 13(1), or 13(2) could, in practice, compel the family mem-bers with the better status to leave the country—and so must be ruled out, by analogy with Case C-34/09 *Ruiz Zambrano* [2011] ECR I-1177.

[284] If there is more than one child involved, then the downgrade takes place (as far as the parent is concerned) when all of the children have finished with the education system: but for each individual child, it takes place as soon as his or her education has finished.

[285] In the event that the parent carer does satisfy the conditions set out in Art 12(1), 12(2), 13(1), or 13(2) for long enough to obtain permanent residence status, he or she should obtain that status even if he or she is *also* within the scope of Art 12(3) of this Directive or Art 10 of Reg 492/2011.

1. Without prejudice to the second subparagraph, divorce, annulment of the Union citizen's marriage or termination of his/her registered partnership, as referred to in point 2(b) of Article 2 shall not affect the right of residence of his/her family members who are nationals of a Member State.

    Before acquiring the right of permanent residence, the persons concerned must meet the conditions laid down in points (a), (b), (c) or (d) of Article 7(1)

Article 13 governs the retention of residence rights by family members in the event of family breakdown, including divorce or annulment of marriage or where a registered partnership, within the meaning of Article 2(2)(b), is terminated. Pursuant to Article 2(2)(b), a registered partner will be regarded as a 'family member' of a Union citizen where the partnership was contracted on the basis of the legislation of a Member State, provided that the legislation of the host Member State treats registered partnerships as equivalent to marriage and in accordance with the conditions laid down in the relevant host Member State.

Given that Article 13(1) refers only to marriage and registered partnerships referred to in Article 2(2)(b), the persons affected by the breakdown of other partnerships such as, for example, durable relationships referred to in Article 3(2)(b), do not benefit from the retention of residence rights provided for by Article 13.[286] Nevertheless, insofar as such partners are also Union citizens, they would in any event be entitled to benefit from free movement rights in accordance with Article 7(1), if they satisfy the relevant conditions. Some of the persons concerned would also be able to benefit from Article 12(3), or from Article 10 of Regulation 492/2011.[287]

Article 13(1) affirms that where a family member is also a Member State national, his or her right of residence shall not be affected by reason of divorce, annulment of the marriage, or termination of the registered partnership. However, similarly to where Union citizen either dies or leaves the host Member State, the burden of compliance with relevant conditions now passes onto the family members. Either the family members concerned must comply with the conditions set out in Article 7(1)(a) to (c) or they must derive such rights indirectly as a family member of another Union citizen who satisfies the applicable conditions, pursuant to Article 7(1)(d).

It is submitted that a family member must be regarded as satisfying the sufficient resources conditions where he or she is in receipt of maintenance payments from a former spouse or registered partner. Indeed, the Union has specifically adopted measures[288] and entered into international agreements[289] intended to facilitate the

---

[286] Case C-45/12 *Radia Hadj Ahmed*, judgment of 13 June 2013.

[287] On the latter possibility, see by analogy *Hadj Ahmed*, ibid, and the commentary on Art 12(3) above.

[288] Council Reg 4/2009 on jurisdiction, applicable law, recognition and enforcement of decisions and cooperation in matters relating to maintenance obligations ([2009] OJ L7/1).

[289] The Convention of 23 November 2007 on the International Recovery of Child Support and other Forms of Family Maintenance ([2011] OJ L 192/39) and the Protocol on the Law Applicable to Maintenance Obligations ([2009] OJ L 331/17).

enforcement of maintenance obligations as between Member States or between Member States and third countries.[290]

It is worth emphasizing that as Article 2(2) recognizes spouses to be 'family members' solely by reference to that legal status (without regard to the underlying conditions or nature of the marriage), individuals will continue to possess 'family member' status for as long as the marriage is in force. Consequently, that status, and the rights which flow from it, will not be affected by the mere fact that spouses decide to live apart or undergo a period of separation, as long as the spouse still resides in the same Member State.[291]

> 2. Without prejudice to the second subparagraph, divorce, annulment of marriage or termination of the registered partnership referred to in point 2(b) of Article 2 shall not entail loss of the right of residence of a Union citizen's family members who are not nationals of a Member State where:
>
> (a) prior to initiation of the divorce or annulment proceedings or termination of the registered partnership referred to in point 2(b) of Article 2, the marriage or registered partnership has lasted at least three years, including one year in the host Member State; or
> (b) by agreement between the spouses or the partners referred to in point 2(b) of Article 2 or by court order, the spouse or partner who is not a national of a Member State has custody of the Union citizen's children; or
> (c) this is warranted by particularly difficult circumstances, such as having been a victim of domestic violence while the marriage or registered partnership was subsisting; or
> (d) by agreement between the spouses or partners referred to in point 2(b) of Article 2 or by court order, the spouse or partner who is not a national of a Member State has the right of access to a minor child, provided that the court has ruled that such access must be in the host Member State, and for as long as is required.
>
> Before acquiring the right of permanent residence, the right of residence of the persons concerned shall remain subject to the requirement that they are able to show that they are workers or self-employed persons or that they have sufficient resources for themselves and their family members not to become a burden on the social assistance system of the host Member State during their period of residence and have comprehensive sickness insurance cover in the host Member State, or that they are members of the family, already constituted in the host Member State, of a person satisfying these requirements. 'Sufficient resources' shall be as defined in Article 8(4).
>
> Such family members shall retain their right of residence exclusively on personal basis.

Article 13(2) provides for the retention of residence rights by third-country national family members in the event of divorce or annulment of marriage or

---

[290] This point is equally relevant to Arts 12(1), 12(2), and 13(2).

[291] Case 267/83 *Diatta* [1985] ECR 567; Case C-40/11 *Iida v Stadt Ulm*, judgment of 8 November 2012, not yet reported, para 58.

where a registered partnership, within the meaning of Article 2(2)(b), is terminated. The persons affected by the breakdown of other kinds of partnerships not provided for in Article 13(2) such as, for example, durable relationships referred to in Article 3(2)(b), do not benefit from the retention of residence rights provided for by Article 13(2).[292] However, again such persons might benefit from Article 12(3) or from Article 10 of Regulation 492/2011.[293] If the individuals satisfy the conditions set out in Article 13(2), they can eventually obtain permanent residence status.[294]

Article 13(2) envisages four situations in which a right of residence of a third-country national family member may be retained in the event of family breakdown: first, where the marriage or registered partnership between the third-country national and the Union citizen has, prior to the initiation of the divorce or annulment proceedings or termination of the partnership, subsisted for at least three years, including one year in the host Member State. Presumably any interruptions from the latter time period must be assessed by analogy with Article 16(3), for the reasons set out above.[295] Besides the latter requirement, the State(s) in which the married couple or partners previously lived is irrelevant (by *a contrario* reasoning), and the Directive does not expressly require that the one year of residence in the host State had to occur immediately before the start of the proceedings. Second: where by agreement or by court order, the third-country national spouse or registered partner has custody of the Union citizen's children. Such cases will often fall within the scope of the more favourable rules set out in Article 10 of Regulation 492/2011.[296] Third: where the divorce, annulment, or termination of the relationship is warranted by particularly difficult circumstances, such as having been a victim of domestic violence while the marriage or registered partnership was subsisting. It is clear from the use of the words 'such as' that this list is not exhaustive. Fourth: where by agreement or by court order, the third-country national family member has the right of access to a minor child, provided that the court has ruled that such access must be in the host Member State, and for as long as is required.[297]

---

[292] Case C-45/12 *Hadj Ahmed*, judgment of 13 June 2013.

[293] On the latter possibility, see Case C-45/12 *Hadj Ahmed*, judgment of 13 June 2013, and the commentary on Art 12(3) above.

[294] See Art 18, discussed in Chapter 4.

[295] See the commentary on Art 11(2) above.

[296] See the commentary on Art 12(3) above. The exception would be where the children are too young to have begun education yet, but as discussed above, those more favourable rules will apply once those children start school.

[297] See, by analogy, Case C-40/11 *Iida v Stadt Ulm*, judgment of 8 November 2012, not yet reported, where the daughter of the applicant in the main proceedings had moved between Member States, while the applicant remained in another Member State. However, this case was not within the scope of Art 13(2), since the applicant was not divorced, had not moved between Member States, and had joint custody of (rather than just access to) his child.

In terms that are identical to Article 12(2),[298] Article 13(2) requires third-country national family members who have not yet acquired permanent residence status, but wish to retain a right of residence following breakdown of marriage or registered partnership, to comply with conditions equivalent to those set out in Article 7(1). In particular, they must show they are workers or self-employed or have sufficient resources for themselves and their family members not to become a burden on the social assistance system of the host Member State during their period of residence as well having comprehensive sickness insurance cover in the host Member State. It is further specified that the definition of 'sufficient resources' must be understood in accordance with the terms of Article 8(4). Even if third-country national family members concerned do not themselves meet the relevant conditions prescribed in the second subparagraph of Article 13(2), they may still retain rights of residence if they are members of a family, already consti-tuted in the host Member State, of a person satisfying the requirements. Where family members are entitled to remain in the host Member State, their right of residence is retained exclusively on a personal basis.[299] Thus their right of residence will be regarded as autonomous as opposed to a right derived through the Union citizen with whom they had previously been married or in a registered partnership.

As noted above, Article 2(2) recognizes spouses to be 'family members' solely by reference to that legal status (without regard to the underlying conditions or nature of the marriage in question). Consequently, individuals may continue to fall within that definition for as long as the marriage endures. Thus 'family member' status, and the rights which flow from it, will not be affected by the mere fact that spouses decide to live apart or undergo a period of separation, as long as the spouse or partner still resides in the same Member State.[300]

Article 14—Retention of the right of residence

1. Union citizens and their family members shall have the right of residence pro-vided for in Article 6, as long as they do not become an unreasonable burden on the social assistance system of the host Member State.
2. Union citizens and their family members shall have the right of residence pro-vided for in Articles 7, 12 and 13 as long as they meet the conditions set out therein.

    In specific cases where there is a reasonable doubt as to whether a Union citizen or his/her family members satisfies the conditions set out in Articles 7, 12 and 13, Member States may verify if these conditions are fulfilled. This verification shall not be carried out systematically

---

[298] Therefore the analysis of the substance of Art 12(2) above applies *mutatis mutandis* to Art 13(2).

[299] Art 12(2), third subparagraph.

[300] Case 267/83 *Diatta* [1985] ECR 567; Case C-40/11 *Iida v Stadt Ulm*, judgment of 8 November 2012, not yet reported, para 58.

3. An expulsion measure shall not be the automatic consequence of a Union citizen's or his or her family member's recourse to the social assistance system of the host Member State.

4. By way of derogation from paragraphs 1 and 2 and without prejudice to the provisions of Chapter VI, an expulsion measure may in no case be adopted against Union citizens or their family members if:

   (a) the Union citizens are workers or self-employed persons, or
   (b) the Union citizens entered the territory of the host Member State in order to seek employment. In this case, the Union citizens and their family members may not be expelled for as long as the Union citizens can provide evidence that they are continuing to seek employment and that they have a genuine chance of being engaged.

Article 14 reinforces the requirement for migrant Union citizens and their family members to be self-supporting in order to retain their right of residence in a host Member State. In particular it sets out the approach that Member States must adopt in assessing whether individuals or families exercising free movement rights under the Directive are meeting the conditions imposed. In addition, the Directive regulates the circumstances in which any failure to meet the relevant criteria may result in the expulsion of the individuals concerned.[301]

Pursuant to Article 14(1), EU citizens and their family members residing for short stays of up to three months on the basis of Article 6 retain a right of residence for so long as they do not become an unreasonable burden on the social assistance system of the host Member State. Article 14(2) provides that Union citizens and their families staying for a longer duration on the basis of Articles 7, 12, or 13 retain a right of residence for as long as they continue to comply with the conditions laid down in those Articles.[302]

These requirements, which imply a limitation on the right of access to social assistance, may be considered to be in tension with Article 24, which provides for the right of Union citizens to be treated equally to nationals of the host Member State. However, such tension is to some extent taken into account by Article 24(2), which recognizes derogations from the principle of equal treatment as regards the right of economically inactive migrant Union citizens to access to social benefits. Moreover, the right to equal treatment in Article 24(1) is stated to apply to Union citizens 'residing on the basis of' the Directive. Thus that provision may be regarded as applying only to individuals who are residing in accordance with the Directive and therefore satisfy the conditions for residence stipulated in Article 7.

---

[301] As regards expulsions on other grounds, see Arts 27–29, discussed in Chapter 6. On expulsions pursuant to Art 14, see N Nic Shiubhne, 'Derogating from the Free Movement of Persons: When can EU Citizens be Deported?' (2005–6) 8 CYELS 187 at 208–227.

[302] See Case C-45/12 *Hadj Ahmed*, judgment of 13 June 2013.

Pursuant to the second subparagraph of Article 14(2), individuals or families exercising free movement rights conferred by the Directive may not be subjected to systematic checks on their compliance with the applicable residence conditions. Such checks may only be carried out in specific cases where there is a reasonable doubt as to whether the individuals concerned satisfy the conditions stipulated. The 2008 Report notes that only ten Member States have explicitly transposed this provision.

Article 14(3) confirms that recourse to the social assistance system of a Member State cannot automatically trigger expulsion measures; the 2008 Report notes that thirteen Member States have not transposed this provision. The requirement for an individualized examination of the particular circumstances of migrant Union citizens (also set out implicitly in Article 8(4)) and the corresponding prohibition on automatic expulsion measures provided for in Article 14 is consistent with the approach adopted by the Court of Justice in its Union citizenship and free movement case law. In a number of different references, the Court of Justice had been asked to consider the extent to which migrant Union citizens that are economically inactive must be self-supporting and the extent to which recourse to social security may affect residence rights.[303] In its judgments, the Court has consistently required Member States to have regard to the particular circumstances of each case with due respect for the principle of proportionality.[304] In each instance, Member States are required to consider the degree of integration that the Union citizen or his or her family members have attained,[305] and whether they have developed genuine or real links[306] with their host State. Further criteria are set out in recital 16 in the preamble (temporary difficulties, duration of stay, personal circumstances, and the amount requested), and the Commission's 2009 guidance on the application of the Directive elaborates further.[307]

Thus, for example, in the case of *Grzelczyk*, the question arose as to whether a final year French university student could be denied access to a minimum subsistence allowance on grounds that the applicant was neither Belgian nor a worker.

---

[303] See, for example, Case C-184/99 *Grzelczyk* [2001] ECR I-6193 and Case C-209/03 *Bidar* [2005] ECR I-2119.

[304] Case C-184/99 *Grzelczyk* [2001] ECR I-6193 and Case C-209/03 *Bidar* [2005] ECR I-2119. Regarding the requirement for proportionality see, in particular: Case C-413/99 *Baumbast and R* [2002] ECR I-7091, para 91; Case C-200/02 *Zhu and Chen* [2004] ECR I-9925, para 32; Case C-408/03 *Commission v Belgium* [2006] ECR I-2647, para 39; and Case C-398/06 *Commission v Netherlands* [2008] ECR I-56.

[305] Case C-209/03 *Bidar* [2005] ECR I-2119 paras 56–59; Case C-158/07 *Förster* [2008] ECR I-8507, paras 49 and 50; and Case C-103/08 *Gottwald* [2009] ECR I-9117, para 35.

[306] Case C-224/98 *D'Hoop* [2002] ECR I-6191, para 38; Case C-138/02 *Collins* [2004] ECR I-2703, para 67; Case C-258/04 *Ioannidis* [2005] ECR I-8275, para 30; Case C-499/06 *Nerkowska* [2008] ECR I-3993, paras 39–43; and Joined Cases C-22/08 and C-23/08 *Vatsouras and Koupatantze* [2009] ECR I-4585, para 38.

[307] COM(2009) 313. See also the judgment of 19 September 2013 in Case C-140/12 *Brey*.

In observations before the Court, the authorities recalled that the right of free movement was limited by the requirement of possessing sufficient financial resources. Moreover, the students' residence Directive expressly excluded any entitlement to maintenance grants in the host Member State. The Court proceeded to interpret the requirement to provide evidence of sufficient resources in light of the Directive's objective which, according to the sixth recital in its preamble, was to ensure that migrant Union citizens did not become an 'unreasonable burden' on the public finances of the host Member State.[308] The Court considered that it followed that there was some scope for solidarity to be shown to migrant Union citizens encountering hardship in a host Member State. As a consequence, despite the express requirement for migrant Union citizen students to possess minimum resources, recourse to social assistance could not automatically entail the termination of a right of residence. It is submitted that this approach applies equally to the interpretation and application of Article 14.[309] Despite the express requirement for migrant Union citizens to possess sufficient resources, national authorities are obliged to consider each application on a case-by-case basis and recourse to social assistance cannot automatically entail the termination of a right of residence.[310]

Article 14(4) serves to reinforce the special status of economically active migrants and confirms that notwithstanding paragraphs (1) and (2) no expulsion measure may be taken against Union citizens or their family members, in circumstances where the Union citizen is a worker or a self-employed person.[311] Such protection also extends to first time job-seekers and their families, provided that the job-seekers entered the host State for the purposes of seeking employment and that they are in a position to provide evidence that they are continuing to seek employment and have a genuine chance of being engaged.[312] While first-time job-seekers may be afforded special protection regarding residence, Member States are not required to grant such persons equal access to social benefits.[313] It should also be recalled that the status of worker or self-employed person can be retained, pursuant to Article 7(3).

---

[308] Case C-184/99 *Grzelczyk* [2001] ECR I-6193, para 44. See also Case C-413/99 *Baumbast and R* [2002] ECR I-7091, para 90. See further, by analogy, the Opinion in Joined Cases C-523/11 and C-585/11 *Prinz and Seeberger*, judgment of 18 July 2013, paras 57–123.

[309] The Directive does not lower standards as compared to prior measures: see Case C-127/08 *Metock* [2008] ECR I-6241.

[310] The incompatibility of automatic expulsion mechanisms with Member States' free movement obligations was similarly emphasized by the Court in Case C-408/03 *Commission v Belgium* [2006] ECR I-2647.

[311] For the definition of 'worker', see the commentary on Art 7(1)(a) above.

[312] This provision ensures consistency with the Court's judgment in Case C-292/91 *Antonissen* [1991] ECR I-745. See also Case C-344/95 *Commission v Belgium* [1997] ECR I-1035, where the Court found that legislation automatically requiring EU citizen job-seekers to leave the territory if they have not found employment within three months following the submission of an application for establishment breached Union law.

[313] Art 24(2).

The Court has confirmed that a Union citizen may equally be regarded as a 'worker' within the meaning of Article 7(1)(a) even if he or she originally entered the Member State as a student pursuant to Article 7(1)(c). The Court has confirmed that the status of 'worker' and 'student' are not mutually exclusive and the mere fact that a person entered a Member State in order to pursue a course of study, does not prevent him or her from qualifying as a worker, provided always that the activities in question are effective and genuine in accordance with the Union law definition of worker.[314]

Article 15—Procedural safeguards

1. The procedures provided for by Articles 30 and 31 shall apply by analogy to all decisions restricting free movement of Union citizens and their family members on grounds other than public policy, public security or public health.
2. Expiry of the identity card or passport on the basis of which the person concerned entered the host Member State and was issued with a registration certificate or residence card shall not constitute a ground for expulsion from the host Member State.
3. The host Member State may not impose a ban on entry in the context of an expulsion decision to which paragraph 1 applies.

Article 15 lays down procedural safeguards that apply to migrant Union citizens and their families in their dealings with the competent authorities of host Member States.

Pursuant to Article 15(1), expulsion decisions on grounds other than public policy, public security, or public health must comply with notification requirements set out in Article 30 and are subject to procedural safeguards provided for in Article 31.[315]

Pursuant to Article 30, relevant decisions must be notified in writing in a comprehensible manner, such that any person to whom the decision is addressed is able to understand its contents and its implications for him or her. Competent authorities are required to specify fully and precisely the grounds upon which such a decision was taken in each particular case.[316] The notification must also provide details of the court or administrative body authorized to determine appeals, as well as applicable limitation periods for lodging any such appeals, and the time limit for leaving the territory (where applicable). Subject to substantiated cases of urgency, competent authorities must allow the individuals concerned not less than one month to leave the territory of the relevant Member State.[317]

---

[314] See Case C-46/12 *LN*, judgment of 21 February 2013.

[315] These Arts (which also apply to Art 35, discussed in Chapter 7) are considered in further detail in the commentary on Chapter 6.

[316] This obligation does, not, however, apply where full disclosure may be contrary to the interests of State security pursuant to Art 30(2), but this exception is clearly not relevant to expulsions which are solely based on failure to satisfy the criteria for residence set out in Chapter 3.

[317] Art 30(3).

Article 31 lays down the procedural safeguards that must be extended to Union citizens and their families in receipt of an expulsion decision. Pursuant to Article 31(1), the persons concerned must be afforded access to judicial and where appropriate administrative redress procedures in the host Member State. Article 31(2) requires that, as a general rule, individuals challenging an expulsion measure and applying for interim relief to suspend enforcement of that measure are not removed pending a decision on that application. However, there is no such prohibition on removal where an expulsion decision is based on a previous judicial decision, where the persons concerned have already had access to judicial review, or where the expulsion decision in question is based on imperative grounds of public security. Here too, the third exception cannot apply to an expulsion decision that falls solely within the scope of Article 15(1), since the latter provision does not apply to expulsions issued on public security grounds. Pursuant to Article 31(3), the redress procedure must permit an examination of the legality of the decision, as well as of the facts and circumstances on which the proposed measures is based. The procedures must in particular ensure that an expulsion decision complies with the principle of proportionality, presumably (in this case) as built in to Article 14. Finally, while an individual may be excluded pending the redress procedure, he or she must be prevented from submitting a defence in person, except where such an appearance is liable to cause serious perturbation to public policy or public security or when the substance of the appeal concerns a denial of entry to the territory. The first exception is again irrelevant to expulsions based on Article 15(1), while the latter exception will only be relevant for expulsions outside the scope of chapter VI where the persons concerned do not have travel documents et al.

Article 15(2) prohibits Member States from ordering expulsions of migrant Union citizens or their families on the grounds that the identity card or passport used to enter their territory has expired. This prohibition was previously enshrined in Article 3(3) of Directive 64/221 and confirmed by the Court of Justice in *MRAX*.[318] Moreover, the Court also clarified that the same must also apply with respect to the expiry of entry visas that may be required of third-country national family members of a Union citizen. The Court considered that an order of expulsion from a national territory on the sole ground that a visa had expired would constitute a sanction manifestly disproportionate to the gravity of the breach of the national provisions concerning the control of aliens.[319]

Finally, pursuant to Article 15(3), individuals who receive an expulsion decision on the basis of Article 15(1), namely, decisions that are not based on public policy, public security, or public health grounds, may not be the subject of an entry ban.[320]

---

[318] Case C-459/99 *MRAX* [2002] ECR I-6591, para 87.
[319] Case C-459/99 *MRAX* [2002] ECR I-6591, para 90.
[320] On entry bans, see further Art 32, discussed in Chapter 6.

F. Evaluation

Chapter III is the core of the citizens' Directive, setting out the conditions for the right of residence up until the acquisition of permanent residence. The Directive has liberalized the conditions for entry and stay modestly as compared to prior legislation, and has also included important new provisions which seek to protect family members in the event of death or departure of the EU citizen whom they joined or accompanied, or following the end of a formal family relationship. As with other aspects of the Directive, there is a continuing close relationship with other legislative measures and the Treaties, both as regards the position of family members of former workers who were EU citizens, and as regards access to social assistance (see further the discussion of Article 24 in Chapter 5), which indirectly impacts upon the satisfaction of the criteria to reside.

4

RIGHT OF PERMANENT RESIDENCE

Section I—Eligibility

A. Function

Article 16, which creates a general status of permanent residence for EU citizens and their family members, is one of the novelties of Directive 2004/38. It builds on the conditional right to permanent residence for workers and the self-employed (upon their termination of their economic activities) and their family members, which already existed and which has been incorporated into the Directive at Article 17. Article 18 provides for a permanent residence right for those third country national family members whose EU citizen principal is no longer available as a source of rights, and who have retained rights of residence under Articles 12(2) or 13(2). A general permanent residence status was not present in the measures which predate the Directive. The purpose of permanent residence is to provide EU citizens and their family members who have moved to another Member State and resided there for five years while fulfilling the conditions of at least one of the grounds of residence for more than three months (Article 7; see Chapter 3) with a secure status which is no longer dependent on the continuing fulfilment of the conditions for residence in Article 7. Once the EU citizen or family member has acquired permanent residence, there is no longer the possibility of negative consequences for being reliant upon social benefits or other public funds. The individual also acquires greater protection against expulsion (see Article 28, discussed in Chapter 6). Permanent residence provides the EU citizen or family member with a status closer to nationality of the host Member State while retaining his or her nationality of origin.

During the negotiation of the citizens' Directive, the Council adopted Directive 2003/109 concerning the status of third country nationals who are long-term residents on 25 November 2003 (six months before the citizens' Directive was adopted), which established an EU status of permanent residence for third-country nationals after five years' residence in a Member State.[1] Therefore, there was pressure to provide a similar status for EU citizens and their family members. Failing to do so would have seemed somewhat incongruous. Further, under Article 6 of Decision 1/80 of the EC–Turkey Association Council, Turkish workers who have completed four years in the labour market of a Member State are entitled to free access to the labour market, which seems to mirror in some ways the status of permanent residence. While the CJEU has held that this right for Turkish workers is not preferential treatment in comparison with EU citizens (which would be unlawful under the terms of the EC–Turkey Agreement),[2] nonetheless, the appearance of preferential treatment may have been a consideration.

In the Commission's explanatory memorandum to the proposal for a Directive,[3] the right of permanent residence (as originally proposed to be acquired after four years' residence in a host Member State) is a corollary of the fundamental personal right conferred by the TFEU (in the form of the EC Treaty, as it then was) on every citizen of the Union. This appears to be an oblique reference to the EU Charter of Fundamental Rights (CFR). Article 45 CFR states that 'every citizen of the Union has the right to move and reside freely within the territory of the Member States'. This does not go further than the right established in Article 21 TFEU. The explanations provided for the Charter provisions seem to support this position. Regarding Article 45 they state: 'The right guaranteed by paragraph 1 is the right guaranteed by Article 20(2)(a) of the Treaty on the Functioning of the European Union (cf. also the legal base in Article 21; and the judgment of the Court of Justice of 17 September 2002, Case C-413/99 *Baumbast* [2002] ECR I-7091). In accordance with Article 52(2) of the Charter, those rights are to be applied under the conditions and within the limits defined by the Treaties.'[4]

Furthermore, the Commission also noted in the explanatory memorandum that each EU citizen's right to remain permanently on the territory of a host Member State under the preceding legislation was 'extremely narrow'.[5] It is this lacuna which the much broader status of permanent residence established by the citizens' Directive seeks to fill in the structure of EU law. If indeed, citizenship of the Union is destined to become the fundamental status of nationals of the Member States as the CJEU has stated,[6] and recital 3 in the preamble to the Directive repeats (in a different form), then a more stable right of residence was considered necessary than one which depended on economic activity or self-sufficiency, as was generally the case

---

[1] [2003] OJ L 16/44.

[2] See, for instance, Case C-451/11 *Dülger*, judgment of 19 July 2012, not yet reported.

[3] COM(2001) 257.

[4] [2007] OJ C 303/29. See the analyses of Arts 45 and 52 of the Charter in S Peers, T Hervey, J Kenner, and A Ward, eds, *Commentary on the EU Charter of Fundamental Rights* (Hart, forthcoming) and by analogy Case C-233/12 *Gardella*, judgment of 4 July 2013, para 39.

[5] COM(2001) 157, p 15.

[6] Case C-184/99 *Grzelczyk* [2001] ECR I-6193.

under the prior legislation. This is confirmed in recital 17 in the preamble to the Directive which states that, '[e]njoyment of permanent residence by Union citizens who have chosen to settle long term in the host Member State would strengthen the feeling of Union citizenship and is a key element in promoting social cohesion, which is one of the fundamental objectives of the Union. A right of permanent residence should therefore be laid down for all Union citizens and their family members who have resided in the host Member State in compliance with the conditions laid down in this Directive during a continuous period of five years without becoming subject to an expulsion measure.' Furthermore, this is reinforced by recital 18 in the preamble, which adds that in order to be a genuine vehicle for integration into the society of the host Member State where the EU citizen resides, the right of permanent residence once obtained, should not be subject to any conditions. Recital 21 in the preamble assists the reader to understand the core of the right. According to that recital, Member States are to be left free to decide to which EU citizens they will grant social assistance, maintenance assistance for studies including vocational training during the first three months of residence (longer for job seekers), other than workers, self-employed persons, persons who have a retained right of residence, or their family members (who are entitled to these benefits). This discretion is only available to Member States prior to an EU citizen acquiring the right of permanent residence.

Thus at the centre of the right of permanent residence lies access to the host Member State's social assistance system. While EU citizens are entitled to equality with nationals of the host State (see Chapter 5), the extension of this equality right to social assistance is highly controversial unless the individuals are workers or self-employed persons or retain that status. Only once they acquire permanent residence do they enjoy without question full equality in the form of solidarity as expressed in the modalities of the social assistance system of the host Member State.

B. Historical development

The provisions of secondary EU law which are the precursors to the right of permanent residence in the citizens' Directive are:

- Regulation 1251/70 on the right of workers to remain in the territory of a Member State after having been employed in that State,[7] which at Article 2 provided that three categories of workers acquired the right to remain permanently in the territory of a Member State: (a) a worker who, at the time of termination of his activity, had reached the age laid down by the law of that Member State for entitlement to an old-age pension and who had been employed in that State

---

[7] [1970] OJ L 142/24.

for at least the last twelve months and had resided there continuously for more than three years; (b) a worker who, having resided continuously in the territory of that State for more than two years, ceased to work there as an employed person as a result of permanent incapacity to work. If such incapacity were the result of an accident at work or an occupational disease entitling him to a pension for which an institution of that State is entirely or partially responsible, no condition could be imposed as to length of residence; and (c) a worker who, after three years' continuous employment and residence in the territory of that State, worked as an employed person in the territory of another Member State, while retaining his residence in the territory of the first State, to which he returned, as a rule, each day or at least once a week.

• Directive 75/34 which contained at Article 2, for self-employed persons, the same permanent residence rights for the same three categories of persons as Article 2 of Regulation 1251/70.[8]

The family members of EU citizens coming within any of the parts of the definition were entitled to permanent residence (Article 3(1) of the Regulation). Further, in the event of the death of the principal, provided certain conditions were fulfilled (Article 3(2) of the Regulation, discussed below) these family members acquired an independent right of permanent residence. The rights of the former workers and self-employed persons, as well as their family members, were incorporated into the new Directive with little change.[9]

There was little jurisprudence (with one exception we will consider below) on Regulation 1251/70,[10] and no jurisprudence on the counterpart provisions in Directive 75/34. Regulation 1251/70 was repealed on 25 April 2006 by Regulation 635/2006,[11] and Directive 75/34 was repealed by Directive 2004/38.[12] Notwithstanding their

---

[8] [1975] OJ L 14/10.

[9] Art 4 of the Regulation concerned continuity of residence, and Art 5 of the Regulation set a deadline to assert the rights set out therein. These provisions were not incorporated in the Directive; on the implication of this, and on the limited changes made to Arts 2 and 3 of the Regulation when they were incorporated into the Directive, see further the commentary on Art 17 below. Art 6 of the Regulation, (administrative formalities), has been superseded by Art 19 of the Directive (see discussion below), and Art 7 of the Regulation (equal treatment), has been superseded by Art 24 of the Directive (see discussion in Chapter 5).

[10] Case C-297/88 *Dzodzi* [1990] ECR I-3763 confirmed that the provision is applicable to those within the scope of EU law and fulfilling the conditions but on the facts of the case the matter was wholly internal to one Member State; Case C-279/89 *Commission v UK* [1992] ECR I-5785 found the UK in breach of the Regulation on account of quotas for fishing vessels but did not deal with our issue; Case C-171/91 *Tsiotras* [1993] ECR I-2925 comes closer with a consideration of Art 2 but the individual did not fulfil the conditions to qualify for permanent residence; Case C-62/96 *Commission v Greece* [1997] ECR I-6725 again concerned registration of vessels as did Case C-151/96 *Commission v Ireland* [1997] ECR I-3327; and Case C-185/96 *Commission v Greece* [1998] ECR I-345 dealt with social benefits for larger families. The judgment in Case C-158/07 *Förster* [2008] ECR I-8507, at paras 25–33, also refers to Art 2 of Regulation 1251/70 but dismisses it immediately as irrelevant to the case as the individual did not fulfil the conditions.

[11] [2006] OJ L 112/9.

[12] See the discussion of Art 38 in Chapter 7.

repeal, the content of the right of permanent residence in both measures was transposed into Directive 2004/38 at Article 17, according to the Commission, in order to maintain the existing *acquis* on the right to remain.[13]

The only substantive jurisprudence on the right of permanent residence under Regulation 1251/70 came in a case regarding the third country national family members of a Portuguese worker who had died in the UK and whose family members sought an EU right to reside on the territory relying on Article 3 of the Regulation.[14] Article 3 read as follows:

1. The members of a worker's family referred to in Article 1 of this Regulation who are residing with him in the territory of a Member State shall be entitled to remain there permanently if the worker has acquired the right to remain in the territory of that State in accordance with Article 2, and to do so even after his death.
2. If, however, the worker dies during his working life and before having acquired the right to remain in the territory of the State concerned, members of his family shall be entitled to remain there permanently on condition that:
   – the worker, on the date of his decease, had resided continuously in the territory of that Member State for at least 2 years; or
   – his death resulted from an accident at work or an occupational disease; or
   – the surviving spouse is a national of the State of residence or lost the nationality of that State by marriage to that worker.

The principal lived and worked in the UK from 15 April 1992 until 10 April 1996, when he went to India for ten months. He returned on 16 February 1996 accompanied by his wife and three children, all Indian nationals. He then died of kidney failure on 11 November 1997 (not an occupational disease even though his occupation was a chef) and the family sought permanent residence under Article 3 of the Regulation. The question which arose was whether the required two years' continuous residence had been fulfilled in this case where there had been a break of ten months. The CJEU confirmed that the death of a worker who has fulfilled the conditions of Article 2 for permanent residence has the effect of transforming the right of residence of the family members into permanent individual rights and that, if the worker died during his working life and before having acquired the right to remain in the territory of the host Member State under Article 2, members of his family were to be entitled to remain there permanently on condition that the worker, on the date of his death, had resided continuously in the territory of that Member State for at least two years. The CJEU found that the two-year continuous residence requirement had not been fulfilled in this case for three reasons:

• The period of two years is expressly linked to the words on the date of death. If it could terminate at any date when the worker was in the host Member State, it would have been superfluous to establish such a link with that date.

---

[13] COM(2001) 157, p 16.
[14] Case C-257/00 *Givane* [2003] ECR I-345.

- The period of two years must be continuous. As the continuity of residence in Article 3(2) is not affected by temporary absences not exceeding a total of three months per year,[15] it follows that longer absences terminate the period of continuous residence.
- The word continuous refers to a minimum period of residence taking place immediately before the event which gives rise to the worker's right to remain in the territory of the host Member State.

The original proposal for Directive 2004/38, while protecting the right of permanent residence as appearing in the previous measures, introduced permanent residence for all EU citizens who exercise their free movement rights, and their family members irrespective of their nationality, after four years of unbroken residence in the host Member State. The proposal noted that several Member States already provided for a form of indefinite leave to remain after a certain period of residence regardless of nationality. This information no doubt was based on a study which the Commission had requested on this type of status which it published in 2001.[16] This study, in turn, built on an in-depth study on secure residence status for non-nationals which the Council of Europe published in 1998.[17] Both these studies had in fact been used as background information for Directive 2003/109 on long-term resident third-country nationals but may have been handy for the Commission in respect of Directive 2004/38 as well. As we will discuss, when analysing the provision, the institutions finally agreed on a period of residence of five years rather than the shorter four-year period proposed by the Commission. This means that while Union citizens and third-country nationals in general both acquire permanent residence on the basis of the same period of residence, Turkish workers, according to Article 6 Decision 1/80 of the EC–Turkey Association Agreement, acquire the equivalent right after four years. There is no mention in the Commission's explanatory memorandum of the advantageous position of Turkish workers and their family members.

The issue of what is continuous residence would turn out to be of substantial importance in particular as regards what kinds of absences affect or break that continuity for the purpose of acquiring the status. No further clarification is provided in the explanatory memorandum.

The Commission's argument in favour of the status was expressed as follows: 'After a sufficiently long period of residence, it may be assumed that the Union citizen has

---

[15] See Art 4(1) of Reg 1251/70, which provided (inter alia) that continuity of residence 'shall not be affected by temporary absences not exceeding a total of three months per year, or by longer periods due to compliance with the obligations of military service'. On the continuity of residence under Directive 2004/38, see the commentary on Art 17 below.

[16] C A Groenendijk, E Guild, and R Barzilay, *The Legal Status of Third Country Nationals who are Long Term Residents in a Member State of the European Union*, Brussels 2001, European Commission.

[17] C A Groenendijk, E Guild, and H Dogan, *Security of residence of long-term migrants, A comparative study of law and practice in European countries*, Strasbourg 1998, Council of Europe.

developed close links with the host Member State and become an integral part of its society, which justifies granting what may be termed an upgraded right of residence. Furthermore, the integration of Union citizens settled long-term in a Member State is a key element in promoting social cohesion, a fundamental objective of the Union.'

This is an interesting departure for EU law as regards acquisition of rights. The principle that EU citizens acquire increasing residence rights with the passage of time in the host Member State was not integral to EU law (leaving aside the two measures Regulation 1251/70 and Directive 75/34). The same quality of rights applied to EU citizens from their arrival in a host Member State until their departure or death there. The idea that the passage of time alone should change the quality of rights was novel. It echoes some of the then well-developed jurisprudence of the European Court of Human Rights on the meaning of Article 8 ECHR—the right to respect for private and family life. In a line of cases commencing in 1991,[18] that Court had established and was refining the principle that the longer a foreigner lives on the territory of a host State, the greater his or her claim to continue to reside because of the strength of the family life ties and, as developed in the second half of the 2000s, the private life ones as well.[19] The EU Charter of Fundamental Rights includes Article 7 which mirrors Article 8 ECHR. However, this Charter right was not specifically mentioned in the Commission's explanatory memorandum to the citizens' Directive. The ECHR itself is only referred to as regards its Article 14 non-discrimination provision. The EU Charter is referred to three times, mostly very vaguely, except as regards the provisions on third-country national family members (see Chapter 1). This issue will arise in further depth in Chapter 6 when we consider the grounds for expulsion in the Directive.

In the Commission's explanatory memorandum, once permanent residence is acquired, it is proposed that the status should not be lost except in the event of more than four years' absence from the host Member State. In the Commission's words: '[T]he right of permanent residence acknowledges the integration of the Union citizen and his family members into the host Member State. Absences of more than four years would suggest a kind of "disintegration".' In the event, as will be discussed in more depth below, the institutions adopted a final text in which the status is lost after more than two years' continuous absence from the host Member State. The concept of 'disintegration' as put forward by the Commission is rather original. There does not appear to be a precedent for it.

The position of third-country national family members of EU citizens acquiring permanent residence was dealt with separately in the Commission's original proposal and remained a separate provision in the final adopted version. The reason for this separation, according to the Commission's explanatory memorandum is for the sake of clarity. This is once again an indication that third-country national

---

[18] *Moustaquim v Belgium* (A-193)–400.
[19] *Uner v Netherlands*, 18 October 2006.

family members required, in the eyes of the Commission officials working on the Directive, special attention to ensure that their situation was not assimilated to that of third-country nationals in general but remained connected to the rights of the principal (see the commentary on Article 3(1) in Chapter 1).

C. Interrelationship of Articles 16–18 with other provisions

Article 16 is intrinsically related to the provisions of chapter III of the Directive, the right of residence, as the acquisition of permanent residence status, which, as will be discussed below, is automatic when the conditions are fulfilled, is subject to satisfying the conditions set out in that chapter. Thus an EU citizen, or an EU citizen's family member, who seeks to rely on his or her permanent residence (particularly where this has not been evidenced by a document from the authorities of the host Member State) will need to show that he or she fulfils and has fulfilled the conditions of chapter III of the Directive over the five-year period. Most of the cases which have come before the CJEU on the interpretation of the right of permanent residence revolve around this issue.[20] We will examine the cases below under the provision of the Article to which they are relevant.

Regarding acquisition of the right of permanent residence by third country national family members in the event of dissolution of family ties during the five-year qualifying period, Article 18 refers to Articles 12(2) and 13(2) as conditions precedent for the acquisition of the right.[21] Article 12(2) sets out the conditions for retention of the right of residence by third-country national family members in the event of death of the Union citizen. However, Article 18 does not refer to Article 12(3), which concerns the death or departure of the EU citizen who leaves behind a child who is undertaking education; the consequences of this omission are discussed further below. Article 13(2) provides for the retention of the right of residence by third-country national family members in the event of divorce, annulment of marriage, or termination of registered partnership. These provisions are discussed in Chapter 3. The interaction between these two provisions relates to the conditions which third-country national family members must fulfil in order to acquire permanent residence. The objective of the intersection of these provisions is to ensure that such third-country national family members who no longer have an EU national principal because of death, divorce, or termination of a registered partnership may still acquire permanent residence.

---

[20] See for instance Cases C-162/09 *Lassal*; C-325/09 *Dias*; C-424/10 and 425/10 *Ziolowski*; and C-378/12 *Onuekwere* (pending), all of which deal with this issue.

[21] The position of family members of EU citizens who are themselves EU citizens, where the EU citizen whom they resided with has died or departed, or the marriage or registered partnership has ended, is governed by Arts 12(1) and 13(1). While these provisions refer expressly to the possible acquisition of permanent residence rights by such family members, Arts 16–18 do not make any further express reference to this category of persons.

Furthermore, the acquisition of permanent residence status may also affect the rules relating to admission of family members,[22] and the Directive provides expressly for greater protection against expulsion,[23] and greater equality rights,[24] for permanent residents. Finally, the rules on the definition of family members in chapter I of the Directive necessarily determine the scope of the persons who can ultimately obtain permanent residence.[25] For the reasons set out in Chapter 1, extended family members as defined in Article 3(2) also ought to be able to obtain such rights.[26]

D. Other relevant EU law rules

First of all, there is another legal instrument that provides for ongoing residence status for a specific category of EU citizens and their family members. Article 12 of Regulation 1612/68 (now Article 10 of Regulation 492/2011)[27] provides for residence status for the children of migrant worker EU citizens who are undertaking education, as well as the primary carer of such children.[28] However, this status does not amount to (or lead to) permanent residence status as set out in the Directive.[29] Article 7(2) of Regulation 492/2011 (the rule on equal treatment for workers as regards social advantages) likewise does not confer a right to equal treatment for EU citizen workers' family members as regards access to permanent residence status as established by national law.[30] Of course, this is now to some extent superseded by access to permanent residence status under the citizens' Directive.

Secondly, third-country national family members of EU citizens might be able to qualify for long-term residence status pursuant to the EU's long-term residence legislation for third-country nationals (Directive 2003/109),[31] even if they cannot (or do not yet) qualify for permanent residence status under the citizens' Directive.[32] Also, as noted already, Turkish citizens (who might also be family members of EU citizens) can qualify for a form of long-term or permanent residence status pursuant to the EC–Turkey Association Council Decision 1/80.

---

[22] See Case E-4/11 *Clauder*, judgment of the EFTA Court of 26 July 2011, discussed further in Chapter 3. See also the questions in Case C-434/09 *McCarthy* [2011] ECR I-3375, which the CJEU did not find it necessary to answer.

[23] See Art 28(2), discussed in Chapter 6.

[24] See Art 24(2), discussed in Chapter 5.

[25] See the commentary on Art 2(2) in Chapter 1.

[26] See the commentary on Art 3(2) in Chapter 1.

[27] [2011] OJ L 141/1.

[28] See the commentary on Art 12(3) in Chapter 3.

[29] Case C-529/11 *Alarape and Tijani*, judgment of 8 May 2013; see the commentary on Art 16(2) below.

[30] Case C-356/98 *Kaba I* [2000] ECR I-2623 and Case C-466/00 *Kaba II* [2003] ECR I-2219.

[31] [2004] OJ L 16/44. On this Directive, see further K Groenendijk, ch 10 of Peers et al, *EU Immigration and Asylum Law: Text and Commentary*, Vol2, 2nd edn, (Brill, 2012).

[32] See particularly Case C-40/11 *Iida*, judgment of 8 November 2012, not yet reported.

Finally, in the context of the EU's criminal law measures, the CJEU has ruled that the provisions on permanent residence status in the Directive can justify a Member State's choice to refuse to execute European Arrest Warrants for nationals of other Member States only when those persons have been residing for five years, ie the same rule as set out in the Directive as regards acquisition of permanent residence status.[33]

E. Analysis—Article 16

Article 16—General rule for Union citizens and their family members

(1) Union citizens who have resided legally for a continuous period of five years in the host Member State shall have the right of permanent residence there. This right shall not be subject to the conditions provided for in Chapter III.

The principle of permanent residence is found here. Where an EU citizen has moved and resided in a Member State other than that of his or her underlying nationality, a new secure residence status which is no longer dependent on continued economic activity or economic self-sufficiency comes into existence. The issue of who counts as an EU citizen has been fully investigated in Chapter 1 (Article 2(1)). The concept of residence is discussed in Chapter 3, although the continuity of such residence (for the purpose of obtaining permanent residence status) is defined in Article 16(3), discussed below. For the purposes of this provision, the additional requirement which appears is the qualification that residence over the five-year period must be 'legal'. This concept is defined by EU law, not national law. It relates back to Articles 6 and 7, which set out the conditions under which the EU citizen has the right of residence. Thus for an EU citizen to fulfil the conditions of this provision, he or she must fulfil the conditions of Article 6 during the first three months of residence in the host Member State (during which time the citizen already starts to accrue time towards the acquisition of legal residence) and then those of Article 7 for the remaining four years and nine months (without prejudice to the rules on interruption of residence set out in Article 16(3)). As the CJEU put it, 'the concept of legal residence implied by the terms "have resided legally" in Article 16(1) of Directive 2004/38 should be construed as meaning a period of residence which complies with the conditions laid down in the directive, in particular those set out in Article 7(1)'.[34] Recital 17 in the preamble to the Directive states that the right of permanent residence is a key element in promoting social cohesion and was provided for by that Directive in order to strengthen the feeling of Union

---

[33] Case C-123/08 *Wolzenburg* [2009] ECR I-9621. See also Art 4(7)(a) of the Framework Decision on the transfer of prisoners ([2008] OJ L 327/27), which provides for an express link to the permanent residence status provided for in the Directive.

[34] Joined Cases C-424/10 and C-425/10 *Ziolowski* and *Szeja*, judgment of 21 December 2011, not yet reported, para 46.

citizenship. This objective is important in the reasoning of the CJEU on the first cases regarding the acquisition of permanent residence.

The first question which was referred to the CJEU regarding this provision was received on 10 March 2009 from a UK court and determined on 7 October 2010.[35] The problem which arose was about Ms Lassal, a French national who had entered the UK in January 1999 to look for work. From September 1999 to February 2005, she was residing and either working or seeking work. From January 1999 to February 2005 all the parties were agreed that Ms Lassal was a worker within the meaning of EU law. However, in February 2005 she left the UK to visit her mother in France, where she stayed for ten months. In December 2005, she returned to the UK and again looked for work. From January to November 2006 she received Job Seeker's Allowance (a social assistance benefit). In November 2006 she applied for income support (another social assistance benefit) on the basis that she was pregnant. That application was refused on the ground that she had no right to reside in the UK. As intimated above, EU citizens seek to rely on their acquisition of permanent residence as it is a status which frees them from the requirement to fulfil the conditions of Articles 6 or 7 and opens up equal access to social benefits in the host State.

The national court sought the answers to two questions—first, could periods of residence before the end of the transposition period (10 April 2006) for Member States to comply with the Directive be counted towards the five years necessary to acquire permanent residence?; and secondly, how should the national court deal with temporary absences which occurred before the end of the transposition period?

The CJEU commenced by noting the objective as set out in the Directive's preamble for the status of permanent residence. It then notes that this status did not exist before the Directive was adopted and is one of the innovations of the measure (aside from the right contained in Article 17, already referred to above, which we will examine below). However, in the CJEU's view this does not lead to the conclusion that only continuous periods of five years' legal residence either ending on 30 April 2006 or thereafter, or commencing after 30 April 2006 are to be taken into account for the purposes of acquisition of the right of permanent residence provided for in Article 16 (para 34). It stated that if time only began to run from the end of the transposition date, the right could be granted only from 30 April 2011. The result would be that residence completed by Union citizens in accordance with EU law instruments pre-dating 30 April 2006 were deprived of any effect for the purposes of the acquisition of that right of permanent residence. The CJEU noted that the concept of permanent residence already existed for some categories of EU citizens, and these rights were retained in Article 17. It found that excluding

---

[35] Case C-162/09 *Lassal* [2010] ECR I-9217.

from the five-year calculation any residence before the end of the transposition period would be contrary to the purpose and effectiveness of the Directive. To the argument that counting any periods before 30 April 2006 would give the provision retroactive effect (which the Member State argued was not intended by the lawmakers) the CJEU replied that 'the taking into account of periods of residence completed before that date does not give retroactive effect to Article 16 of Directive 2004/38, but simply gives present effect to situations which arose before the date of transposition of that directive' (para 38).

In support of this position the CJEU reaffirmed its case law that the provisions on citizenship of the Union are applicable as soon as they enter into force and therefore they must be applied to the present effects of situations arising previously.[36] As a result the CJEU held that for the purposes of the acquisition of the right of permanent residence provided for in Article 16, continuous periods of five years' residence completed before the date of transposition of that Directive, namely, 30 April 2006, in accordance with the earlier EU law instruments, must be taken into account. Regarding the second question on temporary absences, this part of the judgment clarified the interpretation of Article 16(4).

The next case which came before the CJEU was also from a UK court.[37] This time the individual had a very patchy employment history. Ms Dias, a Portuguese national, entered the UK in January 1998. She had five periods of residence:

- January 1998 to summer 2002: in work;
- summer 2002 to 17 April 2003: on maternity leave;
- 18 April 2003 to 25 April 2004: not working;
- 26 April 2004 to 23 March 2007: in work; and
- since 24 March 2007: not working.

The UK authorities issued Ms Dias with a residence document valid for five years until May 2005. In March 2007, Ms Dias applied for income support (a social assistance benefit). The national court held that she was no longer a worker within the meaning of EU law. Thus she could only claim the social assistance benefit if she held permanent residence. As the national judgment pre-dates *Lassal*, the national court considered that permanent residence could only be acquired over a five-year period commencing from 30 April 2006. Further and in any event, the national court found that she could not add together the various periods, for the purposes of the right of permanent residence. The national court asked two questions: first, does residence under a nationally issued residence permit have the effect of making the period of residence, by definition, lawful? The Court of Justice answered that it did not—but the converse is also true, namely, that an individual

---

[36] Case C-224/98 *D'Hoop* [2002] ECR I-6191.
[37] Case C-325/09 *Dias* [2011] ECR I-6387.

can qualify for permanent residence status even if he or she did not hold the formal documentation referred to in Chapter 3.[38]

The second question was whether continuous residence as a worker gives rise to a permanent right of residence directly pursuant to Article 18(1) of the EC Treaty (now Article 21 TFEU) on the grounds that there is a lacuna in the Directive. The CJEU reframed the question in light of its decision in *Lassal* and considered whether the periods of residence of a Union citizen in a host Member State which were completed on the basis solely of a residence permit, without the conditions governing entitlement to any right of residence having been met, and which occurred before 30 April 2006 but after a period of continuous legal residence of five years which ended prior to that date, are such as to affect the acquisition of the right of permanent residence under Article 16(1).

The CJEU repeated its consistent jurisprudence that residence documents do not confer rights, they only evidence them.[39] It noted that the right of permanent residence could be acquired only with effect from 30 April 2006. Consequently, unlike periods of continuous legal residence of five years pursuant to the Directive completed after that date, which confer on citizens of the Union the right of permanent residence with effect from the actual moment at which they are completed, periods completed before that date do not allow those persons to benefit from such a right of residence prior to 30 April 2006. The CJEU held that periods of less than two consecutive years, completed on the basis solely of a residence permit, without the residence conditions equivalent to those set out in Article 7 having been satisfied, which occurred before 30 April 2006 and after a continuous period of five years' legal residence completed prior to that date, do not affect the acquisition of the right of permanent residence under Article 16(1). This confirms that individuals can aggregate periods of employment (including maternity leave) carried out before 30 April 2006 for the purposes of acquiring permanent residence after that date. Again, the Court also referred to the application of Article 16(4) by analogy to events occurring before the transposition date of the Directive; this point is considered further below. It is arguable by extension that Article 16(3), setting out rules on interruption of residence, also applies by analogy to periods of interrupted residence before the transposition date of the Directive. Admittedly the prior legislation had its own interruption clauses,[40] but applying Article 16(3) to interruptions before the transposition date of the Directive is consistent with the rule that residence under the prior Directives has to count towards the acquisition of permanent residence status, even though the latter concept did not exist at all at the time, except as regards Regulation 1251/70 and Directive 75/34.

---

[38] See Case C-123/08 *Wolzenburg* [2009] ECR I-9621 and the commentary on Art 19 below.

[39] Case C-408/03 *Commission v Belgium* [2006] ECR I-2647. See now the discussion of Art 25, in Chapter 5.

[40] See the commentary on Art 16(3) below.

As the adoption of the citizens' Directive, with its creation of a broad concept of permanent residence, coincided with a large enlargement of the EU (namely, the admission of ten new Member States on 1 May 2004), the question rapidly arose whether periods of residence completed before the individual acquired citizenship of the Union (by means of EU enlargement) counted towards the five years necessary to get the status. There are two aspects to this question: (a) do periods of residence completed under national law count towards the calculation of the five-year period?; and (b) do periods when the individual was not an EU citizen (because his or her State of nationality had not yet joined the EU) count for the same purposes? Both parts of this question were resolved by the CJEU on 21 December 2011.[41] In the joined cases of *Ziolowski and Szeja* the facts were as follows: Mr Ziolkowski was a Polish national who arrived in Germany in September 1989. He obtained a residence permit on humanitarian grounds for the period from July 1991 to April 2006. Mrs Szeja was a Polish national who arrived in Germany in 1988. She obtained a residence permit on humanitarian grounds for the period from May 1990 to October 2005. Her children were born in Germany in 1994 and 1996. They obtained residence permits corresponding to their mother's permit. The children's father was a Turkish national who lived separately but had joint custody of the children with Mrs Szeja (the EC–Turkey Association Agreement could have, but did not, play a role in this case, which revolved exclusively around the Directive). The national court asked the CJEU to clarify the meaning of Article 16(1) and whether it applied in either of the cases. While in both cases the individuals had resided in a Member State lawfully for more than five years, in neither case were they citizens of the Union throughout the whole of the five-year period and therefore neither of them could have fulfilled the requirements of Article 7 throughout their qualifying residence period.

The CJEU commenced by re-affirming its consistent jurisprudence that the need for a uniform application of European Union law and the principle of equality require that the terms of a provision of European Union law which makes no express reference to the law of the Member States for the purpose of determining its meaning and scope must normally be given an independent and uniform interpretation throughout the European Union.[42] The Directive does not contain any reference to national laws as regards the meaning of 'who have resided legally'. Therefore according to the standard construction of EU law, the meaning and scope of terms for which European Union law provides no definition must be determined by considering, inter alia, the context in which they occur and the purposes of the rules of which they form part, according to the CJEU.[43]

---

[41] Joined Cases C-424/10 and C-425/10 *Ziolkowski* and *Szeja*, judgment of 21 December 2011, not yet reported.

[42] Cases C-287/98 *Linster* [2000] ECR I-6917 and C-34/10 *Brüstle* [2011] ECR I-9821.

[43] Cases: C-336/03 *easyCar* [2005] ECR I-1947; C-549/07 *Wallentin-Hermann* [2008] ECR I-11061; and C-151/09 *UGT-FSP* [2010] ECR I-7591.

The Court accepted that according to the first recital of the Directive, the objective is to facilitate and strengthen the exercise of the primary and individual right to move and reside freely within the territory of the Member States that is conferred directly on each citizen of the Union. However, it then referred to the second and third recitals which state that the aim of the Directive is to remedy the sector-by-sector piecemeal approach to free movement of persons and to that end introduced a gradual system as regards the right of residence in the host Member State, which reproduces, in essence, the stages and conditions set out in the various instruments of European Union law and case law preceding the Directive and culminates in the right of permanent residence.

In support of the Court's reasoning, recital 18 in the preamble states that, once obtained, the right of permanent residence should not be subject to any further conditions, with the aim of it being a genuine vehicle for integration into the society of the host State. Further, recital 17 in the preamble states that such a right should be laid down for all Union citizens and their family members who have resided in the host Member State 'in compliance with the conditions laid down in this Directive' during a continuous period of five years without becoming subject to an expulsion measure. At this point the CJEU refers to the *travaux preparatoires*, noting that 'the clarification was inserted into that recital during the legislative process that led to the adoption of Directive 2004/38 by Common Position (EC) No 6/2004, adopted by the Council of the European Union on 5 December 2003 (OJ 2004 C 54 E, p 12). According to the Communication to the European Parliament of 30 December 2003 (SEC/2003/1293 final), that clarification was inserted 'in order to clarify the content of the term "legal residence" for the purpose of Article 16(1) of the directive' (para 43).

The CJEU then made a very important move as regards the interpretation of lawful residence. It stated 'a period of residence which complies with the law of a Member State but does not satisfy the conditions laid down in Article 7(1) of Directive 2004/38 cannot be regarded as a "legal" period of residence within the meaning of Article 16(1)' (para 47). The importance of this approach is that while a period of residence under national law which does not fulfil the conditions of Article 7 is excluded from the purposes of calculating the five years, periods of residence under national law which *do* fulfil the conditions of Article 7, even though they are qualified as the application of national law, do qualify in the calculation of the five-year period. This is not a surprising finding as the CJEU had already held that residence in accordance with a residence permit but where the individual no longer fulfilled the conditions of Article 7 did not count. Thus, it is a logical step that residence under a national residence status but which does fulfil the conditions of Article 7 does count. While Member States are always free to apply higher standards than the Directive requires (Article 37, discussed in Chapter 7), the persons who benefit from such higher standards cannot qualify for permanent residence pursuant to the Directive.

The CJEU then turned to the second part of the question—what about the fact that the individuals concerned were only EU citizens throughout part of the five-year period, as their Member States only joined the EU on 1 May 2004? The CJEU relied on the fact that it had already decided that the provisions on citizenship of the European Union are applicable as soon as they enter into force and must therefore be applied to the present effects of situations arising previously.[44] Further, according to the accession treaties, there were no transitional arrangements as regards free movement of persons (only exceptions as regards workers). Thus the provisions of Article 16(1) can be relied upon by Union citizens and be applied to the present and future effects of situations arising before the accession of their Member State to the European Union.[45] This had always been the position of the European Commission which, in its report on the implementation of the Directive,[46] noted that 'Belgium and the UK incorrectly take no account of periods of residence acquired by EU citizens before their countries acceded to the EU' (para 3.7).

As the CJEU had already ruled in *Lassal* and *Dias* that Article 16(4) applies by analogy to the possible loss of permanent residence in the period before the transposition date of the Directive, that provision must equally apply by analogy to the possible loss of permanent residence in the period before EU accession. Furthermore, if, as argued above, the rules on interruption of residence in Article 16(3) also apply by analogy during the period before the transposition date, then logically they must also apply to the period before EU accession.

While the Court of Justice has not yet ruled whether persons who retain the status of workers and self-employed persons pursuant to Article 7(3) can qualify for permanent residence status, it seems obvious that they can, if they satisfy the usual five-year legal residence rule. Article 24(2) expressly assumes that they can qualify for permanent residence, and this is the obvious consequence of retaining their status. It would also be consistent with the logic of Article 17,[47] with the caveat that workers and self-employed persons who cease their economic activities pursuant to Article 7(3) will have a longer wait for permanent residence status than those who cease their economic activities pursuant to Article 17.[48] It should also follow that

---

[44] Case C-224/98 *D'Hoop* [2002] ECR I-6191.

[45] The judgment in *Ziolkowski* was applied by the Court subsequently in Joined Cases C-147/11 and C-148/11 *Czop and Punakova*, judgment of 6 September 2012, not yet reported. Logically, the principle applies equally to the acquisition of permanent residence by the nationals of the 'old' Member States (and the other 'new' Member States) who were residing in each of the 'new' Member States before accession.

[46] COM(2008) 840.

[47] In fact, the precursor to Art 7(3)(a)–(c) was Art 4(2) of Reg 1251/70, which similarly concerned the question of when to count gaps in economic activity for the purpose of acquiring permanent residence status (although see also Art 7 of Directive 68/360, [1968] OJ L 257/13).

[48] See also recital 17 in the preamble, referring to a right of permanent residence for '*all*' EU citizens and their family members who have resided legally and continuously for five years without being subject to expulsion.

time periods spent pursuant to different provisions of Articles 7, 12, and 13 can be added together for the purpose of obtaining permanent residence.

Another question which has arisen as regards the interpretation of Article 16 is whether time spent during imprisonment on the territory of the host Member State counts as 'legal residence' for the purposes of obtaining permanent residence status.[49] The Court of Justice will likely shortly answer this question,[50] but pending this clarification, the best view is that the EU legislature has already clearly addressed this issue in the Directive. Recital 17 in the preamble states that the permanent residence right should be acquired by all EU citizens and their family members who have resided continuously for five years in compliance with the Directive 'without being subject to an expulsion measure'. Even more clearly, Article 21 (discussed further below) states that continuous residence 'is broken by any expulsion decision duly enforced against the person concerned'. Given that exceptions from the rules in the Directive must be interpreted strictly,[51] and that expulsion decisions will most often be linked to convictions for criminal offences,[52] it appears that the drafters of the legislation made a clear choice to permit continuity of residence to be broken *only* where the person concerned is a sufficient public policy or public security threat to justify his or her expulsion pursuant to Articles 27 and 28(1), and such expulsion was actually carried out. This interpretation is confirmed by comparing the citizens' Directive to the long-term residents' Directive; the latter (but not the former) provides expressly for an examination of whether the person concerned is a threat to public policy or public security before granting the status at issue.[53]

If, in the alternative, imprisonment time cannot be counted as 'legal residence', then the obligation to interpret exceptions from the Directive narrowly must at least mean that only imprisonment time spent as the direct consequence of a criminal conviction must be discounted. The effect of the imprisonment time upon the acquisition of permanent residence should be calculated by analogy with

---

[49] Arguably, the effect of any imprisonment *outside* the territory of the host State is simply governed by Art 16(3) (before the acquisition of permanent residence status) or Art 16(4) (after the acquisition of permanent residence status).

[50] See Case C-378/12 *Onuekwere*, pending, where a UK court has asked the CJEU when, if at all, a period of imprisonment counts as 'legal residence' for the purposes of Art 16, and, if a period of imprisonment never counts as legal residence, whether it is possible to aggregate periods of legal residence spent before and after the imprisonment in order to acquire permanent residence status. See also, by analogy, Case C-400/12 *MG*, pending, discussed further in Chapter 6.

[51] See, for instance, Case C-46/12 *LN*, judgment of 21 February 2013, para 33.

[52] See generally Chapter 6. In particular, see the discussion in the commentary on Art 28 as to whether permanent residence could be lost (or never acquired) on the basis of 'hidden crimes'.

[53] Art 6 of Directive 2003/109, [2004] OJ L 16/44; see also recital 8 in the preamble to that Directive: 'The notion of public policy may cover a conviction for committing a serious crime.' See also, by analogy, Case C-340/97 *Nazli* [2000] ECR I-957, where the Court ruled that a Turkish worker could not lose status pursuant to the EU–Turkey association agreement merely because he was detained pending trial and subsequently convicted.

Article 16(3), rather as (as argued above) Article 16(3) applies by analogy to the acquisition of permanent residence before the transposition date of the Directive or the accession of a Member State to the EU.[54]

It should be noted that children who are EU citizens can qualify for permanent residence status before the age of majority, given the interpretation of the 'sufficient resources' requirement set out in Chapter 3.[55]

Finally, it is arguable that, by analogy with the *Ziolkowski* judgment, a person who acquired the nationality of a Member State (and therefore EU citizenship) by the ordinary method of applying for that citizenship should also be able to count any period of lawful residence, before acquiring that citizenship, which is consistent with the rules in Article 7, towards the acquisition of permanent residence under the Directive. This would also impact upon his or her third-country national family members—to whom we now turn.

> (2) Paragraph 1 shall apply also to family members who are not nationals of a Member State and have legally resided with the Union citizen in the host Member State for a continuous period of five years.

This paragraph extends the right to permanent residence to third-country national family members of an EU citizen exercising a free movement right in line with their principal. This rule certainly applies to 'family members' as defined in Article 2(2), and (as noted already) for the reasons set out in Chapter 1, it is arguable that it also applies to third-country national beneficiaries (extended family members) as defined in Article 3(2).[56]

The CJEU has recently ruled for the first time on the interpretation of Article 16(2), in its judgment in *Alarape and Tijani*.[57] This case concerned the third-country national child of an EU citizen migrant worker, who was undertaking education in the United Kingdom following the EU citizen's divorce from his mother, also a third-country national. Pursuant to Article 12 of Regulation 1612/68 (now Article 10 of Regulation 492/2011), the child had the right to reside to undertake education, and his mother had an ancillary right to reside as long as her care was necessary in order to facilitate his access to education.[58] The question was whether

---

[54] See similarly the Court's ruling in *Dias* that in some cases, Art 16(4), which governs the loss of permanent residence status due to time spent *outside* the host State's territory, could in transitional cases apply by analogy to periods of time spent *on* the territory.

[55] See the commentary on Art 7 in Chapter 3.

[56] See the commentary on Art 3(2) in Chapter 1. As explained there, if Member States opt to admit some or all extended family members pursuant to Art 3(2) automatically, they are exercising an option linked to the Directive, rather than granting residence pursuant solely on the basis of national law in accordance with Art 37. So the ruling that residence on the basis of national law does not give rise to permanent residence pursuant to the Directive (Joined Cases C-425/10 and C-425/10 *Ziolkowski and Szeja*, judgment of 21 December 2011, not yet reported) will not be applicable.

[57] Case C-529/11, judgment of 8 May 2013, paras 32–48.

[58] For further analysis of this aspect of the case, see the commentary on Art 12(3) in Chapter 3.

the mother and child had the right to permanent residence status, given that they were residing legally pursuant to EU legislation—although not pursuant to the citizens' Directive as such.

In its judgment, the CJEU first stated that there were 'two different situations' where third-country national family members of an EU citizen could obtain permanent residence: under Article 16(2), if they met the residence condition therein, along with Article 17, which provided for 'exemptions' for former workers; and under Article 18, where third-country national family members remaining on the territory after the death of their EU principal or the end of a marriage or registered partnership with that principal, pursuant to Articles 12(2) or 13(2), could obtain permanent residence status after five consecutive years' legal residence. For Article 16(2) to apply, the EU citizen has to satisfy the conditions set out in Article 16(1), and the family members 'must have resided with him for the period in question'. After reiterating that the EU citizen would have to meet the conditions set out in Article 7(1) to obtain a right of residence for five years, the Court stated that the third-country national family members in turn would have to meet the conditions set out in Article 7(2), applicable to family members joining an EU citizen.[59] So only the periods of residence meeting those conditions would count towards the acquisition of permanent residence. Similarly, for the purposes of Article 18, only the periods of residence meeting the conditions set out in Articles 12(2) and 13(2) would count towards the acquisition of permanent residence.[60] It followed that periods of residence spent purely on the basis of Article 12 of Regulation 1612/68 (now Article 10 of Regulation 492/2011) could not be counted towards acquisition of permanent residence rights.[61]

The Court's judgment, by analogy with *Ziolkowski*, must mean that periods of legal residence by third-country national family members pursuant to purely *national* law (which did not comply with conditions laid down in Article 7 of the Directive) would not count toward the acquisition of permanent residence status under the citizens' Directive. Nor would periods of residence which were solely pursuant to any other EU legislation besides the citizens' Directive, such as the EU's immigration and asylum legislation.[62] On the other hand, the analogy drawn by the Court with its case law on Article 16(1) must mean that any periods of residence by third-country national family members before the transposition of the Directive,[63] or before a Member State joined the EU, which satisfied the conditions of Articles

---

[59] On the interpretation of Art 7(1) and (2), see the commentary in Chapter 3.

[60] On the interpretation of Arts 12(2) and 13(2), see the commentary in Chapter 3.

[61] For criticism of this judgment, see the commentary on Art 12(3) in Chapter 3.

[62] As noted already, however, third-country nationals can qualify for a different form of permanent residence status, pursuant to Directive 2003/109 on long-term residence.

[63] This is the issue in Case C-244/13 *Ogieriakhi*, pending, which also assumes that the conditions set out in prior legislation which were repealed by the Directive must also have been satisfied during that period. However, the *Alarape and Tijani* judgment necessarily means that family

7(2), 12(2), and 13(2),[64] must also count toward the acquisition of permanent residence.[65]

The Court's decision to interpret Article 16(2) consistently with Article 16(1) must also mean that the third-country national family members of EU citizens who qualify for permanent residence status after a period of residence pursuant to Article 7(3) can also qualify for permanent residence. The effect of imprisonment upon the acquisition of permanent residence status must also be the same for third-country national family members as it is for EU citizens, and children could also qualify as permanent residents (see the commentary on Article 16(1) above).

The *Alarape* judgment implicitly also decided an important question as regards the requirement in Article 16(2) that the family members must have 'resided with' the principal in the host State for the qualifying period. The Court interpreted this requirement to mean only that the family members had to satisfy the conditions of Article 7(2), as regards 'accompanying or joining' the principal. As discussed in Chapter 1, the CJEU held that as regards workers' third-country national family members under Regulation 1612/68 (now replaced by Directive 2004/38 and Regulation 492/2011), the family member is not required to live under the same roof as the principal.[66] In light of the rule that the citizens' Directive does not lower standards compared to the prior legislation,[67] this interpretation applies also to Article 7(2).[68]

As with Article 16(1), it must follow from the purely declaratory nature of the residence cards for third-country national family members of EU citizens referred to in Article 10 that the failure to hold such a card will not prevent the acquisition of the right to permanent residence. Similarly, the time to acquire permanent residence status will begin to accrue from the moment that the person concerned becomes a family member of a migrant EU citizen on the territory of the host State.[69] It is, of course, possible that a person will become such a family member after the citizen has become a resident in the host State, and so will acquire permanent residence

---

members would not have to live under the same roof as the worker, since Art 7(2) does not require them to do so: see Case 267/83 *Diatta* [1985] ECR 567, para 18.

[64] On the position of persons with residence rights pursuant to Art 12(3), see the commentary on Art 18 below.

[65] Equally, following *Lassal* and *Dias*, Art 16(4) (and arguably also Art 16(3)) applies to such periods by analogy.

[66] Case 267/83 *Diatta* [1985] ECR 567.

[67] Case C-127/08 *Metock and Others* [2008] ECR I-6241.

[68] See also Case C-40/11 *Iida*, judgment of 8 November 2012, not yet reported, para 58, in which the Court applied *Diatta* to the interpretation of Art 2(2)(a), but did not need (on the facts of that case) to interpret Art 7(2). See further the discussion in Chapter 1. These issues may be clarified in the Court's judgment on Case C-244/13 *Ogieriakhi*, pending.

[69] It is possible that the person concerned was already resident (legally or not) in the host State before becoming the family member of the EU citizen, but that does not matter as regards the acquisition of rights under the Directive: see Case C-127/08 *Metock* [2008] ECR I-6241.

status after the citizen does, but there is no requirement in the Directive that the EU citizen and some or all of his or her family members must acquire permanent residence at the same time.

> (3) Continuity of residence shall not be affected by temporary absences not exceeding a total of six months a year, or by absences of a longer duration for compulsory military service, or by one absence of a maximum of twelve consecutive months for important reasons such as pregnancy and childbirth, serious illness, study or vocational training, or a posting in another Member State or a third country.

Continuity of residence is a particularly important aspect of the acquisition of the right of permanent residence. As a concept, it is divided into two parts—what is continuity for the five years during which the right is being acquired, the rules of which appear in this paragraph, and what it means for the purposes of loss of the status, which is dealt with in the next paragraph. In the absence of any wording to the contrary, Article 16(3) applies to the acquisition of permanent residence both by EU citizens (Article 16(1)) and by their third-country national family members (Article 16(2)).

At the outset, it should be noted that the rules on continuity of residence are more generous than the previous rules which applied to the narrow category of EU citizens and their family members who could obtain permanent residence, in that temporary absences could previously only total three months a year and there was no possibility for a single longer absence.[70] But the rules are less generous than the Commission had proposed, since its proposal did not provide for any limit on the number or length of longer absences.[71] Moreover, Article 16(3) is nearly identical to the rule on absences during the first five years of residence (Article 11(2), discussed in Chapter 3), so the two provisions should logically be interpreted the same way.[72]

In principle, during the qualifying period, for absences to be temporary they must not exceed a total of six months a year. There can be more than one such absence each year, as indicated by the use of the plural ('absences'), and the absence of the word 'consecutive'; multiple absences each year must therefore be cumulated. The *reason* for such temporary absences does not matter—by *a contrario* reasoning with the rules on absences for military service and longer absences. There does not

---

[70] Art 4(1), Reg 1251/70. On the question of whether these older rules still apply to this category of persons, see the commentary on Art 17 below. See also Art 6(2) of Directive 68/360, which provided that absence on military service or 'breaks in residence not exceeding six consecutive months' would not affect the validity of a residence permit.

[71] COM(2001) 257, Art 18(1) of the proposal.

[72] Moreover, as argued in Chapter 3 (see the commentary on Arts 7(1)(b), 7(3)(b), 12(2), and 13(2)), Arts 11(2) and 16(3) are applicable by analogy to the calculation of various waiting periods referred to in that chapter. It should also follow by analogy with Art 16(1) that time periods before accession or the transposition date count for the purposes of calculating time under these provisions of Chapter 3.

seem to be any possibility to 'carry forward' any unused absence time from one year to the next, or to average the total yearly absences over multiple years, as evidenced by the wording ('a total of six months a year'). Presumably the first 'year' begins when an EU citizen and his or her family members first take up residence in the Member State concerned, and each subsequent 'year' starts on the anniversary of that date (this rule applies equally to the rules on absences for military service and longer absences).

However, there are a number of important exceptions. Longer absences do not break the continuity of residence where they are the result of the EU citizen (or family member) having to undertake compulsory military service. This military service does not appear to be limited to such service within the EU or a Member State. Thus a dual national (or a third-country national family member) who is required to undertake military service in, for example, Turkey or Israel, should be equally protected against a claim that his or her absence has affected continuity of residence for this purpose. Implicitly, there can be more than one such absence (as indicated by the plural 'absences' and by comparison with the rules on longer absences), and there is no time limit on each of these absences (as indicated by comparison with the rules on temporary or longer absences).

A second exception is also included in this provision but is limited to a maximum of twelve consecutive months, and for a single occasion during the five-year period. Arguably, it would be possible to cumulate one or two periods of permitted six-month absences with the single twelve-month absence. This is a more flexible exception as it is available to the individual so long as he or she can establish 'important reasons' (although presumably a *single* 'important reason' would be sufficient). Four examples are provided but they do not exhaust the category, as indicated by the words 'such as'.[73] They are: firstly, pregnancy and childbirth and secondly, serious illness—both are related to the body and its functions; thirdly, study or vocational training—these exceptions relate to the acquisition of knowledge and skills and tied to potential future participation in the labour market;[74] fourthly, posting in another Member State or a third country. For the purposes of Directive 96/71 on the regulation of the posting of workers,[75] 'posted worker' means a worker who, for a limited period, carries out his work in the territory of a Member State other than the State in which he normally works (Article 2(1) of that Directive). There is, however, no cross reference to the Posted Workers Directive in Directive 2004/38. Nonetheless, in the interests of consistency one would expect the same definition to apply, and it would be logical to extend the definition by analogy to persons

---

[73] See also N Rogers, R Scannell, and J Walsh, *Free Movement of Persons in the Enlarged European Union*, 2nd edn (Sweet and Maxwell, 2012), para 10-79.

[74] Implicitly the location of such education or training should not matter, by analogy with the interpretation of the military service exception.

[75] [1997] OJ L 18/1.

posted to third countries. As yet there has been no judicial consideration of this provision by the CJEU. As for the 'important reasons' for a long absence which are not mentioned expressly, applying the *ejusdem generis* rule, they could include the adoption of a child, the serious illness of a relative,[76] a fixed-term career-furthering job opportunity, or humanitarian or volunteer work.[77]

Finally, an important issue is the effect of the rule that continuity of residence shall not be '*affected*' by the authorized absences. First of all, does this mean that any periods of absence satisfying the rules in Article 16(3) count towards the acquisition of permanent residence status, or does it mean that the clock stops while such absences are taken, and then restarts where it left off once the person returns? Logically, the former interpretation is correct, in the absence of any wording to the contrary, and because stopping the clock surely would affect the continuity of residence.

Secondly, what is the impact of periods of absence which do *not* satisfy the rules in Article 16(3)? Is the clock simply stopped during those absences, and restarted once the person returns, or does the person concerned have to start from scratch accumulating time which counts toward permanent residence status? The judgment in *Givane*, interpreting a similar previous rule, suggests that the latter interpretation is correct.[78] However, the Directive now includes the rules in recital 17 and Article 21, already discussed above in the context of Article 16(1), which provide that continuity is broken when an expulsion order is enforced. As suggested already, the exceptions to the rules on permanent residence should be interpreted strictly, so it must follow that these are the only circumstances where the clock has to be reset.

> (4) Once acquired, the right of permanent residence shall be lost only through absence from the host Member State for a period exceeding two consecutive years.

Permanent residence is harder to lose on the basis of absences than it is to acquire in the face of absences. There is one single rule for absence leading to loss, which is two years' consecutive absence from the territory of the host Member State. In the absence of any wording to the contrary, Article 16(4) applies to the loss of permanent residence both by EU citizens (Article 16(1)) and by their third-country national family members (Article 16(2)).

As permanent residence relieves the EU citizen (or his or her family member) from the need to fulfil the requirements of Article 7, voluntary absence from the labour market, as distinct from absence from that State's territory, should make

---

[76] In any event, the Directive does not state that the serious illness must be suffered by the person concerned.

[77] The job et al could be either in a Member State or a third State.

[78] Case C-257/00 *Givane* [2003] ECR I-345, para 41.

no difference. In terms of interpreting the rule on loss, from the wording of the provision ('two consecutive years'), every time the EU national (or his or her family member) returns to the territory of the host Member State, the clock is reset for the purposes of calculating the two-year period. Even if the permanent resident leaves again the following day, the provision on its face provides that from the day the permanent resident leaves again, time starts running again from day one to calculate the two-year period for the purposes of the loss of permanent residence.[79] The provision does not appear to require the permanent resident to re-establish residence every time he or she returns to the host Member State within the two-year absence period for the purposes of retaining the right. On this point, the word 'absence' in Article 16(4) can be compared with the word 'resided' in Article 16(1) and (2). This interpretation is in line with the principle that exceptions from the rights in the Directive must be interpreted narrowly, and is consistent with the purpose of permanent residence status as described in recitals 17 and 18 in the preamble (strengthening the feeling of Union citizenship, and becoming a genuine vehicle for integration into the host State's society).

The CJEU first considered this provision in the light of the transposition period of the Directive. In the *Lassal*[80] judgment, the CJEU was asked to clarify the effects of absences on the fulfilment of the residence requirement during a period before the end of that period. The problem was that Ms Lassal had legally resided for a continuous period of more than five years in the host Member State (the UK). However, she had been absent from the UK for ten months after that residence but before the deadline date for transposition of the Directive. For the CJEU the question to be answered was whether an absence prior to 30 April 2006 but following a continuous period of five years' legal residence in the host Member State, prevents a citizen of the Union from relying on the right of permanent residence under Article 16(1). Two Member States, Belgium and the UK, argued that as the status could only be acquired after the end of the transposition date, absence before that date would break the citizen's period of residence as the person can only benefit from Article 16(4) once the status has come into existence, not before. The CJEU did not consider that this followed from the wording and objective of the Directive. In support of this position the CJEU reminded itself that it is necessary to consider not only a measure's wording, but also the context in which it occurs and the objectives pursued by the rules of which it is part.[81] Specifically, the enacting terms of an EU act are indissociably linked to the reasons given for it and therefore preference must be given to the interpretation which ensures that the

---

[79] If the Member State wrongly refused to admit the person concerned to its territory, that person still ought to be able to claim that the two years' period was interrupted and that he or she still retains permanent residence status.

[80] Case C-162/09 [2010] ECR I-9217.

[81] Cases: C-156/98 *Germany v Commission* [2000] ECR I-6857; C-306/05 *SGAE* [2006] ECR I-11519; and Joined Cases C-402/07 and C-432/07 *Sturgeon and Others* [2009] ECR I-10923.

provision retains its effectiveness. Applying this reasoning to the issue to hand, the CJEU held that the objectives and purposes of the Directive (which it restated—to facilitate the exercise of the primary right to move and reside freely on the territory of the Member States and to strengthen that right and to promote social cohesion and to strengthen the feeling of Union citizenship)—would be seriously compromised if the right of residence was refused to Union citizens who had legally resided in the host Member State for a continuous period of five years completed before 30 April 2006, on the sole ground that there had been temporary absence of less than two consecutive years subsequent to the five-year period but before the end date for transposition. The same result, according to the CJEU, is also required by the general scheme of the Directive and spirit of Article 16.

Interestingly, in support of this position the CJEU has regard to the documents on the negotiation of the Directive, noting that: 'According to the *travaux préparatoires* for Directive 2004/38 such a measure [loss of permanent residence] could be justified because after an absence of that duration [two years] the link with the host Member State is loosened (see the Council's statement of reasons for common position (EC) No 6/2004 of 5 December 2003 with a view to the adoption of Directive 2004/38 (OJ 2004 C 54 E, p 12), as far as concerns Article 16 thereof)' (para 55).

Accordingly, Article 16(4) applies independently of whether periods of residence completed before or after 30 April 2006 are concerned.[82] Because Article 16(1) applies to residence periods before the end of the transposition period, so does Article 16(4) as the CJEU helpfully points out, otherwise any period of absence would either have to be admitted, or would extinguish the permanent residence right.

In *Dias*[83] the CJEU held that the rule laid down in Article 16(4) must also be applied by analogy to periods in the host Member State completed on the basis solely of a residence permit, without the conditions governing entitlement to a right of residence of any kind under the Directive having been satisfied, which occurred before 30 April 2006 and after a continuous period of five years' legal residence (for the purposes of Article 16(1)) which was completed prior to that date. What is important here is that the CJEU extended the meaning of absence from one which is territorially restricted to one which includes periods when the individual was absent from the labour market but present in the State. The CJEU considered that even though Article 16(4) refers only to absences from the host Member State, the integration link between the person concerned and that Member State is also

---

[82] As noted above, Art 16(4) should logically also apply to periods of absence after a person has met the criteria for permanent residence during the run-up to his or her Member State's accession to the EU.
[83] Case C-325/09 *Dias* [2011] ECR I-6387.

called into question in the case of a citizen who, while having resided legally for a continuous period of five years, then decides to remain in that Member State without having a right of residence.

This situation must be limited to the transposition period for the Directive (or, as noted above, the period before accession of a Member State) as otherwise it would have the effect of undermining substantially the objective of the status of permanent residence which is to provide security of residence and access to social assistance benefits. If individuals who have been absent from the labour market for two years in a host Member State lose their permanent residence as a result the consequence would be counterproductive, and would undercut the rule in Article 16(1) that permanent residents are no longer subject to the rules in chapter III of the Directive.

It is clear from the text of Article 16(4) (ie the word 'only') that two consecutive years' absence is the sole circumstance which could lead to the loss of permanent residence. Therefore it follows that the expulsion of a permanent resident from the territory pursuant to Article 28(2) (on which, see Chapter 6) will not as such end permanent residence status. Since Article 16(4) does not make any reference to the reasons for absence from the territory (*a contrario* Article 16(3)), it must follow that those reasons do not matter for the purpose of applying Article 16(4).[84] So if a permanent resident is expelled from the territory pursuant to Article 28(2), he or she would retain permanent residence status in the host Member State if he or she returned within two years following the expulsion. Of course, in practice, this return might be difficult if he or she were imprisoned in the State of origin, or if the host State had validly imposed an exclusion order against the permanent resident for a longer period.[85] Any unauthorized return to the host State's territory during the period of validity of the exclusion order would surely not interrupt the two-year period (much as, as argued above, a State's illegal refusal to permit a permanent resident to enter during the two-year period *would* have to be regarded as an interruption).[86]

---

[84] Exceptionally, a period of absence wholly outside the control of the person concerned (such as being held hostage in another country) should not count against the permanent resident for the purposes of Art 16(4), in light of the principle of *force majeure*.

[85] It should be noted that the Directive provides that the person concerned can request the lifting of an exclusion order 'after a reasonable period', at the latest within three years of its adoption, and that Member States must decide upon that request within six months (Art 32(1), discussed in Chapter 6). If a Member State validly makes full use of these possibilities, then the two-year period set out in Art 16(4) will expire and permanent residence will be lost. But if an exclusion order has been imposed for a shorter period or illegally, or if a court rules that it is too lengthy, or if a Member State exceeds either or both of the deadlines set out in Art 32(1) or any shorter deadlines set out in national law, then the relevant time period should not count against the person concerned for the purposes of Art 16(4).

[86] Note that Art 32(2) expressly states that there is no right of entry to the territory of the State which has imposed an exclusion order while waiting for a decision on lifting the order.

If permanent residence status is lost, there is nothing to prevent an EU citizen who meets the criteria set out in Articles 6 and 7 from re-entering the host State and beginning to reacquire that status from scratch—other than an exclusion order which is still valid. However, a third-country national family member of an EU citizen who lost permanent residence status would not have the right to re-enter that State in his or her own name pursuant to the Directive, although of course he or she might still qualify as the family member of an EU citizen,[87] or might have a right to enter pursuant to other provisions of EU or national law.[88]

Finally, in light of the importance of the permanent residence status, surely the host Member State would have the initial burden of proof to show that that status has been lost pursuant to Article 16(4). Once a prima facie case had been made out, the person concerned could then adduce evidence to the contrary.

F. Evaluation—Article 16

As permanent residence (other than the provisions of Article 17) is an innovation of the Directive, there are still quite a few questions outstanding about how it is to be interpreted. There is as yet little jurisprudence from the CJEU on the provisions; and as their wording is not always entirely clear and the traditions of the Member States are quite disparate as regards this kind of status,[89] more clarification will undoubtedly be needed. What does seem certain is that what appears self-evident as the interpretative answer in one Member State may be very foreign indeed in another.

As a status, permanent residence sets a new 'gold standard' for EU citizens and their family members. While EU law has promised EU citizens and their family members equality and non-discrimination on the basis of nationality with nationals of the host Member State since its inception, clearly this has been less than ideally achieved. It is evident that permanent residence is intended to deal with a particularly sensitive issue of equal treatment for EU citizens and their family members in a host Member State—access to social assistance in all forms which are available to nationals of the State. One of the potential dangers of the new status, however, is that it may encourage some Member States to seek to exclude EU citizens and their family members whose underlying nationality is not of the host State from social benefits of a wide variety pending the acquisition of the status. This

---

[87] There is no reason why he or she would have to be a family member of the *same* EU citizen.

[88] For instance, he or she might have acquired the right to long-term residence in another Member State pursuant to Directive 2003/109, and be seeking the right to move between Member States pursuant to the relevant provisions of that Directive.

[89] C A Groenendijk, E Guild, and R Barzilay, *The Legal Status of Third Country Nationals who are Long Term Residents in a Member State of the European Union*, Brussels 2001, European Commission.

would be counterproductive and inconsistent with the existing jurisprudence on the right to equal treatment.[90] This issue is discussed in greater depth in Chapter 5.

Article 17—Exemptions for persons no longer working in the host Member State and their family members

Recital 19 in the preamble provides that certain advantages specific to Union citizens who are workers or self-employed persons and to their family members, which may allow these persons to acquire a right of permanent residence before they have resided five years in the host Member State, should be maintained, as these constitute acquired rights. This objective is fulfilled by Article 17, which imports the right of permanent residence from Regulation 1251/70 and Directive 75/34 concerning the rights of EU citizens to remain on the territory of another Member State after pursuing an activity as a worker or a self-employed person. The preceding measures did not provide for a right of permanent residence otherwise than in the circumstances set out below. The merger of the two separate legislative acts into one Article of this Directive surely suggests that, if it was not already the case before, the rules in question must also benefit those who *switch between* employed and self-employed activities during the relevant time periods.[91] This interpretation is consistent with the objective to 'simplify and strengthen' the free movement rights of EU citizens, as set out in recital 3 in the preamble. Of course, if EU citizens or their family members do not qualify for 'fast-track' permanent residence status pursuant to Article 17, they may still qualify for that status eventually in accordance with Articles 16 or 18.

1. By way of derogation from Article 16, the right of permanent residence in the host Member State shall be enjoyed before completion of a continuous period of five years of residence by:

At the outset, it should be noted that in principle the right to 'permanent residence' set out in Article 17 is the same as the right set out in Article 16, since the same term is used and Article 17 is expressly a 'derogation' from Article 16. Since the only derogation referred to is a reduction in the time period required to qualify for permanent residence status, it must follow that the concept of 'residence' is otherwise the same (ie the requirement that such residence must be in accordance with the rules of the Directive, including the application of these rules to periods before the transposition deadline or accession of a Member State),[92] and that Article 16(3) and (4) apply as regards interruptions of the continuity of residence and the loss of

---

[90] See, for instance, Joined Cases C-22/08 and C-23/08 *Vatsouras and Koupatantze* [2009] ECR I-4585.

[91] Compare with the Court's insistence on enforcing the literal wording of Reg 1612/68, which applies to (the family members of) workers as distinct from self-employed persons: Joined Cases C-147/11 and C-148/11 *Czop and Punakova*, judgment of 6 September 2012, not yet reported.

[92] See the opinion in Case C-162/09 *Lassal* [2010] ECR I-9217, paras 63–67 and 75, which expressly argues that the interpretation of Art 16 as regards the transposition period must also apply to Art 17.

permanent residence status.[93] This reflects the deliberate decision of the drafters of the Directive not to retain the particular rules on continuity of residence or assertion of permanent residence set out in the prior rules (Articles 4 and 5, Regulation 1251/70 and Directive 75/34). Again, this interpretation is consistent with the objective to 'simplify and strengthen' the free movement rights of EU citizens, as set out in recital 3 in the preamble. The impact of this interpretation is that, on the same facts as the *Givane* judgment,[94] the family members who sought permanent residence would now be successful (see further the commentary on Article 17(4) below), as long as they could show that their EU principal's ten-month stay in India was for an 'important reason' (see the commentary on Article 16(3) above).

> a. workers or self-employed persons who, at the time they stop working, have reached the age laid down by the law of that Member State for entitlement to an old age pension or workers who cease paid employment to take early retirement, provided that they have been working in that Member State for at least the preceding twelve months and have resided there continuously for more than three years.
>
> If the law of the host Member State does not grant the right to an old age pension to certain categories of self-employed persons, the age condition shall be deemed to have been met once the person concerned has reached the age of 60;

This first subsection provides for a right of residence for EU citizens who cease to work as a result of reaching pensionable age or taking early retirement. The wording is largely the same as that of Article 2 of Regulation 1251/70 as regards workers, but with one important addition. The previous measure did not also provide for workers who ceased paid employment to take early retirement. The mirror provision in Directive 75/34 provided for an identical right for a self-employed person on the same conditions but again with no provision for early retirement.

There are two conditions to the acquisition of the right: firstly, the citizen must have been working or self-employed in the host State for at least the preceding twelve months and secondly, he or she must have resided in that host State continuously for more than three years. An EU citizen's right to reside in a host Member State after ceasing his or her occupational activity where that activity did not take place in the host State was only created in 1990.[95] However, where the economic activity *did* take place in the host State for at least twelve months before retirement (accompanied by three years' residence in that host State), Regulation 1251/70 or Directive 75/34 applied and the individual acquired a right of permanent residence.

---

[93] Similarly, Art 21, which provides that continuity of residence is broken by any expulsion decision duly enforced against the person, must also be applicable.

[94] See the discussion in Section B of this chapter.

[95] Directive 90/365 ([1990] OJ L 180/28), now incorporated into Art 7(1)(b). This right supersedes Member States' prior obligation to facilitate the readmission of workers or self-employed persons who left the host State for a 'long period' and who seek to return after retirement or permanent incapacity, as set out in Art 8(2) of Reg 1251/70 and Directive 75/34. That presumably explains why these provisions were not incorporated into the citizens' Directive.

The acquisition of permanent residence by the former group (those who only began to reside in the host Member State after retirement in another Member State) is covered by Article 16. Those EU nationals who retired in the host Member State after working and residing in that State for the requisite periods are the subjects of this provision.

The meaning of the terms 'worker' and 'self-employed person' are as defined by the CJEU in relation to Articles 45 and 49 TFEU—see the commentary on Article 7(1), in Chapter 3. The term 'preceding twelve months' means the period immediately before the retirement date. In *Givane*[96] the CJEU considered a similar temporal relationship between a time period and the acquisition of a permanent residence right now incorporated into Article 17(4). It found that the period of two years was expressly linked to the condition (in the latter case the death of the EU principal) (para 40). A similar approach is likely to be the case here, although as noted above, the Directive now provides for a more generous treatment of previous breaks in residence than the previous rules permitted. In this context, the reference to military service in Article 16(3) is interesting as it would only apply in those States where there are continuing military service obligations up to retirement and perhaps beyond.

According to the OECD,[97] official retirement entitlement ages vary substantially across EU Member States and on the basis of gender. The norm was sixty-five in 2010 though women in the Slovak Republic and both men and women in Greece had an official entitlement age of fifty-seven. According to the same source, the average age of labour force exit was about fifty-seven for men and women in Luxembourg but closer to sixty-seven for men in Portugal. These variations, as well as pressure to increase pensionable ages,[98] have made the inclusion of a wider definition in this subsection desirable. The final subparagraph of this subsection makes provision for categories of the self-employed, if they are among the groups where Member States do not provide pensions. For them, the age condition is deemed to have been met once the person concerned reaches sixty. This is a more generous rule than set out in Directive 75/34, which provided instead for a deemed retirement age of sixty-five. A final consideration as regards this subsection is the prohibition on discrimination on the basis of age contained in Directive 2000/78.[99] Interestingly, of all the discrimination grounds covered by that measure, the CJEU

---

[96] Case C-257/00 [2003] ECR I-345.

[97] OECD (2011), 'Pensionable Years', in *Society at a Glance 2011 OECD Social Indicators* OECD Publishing 10.1787/soc_glance-2011-en.

[98] See for instance, OECD 17/03/2011—Recent reforms will still be insufficient to cover increased pension costs in the future, despite increases in retirement ages in half of OECD countries, according to a new OECD report. <http://www.oecd.org/newsroom/pensionreformsmustdeliver-affordableandadequatebenefitswarnsoecd.htm> visited 15 August 2012.

[99] OJ 2000 L 303/16.

has most frequently been requested to interpret this prohibition regarding age.[100] As yet there has been no clarification of how the two Directives intersect.

b. workers or self-employed persons who have resided continuously in the host Member State for more than two years and stop working there as a result of permanent incapacity to work. If such incapacity is the result of an accident at work or an occupational disease entitling the person concerned to a benefit payable in full or in part by an institution in the host Member State, no condition shall be imposed as to length of residence;

This provision is designed to protect the residence right of those who become permanently incapacitated. There is only one requirement: the EU citizen must have resided continuously in the Member State for two years before the incapacity began and stopped working as a result of it. Even this requirement is disapplied where the EU citizen is incapacitated as a result of an accident at work or occupational disease provided that the incapacity entitled him or her to a social benefit related to that accident or disease. Further information about such benefits can be found in Regulation 883/2004 on the coordination of social security and its implementing measures.[101] This Regulation provides an excellent snapshot of the types of benefits available in the Member States.

The previous version of this provision, Article 2(1)(b) of Regulation 1251/70, was the subject of judicial proceedings which resulted in a CJEU judgment on 26 May 1993.[102] The case is somewhat complicated by the enlargement of the EU to include Greece and the fact that the EU citizen's employment record pre-dated that enlargement. A Greek national resident in Germany sought an extension of his residence permit on the basis of his right to reside under Article 2(1)(b) as he had worked in Germany though before his home State acceded to the EU on 1 January 1981. He applied for an extension of his residence permit in December 1981 which application was ultimately refused in August 1986. This took place after he had been refused an invalidity pension in 1983 on the ground that he was not incapable of work. Nonetheless, the national court accepted that it was objectively impossible for him to find employment. The CJEU held that the provision must be interpreted as meaning that a person in his situation did not enjoy a right to remain in the host Member State when he suffered from a permanent incapacity for work which arose during a period of residence authorized on account of judicial proceedings which he had brought against the State for the purposes of obtaining a residence permit. As a general rule, such a situation is likely to arise only in the circumstances of enlargement.

c. workers or self-employed persons who, after three years of continuous employment and residence in the host Member State, work in an employed or self-employed

---

[100] See for instance, Case C-88/08 *Hütter* [2009] ECR I-5325.
[101] [2004] OJ L 166/1.
[102] Case C-171/91 *Tsiotras* [1993] ECR I-2925.

capacity in another Member State, while retaining their place of residence in the host Member State, to which they return, as a rule, each day or at least once a week.

For the purposes of entitlement to the rights referred to in points (a) and (b), periods of employment spent in the Member State in which the person concerned is working shall be regarded as having been spent in the host Member State.

This subsection is designed to protect workers or self-employed EU citizens who have lived and worked for at least three years in a host Member State and then take employment or start self-employed activities in another Member State (which could also be the Member State of the individual's underlying nationality) but retain their residence in the first host Member State. As such, EU citizens will no longer be exercising rights as workers (Article 45 TFEU) or self-employed persons (Article 49 TFEU) in the Member State of residence, and without this protection they would be required to fulfil the self-sufficiency requirements of Article 7 to benefit from a right of residence. This provision is also present in the earlier Regulation and Directive. The category of people who work in one Member State but return once a week to their Member State of residence is defined in Regulation 883/2004 on the coordination of social security as a frontier worker.[103] This definition was enlarged from workers to include the self-employed when the Regulation was modernized in 2004.[104] The final indent specifies how a frontier worker qualifies under Article 17(1)(a) or (b) for permanent residence.

Periods of involuntary unemployment duly recorded by the relevant employment office, periods not worked for reasons not of the person's own making and absences from work or cessation of work due to illness or accident shall be regarded as periods of employment.

This provision applies to all three subparagraphs of Article 17(1). As is apparent from a number of provisions of the Directive, calculating time for the purposes of enjoyment of rights can be a complex business. For the purposes of this provision, there are three time periods which must be counted as periods of employment for the calculation of the permanent residence right. Firstly, periods of involuntary unemployment duly recorded by the relevant employment office: as these periods must be evidenced by the relevant office's records they should be fairly easy to establish. Further, the meaning must be consistent with that of Article 7(3) of the Directive (see Chapter 3). Secondly, periods not worked for reasons not of the person's own making: this category was not present in Regulation 1251/70 but has its origins in Directive 75/34 which provided that periods of inactivity (for self-employed persons) due to circumstances outside the control of the person concerned were counted as periods of activity. The CJEU has not considered this

---

[103] [2004] OJ L 166/1.
[104] The repealed Regulation was 1408/71, [1971] OJ L 149/2.

provision on its substance (on the issue of imprisonment, see the commentary on Article 16(2) above). Thirdly, an absence or cessation of work due to illness or accident counts as employment. This category was present both in Regulation 1251/70 and Directive 75/34 but has not been the subject of judicial interpretation by the CJEU on the substance. This would appear to mean that if a worker moves to, resides, and works in a Member State, even if for a fairly short period, and then, due to illness or accident is no longer able to work, all periods of residence up to the point where permanent residence is acquired under Article 17(1)(b) or (c) count as periods of employment for the calculation of the period of time necessary to acquire the right. This sits very uncomfortably with the wording of Article 17(1)(b), which places substantially more conditions on the acquisition of permanent residence by persons with a permanent incapacity to work as a result of accident or disease.

> (2) The conditions as to length of residence and employment laid down in point (a) of paragraph 1 and the condition as to length of residence laid down in point (b) of paragraph 1 shall not apply if the worker's or the self-employed person's spouse or partner as referred to in point 2(b) of Article 2 is a national of the host Member State or has lost the nationality of that Member State by marriage to that worker or self-employed person.

This provision is repeated from the earlier Regulation and Directive, with the addition of a reference to the 'partner' of the person concerned, as defined in Article 2(2)(b) (see Chapter 1). It means that where an EU citizen who is retiring (a) or has had to stop work because of a permanent incapacity (b) is married to or has a partner who is a national of the host Member State (or was a national of that State but for loss of that citizenship as a result of marriage), the otherwise obligatory length of residence and economic activity requirements do not apply. In such a case, for instance, for the purposes of Article 17(1)(a), the person retiring would not have to show that he or she had worked for the preceding twelve months and resided on the territory of the host State for more than three years. The mere fact of having worked or been self-employed and taking retirement is sufficient. For Article 17(1)(b) those who cease work as a result of permanent incapacity do not have to show that they have been residing for more than two years continuously in the host State. It would seem that the spouse or partner of the EU citizen would need still to be alive at the time the right comes into existence, as evidenced by the use of the present tense ('is').

> (3) Irrespective of nationality, the family members of a worker or a self-employed person who are residing with him in the territory of the host Member State shall have the right of permanent residence in that Member State, if the worker or self-employed person has acquired himself the right of permanent residence in that Member State on the basis of paragraph 1.

This paragraph is of particular importance for third-country national family members of an EU citizen coming within one of the three categories—retiring, permanently incapacitated, and frontier workers, as defined in Article 17(1). It provides for a fast-track to permanent residence status, as compared to the provisions of Article 7(1)(d) or (2), in conjunction with Article 16(1) or (2). The persons concerned must be residing with the EU citizen on the territory of the host State to benefit. Given the close link between Articles 16 and 17,[105] in the absence of any wording to the contrary, the meaning of 'residing with' must have the same meaning as in the CJEU's *Diatta* judgment.[106] This means that the family member(s) need only be residing in the host State, not necessarily under the same roof as the EU citizen.[107] It should be noted that the extended family members referred to in Article 3(2) certainly fall within the scope of Article 17(3) (and (4)), since they were expressly referred to in the prior legislation.[108]

Moreover, there is no waiting period for the family members to acquire this right; it is sufficient that they '*are residing* with him', as distinct from the requirement that they '*have legally resided* with' the EU citizen, set out in Article 16(2). This interpretation reflects the wording of the Directive,[109] as well as its logic: given that the whole point of Article 17(1) is to provide for the enjoyment of a right to permanent residence 'before completion of a continuous period of five years of residence', no such waiting period could logically be applied to family members. It might have been logical to provide for a separate waiting period for family members, matching the waiting periods applicable to workers and self-employed persons, but if the drafters of the Directive (and the prior measures) had wanted to provide for such limits, they would surely have done so expressly.[110] The absence of such provisions may be explained by the social context of the relevant rules,[111] and by the daunting

---

[105] See the commentary above on the *chapeau* of Art 17(1).

[106] Case 267/83 *Diatta* [1985] ECR 567, and Case C-40/11 *Iida*, judgment of 8 November 2012, not yet reported. This interpretation is strengthened by the fact that Art 1 of Reg 1251/70 defined family members by reference to Art 10 of Reg 1612/68, which was interpreted in the *Diatta* judgment; para 33 of the *Givane* judgment also mentions this link. For the same reasons, it should follow that 'family members' includes the extended family members referred to in Art 3(2). See further the commentary on Art 16(2) above, and more generally Chapter 1.

[107] See also the interpretation in the Opinion in *Givane*, para 61, concerning the prior measure: 'it is not necessary that the family members lived with the worker for the entire period which established his right', but the family members 'must in any event have lived with him at the time of his death'.

[108] See the commentary on Art 3(2), in Chapter 1.

[109] The title of Art 17 refers to 'exemptions [from Art 16] for persons no longer working in the host Member State *and their family members*', and recital 19 in the preamble states that the 'advantages' for 'workers or self-employed persons and to their family members, which may allow these persons to acquire a right of permanent residence *before they have resided five years* in the host Member State, should be maintained'. See also the Opinion in *Givane*, and para. 62 of the same Opinion: 'it is not a question of the family members' own minimum period of residence'.

[110] This is clearly evidenced by Arts 12(2) and 13(2)(a), where the drafters of the Directive chose to lay down waiting periods relating to *family members* directly.

[111] See the Opinion in *Givane*, para 63: 'the requirement of a minimum period of residence of the worker alone appears appropriate since it is then possible for him to acquire a secure position with respect to the subsequent right to remain before he arranges for his family to join him'.

complexity of drafting such provisions, given the large number of different waiting periods for workers and self-employed persons set out in Article 17(1) and (2). Therefore, as soon as the EU citizen benefits from the application of Article 17(1) (or the derogation set out in Article 17(2)) to acquire permanent residence, so do the family members.

(4) If, however, the worker or self-employed person dies while still working but before acquiring permanent residence status in the host Member State on the basis of paragraph 1, his family members who are residing with him in the host Member State shall acquire the right of permanent residence there, on condition that:

   a. the worker or self-employed person had, at the time of death, resided continuously on the territory of that Member State for two years; or
   b. the death resulted from an accident at work or an occupational disease or
   c. the surviving spouse lost the nationality of that Member State following marriage to the worker or self-employed person.

This paragraph seeks to provide permanent residence status for the family members, including third-country national family members, of an EU citizen who dies before acquiring permanent residence in the host State. The same rule was present in both the preceding Regulation and Directive, although the protection accorded to spouses who *retain* nationality of the host State has been dropped.[112] The Commission had proposed to reduce the waiting period in Article 17(4)(a) to one year, but the Council rejected this on the grounds that retaining the existing rule would guarantee 'a strong link with the host Member State'.[113] Like Article 17(3), this is another fast-track to permanent residence status for family members.

The first condition for the application of Article 17(4) is that the worker or self-employed EU citizen must be exercising the economic activity at the time when he or she dies (as evidenced by the words 'dies while still working'). The death must precede the acquisition of permanent residence by the EU citizen on any of the grounds set out in Article 17(1). While the EU citizen must be exercising an economic activity at the time of his or her death, that does not mean that the death must take place in the host State, in light of the provisions for permitted interruption of residence set out in Article 16(3).

The right accrues to the family members of the EU citizen on condition that they were residing with him or her in the host Member State. Since Article 17(4) in effect forms a derogation from Article 17(3), the same interpretation will apply as regards the meaning of 'residing with', namely a requirement to reside in the same host State rather than under the same roof as the EU citizen.[114] For

---

[112] Compare Art 17(4)(c) to Art 3(2), third indent, Reg 1251/70. This change was presumably made because, as nationals of the host State, such persons do not need to worry about their immigration law status.

[113] Common Position 6/2004, [2004] OJ C 54 E/12, statement of reasons for Art 17(4)(a).

[114] Case 267/83 *Diatta* [1985] ECR 567 and Case C-40/11 *Iida*, judgment of 8 November 2012, not yet reported. See the commentary on Arts 16(2) and 17(3) above, and generally Chapter 1.

the same reason, family members are not subject to any requirement of prior residence.

There are three circumstances in which the family members will acquire permanent residence; each is independent of the other, as evidenced by the word 'or'. The first is where at the time of the EU citizen's death, he or she had resided on the territory of the host State for at least two years. This is the same period of time as is required under Article 17(1)(b), where the EU citizen is permanently incapacitated. The parallel is obvious. The second is where the death resulted from an accident at work or an occupational disease. Again, this mirrors Article 17(1)(b), regarding the acquisition of the right by EU citizens who suffer accidents at work or occupational diseases but do not die as a result of them. The third circumstance is where the surviving spouse lost nationality of the host State by reason of his or her marriage to the EU citizen. This reflects Article 17(2) which is also designed to protect spouses who lose nationality of the host State on marriage, in this case to cover the situation of death of the EU citizen principal.

The predecessor measure, Article 3(2) of Regulation 1251/70, was the subject of CJEU consideration in *Givane*,[115] which we discussed above. The issue was whether the EU citizen fulfilled the two-year qualifying residence period now incorporated into Article 17(4)(a) at the time of his death. The CJEU considered that the language of the provision (having examined a number of language versions) was not conclusive and therefore interpreted the provision in light of the general scheme of the Article. Supported by an *a contrario* argument and an examination of another provision of the measure, the Treaty, and the objective of EU law generally, the CJEU concluded that the period of two years' continuous residence must immediately precede the EU citizen's death. As this was not the case on the facts, the third-country national family members failed to acquire permanent residence. While the same interpretation would presumably still apply to Article 17(4)(a) as such, in the absence of amendment of this provision, the outcome of the *Givane* case might nonetheless be different because, as noted above,[116] on the facts of the case the Givane family might benefit from the more flexible rules on continuity of residence set out in the citizens' Directive.

Finally, it should be noted that those family members who do *not* satisfy the conditions set out in Article 17(4) upon the death of their principal will still have an opportunity to obtain permanent residence later pursuant to Article 12(1) or (2), if they satisfy the relevant conditions therein.

Article 18—Acquisition of the right of permanent residence by certain family members who are not nationals of a Member State

---

[115] Case C-257/00 *Givane* [2003] ECR I-366.
[116] See the commentary on Art 17(1).

> Without prejudice to Article 17, the family members of a Union citizen to whom Articles 12(2) and 13(2) apply, who satisfy the conditions laid down therein, shall acquire the right of permanent residence after residing legally for a period of five consecutive years in the host Member State.

This provision allows third-country national family members who have a retained right of residence pursuant to Articles 12(2) or 13(2) (see Chapter 3) to obtain permanent residence after five years' legal residence. While the literal wording of Articles 16(2) and 18 might appear to suggest that persons remaining after the death or departure of an EU citizen pursuant to Article 12(3) cannot obtain permanent residence status, this interpretation should not be accepted. Unlike the residence which was at issue in the judgments in *Ziolkowski* and *Alarape*, residence pursuant to Article 12(3) is residence *pursuant to the Directive*, not pursuant to national law or other EU legislation, and so it clearly meets the criteria referred to in recital 17 in the preamble.[117] As with other methods of acquiring permanent residence status, the waiting period could potentially be served before the transposition date of the Directive or date of accession to the EU, and Article 16(3) and (4) will apply to such periods by analogy.[118]

The beneficiaries of Article 18 are, first of all, third-country nationals whose EU citizen principal died before the family member(s) acquired permanent residence. This retained right of residence set out in Article 12(2) comes into existence when the family member(s) lived in the host State as family members for at least one year before the death, but to obtain permanent residence the persons concerned must meet conditions equivalent to those set out in Article 7(1) after that point. For the family members of EU citizens who are working or self-employed at their time of death the provisions of Article 17(4)(a) are more generous (if the conditions are fulfilled). While under this provision the residential requirement is two years, it will always be more favourable as the family members acquire permanent residence immediately and do not have to wait for five years nor do they have to fulfil the other conditions of Article 12(2). However, if the family members do not meet the conditions set out in Article 17(4), or their EU citizen principal was not a worker or self-employed person, then this provision is vital for them.

The Article also provides for the acquisition of permanent residence by the third-country national family members of EU citizens in the event of divorce, annulment of marriage, or termination of a registered partnership. Again, to obtain permanent residence the persons concerned must meet conditions equivalent to those set out in Article 7(1) after the end of their marriage or registered partnership (see the commentary on Article 13(2) in Chapter 3). None of these events were foreseen in the previous measures; nor were the family members protected

---

[117] For an alternative view, see the Opinion in Case C-529/11 *Alarape and Tijani*, judgment of 8 May 2013, paras 85–89.
[118] See the commentary on Art 16(1) above.

in respect of their occurrence, except in the circumstances set out in Article 12 of Regulation 1612/68 (now Article 10, Regulation 492/2011).[119]

In both cases, the family members were not required to live under the same roof as the EU citizen before the family relationship formally ended.[120]

G. Evaluation—Articles 17 and 18

These two provisions are both complex and detailed, in spite of the Directive's objective to simplify and strengthen the right of free movement and residence of all Union citizens. While doubts arise on the question of simplification, certainly in order to maintain the status quo of rights, the incorporation of the rights from the previous measures were necessary. This is explicitly stated in recital 19 in the preamble. It could be argued that the best way to simplify and strengthen the rights of EU citizens and their family members would have been merely to widen the categories of persons eligible for permanent residence under Regulation 1251/70 and Directive 75/34 to all EU citizens, not just workers and the self-employed. Then only a catch-all permanent residence category would apply to everyone who had not already acquired the right otherwise. This approach was not adopted. One must assume that the reason for this was because at least some Member States did not want to widen the categories of persons who would not have had to fulfil all the conditions of Article 16 for five years before enjoying the greater right of permanent residence.

Section II—Administrative Formalities

A. Function

This section consists of three Articles which set out the administrative formalities specific only to permanent residence. Administrative formalities which apply to a right of residence are set out in Articles 8–11 (see Chapter 3). For the general administrative formalities which are common both to a right of residence as well as permanent residence see Chapter 5. This section is needed to clarify the evidencing of permanent residence. However, the general rules of acquisition of residence rights, most importantly that the acquisition is automatic by virtue of fulfilling the conditions, apply equally to permanent residence. This is important as it means that those EU citizens and their family members who have fulfilled the underlying conditions for acquisition of the right but never bothered to seek evidence of the right from the authorities are equally entitled to rely on the right

---

[119] On this issue, see the commentary on Art 12(3) in Chapter 3.
[120] See the commentary on Art 16(2) above.

as compared those who have sought evidence from the authorities of the host State (see Chapter 5, particularly the commentary on Article 25).

B. Historical development

The predecessor measures, Regulation 1251/70 and Directive 75/34, both contained specific provisions on administrative formalities.[121] While these two measures only covered workers and the self-employed, the equivalent provisions of Directive 2004/38 apply to all EU citizens and their family members acquiring permanent residence. There has been no interpretation by the CJEU either of the preceding measures nor of these provisions of the Directive.

C. Interrelationship of Articles 19–21 with other provisions

These provisions must be read in line with Articles 8–11. As regards the underlying principles there needs to be consistency between the two sets of arrangements. Furthermore, they are related to Articles 22–26, which apply also here.

D. Other relevant EU law rules

There are no other EU rules relevant to this section.

E. Analysis

Article 19—Document certifying permanent residence for Union citizens

1. Upon application Member States shall issue Union citizens entitled to permanent residence, after having verified duration of residence, with a document certifying permanent residence.
2. The document certifying permanent residence shall be issued as soon as possible.

While the Commission had proposed that EU citizens would have to apply for permanent residence cards, the Council decided to make this optional, arguing that its 'approach meets the objective of reducing administrative formalities for Union citizens'.[122] Member States are under a duty to evidence permanent residence where Union citizens so request, as this is an entitlement of the citizen. The document does no more than certify that the individual has acquired permanent residence. It does not have the effect of conferring any status on the individual (see

---

[121] See Art 6 of each measure.
[122] Common Position 6/2004, [2004] OJ C 54/12, statement of reasons regarding Arts 19 and 20.

the commentaries on Article 8, in Chapter 3, and Article 25, in Chapter 5).[123] The Court of Justice has confirmed that Article 19 does not require EU citizens who have acquired permanent residence status to hold a residence permit of indefinite duration, that there is no obligation to apply for the card, and that the document 'has only declaratory and probative force but does not give rise to any right'.[124]

The Member State is entitled to verify the duration of residence. Taking into account the CJEU's approach to qualifying residence and the possession of residence cards,[125] Member States must be entitled to verify also the legality of the residence over the period and thus require substantial documentation regarding the exercise of Article 7 rights throughout the five-year period. In *Dias* the CJEU found that periods of residence enjoyed when the EU citizen was in possession of a residence permit pursuant to prior legislation, but was not exercising residence rights under that prior legislation (which is equivalent to residence under Article 7 of the Directive), did not qualify as legal residence for the purposes of the Directive (and so could not be counted towards the five years for permanent residence). Therefore even where the EU citizen has a residence card issued under Article 10, the host Member State may be entitled to verify that at the end of the five-year period the individual has fulfilled the underlying conditions. Nonetheless, EU principles of proportionality apply here and excessive documentation must be prohibited—for instance, were a Member State to demand weekly payslips over the total five-year period to be presented. Article 25 provides that permanent residence cards must be issued free of charge or for a charge not exceeding that imposed on nationals for the issuing of similar documents (see Chapter 5).

Article 19(2) obliges Member States to issue the document 'as soon as possible'. This too must be read in light of Articles 8 and 10(1), which require a registration certificate for an EU citizen to be issued 'immediately' and a residence card for any third-country national family members to be issued as soon as possible and in any event within six months of the request (see Chapter 3). Third-country nationals entitled to a permanent residence card must also receive their cards within six months of the submission of their application, according to Article 20(2). While there is no time limit specified in Article 19(2), 'as soon as possible' must, by analogy with these other provisions of the Directive, mean somewhere between immediately and six months.

Both Regulation 1251/70 and Directive 75/34 included provisions on administrative formalities, which were an amalgam of Articles 19 and 22–25.

---

[123] See by analogy Case 48/75 *Royer* [1976] ECR 497.
[124] Case C-123/08 *Wolzenburg* [2009] ECR I-9621, paras 50 and 51. See also the Opinion in Case C-480/08 *Teixeira* [2010] ECR I-1107, para 120.
[125] Case C-325/09 *Dias* [2011] ECR I-6387.

Article 20—Permanent residence card for family members who are not nationals of a Member State

1. Member States shall issue family members who are not nationals of a Member State entitled to permanent residence with a permanent residence card within six months of the submission of the application. The permanent residence card shall be renewable automatically every ten years.
2. The application for a permanent residence card shall be submitted before the residence card expires. Failure to comply with the requirement to apply for a permanent residence card may render the person concerned liable to proportionate and non-discriminatory sanctions.
3. Interruption in residence not exceeding two consecutive years shall not affect the validity of the permanent residence card.

This is the mirror-image provision to Article 10, which regulates the issue of residence cards for the first five-year residence period to third-country national family members. Again, the card must be issued within six months of the date of application. These residence cards are automatically renewable (if the Member State does not have a system of permanent cards). However, as the renewal is automatic the individual is not required to fulfil any of the conditions which underlay the first issue of the card.

The provision requires third-country national family members to apply for their permanent residence cards before their residence card expires. This is somewhat odd because either card merely evidences a right which the individual holds and does not confer any right (see the commentary on Articles 10 and 25, in Chapters 3 and 5). The Member State is permitted to apply proportionate and non-discriminatory sanctions, if the person concerned does not comply with the obligation. The comparator for the evaluation of discrimination must be those sanctions which apply to nationals of the State regarding their own identity cards and documents (see Chapter 3).

Paragraph 3 provides that third-country nationals who have a permanent residence permit will only place in jeopardy the validity of the permit if they do not reside in the host State for a period exceeding two consecutive years. The meaning of 'residence' here must be consistent with that in Article 7 (see Chapter 3), as well as Article 16(4), which concerns the loss of permanent rights for exactly the same reason.

Article 21—Continuity of residence

For the purposes of this Directive, continuity of residence may be attested by any means of proof in use in the host Member State. Continuity of residence is broken by any expulsion decision duly enforced against the person concerned.

The objective of the first sentence of Article 21 is to permit EU citizens and their family members to evidence the acquisition of their right of permanent residence (though this provision applies to the whole Directive) by any means of proof in use in the host State.[126] This does not mean that the host State is entitled to require only one type of evidence which it uses but rather that it cannot limit evidence to any specific kind, and must permit EU citizens and their family members to choose between any of the means of proof in use in that State. It is very common for Member States to have a variety of means to evidence residence, not simply a population register.

According to the second sentence of Article 21, the enforcement of an expulsion decision has the effect of breaking continuity of residence. For the reasons discussed above, these are the only circumstances in which continuity of residence can be considered broken.[127] Therefore, the fact that a host State has made an expulsion decision but has not enforced it does not have this consequence. This is different from the proposal originally put forward by the Commission which suggested that the status would be lost on the taking of an expulsion decision, unless the enforcement of that decision were deferred.[128]

F. Evaluation—Articles 19–21

The administrative formalities are an important part of the protections for EU citizens and their family members. In practice, it is common for Member State authorities to have backlogs of applications (usually relating to third-country national family members) and trouble complying with their time limits under the Directive. The inclusion of such provisions is thus vital for EU citizens and their family members who, in the event that the time limits are not respected by the Member State, will potentially have a claim to damages for loss caused as a result of that failure in accordance with EU law principles.[129]

---

[126] This sentence is taken from Art 4(1) of Reg 1251/70 and Directive 75/34; these provisions have not been interpreted by the CJEU.

[127] See the commentary on Art 16.

[128] COM(2001) 257.

[129] Joined Cases C-6/90 and 9/90 *Francovich and Bonifaci* [1991] ECR I-5357. See by analogy the commentary on Art 10 in Chapter 3.

5

PROVISIONS COMMON TO THE RIGHT OF RESIDENCE AND THE RIGHT OF PERMANENT RESIDENCE

A. Function

Chapter V of the citizens' Directive sets out a number of overarching principles that apply both to the right of residence and the right of permanent residence. The Articles in this chapter define the territorial scope of residence rights (Article 22) and confirm the entitlement of family members of EU citizens who move within the EU to engage in economic activity (Article 23). Further provisions elaborate on the application of the principle of equal treatment to migrant Union citizens and their family members (Article 24) and clarify the status of residence documents issued by national authorities (Article 25). This chapter also regulates the entitlement of Member States to carry out checks on non-nationals (Article 26).

Of these principles, the principle of equality, to which Article 24 gives expression, has been particularly critical in the development of the status of Union citizenship. The right of migrant Union citizens to be treated equally to nationals of a host Member State permeates a great number of the Directive's provisions and has dominated the citizenship case law of the Court of Justice. The right to equal treatment is therefore afforded particular consideration in this chapter.

B. Historical development

The overarching principles contained in Articles 22 to 26 essentially have their source in provisions contained in preceding residence Directives as well as in the case law of the Court of Justice.

A clause on territorial scope, such as that provided for in Article 22, had already featured in the first Directive on the free movement of workers adopted in 1961.[1] The 1961 Directive required residence permits to be valid throughout the territory of a Member State,[2] but permitted restrictions on the territorial scope of work permits, albeit for important reasons.[3] The entitlement of migrant Member State workers to reside throughout the entire territory of a host Member State was carried through in successive legislative measures, in particular Directive 64/240[4] and Directive 68/360.[5] It was also extended to individuals exercising the right of establishment or the provision of services by Directive 64/220.[6] While this latter Directive permitted Member States to restrict the territorial scope of residence rights in individual cases on public policy or security grounds, such an exception was not included in legislation concerning workers or re-enacted in subsequent Directives governing the right of establishment and the provision of services.[7] Indeed, in the case of *Rutili*, the Court held that any restrictions on residence on the basis of justifications set out in what is now Article 45(3) TFEU may only be imposed in respect of the whole of the national territory. The Court held that restrictions on residence within a particular part of a territory could only be permitted where they did not apply exclusively to migrant Union citizens but also to nationals of the host Member State.[8] This case law is reflected in the terms of Article 22 of the Directive. While affirming that the right of residence and permanent residence covers the whole territory of a host Member State, Article 22 expressly authorizes the imposition of territorial restrictions provided that the same restrictions also apply to nationals of the host Member State.

The right that Article 23 confers on family members of a Union citizen to engage in economic activities in the host Member State, irrespective of nationality, similarly re-enacts a right that had been granted to family members of migrant Member State national workers since the very first instruments on free movement were adopted in 1961.[9] Article 12 of Regulation 15 provided that the spouse and children of

---

[1] Council Directive of 16 August 1961 on administrative procedures and practices governing the entry into and employment and residence in a Member State of workers and their families from other Member States of the Community ([1961] OJ 80/1513, hereinafter 'the 1961 Directive').

[2] See Art 5(1) of the 1961 Directive.

[3] See Art 4(2) of the 1961 Directive.

[4] See Art 5(1)(a) of Directive 64/240 of 25 March 1964 on the abolition of restrictions on the movement and residence of Member States' workers and their families within the Community ([1964] OJ 64/981).

[5] Art 6(1)(a) of Directive 68/360/EEC on the abolition of restrictions on movement and residence within the Community for workers of Member States and their families ([1968] OJ L 257/13).

[6] Art 4 of Directive 64/220/EEC of 25 February 1964 on the abolition of restrictions on movement and residence within the Community for nationals of Member States with regard to establishment and the provision of services ([1964] OJ 64/845).

[7] Case 36/75 *Roland Rutili v Minister for the Interior* [1975] ECR 1219, para 44.

[8] Case 36/75 *Roland Rutili v Minister for the Interior* [1975] ECR 1219, para 50.

[9] Regulation 15 of 16 August 1961 on initial measures to bring about free movement of workers within the Community ([1961] OJ 57/1073, hereinafter 'Regulation 15').

migrant workers were entitled to take up employment in another Member State under the same conditions as applied to the workers they were accompanying. This entitlement was carried through in subsequent free movement legislation, namely, Regulation 38/64[10] and Regulation 1612/68[11] and was also extended to family members of self-employed Member State nationals by the latter Regulation.[12] As the right of free movement provided for in Union law became detached from the requirement to exercise an economic activity, the rights of family members became similarly decoupled from the economic status of the Union citizen they were accompanying. The right accorded to family members of Union citizens to engage in economic activities became exercisable regardless of whether a migrant Union citizen was economically active.[13] Significantly, the Directive has also expanded the category of individuals who can rely on the right provided for in Article 23,[14] as well as the material scope of the right: it now applies to access to self-employment, whereas it previously applied (for family members of workers and self-employed persons) only to access to employment.

Pursuant to Article 24, migrant Union citizens and their family members are, as a general rule,[15] entitled to be treated equally to nationals of the host Member State. Article 24 gives expression to a long-established principle of equality and non-discrimination enshrined in the founding Treaties. At the outset, Article 7 of the EEC Treaty had prohibited discrimination on grounds of nationality falling within the scope of application of that Treaty.[16] In addition, a more specific expression of the principle featured in Treaty provisions on the freedom of movement of workers.[17] Article 48(2) of the EEC Treaty specified that any discrimination on the basis of nationality between workers of Member States was prohibited as regards

---

[10] Art 18(1) of Reg 38/64/EEC.

[11] Art 11 of Reg 1612/68 of 15 October 1968 on freedom of movement for workers ([1968] OJ L 257/2).

[12] Art 11 of Reg 1612/68 refers expressly to employed and self-employed persons.

[13] Art 2(2) of each of Directives 90/364, 90/365, and 93/96 ([1990] OJ L 180/26 and 28; [1993] OJ L 317/59) provided for the Union citizen's spouse and minor or dependent children to exercise employed or self-employed activities.

[14] Previously such rights had been confined to the Union citizen's spouse and minor or dependent children. See also the 2001 Proposal, p 18.

[15] Permitted derogations are provided for in Art 24(2). They include the right to social assistance during the first three months of residence, or indeed to job-seekers who may remain for longer periods so long as they comply with the conditions specified in Art 14(4)(b). The Directive further states that prior to the acquisition of the right of permanent residence, Member States are not required to grant maintenance aid for studies, including vocational training consisting of student grants or student loans, to persons other than workers or self-employed persons, including former workers or self-employed persons, and their family members.

[16] The prohibition of discrimination on grounds of nationality was first enshrined in Art 7 EEC (which subsequently became Art 6 EC following the entry into force of the 1992 Maastricht Treaty). The provision was then renumbered by the Amsterdam Treaty as Art 12 EC. Since the entry into force of the Lisbon Treaty, the principle of non-discrimination on grounds of nationality is set out in Art 18 TFEU.

[17] Case C-94/07 *Raccanelli* [2008] ECR I-5939, para 45.

employment, remuneration, and other conditions of employment.[18] The principle of equality and non-discrimination has also long been recognized as constituting a general principle of Union law.[19]

The right of migrant Member State workers to be afforded equal treatment in a host State was incorporated into successive legislative instruments on free movement. Already, the very first regulation on workers, Regulation 15 of 1961, contained a specific chapter[20] on equal treatment, requiring that migrant Member State workers benefit from the same protection and the same treatment with respect to all conditions of employment, in particular remuneration and dismissal.[21] The right of equal treatment was also extended to membership of trade unions.[22] The Regulation further provided that any collective or individual agreement or any other collective regulation concerning employment, remuneration, and other conditions of work shall be null and void in so far as it lays down or authorizes conditions that are discriminatory against migrant Member State workers.[23] Such provisions were re-enacted and enhanced in subsequent free movement of workers' legislation including Regulation 38/64[24] and Regulation 1612/68.[25] Article 21 of Regulation 38/64 and subsequently Article 12 of Regulation 1612/68 required children of migrant or frontier workers to be treated equally as regards admission to courses of general education, apprenticeship, and vocational training.[26] Regulation 1612/68 expressly conferred on migrant Member State national workers the same social and tax advantages as national workers and the same entitlement to access training in vocational schools or retraining centres.[27]

In its case law on the free movement of workers, the Court of Justice interpreted equality rights of workers expansively. Thus, for example, when considering the entitlement of migrant workers to equal access to social advantages, the Court, after initial reluctance,[28] proceeded to hold that this entitlement must be regarded

---

[18]   Art 48(2) was subsequently renumbered Art 39(2) EC and is now Art 45(2) TFEU. On the right to equal treatment of workers, see: Case C-281/98 *Angonese* [2000] ECR I-4139, para 29; Case C-94/07 *Raccanelli* [2008] ECR I-5939, para 41; and Case C-276/07 *Delay* [2008] ECR I-3635, para 18.

[19]   See: Joined Cases 117/76 and 16/77 *Ruckdeschel* [1977] ECR 1753; Case 175/78 *La Reine v Vera Ann Saunders* [1979] ECR 1129; and Joined Cases C-92/92 and C-326/92 *Phil Collins* [1993] ECR I-5145. Similarly, the Treaty has always contained a provision on equal treatment on grounds of gender: Art 119 EEC/EC (subsequently Art 141 EC and now Art 157 TFEU) required men and women to receive equal pay for equal work.

[20]   Chapter 3 of Regulation 15.

[21]   Art 8(1) of Regulation 15.

[22]   Art 8(2) of Regulation 15.

[23]   Art 8(3) of Regulation 15.

[24]   Chapter 2, Arts 8–14 of Reg 38/64.

[25]   Title II, Arts 7–9 of Reg 1612/68. After over forty years, Reg 1612/68 was repealed and recast by Reg 492/2011 ([2011] OJ L 141/1).

[26]   On the immigration aspects of this provision, see the commentary on Art 12(2) in Chapter 3.

[27]   Art 7(2) and (3) of Reg 1612/68.

[28]   Case 76/72 *Michael S* [1973] ECR 457, para 9. In that case, the Court took a restrictive view, holding that the right of equal access to benefits provided for by Art 7 of Reg 1612/68 referred

as encompassing all advantages which were generally granted to national workers because of their objective status as workers or by virtue of the mere fact of their residence on the national territory.[29] In this context, it was immaterial whether or not these advantages are linked to an employment contract. The decisive criterion was whether the extension of such rights to migrant workers who were Member State nationals would likely facilitate their mobility within the Union. Adopting such an approach, the Court held that travel reduction cards for large families,[30] child raising allowances,[31] student finance,[32] first-time job-seeker's allowance,[33] admission of unmarried partners,[34] and unemployment benefits[35] were all qualified as social advantages within the meaning of Article 7(2) of Regulation 1612/68. Significantly, an allowance could still qualify as a 'social advantage' notwithstanding the fact that it was primarily intended to benefit a family member of a worker as opposed to the worker himself or herself.[36]

The Court has confirmed that prohibition on discrimination against migrant Member State national workers did not merely prohibit direct discrimination on grounds of nationality but also all indirect forms of discrimination which, by the application of other criteria of differentiation, lead in fact to the same result.[37] National rules that made certain rights conditional on residence requirements,[38] or on having completed secondary education in particular establishments,[39] or which refused to recognize qualifications or experience obtained in another Member State[40] have, for example, been held by the Court to be capable of giving rise to indirect discrimination.

---

exclusively to benefits aimed at the workers themselves and was required to be connected with the contract of employment. Art 7 was therefore considered to exclude benefits reserved to family members.

[29] Case 32/75 *Cristini* [1975] ECR 1085, para 13; Case C-249/83 *Hoeckx v Openbaar Centrum voor Maatschappelijk Welzijn Kalmthout* [1985] ECR 973, para 20; Case C-310/91 *Schmid v Belgian State* [1993] ECR I-3011, para 18; and Case C-57/96 *Meints* [1997] ECR I-6689, para 39.

[30] Case 32/75 *Cristini* [1975] ECR 1085.

[31] Case C-85/96 *Martínez Sala* [1998] ECR I-2691 and Case C-212/05 *Hartmann* [2007] ECR I-6303.

[32] Case 39/86 *Lair* [1988] ECR 3161; Case C-3/90 *Bernini* [1992] ECR I-1071; C-337/97 *Meeusen* [1999] ECR I-3289; Case C-413/01 *Ninni-Orasche* [2003] ECR I-13187; and Case C-542/09 *Commission v Netherlands*, judgment of 14 June 2012, not yet reported, para 35.

[33] Case C-224/98 *D'Hoop* [2002] ECR I-6191, para 17.

[34] Case 59/85 *Reed* [1986] ECR 1283.

[35] Case 94/84 *Deak* [1985] ECR 1873 and Case C-57/96 *Meints* [1997] ECR I-6689.

[36] Case 94/84 *Deak* [1985] ECR 1873, paras 22 to 24, and Case C-3/90 *Bernini* [1992] ECR I-1071, paras 25 and 26.

[37] Case 152/73 *Sotgiu* [1974] ECR 153, para 1; Case C-57/96 *Meints* [1997] ECR I-6689, paras 44–46; Case C-209/03 *Bidar* [2005] ECR I-2119, para 51; C-212/05 *Hartmann* [2007] ECR I-6303, paras 28–30; Case C-269/07 *Commission v Germany* [2009] ECR I-7811, para 53; and Case C-542/09 *Commission v Netherlands*, judgment of 14 June 2012, not yet reported, para 37.

[38] See, for example, Cases C-57/96 *Meints* [1997] ECR I-6689 and C-212/05 *Hartmann* [2007] ECR I-6303.

[39] Case C-278/94 *Commission v Belgium* [1996] ECR I-4307.

[40] Case C-419/92 *Scholz* [1994] ECR I-505; Case C-340/89 *Vlassopoulou* [1991] ECR I-2357, para 15; and Case C-104/91 *Colegio Nacional de Agentes de la Propiedad Inmobiliaria* [1992] ECR I-3003, para 10.

Following the introduction of Union citizenship by the 1992 Maastricht Treaty, there was some uncertainty as to whether migrant Union citizens, who were economically inactive, could be considered to fall within the personal scope of the Treaty and thereby rely upon the right to equal treatment conferred by Union law. An early opportunity for clarification arose in the case of *Martínez Sala*.[41] Here, the applicant was an economically inactive Union citizen resident in Germany whose request for a child raising allowance was rejected on the ground that she failed to furnish a specific type of residence document, even though an equivalent document was not required from German nationals. The question arose as to whether the applicant could rely on the right to non-discrimination enshrined in the Treaty. Although accepting that the legislation was discriminatory, the German government argued that as a consequence of her economically inactive status, Ms Martínez Sala did not fall within the scope of application of the Treaty and therefore could not rely upon its provisions.

The Court, however, disagreed. In its judgment, the Court noted that the applicant was a Union citizen lawfully resident in another Member State. It considered that this factual circumstance was sufficient to bring Ms Martínez Sala within the scope of the Treaty such that she could rely upon its provisions, and in particular, the right to equal treatment and non-discrimination enshrined in what is now Article 18 TFEU.[42] In its subsequent case law, the Court continued to connect citizenship of the Union with the right to equal treatment and non-discrimination. Once Union citizens exercised free movement rights, they were to be regarded as falling within the scope of Union law and were entitled to rely on the rights enshrined in the Union Treaties.[43] The Court has proceeded to apply the right of migrant Union citizens and their families to equal treatment in a variety of contexts, for example, in the context of provisions regulating eligibility for tax advantages,[44] the choice of a language in which a criminal trial is to be held,[45] the taking and processing of data of Union citizens entering or residing in a host Member State,[46] the naming of a child,[47] the right to stand and vote for European Parliament elections,[48] the right of access to higher education,[49] and the right to discounted travel fares for students.[50]

---

[41] Case C-85/96 *Martínez Sala* [1998] ECR I-2691.

[42] The prohibition of discrimination on grounds of nationality was first enshrined in Art 7 EEC (which subsequently became Art 6 EC following the entry into force of the 1992 Maastricht Treaty). The provision was then renumbered by the Amsterdam Treaty and appeared under Art 12 EC.

[43] See, for example, Case C-274/96 *Bickel and Franz* [1998] ECR I-7637; Case C-184/99 *Grzelczyk* [2001] ECR I-6193; Case C-224/98 *D'Hoop* [2002] ECR I-6191; Case C-76/05 *Schwarz and Gootjes-Schwarz* [2007] ECR I-6849; Case C-524/06 *Heinz Huber* [2008] ECR I-9705; Case C-56/09 *Zanotti* [2010] ECR I-4517.

[44] Case C-56/09 *Zanotti* [2010] ECR I-4517.

[45] Case C-274/96 *Bickel and Franz* [1998] ECR I-7637.

[46] Case C-524/06 *Heinz Huber* [2008] ECR I-9705.

[47] Case C-353/06 *Grunkin and Paul* [2008] ECR I-7639.

[48] Case C-300/04 *Eman and Sevinger* [2006] ECR I-8055, paras 57–61.

[49] Case C-73/08 *Bressol and Others* [2010] ECR I-2735.

[50] Case C-75/11 *Commission v Austria*, judgment of 4 October 2012, not yet reported.

Even if the principle of equal treatment has been applied extensively to migrant Union citizens, its application has been circumscribed with respect to the entitlement of economically inactive Union citizens and their family members to access social benefits. The residence Directives of the early 1990s, which conferred residence rights on various categories of economically inactive Union citizen, made such rights conditional on beneficiaries possessing sufficient resources and health insurance cover.[51] Moreover, the students' Directive contained specific measures restricting the right of students' access to maintenance grants.[52] Nevertheless, in spite of such restrictions, in a number of instances, Union citizens and their family members proceeded to challenge decisions of national authorities excluding them from a particular social benefit. In numerous references before the Court of Justice, nationals of the Member States sought to rely on their Union citizenship status to claim a right of equal access to social assistance.[53]

In resolving such cases, the Court of Justice was confronted with the delicate task of striking a balance between facilitating the exercise of free movement rights with preserving the effective functioning of Member States' social security systems. An overly expansive interpretation of social welfare entitlements in favour of economically inactive, and therefore non-economically contributing, migrant Union citizens and their family members, risked overextending Member States' social welfare systems. However, it was equally apparent that a blanket prohibition on accessing social assistance or the automatic application of expulsion measures in the event of a request for assistance would be liable to force the departure of migrant Union citizens who had settled and made their home in another Member State.

The Court essentially adopted a compromise position. It recognized that Union law allows for a certain degree of financial solidarity amongst migrant Union citizens and the nationals of a host Member State insofar as such citizens do not become an unreasonable burden on the public finances on the Member State concerned.[54] In assessing the rights of migrant Union citizens, Member States are required to have regard to the circumstances of each case with due respect for the principle of proportionality.[55] More particularly, in each instance, Member States are to assess the degree of integration that a particular Union citizen or his or her family

---

[51] See Art 1(1) of Directive 90/364, Art 1(1) of Directive 90/365, and Art 1 of Directive 93/96.

[52] Art 3 of Directive 93/96.

[53] See, for example: Case C-184/99 *Grzelczyk* [2001] ECR I-6193; Case C-209/03 *Bidar* [2005] ECR I-2119; Case C-138/02 *Collins* [2004] ECR I-2703; Case C-158/07 *Förster* [2008] ECR I-8507; and Case C-103/08 *Gottwald* [2009] ECR I-9117.

[54] Case C-184/99 *Grzelczyk* [2001] ECR I-6193.

[55] See for example Case C-184/99 *Grzelczyk* [2001] ECR I-6193 and Case C-209/03 *Bidar* [2005] ECR I-2119. Regarding the requirement for proportionality see, in particular: Case C-413/99 *Baumbast and R* [2002] ECR I-7091, para 91; Case C-200/02 *Zhu and Chen* [2004] ECR I-9925, para 32; Case C-408/03 *Commission v Belgium* [2006] ECR I-2647, para 39; and Case C-398/06 *Commission v Netherlands* [2008] ECR I-56.

members have attained,[56] and in particular whether they have developed genuine or real links[57] with their host State. For the purposes of assessing an individual's links with their host Member State, national authorities may have regard to a number of different factors, such as, whether the individual concerned has spent time living,[58] being educated,[59] working,[60] or seeking work[61] in that State or indeed whether he or she is a national of the Member State.[62] The length of time spent in another Member State may also be indicative of the degree to which a Union citizen has developed ties with that State.[63] In the case of *Förster*, the Court upheld national legislation which made access to social assistance subject to a period of five years' residence in a host Member State.[64] While Member States may introduce restrictions on access to social benefits, the eligibility conditions for a particular benefit must be sufficiently nuanced to be able to take into account the extent of a Union citizen's ties with his or her Member State of residence with due regard to the specific nature and purpose of that benefit.[65]

Thus while, as a general rule, migrant Union citizens could rely on the right to equal treatment, regardless of economic activity, Union law recognized a differentiation and limitation on that right in the specific context of accessing social benefits.

---

[56] Case C-209/03 *Bidar* [2005] ECR I-2119 paras 56–59; Case C-158/07 *Förster* [2008] ECR I-8507, paras 49–50; and Case C-103/08 *Gottwald* [2009] ECR I-9117, para 35.

[57] Case C-224/98 *D'Hoop* [2002] ECR I-6191, para 38, Case C-138/02 *Collins* [2004] ECR I-2703, para 67; Case C-258/04 *Ioannidis* [2005] ECR I-8275, para 30; Case C-499/06 *Nerkowska* [2008] ECR I-3993, paras 39–43; and Joined Cases C-22/08 and C-23/08 *Vatsouras and Koupatantze* [2009] ECR I-4585, para 38.

[58] In Case C-499/06 *Nerkowska* [2008] ECR I-3993, the Court found the applicant for a benefit granted by the Polish authorities had sufficient links with that Member State. The Court noted she was a Polish national and had lived for over twenty years in Poland, during which time she had studied and worked there.

[59] In Joined Cases C-11/06 and C-12/06 *Morgan and Bucher* [2007] ECR I-9161, at para 45 the Court noted that the applicants in the main proceedings, who were German nationals, were raised and completed their schooling in Germany and that they therefore satisfied the sufficient link requirement.

[60] Case C-499/06 *Nerkowska* [2008] ECR I-3993.

[61] Case C-138/02 *Collins* [2004] ECR I-2703, paras 69 and 70.

[62] In Case C-224/98 *D'Hoop* [2002] ECR I-6191, the applicant in the main proceedings was a national of the State in which she sought the benefit, who had resided for a period in another Member State. See generally the discussion of 'returnees' in the commentary on Art 3(1) in Chapter 1.

[63] Case C-209/03 *Bidar* [2005] ECR I-2119, para 59; Case C-158/07 *Förster* [2008] ECR I-8507, para 50; and Case C-103/08 *Gottwald* [2009] ECR I-9117, para 35.

[64] Case C-158/07 *Förster* [2008] ECR I-8507. In this context, the Court had specific regard to the fact that in adopting the citizens' Directive, which had not yet entered into force, the Union legislature had considered it appropriate to make the right to permanent residence status conditional on five years' residence in the territory of the host Member State.

[65] In relation to job-seekers' allowance, for example, claimants may be required to demonstrate a link with the employment market of the Member State in which they are seeking work. See: Case C-224/98 *D'Hoop* [2002] ECR I-6191, para 38; Case C-138/02 *Collins* [2004] ECR I-2703, para 69; and Case C-258/04 *Ioannidis* [2005] ECR I-8275, para 30. If a particular benefit falls within the competence of Member States, then the Court has accepted that Member States are conferred with a wider margin of appreciation in determining the nature and extent of connection that a claimant may be required to demonstrate: Case C-103/08 *Gottwald* [2009] ECR I-9117, para 34.

Workers who were economically contributing were entitled to equal treatment as a matter of course because their participation in the employment market of a Member State is regarded as implying, in principle, a sufficient link of integration with the society of the host Member State.[66] However, for economically inactive citizens, such a right was not automatic and required an individual assessment of the ties that a Union citizen possessed with his or her Member State.

This case law was largely incorporated into the provisions and even the scheme underpinning the citizens' Directive, namely, in the distinction between a right of residence and the right of permanent residence.[67] The Union legislature considered that prior to fulfilling five years of residence in a host State, migrants may be required to be self-supporting and have their right to social benefits curtailed. However, the status of permanent residence provides systematic recognition that individuals who have lived in excess of five years have by that time developed sufficient links with a host Member State and are to be accorded the same right of access to benefits as nationals of the host Member State. Crucially, the fact that a Union citizen or family members of a Union citizen have not yet obtained permanent residence does not, however, mean that they may be excluded a priori from access to benefits. The Court has made it clear that in each case it remains necessary to examine the individual circumstances of the applicant and the nature of his or her links with the host Member State in the light of the specific characteristics of the benefit at issue.[68]

Article 25 prohibits national authorities from making the exercise of a right or the completion of an administrative formality conditional on the possession of residence documentation issued by national authorities. Although this is a new clarifying provision,[69] it serves to give effect to the well-established case law of the Court, dating from 1976, according to which national residence documents do not

---

[66] See Case C-542/09 *Commission v Netherlands*, judgment of 14 June 2012, not yet reported, para 65, although on occasion, the Court has not always respected the boundaries between its case law on workers and case law on citizenship and applied the 'real link' test to workers: Case C-213/05 *Geven* [2008] ECR I-6347, paras 28–30 and again in Case C-20/12 *Giersch and others*, judgment of 20 June 2013. In *Geven*, the Court found that the limited hours performed by a frontier worker did not provide evidence of sufficient connection to enable her to qualify for a family benefit. For detailed comment on this case, see S O'Leary, 'Developing an Ever Closer Union between the People's of Europe? A reappraisal of the case-law of the Court of Justice on the free movement of persons and EU citizenship' (2008) 27 YEL 167–194.

[67] However, there are possible points of tension between the wording of Art 24 and the case law on equal treatment for EU citizens according to the prior legislation and the Treaties. See N Nic Shiubhne, 'Derogating from the Free Movement of Persons: When can EU citizens be Deported?' (2005–06) 8 CYELS 187 at 223–226, and E Fahey, 'Interpretive Legitimacy and the Distinction Between "Social Assistance" and "Work-Seekers' Allowance": Comment on *Vatsouras*' (2009) 34 ELRev 933.

[68] Case C-503/09 *Lucy Stewart v Secretary of State for Work and Pensions* [2011] ECR I-6497 and Case C-75/11 *Commission v Austria*, judgment of 4 October 2012, not yet reported. This point is considered in greater detail below in Section E of this chapter relating to Art 24.

[69] See the 2001 Proposal, p 19.

create rights of movement or residence; they merely serve to attest existing rights conferred directly on Union citizens by the Treaties and secondary legislation adopted to give them effect.[70] It follows that the possession of such documents cannot be made a precondition for the acquisition or enjoyment of substantive rights provided for in Union law. Article 25(2) further requires that residence documentation must be issued free of charge or for a charge not exceeding that imposed on nationals for the issuing of comparable documentation.[71]

Article 26 affirms the entitlement of Member States to verify compliance by non-nationals with requirements in domestic law to carry a registration certificate or residence card. Significantly, it stipulates that such checks are permissible only insofar as equivalent requirements apply to nationals of the Member State as regards their identity card. This extension of the principle of equal treatment to the obligation to carry residence or identity documentation gives effect to the judgment of the Court of Justice in *Commission v Belgium*.[72] Pursuant to the second sentence of Article 26, sanctions that may be imposed for failure to comply with the requirement to carry residence documentation must be the same as those imposed on nationals of the host Member State for failure to carry their identity card. In its 2001 proposal, the Commission observed that this requirement was introduced to give effect to the judgments of the Court in *Messner*[73] and in *Commission v Germany*.[74]

C. Interrelationship of Articles 22–26

As the title to chapter V of the Directive indicates, the provisions contained in Articles 22 to 26 contain overarching principles that are common to both the right of residence and the right of permanent residence. Such principles supplement and in certain cases inform the interpretation and application of administrative procedures governing the exercise of rights provided for in Articles 6 to 15 (rights of residence; see Chapter 3) and Articles 16 to 21 (right of permanent residence; see Chapter 4).

The principle of equal treatment as expressed in Article 24 finds specific expression in a number of different provisions of the Directive.[75] In particular, the Directive repeatedly stipulates that any sanctions imposed on Union citizens and their

---

[70] Case 48/75 *Royer* [1976] ECR 497, paras 31–33; Case C-357/89 *Raulin* [1992] ECR I-1027, paras 36 and 42; Case C-459/99 *MRAX* [2002] ECR I-6591, para 74; and Case C-215/03 *Oulane* [2005] ECR I-1215, paras 17 and 18.

[71] This rule appeared in the prior legislation: see Art 9(1) of Directive 68/360.

[72] Case 321/87 *Commission v Belgium* [1989] ECR 997, para 12.

[73] Case C-265/88 *Messner* [1989] ECR 4209.

[74] Case C-24/97 *Commission v Germany* [1998] ECR I-2133.

[75] See, for example, Arts 5(5), 8(2), 8(4), 9(3), 20(2), 22, 25(2), and 26.

families for breaches of national law regulating the exercise of free movement rights must not be discriminatory and must be the same as sanctions that may be imposed on nationals of the host Member State for comparable breaches.[76] The principle of equal treatment also forms part of other provisions appearing under chapter V, such as Article 22 concerning the extent to which geographical restrictions may be imposed, Article 25(2), concerning the fees that may be charged for issuing national residence documentation, and Article 26 concerning the entitlement of Member States to carry out identity checks on migrant Union citizens and their family members.

The clarification laid down in Article 25 concerning the function and status of national residence documentation is of critical importance in the context of accessing rights provided throughout the Directive. As possession of national residence documents cannot be a precondition for the enjoyment of a substantive right or the completion of a formality, it follows that any delays or errors in the issuing of residence cards or residence certificates cannot prevent or adversely affect the exercise of rights of residence (Article 7), the acquisition of permanent residence status (Article 16), or the right of third-country national family members to engage in economic activities (Article 23), once the substantive conditions laid down by the Directive are satisfied.

D. Other relevant norms

Insofar as Articles 22 to 26 concern the conditions governing the exercise of the right of freedom of movement, they give effect to rights enshrined in Articles 20(2)(a) and 21 TFEU. Moreover, Article 24 and also the formulation of Articles 22, 25(2), and 26 reflect and give specific expression to the principle of equality and non-discrimination enshrined in Article 18 TFEU.[77]

In parallel to the general right to equal treatment provided for in Article 24, Union citizens who are workers, and their family members, benefit from more specific and extensive equality rights provided for in Regulation 492/2011 on the freedom of movement for workers.[78] The right of migrant Union citizen workers to equal treatment covers conditions of employment including remuneration, dismissal, and in the event of unemployment, reinstatement or re-employment.[79] In

---

[76] See, for example, Arts 5(5), 8(2), 9(3), 20(2), and 26.

[77] Case C-75/11 *Commission v Austria*, judgment of 4 October 2012, not yet reported.

[78] [2011] OJ L 141/1. For consideration of potentially overlapping and parallel rights, see Case C-46/12 *LN*, judgment of 21 February 2013. Here the Court held that the fact that Union citizens may initially have entered as students does not preclude them from taking up employment subsequently and acquiring 'worker' status. The Commission has proposed to supplement this Reg with a Directive which would ensure its effective enforcement (COM(2013) 236, 23 April 2013).

[79] Art 7(1) of Reg 492/2011.

addition, it entitles workers to the same tax and social advantages as enjoyed by national workers[80]—a right which does not automatically apply to economically inactive Union citizens who have not yet acquired permanent residence status. Migrant Union citizen workers are also granted the same right as national workers to access to training in vocational schools and retraining centres.[81] Article 7(4) of Regulation 492/2011 clarifies that any clause of a collective or individual agreement or of any other collective regulation concerning the eligibility for employment, remuneration, and other conditions of work or dismissal shall be null and void insofar as it lays down or authorizes conditions that are discriminatory in favour of workers who are nationals of the host Member State. Also, Article 10 of Regulation 492/2011 requires equal treatment as regards study finance for migrant workers' children.[82]

Aside from the right of equal access to social and tax advantages conferred by Article 7(2) of Regulation 492/2011, economically active migrant Union citizens may also be entitled to benefits on the basis of Regulation 883/2004 coordinating the application of social security schemes as between Member States.[83] Regulation 883/2004 sets out the criteria determining the social security system applicable to migrant workers or self-employed persons. In general, the application of the conflict rules provided for in the Regulation entitles a migrant worker or self-employed person to social security benefits administered by the Member State in which they are economically active. Pursuant to its Article 4, unless otherwise provided for in the Regulation, the persons to whom the Regulation applies shall enjoy the same benefits and be subject to the same obligations under the legislation of any Member State as the nationals of that Member State.

It will be apparent from the norms cited above that migrant Union citizens may be subject to different sets of rules from a variety of different legislative sources on the basis of their status as citizens on the one hand, or as workers and self-employed persons on the other.[84] It is not uncommon for the scope of legislative measures to overlap and for rights to intertwine as a particular benefit may fall within the scope of more than one piece of legislation. Thus, for example, it is well established in the case law of the Court that the fact that a benefit constitutes an allowance falling within the scope of Regulation 883/2004 coordinating social security systems does not preclude it from also being a 'social advantage' within the meaning of Regulation 492/2011;[85] nor does it prevent the benefit from being subject to

---

[80] Art 7(2) of Reg 492/2011.

[81] Art 7(3) of Reg 492/2011.

[82] Case law starting with Case 9/74 *Casagrande* [1974] ECR 773.

[83] [2004] OJ L 166/1. Reg 883/2004 repealed and recast Reg 1408/71, as amended and updated by Reg 118/97 ([1997] OJ L 28/1).

[84] See Case C-503/09 *Lucy Stewart v Secretary of State for Work and Pensions* [2011] ECR I-6497, paras 75–78. See also Case C-75/11 *Commission v Austria*, judgment of 4 October 2012, not yet reported and Case C-46/12 *LN*, judgment of 21 February 2013.

[85] Case C-75/11 *Commission v Austria*, judgment of 4 October 2012, not yet reported.

scrutiny from the perspective of the right to equal treatment pursuant to Article 24 of the citizens' Directive.[86] The same factual situation may thus be approached from a variety of different legal perspectives, each governed by distinct legislative measures which fall to be considered independently in accordance with their particular objectives and their field of application.

E. Analysis

Article 22—Territorial scope

The right of residence and the right of permanent residence shall cover the whole territory of the host Member State. Member States may impose territorial restrictions on the right of residence and the right of permanent residence only where the same restrictions apply to their own nationals.

Pursuant to Article 22, the right of residence and the right of permanent residence conferred by the Directive extends to the whole territory of a host Member State. As such it is consistent with the terms of preceding residence Directives,[87] and corresponds to the scope of free movement rights provided for in the Union Treaties.[88]

In its case law, the Court initially imposed a requirement for symmetry as regards the territorial scope of the right of residence and the scope of any restriction of such right. In particular, in the case of *Rutili*, the Court held that since the right of free movement provided for in (what is now) Article 45(1) TFEU covers the whole territory of a host Member State, any restrictions on that right of movement, where justified on public policy, public security, or public health grounds in accordance with what is now Article 45(3) TFEU, must equally apply to the whole territory of a Member State.[89] Having regard to the principle of equality and non-discrimination, the Court considered that measures in secondary legislation restricting residence in certain parts of a national territory will only be permitted if the same measures apply both to migrant Member State nationals and nationals of the host Member State. The second sentence of Article 22 gives effect to this case law. Nevertheless, it should be noted that the Court qualified this case law in the judgment in *Olazabal*, delivered while the Directive was being negotiated.[90] In this judgment, the Court stated that notwithstanding its prior *Rutili* ruling, the right

---

[86] Case C-503/09 *Lucy Stewart v Secretary of State for Work and Pensions* [2011] ECR I-6497 and Case C-75/11 *Commission v Austria*, judgment of 4 October 2012, not yet reported.

[87] For the historical background to Art 22, see Section B of this chapter.

[88] Case 36/75 *Roland Rutili v Minister for the Interior* [1975] ECR 1219, para 46. The Court observed, 'Right of entry into the territory of Member States and the right to stay there and to move freely within it is defined in the Treaty by reference to the whole territory of these States and not by reference to its internal subdivisions.'

[89] Case 36/75 *Roland Rutili v Minister for the Interior* [1975] ECR 1219. For detailed consideration of the power to restrict rights of free movement, see the commentary on Art 27 in Chapter 6.

[90] Case C-100/01 *Olazabal* [2002] ECR I-10981.

of residence of a citizen of another Member State could be limited to only part of the national territory, provided that: 'such action is justified by reasons of public order or public security based on his individual conduct'; 'by reason of their seriousness, those reasons could otherwise give rise only to a measure prohibiting him from residing in, or banishing him from, the whole of the national territory'; and 'that the conduct which the Member State concerned wishes to prevent gives rise, in the case of its own nationals, to punitive measures or other genuine and effective measures designed to combat it'.[91]

The Court has, moreover, clarified that even if territorial restrictions apply equally to migrant Union citizens and nationals of the host Member State, they may still be precluded if they restrict the right of free movement and are not considered justified by an objective in the public interest or proportionate. In joined cases *Libert and others* and *All projects & Developments NV and others*,[92] the Court was asked to consider the compatibility of national measures which made the right to transfer buildings and land situated in particular communes conditional on the existence of a 'sufficient connection' between the individuals concerned and the commune in which they resided. The Court observed that such measures served to deter Union citizens who own or rent a property in the relevant communes from exercising free movement rights because their departure may deprive them of the right to acquire property should they wish to return in the future.[93] The Court considered that the rule constituted restrictions on fundamental free movement rights as well as on the territorial scope of the Directive pursuant to Article 22 and the right to equal treatment enshrined in Article 24.[94] Nevertheless, the Court acknowledged that the measure could still be permitted if it was justified and respected the principle of proportionality.[95]

In support of the legislation at issue, it was submitted that the 'sufficient connection' requirement was justified by the objective of facilitating the access of lower income groups and disadvantaged members of society to property in the target communes. While the Court accepted that requirements relating to social housing policy were capable of constituting overriding reasons in the public interest, it considered that the national law in question was neither necessary nor appropriate for the objective stated. In particular, the Court observed that none of the conditions establishing the connection directly reflected the socio-economic aspects relating to the objective advanced. The Court noted that the national measure as formulated could benefit (or restrict) individuals regardless of the level of their income. In addition, the Court noted that other less restrictive measures would have been

---

[91] Case C-100/01 *Olazabal* [2002] ECR I-10981, para 45.
[92] Joined Cases C-197/11 and C-203/11, judgment of 8 May 2013.
[93] Joined Cases C-197/11 and C-203/11, judgment of 8 May 2013, para 40.
[94] Joined Cases C-197/11 and C-203/11, judgment of 8 May 2013, para 41.
[95] Joined Cases C-197/11 and C-203/11, judgment of 8 May 2013, para 49.

possible, for example, the granting of subsidies specifically designed to assist less affluent persons. The Court considered that the legislation did not justify a derogation from fundamental freedoms and breached numerous provisions providing for freedom of movement as well as Article 22 of the Directive.

Article 23—Related rights

Irrespective of nationality, the family members of a Union citizen who have the right of residence or the right of permanent residence in a Member State shall be entitled to take up employment or self-employment there.

Article 23 provides for the right of family members of a Union citizen to pursue economic activities in the host Member State, irrespective of nationality. As noted above, the Directive expanded the personal scope of the right provided for in Article 23 beyond the spouses of Union citizens or their minor or dependent children,[96] to apply to all family members. Arguably, this includes not only the family members defined in Article 2(2), but also the extended family members referred to in Article 3(2).[97] As also noted above, the material scope of the right extends now to self-employed activities. The right applies to any field of employment and entails equal treatment for family members as regards recognition of qualifications,[98] but only applies to the Member State where the EU citizen is residing, not to any other Member State.[99] Member States may not oblige the persons concerned to obtain work permits.[100] Significantly, Article 23 is triggered by citizens' exercise of free movement rights and applies irrespective of whether or not the Union citizen is economically active in the host Member State.[101]

Article 24—Equal treatment

1. Subject to such specific provisions as are expressly provided for in the Treaty and secondary law, all Union citizens residing on the basis of this Directive in the territory of the host Member State shall enjoy equal treatment with the nationals of that Member State within the scope of the Treaty. The benefit of this right shall be extended to family members who are not nationals of a Member State and who have the right of residence or permanent residence.
2. By way of derogation from paragraph 1, the host Member State shall not be obliged to confer entitlement to social assistance during the first three months of

---

[96] As regards EU citizens who were not carrying out economic activities, only the citizen's spouse and dependent children had this right (ie minor children who were *not* dependent did not have it).

[97] On the latter issue, see the commentary on Art 3(2), in Chapter 1. See also the 2001 Proposal, p 18. In any event, even if the right is limited to the family members defined in Art 2(2), it now includes registered partners, who were not within the scope of the previous legislation expressly.

[98] Case 131/85 *Gul* [1986] ECR 1573.

[99] Case C-10/05 *Mattern and Cikotic* [2006] ECR I-3145.

[100] Case C-165/05 *Commission v Luxembourg*, judgment of 27 October 2005, unreported.

[101] For discussion concerning the extent to which third-country nationals may invoke a right to work in order to assist the Union citizen in proving he or she has sufficient resources to retain a right of residence, see the commentary on Art 7(1) in Chapter 3. See also the commentary on Arts 7(3), 12(2), and 12(3).

residence or, where appropriate, the longer period provided for in Article 14(4)(b), nor shall it be obliged, prior to acquisition of the right of permanent residence, to grant maintenance aid for studies, including vocational training, consisting in student grants or student loans to persons other than workers, self-employed persons, persons who retain such status and members of their families.

Pursuant to Article 24, Union citizens and their third-country national family members, residing in another Member State in accordance with the Directive, have the right to be treated equally to nationals of the State concerned.

Article 24 reflects the well-established case law of the Court of Justice, according to which Union citizenship, destined to be the fundamental status of Member State nationals, confers on all such nationals, who find themselves in situations falling within the material scope of the Treaty, the right to equal treatment subject to such exceptions as are provided for in that regard.[102] The Court has held that situations falling within the material scope of the Treaty include the exercise of fundamental freedoms such as the freedom to move and reside conferred directly by the Treaties.[103] Article 24(1) has been recognized as giving specific expression to the principle of non-discrimination on grounds of nationality enshrined in Article 18 TFEU.[104] It should also be recalled that as discussed in Section D of this chapter, Article 24 overlaps in particular with the right to equal treatment for migrant workers set out in Regulation 492/2011.

While cases of direct discrimination on grounds of nationality do arise,[105] the Court has more often been required to examine situations in which indirect discrimination is alleged. Indirect discrimination occurs when national legislation of a Member State, though framed in neutral terms, nevertheless disadvantages or is likely to disadvantage non-nationals to a greater extent than it does nationals. The Court has consistently held that Union law not only prohibits overt discrimination on grounds of nationality, but all covert forms of discrimination which, by applying other distinguishing criteria, leads in fact to the same result.[106] National rules

---

[102] Case C-103/08 *Gottwald* [2009] ECR I-9117, para 23; Case C-544/07 *Rüffler* [2009] ECR I-3389, para 62; Case C-503/09 *Lucy Stewart v Secretary of State for Work and Pensions* [2011] ECR I-6497, para 80, and Case C-46/12 *LN*, judgment of 21 February 2013, para 27. On the interpretation of Art 24 in light of the prior case law, see M Dougan and E Spaventa, ' "Wish you weren't here"...New Models of Social Solidarity in the European Union', in M Dougan and E Spaventa, eds, *Social Welfare and EU Law* (Hart, 2005), 181 at 212–216.

[103] Case C-103/08 *Gottwald* [2009] ECR I-9117, para 25 and Case C-46/12 *LN*, judgment of 21 February 2013, para 28.

[104] Case C-75/11 *Commission v Austria*, judgment of 4 October 2012, not yet reported, para 44 and Case C-46/12 *LN*, judgment of 21 February 2013, not yet reported, para 28. See also Case C-73/08 *Bressol and Others* [2010] ECR I-2735, paras 33 and 34.

[105] For example, Case C-118/92 *Commission v Luxembourg* [1994] ECR I-1891 and Case C-465/01 *Commission v Austria* [2004] ECR I-8291, where national rules precluded anyone other than the host Member State's nationals from standing for election to certain employees' representative bodies.

[106] Case C-73/08 *Bressol and Others* [2010] ECR I-2735, para 40; Case C-103/08 *Gottwald* [2009] ECR I-9117, para 27; and Case C-75/11 *Commission v Austria*, judgment of 4 October 2012, not yet

that have been considered to be indirectly discriminatory include provisions that make the enjoyment of rights subject to a residence requirement,[107] or subject to conditions which necessarily imply residence, in the host Member State. Thus, for example, in the case of *Commission v Austria*,[108] the Court considered that national rules limiting reduced travel fares to students whose families were in receipt of Austrian family allowances, and therefore resident in that Member State, may be regarded as indirectly discriminatory. The Court reasoned that Austrian students were much more likely to be in a position to benefit from the travel discount, as they were also more likely to have families in receipt of that allowance than students who left their Member States of origin to pursue studies in Austria.[109] However, indirectly discriminatory measures will not necessarily be prohibited if they are accepted as being justified by objective considerations independent of nationality and are proportionate to the legitimate objective pursued.[110]

The means by which Member States may justify indirectly discriminatory measures was considered extensively by the Court in the case of *Bressol and others*.[111] This case concerned the compatibility of national rules which favoured access of individuals whose primary residence was in Belgium to third-level medical or paramedical courses. The Court considered the national rules to be indirectly discriminatory because they were more easily satisfied by Belgian nationals who more often than not resided in Belgium, compared with nationals of other Member States who typically resided in a Member State other than Belgium.[112] However, the question arose as to whether the restriction could be considered as objectively justified and proportionate.

In its observations, the Belgian government advanced numerous justifications for the restriction imposed, including the objective of avoiding excessive burdens on the financing of higher education and the protection of the homogeneity of the higher education system. It was further submitted that the measure was necessary

---

reported, para 49. For case law concerning the prior legislation, see Case 152/73 *Sotgiu* [1974] ECR 153, para 1; Case C-57/96 *Meints* [1997] ECR I-6689, paras 44–46; Case C-209/03 *Bidar* [2005] ECR I-2119, para 51; and Case C-212/05 *Hartmann* [2007] ECR I-6303, paras 28–30.

[107] Case C-212/05 *Hartmann* [2007] ECR I-6303; Case C-499/06 *Nerkowska* [2008] ECR I-3993; Case C-192/05 *Tas-Hagen and Tas* [2006] ECR I-10451; Case C-221/07 *Krystyna Zablocka-Weyhermüller* [2008] ECR I-9029; and Case C-73/08 *Bressol and Others* [2010] ECR I-2735.

[108] Case C-75/11, judgment of 4 October 2012, not yet reported.

[109] Case C-75/11 *Commission v Austria*, judgment of 4 October 2012, not yet reported. See also Case C-544/07 *Rüffler* [2009] ECR I-3389.

[110] See Case C-73/08 *Bressol and Others* [2010] ECR I-2735, para 48 and Case C-103/08 *Gottwald* [2009] ECR I-9117. See also: Case C-499/06 *Nerkowska* [2008] ECR I-3993; Case C-192/05 *Tas-Hagen and Tas* [2006] ECR I-10451, para 33; C-221/07 *Krystyna Zablocka-Weyhermüller* [2008] ECR I-9029, para 37; Case C-544/07 *Rüffler* [2009] ECR I-3389, para 74; and C-503/09 *Lucy Stewart v Secretary of State for Work and Pensions* [2011] ECR I-6497, para 87.

[111] Case C-73/08 *Bressol and Others* [2010] ECR I-2735.

[112] Case C-73/08 *Bressol and Others* [2010] ECR I-2735, para 45.

to ensure the quality and continuing provision of medical and paramedical care within the French Community in Belgium and to prevent a shortage of qualified medical personnel.[113] Although considering that the financial burden claim had not been substantiated,[114] the Court did not exclude the possibility that public health considerations could conceivably justify the adoption of the restrictive measures at issue.[115] The Court further considered that, having regard to their substance, justifications advanced concerning the maintenance of homogeneity of the education system were more appropriately considered from a public health perspective.[116]

The Court recalled that to be justified, a measure such as that at issue in the main proceedings must be appropriate for securing the attainment of the legitimate objective it pursues and must not go beyond what is necessary to ensure that objective is attained.[117] In particular, the Court held that the competent authorities must be able to demonstrate the existence of a genuine risk to the protection of public health and that the restrictive measure would constitute an appropriate means of countering the risk identified.[118] In the present case, the risk of a shortage of qualified graduates servicing a particular territory fell to be substantiated by means of an assessment of the health service, both in its present state and as it was likely to develop in the future.[119] The Court cautioned, however, that in calculating future risk, a causal connection between the measures adopted and the development of the health service is less easily established when they concern future healthcare professionals as opposed to professionals already active on the market.[120] In the Court's view, as a matter of principle, Member States must be entitled to take precautionary protective measures without having to wait for anticipated risks to materialize.[121] Nevertheless, ultimately it was for the authorities to justify restrictions. Justifications were to be accompanied by an analysis of the appropriateness and proportionality of the measure adopted by that State and by specific evidence substantiating its arguments. The Court concluded that an objective detailed analysis, supported by figures, must be capable of demonstrating with solid and consistent data that there are genuine risks to public health.[122]

In practice, as the Court itself has implicitly acknowledged,[123] there will be limits on the extent to which Member States may be able to foresee, let alone provide solid

---

[113] Case C-73/08 *Bressol and Others* [2010] ECR I-2735, paras 49, 52, and 55.
[114] Case C-73/08 *Bressol and Others* [2010] ECR I-2735, para 51.
[115] Case C-73/08 *Bressol and Others* [2010] ECR I-2735, paras 62–64.
[116] Case C-73/08 *Bressol and Others* [2010] ECR I-2735, para 54.
[117] Case C-73/08 *Bressol and Others* [2010] ECR I-2735, paras 47, 48, and 63.
[118] Case C-73/08 *Bressol and Others* [2010] ECR I-2735, paras 66 and 71.
[119] Case C-73/08 *Bressol and Others* [2010] ECR I-2735, para 69.
[120] Case C-73/08 *Bressol and Others* [2010] ECR I-2735, para 69.
[121] Case C-73/08 *Bressol and Others* [2010] ECR I-2735, para 70.
[122] Case C-73/08 *Bressol and Others* [2010] ECR I-2735, paras 71–74.
[123] Case C-73/08 *Bressol and Others* [2010] ECR I-2735, para 69.

and consistent data on, the career and lifestyle decisions that health graduates are likely to make in the future. It is submitted, however, that the judgment may be understood as exhorting Member States wishing to invoke derogations on the basis of an identified risk to refrain from making unsubstantiated assertions. Rather, Member States are required to make every effort to demonstrate that there are objectively justifiable grounds for considering that the risk pleaded is real and that the derogatory measures adopted constitute an appropriate means of preventing that risk from materializing.[124]

Aside from indirectly discriminatory measures that are objectively justified and proportionate, certain limited derogations to the principle of equal treatment are also expressly authorized by the Directive, in particular, as regards the entitlement of economically inactive Union citizens to access social benefits.[125] Article 24(2) confirms that Member States are not obliged to confer migrant Union citizens or their family members with an entitlement to social assistance during the first three months of residence, or for the longer period afforded to job-seekers by virtue of Article 14(4)(b). The Directive further states that prior to obtaining the right of permanent residence, Member States are not required to grant maintenance aid for studies, including vocational training consisting in student grants or student loans to persons other than workers or self-employed persons, including former workers or self-employed persons, and their family members. As the concept of 'worker' and 'self-employed person' are not expressly defined by Article 24(2), they must be regarded as corresponding to those terms as defined in the context of Articles 45 and 49 TFEU, which are among the Treaty provisions to which the Directive gives effect. Consequently, the limitations provided for in Article 24(2) may only apply to individuals who do not fall within the Treaty definition of worker or self-employed person as developed in the case law of the CJEU.[126]

More fundamentally still, a difference in the right of economically inactive Union citizens to access social benefits may be considered to underpin the entire scheme

---

[124] For detailed consideration of the extent to which Member States may invoke public policy exceptions to justify derogations to fundamental freedoms, see N Nic Shuibhne and M Maci, 'Proving Public Interest: The Growing Impact of Evidence in Free Movement Case-Law', (2013) 50 CMLRev 965.

[125] Such derogations have been applied since freestanding residence rights were first extended to economically inactive migrant Member State nationals and are considered in Section B of this chapter.

[126] For discussion concerning the definition of 'worker', see the commentary on Art 7(1) in Chapter 3. Notably, the limitation on rights provided for in Art 24(2) also excludes former workers or self-employed persons. This approach is consistent with the settled case law of the Court according to which migrant Union citizens may continue to derive certain rights linked to the status of 'worker' even when they are no longer in an employment relationship. Such rights will be extended to categories of persons referred to in Art 7(3), but arguably may not be limited to those categories of persons: see the commentary on Art 7(3) and Case C-507/12, *Jessy Saint Prix v Secretary of State for Work and Pensions,* pending before the Court of Justice at the time of writing.

of the Directive as reflected in its differentiation between the right of residence and the right of permanent residence. As is apparent from the terms of Articles 7, 12, 13, and 14, economically inactive citizens residing on the basis of 'ordinary' rights of residence (prior to having obtained permanent residence status after having fulfilled five years' residence) are required to be self-supporting as a condition for their continued residence in the host Member State. Thus, in principle, their entitlement to equal access to social benefits may be curtailed, subject to the principle of proportionality and the obligation to assess the applicant's individual circumstances.[127] By contrast, the condition for self-sufficiency, and the resulting restriction on equal access to social benefits, does not apply to permanent residents. It follows therefore that the scheme of the Directive permits a certain limitation on the right of equal treatment enshrined in Article 24(1) as regards economically inactive Union citizens who are within the first five years of their residence in a host Member State.

However, even if self-sufficiency is a condition that economically inactive migrant Union citizens must satisfy to enjoy a right of residence under the Directive, unless they are family members of EU citizens with primary residence rights, it does not follow that their right to benefits may be automatically or systematically restricted. As the Court itself has observed, the mere fact that Union citizens or their families seek access to a particular grant or allowance does not necessarily mean that they do not possess sufficient resources.[128] Benefits, grants, and financial incentives may be provided to promote a variety of different policy objectives unrelated to the provision of minimum resources necessary for subsistence. Moreover, any derogation from the principle of equal treatment, including the expression of that principle in Article 24(1), is to be interpreted narrowly.[129] Union law relating to the free movement of persons allows for a certain degree of financial solidarity amongst nationals of the host Member State and nationals of other Member States.[130] Member States are under an obligation to examine the individual circumstances of a migrant Union citizen and the nature of his or her links with the host Member State.[131] While it may be legitimate for Member States to make the right of access to benefits conditional on the existence of a genuine link with the society of the host Member

---

[127] Since recourse to social assistance could disclose a failure to comply with the self-sufficiency requirement, which itself is condition for the retention of residence rights. See the judgment of 19 September 2013 in Case C-140/12 *Brey* and the commentary on Arts 7(1)(b), 8(4), and 14 in Chapter 3.

[128] Case C-75/11 *Commission v Austria*, judgment of 4 October 2012, not yet reported, para 58.

[129] Case C-75/11 *Commission v Austria*, judgment of 4 October 2012, not yet reported, para 54.

[130] Case C-184/99 *Grzelczyk* [2001] ECR I-6193, para 44 and Case C-75/11 *Commission v Austria*, judgment of 4 October 2012, not yet reported, para 60.

[131] Case C-103/08 *Gottwald* [2009] ECR I-9117; Case C-73/08 *Bressol and Others* [2010] ECR I-2735; and Case C-75/11 *Commission v Austria*, judgment of 4 October. 2012, not yet reported. On these principles, see C O'Brien, 'Real links, abstract rights and false alarms: the relationship between the ECJ's "real link" case law and national solidarity' (2008) 33 ELRev 643.

State, such a connection must not be too exclusive in nature or unduly favour an element which is not necessarily representative of the real and effective degree of connection in existence.[132] The genuine link required for a particular benefit is not required to be fixed in a uniform manner for all benefits, but should be established in the light of the constitutive elements of the benefit in question, including its nature and purpose or purposes.[133]

The Court has shown itself willing to scrutinize national provisions limiting access to social benefits in order to establish whether the links required of migrant Union citizens were appropriate having regard to the specific nature of the particular benefit to which access was sought. In the case of *Lucy Stewart*, for example, a United Kingdom national resident in Spain was excluded from receipt of a short-term incapacity benefit in youth as she had not resided in the UK for a minimum period of twenty-six weeks within fifty-two weeks of having made the claim.[134] The UK government had submitted that the legislation was intended to guarantee the existence of a continuous effective link between that Member State and the recipient of the benefit as well as the financial balance of the national social security system. In its judgment, the Court acknowledged that while the rules applying the condition of past presence did not appear to be unreasonable, the condition was nonetheless too exclusive and unduly favoured one connecting factor which was not necessarily representative of the real and effective degree of connection between a claimant and the Member State concerned.[135]

The Court considered that the existence of a link could be established from other elements, such as the claimant's relationship with the social security system of the host Member State. It was apparent that the claimant was already entitled to disability living allowance under UK legislation and was further credited with UK national insurance contributions, which revealed a certain link to the national security system in question.[136] The Court further considered that the claimant's personal and family circumstances also implied a link with the competent Member State.[137] In particular, the claimant was dependent on her parents as carers, both

---

[132] Case C-503/09 *Lucy Stewart v Secretary of State for Work and Pensions* [2011] ECR I-6497, para 95, and Case C-75/11 *Commission v Austria*, judgment of 4 October 2012, not yet reported, para 62.

[133] Joined Cases C-22/08 and C-23/08 *Vatsouras and Koupatantze* [2009] ECR I-4585, paras 41 and 42, and Case C-75/11 *Commission v Austria*, judgment of 4 October 2012, not yet reported, para 63.

[134] In particular, pursuant to Reg 16(1) and (6) of the Social Security (Incapacity Benefit) Regulations 1994, a claimant was required to have been present in Great Britain for a period of, or for periods amounting in aggregate to, not less than twenty-six weeks in the fifty-two weeks immediately preceding the date of the claim.

[135] Case C-503/09 *Lucy Stewart v Secretary of State for Work and Pensions* [2011] ECR I-6497, para 95.

[136] Case C-503/09 *Lucy Stewart v Secretary of State for Work and Pensions* [2011] ECR I-6497, paras 97–99.

[137] Case C-503/09 *Lucy Stewart v Secretary of State for Work and Pensions* [2011] ECR I-6497, para 100.

of whom received retirement pensions under UK legislation. Finally, the Court observed that the claimant, a UK national, had passed a significant part of her life in the UK. The Court considered that these elements were indicative of a genuine and sufficient connection between the claimant and the competent Member State.[138]

The nature of the link imposed by a Member State as a condition for obtaining access to a particular benefit was also scrutinized by the Court in the *Commission v Austria* student travel fares case.[139] Here the Court considered that making access to student travel discounts conditional on belonging to a family in receipt of Austrian family allowance was inappropriate and excessive having regard to the nature of the benefit in question. Given that the travel discount was conferred on students, the Court considered a more relevant criterion would have been whether the person in question was enrolled at a private or public educational institution for the principal purpose of following a course of studies.[140]

The real link test has equally been applied in considering the extent to which restrictions may be placed on job-seekers' rights to equal treatment. In particular, the Court has held that the derogation provided for in Article 24(2) may not be applied to job-seekers who are able to provide evidence of a real link with the labour market of the State in which they are seeking employment. The existence of such a link may be determined by establishing that the person concerned has, for a reasonable period, genuinely sought work in the Member State in question.[141] Moreover, it is to be recalled that pursuant to Article 7(3)(b) and (c), job-seekers who were in employment previously and became unemployed involuntarily, in circumstances laid down in those subparagraphs,[142] will retain their worker status. Such job-seekers may not in any event be made subject to the derogation provided for in Article 24(2) as that provision is stated not to apply inter alia to workers including persons who retain that status.

The Court has emphasized that even if Article 24(2) permits limitations to the right to student maintenance aid, it refers only to aid that consists in student grants or student loans. Given that derogations are to be interpreted narrowly, the Court has clarified that other forms of aid will not fall within the scope of the derogation provided for in Article 24(2).[143] The Court has also held that the application

---

[138] Case C-503/09 *Lucy Stewart v Secretary of State for Work and Pensions* [2011] ECR I-6497, paras 101 and 102.

[139] Case C-75/11, judgment of 4 October 2012, not yet reported.

[140] Case C-75/11, judgment of 4 October 2012, not yet reported, para 64.

[141] Case C-138/02 *Collins* [2004] ECR I-2703, para 70; Joined Cases C-22/08 and C-23/08 *Vatsouras and Koupatantze* [2009] ECR I-4585, para 39; and Case C-367/11 *Prete*, judgment of 25 October 2012, not yet reported, para 46.

[142] See the commentary on Art 7, in Chapter 3.

[143] Case C-75/11 *Commission v Austria*, judgment of 4 October 2012, not yet reported, paras 55 and 56. For an analogous approach predating the entry into force of the Directive see Case C-184/99 *Grzelczyk* [2001] ECR I-6193.

of Article 24(2) cannot prejudice the rights of students who, although entering a Member State for the purposes of engaging in full-time studies, have also engaged in employed activities and consequently acquired the status of 'worker' within the meaning of Article 45 TFEU.[144] However, in order to acquire worker status, the citizen must of course satisfy the well established criteria set out in the case law of the Court. In particular, the citizen must for a certain period of time, have been performing services for and under the direction of another person, in return for which he or she received remuneration. The activities must further be genuine and effective and cannot be on such a small scale as to be regarded as purely marginal or ancillary.[145]

Article 25—General provisions concerning residence documents

1. Possession of a registration certificate as referred to in Article 8, of a document certifying permanent residence, of a certificate attesting submission of an application for a family member residence card, of a residence card or of a permanent residence card, may under no circumstances be made a precondition for the exercise of a right or the completion of an administrative formality, as entitlement to rights may be attested by any other means of proof.
2. All documents mentioned in paragraph 1 shall be issued free of charge or for a charge not exceeding that imposed on nationals for the issuing of similar documents.

Article 25 prohibits national authorities from making the exercise of a right or the completion of an administrative formality conditional on the possession of residence documentation issued by national authorities. In so doing, it reflects the well-established case law of the Court according to which national residence documents do not create rights of movement or residence. They merely serve to attest existing rights conferred directly on Union citizens by the Treaties and secondary legislation adopted to give them effect.[146] By way of derogation, though, it is necessarily implicit that a Member State cannot be obliged to waive a visa requirement unless the person concerned holds the residence card referred to in Article 10.

It follows that the possession of national residence documents cannot be made a precondition for the acquisition or enjoyment of substantive rights provided for in Union law. Errors or delays connected with the issuing of residence permits or

---

[144] Case C-46/12 *LN*, judgment of 21 February 2013, para 27.

[145] Case 66/85 *Lawrie-Blum* [1986] ECR 2121, paras 16 and 17; Case C-337/97 *Meeusen* [1999] ECR I-3289, para 13; Case C-138/02 *Collins* [2004] ECR I-2703, para 26; Case C-456/02 *Trojani* [2004] ECR I-7573, para 15; and Case C-208/07 *von Chamier-Glisczinski* [2009] ECR I-6095, para 69; Joined Cases C-22/08 and C-23/08 *Vatsouras and Koupatantze* [2009] ECR I-4585, para 26; and Case C-46/12 *LN*, judgment of 21 February 2013, paras 40–43.

[146] Case 48/75 *Royer* [1976] ECR 497, paras 31–33; Case C-357/89 *Raulin* [1992] ECR I-1027, paras 36 and 42; Case C-459/99 *MRAX* [2002] ECR I-6591, para 74; and Case C-215/03 *Oulane* [2005] ECR I-1215, paras 17 and 18. As regards Art 19 of the citizens' Directive (referring to a document certifying permanent residence status for EU citizens), see Case C-123/08 *Wolzenburg* [2009] ECR I-9621, paras 50 and 51.

residence certificates may not prevent beneficiaries of the Directive from the enjoyment or exercise of residence rights, or the right of third-country national family members to engage in economic activity. Equally, as duration of residence may give rise to substantive rights, such as the right to permanent residence, the calculation of the period of lawful residence in a host Member State cannot be determined by reference to the date of application or the date of issuing of a residence card, but must take into account the entire duration of the period of actual residence in that Member State on the basis of the relevant Treaty right. An interpretation of domestic law that would only recognize periods of residence by reference to national residence documentation would essentially be attributing to such documents substantive or constitutive qualities they do not possess.

Article 25(2) requires national residence documents to be issued free of charge or for a charge not exceeding that which is imposed on nationals of the host Member State for the issuing of similar documents.

Article 26—Checks

Member States may carry out checks on compliance with any requirement deriving from their national legislation for non-nationals always to carry their registration certificate or residence card, provided that the same requirement applies to their own nationals as regards their identity card.

In the event of failure to comply with this requirement, Member States may impose the same sanctions as those imposed on their own nationals for failure to carry their identity card.

Article 26 affirms Member States' entitlement to carry out checks on the compliance with requirements in national law for non-nationals to carry their registration certificate or residence card. However, it stipulates that such checks are only permissible insofar as equivalent requirements apply to nationals of that Member State as regards their identity card. Moreover, any sanctions applicable for failure to comply with the requirement to carry documentation must be the same for migrant Union citizens and nationals of the host Member State.

Article 26 gives effect to the judgment of the Court of Justice in *Commission v Belgium*[147] and is also consistent with the judgments in *Wijsenbeek*[148] and *Oulane*, in which the Court essentially upheld the entitlement of Member States to carry out checks, provided they did so in compliance with the principle of equal treatment and non-discrimination.[149] The Court has emphasized that controls carried out in a systematic, arbitrary, or unnecessarily restrictive manner are liable to be incompatible with what is now Article 18 TFEU.[150]

---

[147] Case 321/87 *Commission v Belgium* [1989] ECR 997.
[148] Case C-378/97 *Wijsenbeek* [1999] ECR I-6207.
[149] Case C-215/03 *Oulane* [2005] ECR I-1215.
[150] See Case 321/87 *Commission v Belgium* [1989] ECR 997, para 15.

In *Wijsenbeek*, a Dutch national travelling between Strasbourg and Rotterdam refused to present his passport on arrival on the ground that the requirement to present evidence of identity and nationality breached free movement rights enshrined in the Treaty. In its judgment, the Court observed that since not every traveller will be a beneficiary of free movement rights, a Member State must be able to require presentation of a valid identity card or passport in order to ascertain whether the person concerned is in fact such a beneficiary.[151] The Court held, however, that any penalties for the breach of the obligation to present a valid card must be comparable to those which apply to similar infringements under national law. In addition, any penalty must not be disproportionate such that it would create an obstacle to the free movement of persons.[152]

In the case of *Oulane*,[153] the Court confirmed that Union citizens may be required to provide evidence of their identity and nationality at any time during their stay in another Member State,[154] provided always that any such requirement applies equally to nationals of the Member State concerned.[155] The Court acknowledged that ascertaining the identity and nationality of persons exercising free movement rights could be necessary to resolve any questions relating to evidence of a person's right of residence.[156] Moreover, this would assist national authorities in ensuring that they respect the applicable limits regarding the information they are entitled to seek from the persons concerned.[157] However, the Court confirmed that for the purpose of ascertaining an individual's nationality, the competent authorities cannot insist on the presentation of a valid identity card or passport, but must accept any form of unequivocal proof.[158] Any sanctions imposed on nationals of other EU Member States who fail to produce identification as required must be comparable to sanctions imposed under national law against nationals for similar infringements and must respect the principle of proportionality.[159] In particular, detention with a view to deportation would be disproportionate.

---

[151] Case C-378/97 *Wijsenbeek* [1999] ECR I-6207, para 43 and C-215/03 *Oulane* [2005] ECR I-1215, para 21.

[152] Case C-378/97 *Wijsenbeek* [1999] ECR I-6207, para 44.

[153] Case C-215/03 *Oulane* [2005] ECR I-1215.

[154] Case C-215/03 *Oulane* [2005] ECR I-1215, para 21. Although this case concerned a Union citizen, it is submitted that the reasoning underpinning the judgment would apply *a fortiori* to third-country national family members. Moreover, pursuant to the second sentence of Art 24(1), the benefit of the right to equal treatment extends to family members who are not nationals of a Member State and who have a right of residence or permanent residence.

[155] Case 321/87 *Commission v Belgium* [1989] ECR 997, para 12, and Case C-215/03 *Oulane* [2005] ECR I-1215, paras 32–35.

[156] Case C-215/03 *Oulane* [2005] ECR I-1215.

[157] Case C-215/03 *Oulane* [2005] ECR I-1215, para 22.

[158] Case C-215/03 *Oulane* [2005] ECR I-1215, para 23.

[159] Case C-378/97 *Wijsenbeek* [1999] ECR I-6207, para 44; Case C-215/03 *Oulane* [2005] ECR I-1215, para 38.

F. Evaluation

The provisions of chapter V set out important rules governing the lives of all EU citizens and their family members who fall within the scope of the Directive. Chief among these is the principle of equality, which also overlaps with equal treatment rules in legislation governing the free movement of workers and the Treaty rules on equal treatment in relation to EU citizenship. It is essential for the CJEU to ensure that it interprets these rules in a coherent manner that guarantees legal certainty for both the individuals concerned and the national administrations that have to implement these provisions.

6

RESTRICTIONS ON THE RIGHT OF ENTRY AND THE RIGHT OF RESIDENCE ON GROUNDS OF PUBLIC POLICY, PUBLIC SECURITY, OR PUBLIC HEALTH

A. Function—Articles 27–29

The EU Treaties have always provided for exceptions to the free movement of persons on grounds of public policy, public security, and public health. This exception can be found, for instance, in Article 45(3) TFEU on the free movement of workers, which specifies that this freedom is 'subject to limitations justified on grounds of public policy, public security or public health'. The secondary legislation adopted specifically to give precision to this exception was Directive 64/221,[1] which continued to apply until it was ultimately repealed by Directive 2004/38—thus making it one of the longest surviving measures of secondary legislation in this field.[2] It set out the meaning of and limitations upon the right of Member States to exclude or expel EU citizens or their family members on grounds of public policy, public security, and public health.[3]

All EU citizens (and their family members) who move from their home Member State to another Member State are entitled to enter and reside unless the host Member State can establish that one of these three grounds applies. These exclusions are foremost among the 'limitations' referred to in Article 21 TFEU on citizenship of the Union. The three exceptions apply to all measures of exclusion,

---

[1] OJ English special edition: Series I Chapter 1963–1964 p 117.

[2] An earlier measure from 1961 was repealed by Directive 64/221 JO 57 of 26.8.1961, p 1073–1084 (DE, FR, IT, NL).

[3] See also N Fennelly, 'The European Union and Protection of Aliens from Expulsion' (1999) 3 EJML 313, where he reviews the rules relating to Community nationals before considering their potential application to third-country nationals.

including refusal of entry onto the territory, prevention of exit from a territory, the issue and renewal of residence cards, permits (as regards cases like *Ruiz Zambrano*, which arguably fall inside the scope of chapter VI even if they are outside the scope of the rest of the Directive), and expulsion. Thus rather than setting out what States can do, EU law focuses on what States cannot do. This is important from the perspective of implementation at the national level. It is sometimes easier to indicate instructions to civil servants explaining exactly how they must act and what they are entitled to do rather than draft circulars and instructions on what they cannot do, particularly when the limitations are subtle.

The objective of the three grounds on the basis of which the rights of Union citizens (and their family members) to move and reside can be limited is to provide Member States with a long stop of State sovereign decision-making about which non-citizens they wish to exclude from their territory. As the European Court of Human Rights has frequently confirmed, State sovereignty permits States to determine whether they will permit foreigners to enter or remain on their territory or not. However, given the creation of citizenship of the Union, this continuing right to refuse entry to or expel EU citizens whose underlying nationality is not that of the host Member State may be considered somewhat anachronistic. One would need to assimilate this expulsion power to a power to restrict the residence of citizens to certain parts of a State for this power to be consistent with the principles of citizenship as contained in international law.

This power to expel has been the matter of much jurisprudence of the CJEU seeking to find the balance between the principle of equality and the express derogation contained in these provisions. Because the EU citizen or his or her family member remains for these purposes a 'foreigner', he or she is liable to expulsion or exclusion. This jurisprudence will be considered as we examine each of the provisions in detail. However, while Member States are permitted a residual State sovereign control over the EU citizens and their family members (other than their own nationals) who enter and reside on their territory, there are strict EU rules on the procedures which must be respected as regards any Member State's attempt to use these powers. These procedural obligations (which are examined in the second part of this chapter) include written notification requirements, and procedural safeguards which entitle the individual subject to the decision to appeal against it before an independent authority. Further, limitations are placed on how long an EU citizen or his or her family member can be banned from the territory of another Member State before a reconsideration of the material facts must be carried out.

The preamble to the Directive expressly notes that the Treaty itself allows restrictions to be placed on the right of free movement and residence on the three grounds. However, these restrictions are more precisely regulated by the provisions of the citizens' Directive which we will consider in this chapter. According to recital 22 in the preamble to the Directive, these rules are designed 'to ensure a tighter definition of the circumstances' of the use of the restrictions, as well as 'procedural safeguards'. The preamble also recognizes (in recital 23) that expulsion of EU citizens and their family members 'is a measure that can seriously harm' persons who have used their rights and 'have become genuinely integrated into the host Member State'. For this reason, expulsion measures must be 'limited in accordance with the principle of proportionality to take into account the degree of integration of the persons concerned' which is stated to include (at least) 'the length of their residence in the host Member State, their age, state of health, family and economic situation and the links with their country of origin'. This list of considerations tallies very closely with the list set out by the European Court of Human Rights in its judgment in *Boultif*[4] and refined in *Uner*.[5] Undoubtedly the ever closer alignment of fundamental rights of citizens of the Union, now contained in the Charter, with the ECHR and the anticipated (at the time of writing) accession of the EU to the ECHR, has led to greater attention to ensuring that EU legislation is ECHR proof. Thus according to the preamble to the Directive (recital 24), the objective is to ensure that only in 'exceptional circumstances . . . should an expulsion measure be taken against' an EU citizen who has 'resided for many years' on the host Member State's territory. Extra protection is also required for minors.

As regards procedural safeguards, recital 25 in the preamble states that EU law requires 'a high level of protection of the rights' of EU citizens and their family members 'in the event of their being denied leave to enter or reside in another Member State'. It is also necessary 'to uphold the principle that any action taken by the authorities must be properly justified' in this field. Next, the preamble specifies that 'judicial redress procedures' are required for EU citizens and their family members 'who have been refused leave to enter or reside in a Member State' (recital 26).

Finally, recital 27 in the preamble also provides some explanation for the limitation on re-entry bans which the Directive sets out. It confirms that this provision is the result of the case law of the CJEU,[6] which prohibits Member States from issuing orders excluding for life EU citizens and their family members from a Member State's territory. EU citizens or their family members who have been excluded always have the right 'after a reasonable period' of time, 'and in any event after a three year period from the enforcement of the final exclusion order', to 'submit a fresh application' to seek re-entry to the host Member State.

Of course within the Schengen area, where border controls on the movement of persons within the area are not permitted in principle (see Chapter 2), expulsion orders and bans on re-entry are difficult to police. Although an individual may

---

[4] *Boultif v Switzerland* (Reports 2001-IX)—400-1, 406.
[5] *Uner v Netherlands* 18 October 2006—401-2, 406.
[6] See in particular Case C-348/96 *Calfa* [1999] ECR I-11.

be expelled to another Schengen area Member State, there is no practical way to ensure that the person does not reappear the next day back in the State from which he or she had been expelled. Other mechanisms such as controls on population registers seem to be the way in which such efforts are carried out. Even among those few Member States which are not part of the Schengen area, keeping out of the territory an individual who has been expelled but seeks to return presents difficulties, as it means that information about EU nationals and their family members has to be immediately available to border guards at the light control which takes place at the borders, which is not always easy.

B. Historical development

The right of free movement of persons is subject to two limitations, one territorial and the other occupational (which is not relevant here). Member States are permitted to limit the entry and residence of a national of another Member State or that person's family members to its territory on the grounds of public policy, public security, and public health (the latter exception can only be applied on first admission or within the first three months of residence). Most commonly pleaded by Member States seeking to expel EU nationals or their family members is 'public policy', which includes criminal behaviour. The implementing legislation in respect of restrictions on free movement (Directive 64/221, which was repealed with the introduction of Directive 2004/38,[7] where the rules are now found) prohibits Member States from using restrictions on free movement to achieve 'economic ends'.[8] Thus Member States cannot expel nationals of other Member States simply because the latter persons are unemployed and claiming social benefits, except to the extent that this is permitted in accordance with the provisions of chapter III of the Directive,[9] for persons who do not yet have the right of permanent residence. Where the ground is criminality, the individual needs not only to have been convicted by a duly constituted criminal court, but must also be a present and immediate threat to a fundamental interest of society. This is a high threshold which, sadly, is not always respected by all Member States.

The protection of EU citizens and their family members from expulsion by a Member State was strengthened on the revision of rights contained in Directive 2004/38. A three-step approach has been incorporated into the law: for the first five years, the EU citizen or family member is protected under the general rules. After five years, if the person concerned qualifies for permanent residence status pursuant to the Directive,[10] the Member State can only justify the expulsion of an

---

[7] See Art 38, discussed in Chapter 7.
[8] Art 2(2), Directive 64/221.
[9] See in particular the commentary on Arts 14 and 15 in Chapter 3.
[10] For details, see Chapter 4.

individual on the basis of 'serious grounds of public policy or security'. After ten years of residence on the territory of a host Member State, the only permitted reason to commence expulsion proceedings against an EU national is 'imperative grounds of public security'. This increasing level of protection is intended to reflect the ever greater integration of the individual in the host community. As noted in Chapter 4, this concept of the individual becoming ever more integrated into the host Member State with the passage of time is one of the innovations of Directive 2004/38.

While, to date, there has only been limited judicial consideration of the protection against expulsion in Articles 27 to 33, the corresponding provisions of Directive 64/221 have been the subject of a great deal of jurisprudence. As the purpose of the Directive is 'to simplify and strengthen the right of free movement and residence of all Union citizens' and their family members, as stated in the preamble to the Directive (recital 3), the preceding jurisprudence of the CJEU which sets out the protection of citizens must still be valid for the interpretation of the counterpart provisions of this Directive, except to the extent that this Directive sets higher standards than its predecessor.[11] Accordingly, when considering each provision of the citizens' Directive, we will have regard to the jurisprudence relating to its counterpart in the previous Directive.

C. Interrelationship of Articles 27–33 with other provisions

These provisions are closely related to Articles 7 and 16, regarding the conditions of the right of residence and permanent residence. There is a specific reference in Article 27(3) to Article 5(5). In the rest of the Directive, the application of Articles 15(1) and 35 are subject to the procedural safeguards set out in Articles 30 and 31, and Articles 14(1), 15(2), and 15(3) concern expulsions and entry bans for reasons other than public policy, public security, or public health. Arguably Article 29 restricts the reasons related to public health which Member States could rely upon to deny admission to an extended family member who seeks to live with an EU citizen on 'serious health grounds'.[12] Otherwise these provisions are surprisingly self-contained.

D. Other relevant international law rules

There are two international law references in these Articles. Firstly, Article 28(3)(b) requires that any decision on the expulsion of a minor must be 'necessary for the best interests of the child' as provided for in the UN Convention on the Rights of

---

[11] Recital 3 in the preamble confirms that the citizens' Directive does not *lower* standards compared to the prior legislation: see Case C-127/08 *Metock* [2008] ECR I-6241.

[12] See the commentary on Art 3(2) in Chapter 1.

the Child. This clearly indicates that a common interpretation of the meaning of 'the best interests of the child' applies here, and the EU definition must be consistent with that contained in the UN Convention. Secondly, as regards public health, this ground of exclusion is defined in Article 29(1) by reference to the relevant instruments of the World Health Organization (WHO). This reference is to the meaning of the concepts of 'diseases with epidemic potential' and 'other infectious diseases or contagious parasitic diseases' which are the only ones on the basis of which an exclusion or expulsion decision can be taken against an EU citizen or his or her family members.

E. Analysis—Article 27

Article 27—General principles

1. Subject to the provisions of this Chapter, Member States may restrict the freedom of movement and residence of Union citizens and their family members, irrespective of nationality, on grounds of public policy, public security or public health. These grounds shall not be invoked to serve economic ends.

Article 27(1) sets out the general rule that freedom of movement of Union citizens and their family members may be restricted on three grounds: public policy, public security, and public health. This general rule is specified in further detail in the rest of chapter VI, as the opening words of Article 27(1) ('[s]ubject to the provisions of this Chapter') indicate. The first sentence of Article 27(1) reflects Article 45 TFEU and is the substantive content of Article 21(1) TFEU's reference to limitations upon the free movement of EU citizens, while the second sentence has been retained from Directive 64/221.[13] During negotiation of the Directive, the scope of Article 27(1) was widened: the original proposal applied more specifically to 'decisions whereby... [EU citizens and their family members]... are *refused entry or expelled*',[14] but when the Commission revised its proposal, it accepted an amendment suggested by the European Parliament, in order to 'make a more general reference to all types of decision restricting freedom of movement', to cover 'all types of measure—removal, refusal of leave to enter the territory and refusal to leave'.[15] Indeed, the case law of the CJEU has confirmed that Article 27(1) applies to restrictions on entry, exit, or residence.[16] As for the personal scope of Article 27 (and the rest of chapter VI), in light of its wide reference to all EU citizens and their family members, it clearly applies to all persons within the scope of the citizens'

---

[13] Art 2(2), Directive 64/221.
[14] COM(2001) 257 (emphasis added).
[15] COM(2003) 199, explanatory memorandum.
[16] As regards exit, see, for instance, Case C-33/07 *Jipa* [2008] ECR I-5157, which links Art 27(1) to the right to leave the territory of a Member State set out in Art 4 (on which, see Chapter 2).

Directive,[17] and arguably also to those EU citizens and their family members *outside* the Directive's scope,[18] given that the case law on the prior Directive confirmed its application to those who were not legally resident.[19]

The starting place to understand this provision is the fact that what is at stake is the restriction of a right. Thus while every EU national (with his or her family members) has the right of free movement, Member States are limited as regards the grounds on which they can seek to restrict that right to those which are justified on the basis of public policy, public security, and public health.[20] This means that EU citizens and their family members are protected against restrictions on exit, entry, and residence in the same way under this provision and in equal measure. However, as is clarified below, according to Article 29 the ground of public health can only be used on entry and within three months of entry. The power of a Member State to restrict free movement of an EU citizen or his or her family member on any one of the three grounds is subject to an EU interpretation. The definition of the three provisos is the subject of the next paragraph (as regards public policy and public security) and Article 29 (as regards public health). Before moving to that aspect, it is worth considering the relationship of the proviso which permits Member States to take exclusion/expulsion action against an EU citizen in light of the right to non-discrimination on the basis of nationality set out in Article 18 TFEU. As the prospect of restricting free movement is largely an exception to the right to non-discrimination (States cannot exclude or expel their own nationals, although there is a limited possibility for them to restrict their nationals' exit from the territory) it comes among the exceptions which must be subject to particular attention.

Indeed, in the first case the Court considered on the public policy proviso contained in Directive 64/221, it recognized that 'it is a principle of international law, which the EEC Treaty cannot be assumed to disregard in the relations between Member States, that a State is precluded from refusing its own nationals the right of entry or residence'.[21]

The application of exclusion/expulsion specifically permitted on grounds of public policy, public health, and public security must be reconciled with the right to non-discrimination. A first attempt was to consider the underlying subject matter

---

[17] In particular, it applies to those EU citizens and their family members subject to Art 12(3), irrespective of whether such persons can qualify for permanent residence under the Directive (see the commentary on Art 18 in Chapter 4).

[18] For instance, the persons solely subject to Art 10 of Reg 492/2011 ([2011] OJ L 141/1). On this category of persons, see the commentary on Art 12(3) in Chapter 3.

[19] Case C-50/06 *Commission v Netherlands* [2007] ECR I-4383. See also Case C-459/99 *MRAX* [2002] ECR I-6591, paras 100–104.

[20] See the explanatory memorandum to the original proposal (COM(2001) 257): '[t]his article states the principle already contained in the Treaty that restrictions on freedom of movement and residence are permitted *only* on grounds of public policy, public security or public health' (emphasis added).

[21] Case 41/74 *Van Duyn* [1974] ECR 1337.

of the expulsion/exclusion decision. In what Mancini described as a false step,[22] the CJEU rejected this approach in 1974.[23] In *Van Duyn*, the Member State (the UK) refused admission to a national of another Member State (the Netherlands) who was seeking to take up employment with a religious organization of which the host Member State disapproved but which was not proscribed by law. It was argued that exclusion on the basis of economic (and religious) activities with a religious organization where no penalty accrues to own nationals for such activities constituted prohibited discrimination on the basis of nationality. The CJEU rejected that argument and found that the Member State could justify exclusion on the grounds of public policy even for activities in respect of which own nationals were under no restriction without violating the principle of non-discrimination. The Court's reasoning was: 'Where the competent authorities of a Member State have clearly defined their standpoint as regards the activities of a particular organisation and where, considering it to be socially harmful, they have taken administrative measures to counteract these activities, the Member State cannot be required, before it can rely on the concept of public policy, to make such activities unlawful, if recourse to such a measure is not thought appropriate in these circumstances.'[24]

This interpretation of the non-discrimination principle indicated a great sensitivity to each Member State's appreciation of the social consequences of a migration right. The difficulty was that such an interpretation blocked the effectiveness of the non-discrimination tool.[25] However, in the following year the CJEU at least in part rejected this limitation on the principle and found that only where penalties are applicable to own nationals for the behaviour upon which the expulsion decision is based could penalties be applied to Union citizens for similar behaviour.[26] The CJEU set out its reasoning: 'Although Community law does not impose upon Member States a uniform scale of values as regards the assessment of conduct which may be considered as contrary to public policy, it should nevertheless be stated that conduct may not be considered as being of a sufficiently serious nature to justify restrictions on the admission to or residence within the territory of a Member State of a national of another Member State in a case where the former Member State does not adopt, with respect to the same conduct on the part of its own nationals, repressive measures or other genuine and effective measures intended to combat such conduct.'[27]

---

[22] G F Mancini, 'The Free Movement of Workers in the Case Law of the European Court of Justice', in *Constitutional Adjudication in European Community and National Law, Essays for the Hon. Mr Justice T. F. O'Higgins*, D Curtin and D O'Keeffe, eds (Butts, London, 1992).

[23] Case 41/74 *Van Duyn* [1974] ECR 1337.

[24] Case 41/74 *Van Duyn*. The EFTA Court has recently been called upon to decide a case raising similar issues: Case E-15/12 *Wahl*, pending.

[25] Mancini, n 22.

[26] Case 36/75 *Rutili* [1975] ECR 1219.

[27] Joined Cases 115/81 and 116/81 *Adoui and Cornuaille* [1982] ECR 1665.

It is worth noting that the requirement that a Member State which intends to interfere with a free movement right of an EU citizen or his or her family member justify its action in accordance with at least one of the provisos applicable to any action taken by the State.[28] In the *Rutili* case the Member State sought to limit the residence of the EU citizen to a specific part of the country. The CJEU found that such an action would be lawful only if it was applicable also to nationals of the State.[29] Nonetheless, the CJEU has recognized that the needs of public policy and public security can vary from Member State to Member State and from one period to another. Thus there is a degree of flexibility in the meaning of the two terms. However, the CJEU obliges Member States to interpret those needs or requirements strictly. It will apply a particularly stringent investigation into the necessity of a restriction.[30] To this end, Member States are required to define clearly what the protected interests of society are on the basis of which they seek to interfere with the EU citizen's (or family member's) right and in so doing clearly distinguish between public policy and public security. The two concepts are not interchangeable.

Public policy

Public policy is related to the prevention of disturbances to social order. In a 1977 decision,[31] however, the CJEU did not rule out that the possibility that the concept of public policy could extend beyond reasons of State that related to some threatened breach of the public peace, order, or security. The Court considered that particular circumstances justifying recourse to the concept of public policy may vary from one country to another and from one period to another and competent national authorities must therefore be afforded a degree of discretion within the limits imposed by the Treaty and the provisions adopted for its implementation. Nevertheless, insofar as that concept was invoked as a derogation to the exercise of free movement rights, it was to be interpreted strictly. To justify a restriction, recourse by a national authority to the concept of public policy was required to presuppose, in any event, the existence, in addition to the perturbation of the social order which any infringement of the law involves, of a genuine and sufficiently serious threat to the requirements of public policy affecting one of the fundamental interests of society.

The judgment was clarified further in subsequent jurisprudence. In the *Orfanopoulos and Oliveri* judgment[32] the two EU citizens concerned, one Greek and the other Italian, had lived for many years in Germany. The first had arrived in the host State as a child of thirteen in 1972 and at the time of the judgment was married with three children in Germany. The second had been born in Germany in 1977 and

---

[28] Case 36/75 *Rutili* [1975] ECR 1215.
[29] This rule is now set out expressly in Art 22; see Chapter 5.
[30] Case 30/77 *Bouchereau* [1977] ECR 1999.
[31] Case 30/77 *Bouchereau* [1977] ECR 1999.
[32] Joined Cases C-482/01 and C-493/01 [2004] ECR I-5257.

always lived there. Mr Orfanopoulos had accumulated nine convictions for narcotics offences and acts of violence and spent increasing periods of time in prison with each conviction. Eventually the German authorities decided to expel him on the basis of the number of convictions and their seriousness which indicated a real risk of offending in the future by reason of his dependency on drugs and alcohol. Mr Oliveri had been addicted to drugs for several years and had become infected with the HIV virus (though that could not justify expulsion on grounds of public health: see the commentary on Article 29 below). He committed numerous offences including theft and sale of narcotics and spent time in prison for these offences. He also received an expulsion decision from the German authorities based on the frequency and seriousness of the offences he had already committed and the real risk that he would re-offend in the future.

The CJEU took the opportunity of these two cases to review and reinforce its jurisprudence on the meaning of public policy. It again confirmed that because the principle of freedom of movement of workers must be given a broad definition any derogations from it must be interpreted strictly. It added that a particularly restrictive interpretation of the derogations from free movement is also required because of the person's status as a citizen of the Union which, the CJEU, repeated, is destined to be the fundamental status of nationals of the Member States. In order for measures on the basis of public policy to be justified, they must be based exclusively on the personal conduct of the individual concerned. Previous criminal convictions in themselves cannot justify such measures as the concept of public policy presupposes the existence, in addition to the perturbation of the social order which any infringement of the law involves, of a genuine and sufficiently serious threat to the requirements of public policy affecting one of the fundamental interests of society.[33] This phrase is now repeated in the Directive itself at Article 27(2), second subparagraph (see section entitled 'Decisions serving economic ends'). Even in the case of the use of prohibited narcotics, which the CJEU accepted constitutes a danger for society such as to justify special measures against foreign nationals who contravene laws against narcotic use, the 'public policy' exception must be interpreted restrictively.[34] The existence of previous criminal convictions can only justify an expulsion insofar as the circumstances which gave rise to the conviction are evidence of personal conduct constituting a present threat to the requirements of public policy.[35] An EU citizen or his or her family member may only be expelled for conduct punished by the law of the host Member State or against which genuine and effective measures have been taken by the State in order to combat such conduct.[36] In any event, the CJEU has held that failure to comply with registration

---

[33] Case 30/77 *Bouchereau* [1977] ECR 1999.
[34] Joined Cases C-482/01 and C-493/01 *Orfanopoulos and Oliveri* [2004] ECR I-5295.
[35] Case C-348/96 *Calfa* [1999] ECR I-11.
[36] Joined Cases 115/81 and 116/81 *Adoui and Cornuaille* [1982] ECR 1665.

requirements is not of such a nature as to constitute in itself conduct threatening public policy and this cannot justify expelling an EU citizen.[37]

Furthermore, the CJEU has ruled that a Member State's decision to restrict free movement can only be 'adopted in the light of considerations pertaining to the protection of public policy or public security in the *Member State imposing the* measure', and so cannot rely 'exclusively on reasons advanced by *another Member State* to justify' restrictions on free movement on the grounds of public policy or public security, although it is possible for the other Member State's view to be 'taken into account in the context of the assessment which the competent national authorities undertake for the purpose of adopting the measure restricting freedom of movement'.[38] This rule applies *a fortiori* to reasons advanced by third States (or the organs of international organizations, like the United Nations Security Council).[39]

Public security

Public security has a content distinct from that of public policy. It is generally interpreted as covering both internal and external security.[40] In a case which revolved around free movement of capital and whether (non-Italian) EU citizens should be entitled to buy land surrounding Italian military bases, the CJEU held that a mere reference to the requirements of defence of the national territory was insufficient to trigger the public security proviso. The CJEU found that the position would be different only if it could be demonstrated that the non-discriminatory treatment of the nationals of all the Member States would expose the military interests of Italy to real, specific, and serious risks which could not be countered by less restrictive procedures. Criminal behaviour, however, can come within the ambit of public security. In a judgment on the scope of Article 28(3) (see Section G), the CJEU held that criminal offences such as those referred to in the second subparagraph of Article 83(1) TFEU could constitute a particularly serious threat to one of the fundamental interests of society, which might pose a direct threat to the calm and physical security of the population and thus be covered by the concept of 'imperative grounds of public security', capable of justifying an expulsion measure under Article 28(3). However, this would be the case only as long as the manner in which such offences were committed disclosed particularly serious characteristics. We will discuss this in more depth under Article 28(3).

---

[37] Case 48/75 *Royer* [1976] ECR 497. See Arts 8(2) and 9(3), discussed in Chapter 3.

[38] Case C-33/07 *Jipa* [2008] ECR I-5157, para 25 (emphasis added), referring 'by analogy' also to Case C-503/03 *Commission v Spain* [2006] ECR I-1097.

[39] See Case C-430/10 *Gaydarov*, judgment of 17 November 2011, not yet reported, where a decision to limit free movement based solely on a prior conviction in Serbia without an assessment of personal conduct did not satisfy the requirements of Art 27(2).

[40] Case C-423/98 *Albore* [2000] ECR I-5965.

Public health

Public health has been the subject of the least attention. It is provided greater clarity in Article 29 where the Directive specifies that only diseases with epidemic potential as defined by the relevant instruments of the WHO and other infectious diseases or contagious parasitic diseases are covered by the concept.

Decisions serving economic ends

The second sentence of Article 27(1) confirms that such decisions cannot be invoked to serve economic ends. This is particularly important as it means that just because an individual is unemployed or that there is a high rate of unemployment in a particular Member State, a host State cannot refuse entry or seek to expel an EU citizen or his or her family members in order to diminish the number of unemployed people on the territory, without prejudice to the possible loss of free movement rights pursuant to Article 14, due to becoming a 'burden on the social assistance system' and so no longer meeting the conditions of Articles 7(1)(b) or (c), 12(1) or (2), or 13.[41] Restrictions on free movement which are taken either on the stated grounds of protecting the labour market or on indirect labour market grounds are equally prohibited. This is critical to the enjoyment of free movement rights for job-seekers among others. One of the problematic aspects of the exercise of free movement rights beyond the three-month period set out in Article 6 (discussed in Chapter 3) is where Member States are reluctant to recognize an individual's status as a job-seeker or potentially as a person exercising a self-employed activity albeit one on a small scale.

In a decision of the CJEU primarily about the right to leave a Member State (see Chapter 2) the Court also cast some light on the question of measures taken exclusively to serve economic ends.[42] The CJEU considered whether an interference with the right to exit, which was taken for the purpose of recovery of debts owed to a public authority (recovery of taxes), should be classified as a measure taken exclusively to serve economic ends. It held that 'since the purpose of recovery of debts owed to a public authority, in particular the recovery of taxes, is to ensure the funding of actions of the Member State concerned on the basis of the choices which are the expression of, inter alia, its general policy in economic and social matters . . . the measures adopted by the public authorities in order to ensure that recovery also cannot be considered, as a matter of principle, to have been adopted exclusively to serve economic ends'. However, on the facts there was insufficient information for the CJEU to determine whether the measures taken had in fact been adopted solely to serve economic ends, and so it left this issue to the national

---

[41] See the commentary on Arts 7 and 12–14 in Chapter 3. Art 15(1) specifies that in such a case the person concerned will still benefit from the procedural safeguards set out in Arts 30 and 31.
[42] Case C-434/10 *Aladzhov*, judgment of 17 November 2011, not yet reported.

court to determine.[43] However, the Court was more willing to clarify the interpretation of the second sentence of Article 27(1) in a later case, involving an exit ban for the purpose of enforcing an unsecured *private* debt. The Court held that such a restriction was precluded by EU law, taking account also of the criteria set out in Article 27(2)—personal conduct, the seriousness of the threat to public policy, and proportionality—along with the existence of EU measures on recognition of judgments which 'are capable of protecting creditors' rights without necessarily restricting the debtor's freedom of movement'.[44] Its approach in this case suggests that the CJEU will not interpret the prohibition on serving 'economic ends' separately from the provisions in Article 27(2)—to which we now turn.

> 2. Measures taken on grounds of public policy or public security shall comply with the principle of proportionality and shall be based exclusively on the personal conduct of the individual concerned. Previous criminal convictions shall not in themselves constitute grounds for taking such measures.
>
> The personal conduct of the individual concerned must represent a genuine, present and sufficiently serious threat affecting one of the fundamental interests of society. Justifications that are isolated from the particulars of the case or that rely on considerations of general prevention shall not be accepted.

The first subparagraph of Article 27(2) previously appeared in Directive 64/221, although the citizens' Directive has added an express reference to proportionality.[45] The second subparagraph has also been added by the citizens' Directive. However, all these amendments codify the CJEU's jurisprudence concerning the previous Directive.[46]

The concepts of 'public policy' and 'public security' have already been examined above, in the context of Article 27(1). There are five additional elements set out in Article 27(2): the 'principle of proportionality'; the requirement that a restriction be based on 'personal conduct'; the rule concerning previous criminal convictions; the degree of threat posed; and the ban on general preventative measures. These elements are closely linked, and so some of them should be grouped together.

Personal conduct and general prevention

The principle that restrictions on free movement can only be based on the 'personal conduct' of the EU citizen (or his or her family members) was interpreted early in the CJEU's jurisprudence.[47] The *Bonsignore* case revolved around an Italian national who caused the accidental death of his brother by his careless handling of a firearm

---

[43] Paras 38 and 39 of the judgment.

[44] Case C-249/11 *Byankov*, judgment of 4 October 2012, not yet reported, paras 29–48 of the judgment.

[45] Art 3(1) and (2), Directive 64/221.

[46] In the words of N N Shuibhne, the Directive 'absorbs phrases plucked straight from the case law' in this area: 'Derogating from the Free Movement of Persons: When can EU Citizens be Deported?' (2005–06) 8 CYELS 187 at 191.

[47] Case 67/74 *Bonsignore* [1975] ECR 297.

unlawfully in his possession. While Mr Bonsignore was convicted of the criminal offence, the national court did not impose a punishment as it considered that under the circumstances the mental suffering caused to the individual by his own behaviour was sufficient. The German authorities then commenced expulsion proceedings against Mr Bonsignore which the national court clarified as being on general preventative grounds: the expulsion of a foreigner would have a deterrent effect in immigrant circles, having regard to the resurgence of violence in large urban centres in Germany. The CJEU held that the provisions must be interpreted in light of the objective of the Directive (at that time Directive 64/221), which seeks to coordinate measures justified on public policy grounds in order to reconcile them with the basic principle of free movement of persons and the elimination of all discrimination based on nationality. As the objective of the expulsion order was to deter other people from certain acts, it did not relate specifically to the conduct of Mr Bonsignore and thus could not justify an expulsion decision. Accordingly, general preventative grounds cannot justify an expulsion decision against an EU citizen; this rule now appears in the second subparagraph of Article 27(2). There must be a case-by-case assessment of each individual where the authorities of a Member State contemplate restricting free movement.[48] Automatic expulsion or refusal of entry is prohibited.[49]

Degree of the threat and proportionality

The threat which the individual is accused of representing must be more than presumed, it must be 'genuine', as the Commission notes in its guidelines on the Directive.[50] Further the threat must also be 'present', not presumptive. The requirements of proportionality must be respected. According to the Commission's guidance on the implementation of the Directive, the proportionality assessment requires the national authorities to identify the interests which are to be protected by the restriction of free movement. In light of those interests, the authorities are required to carry out an analysis of the characteristics of the threat. The Commission proposes three factors to be taken into account:

- the degree of social danger resulting from the presence of the person on the territory of the State;

---

[48] See, for instance, Case C-33/07 *Jipa* [2008] ECR I-5157, para 27, where the Court noted that there had been no such assessment, the Romanian authorities having based their decision entirely on the Belgian government's previous expulsion of the person concerned due to his unauthorized residence. See also Cases C-434/10 *Aladzhov*, judgment of 17 November 2011, not yet reported, paras 44 and 45, where the Court criticized a national rule imposing an exit restriction for tax debts without any requirement to examine personal conduct.

[49] The Commission's report on the application of the Directive (COM(2008) 840) states that two Member States provide for automatic expulsions, and one Member State aggravates detention periods if a person was staying irregularly at the time of the crime. The latter rule violates Arts 8(2), 9(3), and 20(2), if the persons concerned satisfy the conditions to obtain an underlying right to reside: see Chapters 3 and 4.

[50] COM(2009) 313 final.

- the nature of the offending activities, their frequency, cumulative danger, and damage caused;
- the time lapsed since the acts committed and behaviour of the person concerned.

Additionally, the proportionality test requires the personal and family situation of the individual to be assessed carefully to see whether the proposed expulsion is appropriate and does not go beyond what is strictly necessary to achieve the objective pursued. The factors set out in Article 28(1) are:

- the impact of the expulsion on the economic, personal, and family life of the individual taking into account also the impact on those family members who would remain after the departure of the EU citizen;
- the seriousness of the difficulties which the spouse/partner and any of their children risk facing in the country of origin of the person concerned;
- the strength of ties or lack of them with the Member State of origin and with the host Member State;
- the length of residence in the host Member State (though under the structure of the Directive there is greater protection against expulsion after five years' residence and acquisition of permanent residence and then again after ten years' residence; see Article 28);
- the age and state of health of the individual and any family members.

In two recent judgments, the Court of Justice has elaborated more upon the concept of proportionality in the context of Article 27(2). First of all, in the *Aladzhov* judgment, concerning a company director prevented from leaving the country until the company's tax debts were paid, the Court stated that is was for the national court to decide whether, by 'depriving Mr Aladzhov of the possibility of pursuing part of his professional activity abroad and thereby depriving him of part of his income, the measure of prohibition at issue is both appropriate to ensure the recovery of the tax sought and necessary for that purpose'. Also, the national court had to examine whether there were 'measures other than that of a prohibition on leaving the territory which would have been equally effective to obtain that recovery, but would not have encroached on freedom of movement', in particular the use of EU legislation on cross-border recovery of tax debts.[51] Secondly, in its *Byankov* judgment, concerning an exit restriction placed upon a private debtor, the Court ruled definitively that the Directive precluded the national measure in question partly on the grounds of proportionality, since its application was 'absolute' without any exceptions and applied 'indefinitely', with no 'possibility of regular review', and the recovery of civil debts could be enforced by means of the EU's legislation on recognition of judgments.[52]

---

[51] Case C-434/10, judgment of 17 November 2011, not yet reported, paras 47 and 48.
[52] Case C-249/11, judgment of 4 October 2012, not yet reported, paras 43-45.

Prior criminal convictions

In *Bouchereau*,[53] the CJEU set out the correct interpretation of the prohibition of expulsion on grounds of a simple criminal conviction. In that case a French national had been found guilty by a UK criminal court of unlawful possession of drugs. This was the second time in twelve months that Mr Bouchereau had pleaded guilty to the same offence. The criminal court, faced with the possibility of making a recommendation for deportation under national law, referred to the CJEU for clarification of the grounds on which it should be exercising its jurisdiction. The national court asked whether previous criminal convictions are solely relevant insofar as they manifest a present or future intention to act in a manner contrary to public policy or public security, or on the other hand, whether although the court cannot make a recommendation for expulsion on grounds of public policy based on the fact alone of a previous conviction, it is entitled to take into account the past conduct of the individual which resulted in the previous conviction. The CJEU held that the prohibition on reliance on previous convictions in themselves must be understood as requiring the national authorities to carry out a specific appraisal from the point of view of the interests inherent in protecting the requirements of public policy, which, it stated, does not coincide with the appraisals which formed the basis of the criminal conviction. This means, the CJEU continued, that the existence of a previous conviction can only be taken into account insofar as the circumstances which gave rise to that conviction are evidence of a personal conduct constituting a present threat to the requirements of public policy. A finding that a threat of this kind exists implies the existence of a propensity in the individual to act in the same way again in future. In such a case, it is possible that past conduct alone may constitute a threat to the requirements of public policy.

In quite a decisive move, the CJEU held in *Orfanopoulos*[54] that this provision precluded national legislation which requires a national authority to expel a national of another Member State who had been finally sentenced to a term of youth custody of two years for an intentional offence against narcotics laws. Of course the main mischief which the CJEU was addressing was the automatic effect of the sentence; nonetheless, the question of the seriousness of the offence is also taken into account. Of key importance is the propensity of the individual to act in the same way in the future. The CJEU noted that the threat to public security (and by extension public policy) requires on the one hand an assessment of the threat on the basis of the penalties, sentences imposed, degree of involvement in the criminal activity, and the risk of re-offending and on the other hand the risk of compromising the social rehabilitation of the Union citizen in the State where he or she has become genuinely integrated, something which is not only in the

---

[53] Case 30/77 [1977] ECR 1999.
[54] Joined Cases C-482/01 and C-493/01 [2004] ECR I-5257.

individual's interest but also in the interests of the Union in general.[55] Further, the right to private and family life as contained in Article 7 of the Charter and Article 8 ECHR, as fundamental rights whose observance the CJEU ensures, must be respected.[56]

> 3. In order to ascertain whether the person concerned represents a danger for public policy or public security, when issuing the registration certificate or, in the absence of a registration system, not later than three months from the date of arrival of the person concerned on its territory or from the date of reporting his/her presence within the territory, as provided for in Article 5(5), or when issuing the residence card, the host Member State may, should it consider this essential, request the Member State of origin and, if need be, other Member States to provide information concerning any previous police record the person concerned may have. Such enquiries shall not be made as a matter of routine. The Member State consulted shall give its reply within two months.

Article 27(3) is taken from Directive 64/221, with amendments.[57] This provision is based on the principle of cooperation among Member States. It permits a host Member State where an EU citizen or his or her family member has applied for a registration certificate or has remained for more than three months to request information from the Member State of origin concerning any previous police record on the person. However, the provision makes it clear that such inquiries must not be made as a matter of course, only in situations where this is essential in order to ascertain the danger posed by the person concerned. The Directive provides no indication of what circumstances might make such inquiries essential, although EU data protection law would apply.[58] Further it is not entirely clear what the procedure is for a Member State to make such inquiries.[59] What is clear is that an EU citizen who has criminal convictions in his or her State of origin or another Member State may find those convictions used as a basis for expulsion action in the host Member State. In *Gaydarov*[60] the CJEU examined whether a

---

[55] Case C-145/09 *Tsakouridis* [2010] ECR I-11979.

[56] Case C-145/09 *Tsakouridis* [2010] ECR I-11979.

[57] Art 5(2), Directive 64/221. The citizens' Directive has set out a precise time frame for making such requests, and has more clearly specified the grounds for making them, ie adding the proviso that the purpose of such requests is to ascertain whether the person concerned is a threat to public policy or public security.

[58] See the Framework Decision on data protection in the policing and criminal law context, [2008] OJ L 350/60. The Commission has proposed a Directive to replace this Framework Decision (COM(2012) 10, 25 January 2012); this proposal is currently under discussion.

[59] There is EU legislation on the process of requesting *criminal* records from other Member States ([2009] OJ L 93/23 and 33), but Art 27(3) refers to the broader notion of a *police* record, which might include information on suspicions or investigations relating to the person concerned that have not been tested in court. Currently, there are a number of different EU mechanisms for the exchange of information among police forces, but not a general system for the exchange of information on police records, and the Commission has ruled out proposing such a measure for the time being: see the Communication on exchanges of police information, COM(2012) 735, 7 December 2012. The proposed Regulation on Europol, the EU's police agency (COM(2013) 173, 27 March 2013) does not provide for Europol to handle such inquiries.

[60] Case C-430/10 *Gaydarov*, judgment of 17 November 2011, not yet reported.

home State could prevent one of its nationals from travelling elsewhere in the EU on account of a criminal conviction in a third country (see the commentary on Article 27(2)). While Article 27(3) was not referred to in the judgment, the CJEU held that such interference could be justified provided that it was appropriate to ensure the achievement of the objective it pursued and did not go beyond what was necessary to attain it, and once the national authorities examined the citizen's personal conduct. Furthermore, the principle of proportionality must be strictly adhered to. It could be argued that similar criteria should apply also to Member States' inquiries about the police records of EU citizens, nationals of other Member States but present on their territory. The impact of any evidence of criminal convictions in the home Member State could only justify a host Member State finding that the individual's presence was a threat to public policy or security if all the criteria set out in Articles 27(2) and (3) and 28 were fulfilled.[61] The mere fact of a conviction in the State of origin could not justify interference, on its own, with the individual's right of residence in the host Member State, since the rule concerning previous criminal convictions set out in Article 27(2) applies regardless of the State in which the criminal conviction took place.[62]

> 4. The Member State which issued the passport or identity card shall allow the holder of the document who has been expelled on grounds of public policy, public security, or public health from another Member State to re-enter its territory without any formality even if the document is no longer valid or the nationality of the holder is in dispute.

This final paragraph of Article 27, which has been taken over from Directive 64/221,[63] embodies the rule of customary international law that States must allow their own nationals entry to their territory. Article 12(4) of the UN Covenant on Civil and Political Rights (ICCPR) 1966 contains a similar right for every national to enter the territory of his or her country of nationality. For European purposes this duty is found in Article 4 Protocol 4 ECHR, although not all Council of Europe States have ratified this provision.[64] Quite simply, this provision means that when a Member State seeks to expel an EU citizen who holds the underlying nationality of another Member State, or a third-country national family member of an EU citizen who has been issued an identity card by another Member State, the Member State of nationality is not permitted to stand on ceremony and refuse to take back its citizen. However, the wording of this provision follows that of the

---

[61] The CJEU has confirmed this approach as regards entry bans for third-country national family members of EU citizens, as set out in the Schengen Information System: see Case C-503/03 *Commission v Spain* [2006] ECR I-1097, and now Art 25 of Reg 1987/2006 establishing the second-generation Schengen Information System ([2006] OJ L 381/4), which began operations on 9 April 2013.

[62] Case C-430/10 *Gaydarov* [2011] ECR I-11637, paras 34 and 38 of the judgment.

[63] Art 3(4) of that Directive.

[64] Notably, Greece, Switzerland, Turkey, and the UK have not done so. However, all of them have ratified the ICCPR.

international commitments in that the right belongs to the individual to enter the State of his or her nationality.

F. Evaluation—Article 27

This provision of the Directive, along with the similar provisions in the prior legislation, has given rise to substantial jurisprudence over a forty-year period. This is perhaps an indication of two factors. Firstly, some Member States remain partial to the idea of expelling the nationals of other Member States where they are involved in criminal activities or suspected of so being. It is clear that this seems to be a central issue for some Member States more than others. For instance the UK likes to expel foreign criminals, while Germany appears to have a propensity for automatic expulsion grounds on the basis of certain criminal convictions which it applies to EU citizens as well as third-country nationals. Secondly, the CJEU has perhaps not been as clear as it could be on how Member States are obliged to apply the restrictions on expulsion. While it has provided general grounds which sound good on paper, when officials at the Member State level try to apply them to the facts of cases before them, there appear always to be questions about the best approach. This has resulted in a continuing series of references over the whole of the period to the CJEU from national courts, which clearly remain in doubt as to what expulsion measures may be regarded compatible with obligations under Union law.

A number of clarifications could have assisted national courts, such as requiring at the very least a criminal conviction before the 'public policy' ground can be invoked, but the CJEU has not done this (or at least has not *yet* done this). This has resulted in the Commission stating in its guidelines on the application of the Directive that in certain circumstances persistent petty criminality may represent a threat to public policy despite the fact that any single crime/offence, taken individually, would be insufficient to represent a sufficiently serious threat.[65] However, this assertion has no express support in the case law of the CJEU. The proportionality assessment turns up in this provision but will arise again a few more times before we leave the provisions of chapter VI. It is not entirely clear exactly what the different proportionality tests require, nor what the difference among them may be.

As the provisions on restriction of free movement have become more elaborate with Directive 2004/38, there would be additional scope for the CJEU to take the opportunity to develop more easily identifiable rules which can be applied with greater confidence by national officials in respect of the meaning of public policy and the role of criminal convictions in the decision-making on restricting free movement.

---

[65] COM(2009) 313.

G. Analysis—Article 28

Article 28—Protection against expulsion

Article 28 is an entirely new provision as compared to the previous legislation. It implements the objective (set out in the preamble) of setting out a 'tighter definition of the circumstances' in which EU citizens and their family members can be expelled (recital 22), recognizing also that expulsion 'can seriously harm persons' exercising free movement rights and 'should therefore be limited' (recital 23), and putting into place the principle that 'the greater the degree of integration of Union citizens and their family members in the host Member State, the greater the degree of protection against expulsion should be' (recital 24). It starts with general rules concerning all expulsions within the scope of the Directive (Article 28(1)), then raises the threshold for expulsion where EU citizens or their family members are permanent residents (Article 28(2)), and finally raises that threshold even further where EU citizens have resided for ten years in the host Member State, or are minors (Article 28(3)). Although Article 28 only concerns expulsion, presumably it would also apply if a State refuses to *re-admit* a person who still retains a right of residence or permanent residence in the host State, and is returning there after a visit to another State. If it did not, the effectiveness of Article 28 would be completely undermined, since the protection it provides for could be lost any time that a person takes (for example) a holiday or business trip to another country—a journey which might itself entail an exercise of free movement rights within the Union. Finally, it should be noted that Article 15(2) specifies that the expiry of an identity card or passport which the person used to enter the host Member State and then used to obtain a registration certificate or residence card (see Articles 8 and 10, discussed in Chapter 3) is not a valid ground for expulsion from that State,[66] and Article 14(3) bans the automatic expulsion of EU citizens purely because they have applied for social assistance.

> 1. Before taking an expulsion decision on grounds of public policy or public security, the host Member State shall take account of considerations such as how long the individual concerned has resided on its territory, his/her age, state of health, family and economic situation, social and cultural integration into the host Member State and the extent of his/her links with the country of origin.

This provision includes the second proportionality test to be found in this chapter of the Directive, in this case examining proportionality from the perspective of the individual. Here the criteria which are relevant to the assessment of the appropriateness of an expulsion decision are set out in detail, although the list

---

[66] This provision takes over the wording of Art 3(3) of Directive 64/221. According to the case law, the same rule applies if a visa expires before a person applies for a residence permit (now a residence card): see Case C-459/99 *MRAX* [2002] ECR I-6591, paras 86–91.

in Article 28(1) is not exhaustive ('such as'). The relevant criteria set out in the provision are:

- length of residence on the territory of the host State;
- the age of the individual;
- the state of his or her health;
- the family and economic situation of the individual;
- the social and cultural integration of the individual into the host Member State;
- the extent of the individual's links with his or her country of origin.

These criteria will be considered in turn.

Length of residence

Although EU citizens and their family members will get enhanced protection against expulsion after they acquire permanent residence with the completion of five years' lawful residence in the host Member State (Article 28(2)), and EU citizens obtain further protection against expulsion after ten years' residence in that State (Article 28(3)), the first criterion might still be relevant to them in such circumstances, for instance ensuring that there is greater protection against expulsion for persons who have resided on the territory for thirty years as compared to those who have resided there for ten years. Indeed, the CJEU has confirmed that Article 28(1) applies to all expulsions, even when the person concerned falls within the scope of Article 28(2) or (3).[67] Moreover, the Court has stated that '[i]n the case of a Union citizen who has lawfully spent most or even all of his childhood and youth in the host Member State, very good reasons would have to be put forward to justify the expulsion measure'.[68]

Age and state of health of the individual

Exactly how one is to assess the importance of the age of the individual is less than entirely clear. In Article 28(3)(b), minors are provided with specific protection against expulsion, so presumably they are not the target group here. It may be, though, that this is no more than a supposition, that like minors, the elderly could be among those whose expulsion should be the subject of even more anxious scrutiny than of younger people. Equally, young people who are no longer minors might still be considered particularly vulnerable in the face of an expulsion decision. Recital 23 in the preamble to the Directive does no more than repeat the fact that the age of the individual is a relevant factor, without providing further explanation. Similarly, there is no indication on how the state of health of an individual is

---

[67] Case C-145/09 *Tsakouridis* [2010] ECR I-11979, para 26; Case C-348/09 *PI*, judgment of 22 May 2012, not yet reported, paras 32 and 34.
[68] Case C-145/09 *Tsakouridis* [2010] ECR I-11979, para 53, referring to the jurisprudence of the ECtHR.

supposed to impact on any decision to expel him or her. One can surmise that the intention is that people who are seriously unwell should not be subject to expulsion orders.

Family and economic situation

The family and economic situation of the individual also raise complicated questions. Presumably the intention is that expulsion action should not have the effect of separating families without careful consideration of all the potential impacts. But a consideration of the economic situation of the individual sits uncomfortably with the prohibition in Article 27(1) of expulsions which are invoked to serve economic ends.

Social and cultural integration

The factor of social and cultural integration into the host Member State opens another can of worms. EU citizens cannot be the subject of 'integration' measures or conditions as referred to in Directive 2003/109 on long-term resident third-country nationals or Directive 2003/86 on family reunification for third-country nationals.[69] The reason for this is because EU citizens are entitled to equality with nationals of the Member States by virtue of Article 18 TFEU and thus as own nationals of Member States are not (or not yet) subject to integration conditions and measures, so EU citizens cannot be either. So what does this provision mean? In *Kahveci*[70] the CJEU found that Turkish workers who had been naturalized in the Netherlands were entitled to continue to rely on their Turkish citizenship to enjoy better family reunification rights under the EC–Turkey Association Agreement than under Dutch national law applicable to Dutch citizens because this enhanced the integration of these people into the EU.[71] The objective of the Agreement was to deepen the lasting integration of the Turkish migrant worker's family in the host Member State by granting to the family member concerned, after three years of legal residence, the possibility of him- or herself gaining access to the labour force. The fundamental objective thus pursued is that of consolidating the position of that family member, who is, at that stage, already legally integrated in the host Member State, by giving him or her the means to earn his or her own living in that State and therefore to establish a position which is independent of that of the migrant worker, according to the CJEU. So it would seem that integration cannot be equated with equal status with the nationals of the host State. Security of residence and a right to work seem to be at the heart of the EU concept of integration which was at work in that judgment at least.

---

[69] Respectively [2003] OJ L 251/12 and [2004] OJ L 16/44.
[70] Joined Cases C-7/10 and 9/10, judgment of 29 March 2012, not yet reported.
[71] See further the commentary on Arts 2(1) and 3(1) in Chapter 1.

Extent of links with the country of origin

The extent of links with the host and home States also raise similar questions about how these links are to be identified and what weight is to be placed on them. One easy solution is to seek to apply the jurisprudence of the European Court of Human Rights in the Article 8 cases on interferences by States with the right to private and family life of foreigners by reason of expulsion decisions. There are many judgments of that Court on the subject, but two stand out as setting the criteria for consideration of expulsion measures—*Boultif* [72] and *Uner* [73]—and there is a suspicious similarity to the criteria set out in this part of Article 28 and those two judgments. Suffice it to recognize that the ECtHR consistently commences with the sentence: 'The Court recalls that the Convention does not guarantee the right of an alien to enter or to reside in a particular country. However, the removal of a person from a country where close members of his family are living may amount to an infringement of the right to respect for family life as guaranteed in Article 8 § 1 of the Convention (see Moustaquim v. Belgium, judgment of 18 February 1991, Series A no. 193, p. 18, § 36)'. [74] This means that the starting place is entirely different than in EU law where the individual has a right of entry and residence and it is for the Member State to justify the interference. Thus it is apparent that a simple transposition of the jurisprudence of the ECtHR to apply the Article 28 test would not necessarily result in the correct outcome. Instead the ECtHR guidelines to the correct application of Article 8 ECHR need to be modified to reflect the fundamentally different starting place in EU law than in human rights law. In particular, although (as noted above) the Court of Justice accepted the ECtHR guidelines in *Orfanopoulos* and *Tsakouridis*, for the purposes of EU law these guidelines must be applied while taking account of the right of entry for EU citizens into other Member States, so the application of that balancing test in the EU law context might in particular be more favourable for people who have resided for a fairly short period.

> 2. The host Member State may not take an expulsion decision against Union citizens or their family members, irrespective of nationality, who have the right of permanent residence on its territory, except on serious grounds of public policy or public security.

This paragraph provides for a higher level of protection against expulsion, which is designed to reflect the increased recognition of belonging in the host State which the status of permanent residence evidences (see Chapter 4). The Commission originally proposed that anyone who acquired permanent residence should have an absolute protection against expulsion on any grounds. [75] This was a step too far

---

[72] Reports 2001–IX–400-1, 406.
[73] 18 October 2006.
[74] *Boultif*, para 39.
[75] COM(2001) 257.

for the Council,[76] and the provision was divided into two parts—a heightened protection for those EU citizens and their family members with permanent residence (Article 28(2)) and an even higher protection for those EU citizens who have resided in the host Member State for ten years or more or are children (Article 28(3), discussed further below). As noted already, the rationale, contained in recital 24 in the preamble, is that the greater the degree of integration of the Union citizens and their family members into the host Member State (as evidenced, inter alia, by length of residence) the greater the degree of protection against expulsion should be. According to the Commission's report on the implementation of the Directive ('the 2008 report'), this protection expressed the underlying principle of proportionality by strengthening the protection against expulsion for those EU citizens or family members who have resided in a host Member State for a longer period of time.[77] The Commission's main concern regarding the implementation of the Directive, as recorded in its 2008 Report, is that the implementation of Article 28(2) (and (3)) must not trivialize the degree of protection afforded by Article 28(1). According to the Commission, there needs to be a clear distinction between the normal, 'serious', and 'imperative' grounds on which expulsion can be taken.[78]

Personal scope of Article 28(2)

First, Article 28(2) applies not only to EU citizens but to their third-country national family members, as does Article 28(1). Family members are at least those persons included in the definition in Article 2(2), and arguably also those covered by Article 3(2) (see Chapter 1). As permanent residence is acquired as soon as the conditions set out in chapter IV of the Directive are fulfilled, an EU citizen or his or her family member may well have acquired permanent residence without any specific act by the host Member State or even necessarily with the knowledge of the host Member State (see Article 25, discussed in Chapter 5). Thus the issue of how to count time for the purpose of the acquisition of permanent residence is a matter of some concern. Article 28(2) implicitly refers back to chapter IV of the Directive on this point, which has already been the subject of case law. Equally, the loss of permanent residence status—which would logically entail also the loss of increased protection against expulsion pursuant to Article 28(2)—is also addressed explicitly in chapter IV.[79] The issue of how to count time also arises as regards Article 28(3),

---

[76] See Common Position 6/2003, [2004] OJ C 54 E/25, statement of reasons on Art 28: 'the Council is almost unanimously against the absolute protection against expulsion'.

[77] COM(2008) 840.

[78] COM(2009) 313.

[79] The effect of imprisonment and/or expulsion upon the acquisition or loss of permanent residence rights is also discussed at length in Chapter 4. Although the Advocate-General's Opinion in the case of C-348/09 *PI*, judgment of 22 May 2012, not yet reported, argued that permanent residence status (and so the protection of Art 28(2)) could not be obtained where a period of hidden criminality began before the person concerned was resident for five years, the Court implicitly rejected this view (see the commentary on Art 28(3) below).

where there is increased protection against expulsion after ten years' residence. As ten years' residence does not correspond with any specific status recognized in the Directive, counting it becomes particularly important.

Finally, the CJEU has ruled that like the right to permanent residence, enhanced protection against expulsion on the basis of ten years' residence pursuant to Article 28(3) can be lost. However, where a national court in a finding of fact determines that an individual has lost that greater protection, he or she may still be entitled to the enhanced protection under Article 28(2) because he or she holds permanent residence status. According to the CJEU it is for the national court to determine, taking into account all the factors set out, whether the EU citizen falls within the scope of in Article 28(2) or Article 28(3).[80]

Substance of Article 28(2)

First of all, the grounds for expulsion set out in Article 28(2) are exhaustive ('may *not* take an expulsion decision . . . *except* on serious grounds'). The CJEU first considered the meaning of 'serious grounds of public policy' in the case of *Tsakouridis*.[81] In this case a Greek national was born in Germany in 1978. He finished secondary school in Germany in 1996 and was issued an unlimited residence permit in that host Member State in 2001. However, from March to October 2004 he ran a pancake stall on Rhodes then returned to Germany and worked from December 2004. He returned to Greece to run the pancake stall in October 2005. On 22 November 2005 a German court issued an international arrest warrant against him and on 19 November 2006 he was arrested in Greece and transferred to Germany on 19 March 2007. Mr Tsakouridis had acquired a number of convictions for crimes of violence, possession of illegal objects and prohibited drugs, and dealing in prohibited drugs. A German court determined on 19 August 2008 that Mr Tsakouridis had lost his right of entry and residence in Germany because he had been sentenced to five years' imprisonment thus the measures were justified on grounds of 'imperative grounds of public security', applying the ten-year rule which we will discuss below under Article 28(3). We will return to this case below, as regards the clarification it provides for Article 28(3). However, the CJEU did state that 'since the use of drugs constitutes a danger for society such as to justify special measures against foreign nationals who contravene its laws on drugs [referring to prior case law] . . . it must follow that dealing in narcotics as part of an organised group is *a fortiori* covered by the concept of "public policy" for the purposes of Article 28(2)'.[82] Possibly the Court meant here to draw a distinction between *using* drugs (which might justify an expulsion of a person who does not have permanent residence) and *dealing* in them, which was a more serious offence that (unlike simply using drugs) could

---

[80] Case C-145/09 *Tsakouridis* [2010] ECR I-11979.
[81] Case C-145/09 *Tsakouridis* [2010] ECR I-11979.
[82] Case C-145/09 *Tsakouridis* [2010] ECR I-11979, para 54.

constitute a 'serious ground' of public policy which could justify the expulsion of a person within the scope of Article 28(2).

> 3. An expulsion decision may not be taken against Union citizens, except if the decision is based on imperative grounds of public security, as defined by Member States, if they:
> (a) have resided in the host Member State for the previous ten years; or
> (b) are a minor, except if the expulsion is necessary for the best interests of the child, as provided for in the United Nations Convention on the Rights of the Child of 20 November 1989.

Following the logic set out above as regards Article 28(2), this paragraph provides the highest level of protection against expulsion for an EU citizen from a host Member State. Recital 24 in the preamble states, as noted above, that 'the greater the degree of integration of Union citizens and their family members in the host Member State, the greater the degree of protection against expulsion should be', and that 'only in exceptional circumstances, where there are imperative grounds of public security, should an expulsion measure be taken against Union citizens who have resided for many years in the territory of the host Member State, in particular when they were born and have resided there throughout their life'. It further states that 'such exceptional circumstances should also apply to an expulsion measure taken against minors in order to protect their links with their family, in accordance with the United Nations Convention on the Rights of the Child (CRC) 1989'. In its 2008 Report on the implementation of the Directive the Commission provided no further clarification of this provision.[83] In its 2009 guidance on the Directive, it specified that there must be a clear distinction between 'normal', 'serious', and 'imperative' grounds.[84]

Personal scope of Article 28(3)

First of all, it seems clear that from the wording of Article 28(3), as compared to the remaining provisions of Article 28(2) and the rest of this chapter (and the rest of the Directive), Article 28(3) applies *only to EU citizens*, and not to their third-country national family members. But the latter persons could clearly still qualify for enhanced protection pursuant to Article 28(2), which applies 'irrespective of nationality', and could benefit from extra protection pursuant to Article 28(1) in light of their length of residence on the territory.

Secondly, in order for an EU citizen to qualify for the enhanced protection of Article 28(3) at least one of two conditions must be fulfilled:[85] either the individual has resided in the host Member State for the previous ten years, or he or she is a

---

[83] COM(2008) 840.
[84] COM(2009) 313.
[85] It is technically possible to satisfy *both* these criteria, in which case there is arguably a prima facie case for an even greater degree of protection against expulsion.

'minor'. With the passage of time, the former condition will eventually be satisfied, while the latter status will inevitably be lost. If either development takes place during the course of expulsion proceedings or a prosecution that leads up to them, the wording of the Directive suggests that the decisive point is when the expulsion decision was taken.[86] Arguably, however, Article 33(2), which requires authorities to review the situation of the individual if an expulsion order is not enforced more than two years after it has been issued, would require those authorities to take such changes of circumstances into account.

The term 'minor' is not defined in the Directive, but arises first in Article 13 on retained rights of residence (see Chapter 3). A consistent meaning of 'minor' throughout the Directive is likely. However, as there is a specific reference in Article 28(3) to the UN CRC, at least this provision of the Directive should be interpreted in line with that Convention, Article 1 of which provides that a 'child' means every human being below the age of eighteen years, unless under the law applicable to the child, majority is attained earlier.

Regarding the requirement that the individual has resided in the Member State for the previous ten years, this was an issue in only one of the two cases on Article 28(3) which the CJEU has decided to date.[87] In the first case (*Tsakouridis*), the individual had been born in the host Member State, undertaken all his schooling there and lived there for about twenty-six years before going to his country of nationality, it would seem, for the purpose of self-employment for a period of about seven months, over the tourist season, after which he returned to the host Member State and worked there for some months. At the start of the next tourist season he went back to his Member State of nationality again for self-employment and during that period of residence he was the subject of an international arrest warrant from his host Member State and was sent back there. The national authorities of his host Member State withdrew his residence permit, determined he no longer had the right to enter the country, and proceeded directly to the assessment of the proportionality of the expulsion decision and entry ban on the basis of the individual's personal circumstances. The CJEU found that the Directive, while making the enjoyment of enhanced protection subject to the person's presence in the Member State concerned for ten years preceding the expulsion measure, is silent as to the circumstances which are capable of interrupting the period of ten years' residence for the purposes of the acquisition of the right to enhanced protection against expulsion. The CJEU did not simply apply by analogy Article 16(4) (see Chapter 4), which regulates how an EU citizen (or his or her family members) can

---

[86] 'An expulsion decision may not be taken... if they... (a) have resided... or (b) are a minor.' See also recital 24 ('[o]nly in exceptional circumstances should an expulsion measure be taken against...'), and the judgment in C-145/09 *Tsakouridis* [2010] ECR I-11979, paras 31, 32, and 38 ('preceding the expulsion decision').

[87] Cases C-145/09 *Tsakouridis* [2010] ECR I-11979 and C-348/09 *PI*, judgment of 22 May 2012, not yet reported.

lose permanent residence status. Instead, the central issue as regards Article 28(3) is whether the person is genuinely integrated into the host Member State. Referring to recitals 23 and 24 in the preamble, the CJEU noted the reference to those who were born in a host Member State and have spent all their life there. However, it considered that the fact remained that, in view of the wording of Article 28(3), the decisive criterion is whether the Union citizen has lived in that Member State for the ten years preceding the expulsion decision. This first finding appears to give preference to formalism over the content of integration, and disregards the wording of the preamble, even though the Court gives the preamble great weight as regards interpreting the similar issue of the acquisition of permanent residence status (see Chapter 4).

According to the CJEU, as regards the question of the extent to which absences from the host Member State during the ten-year period preceding the expulsion decision prevent the individual from enjoying enhanced protection pursuant to Article 28(3), an overall assessment of the person's situation must be made on each occasion at the precise time when the question of expulsion arises. Therefore, according to the CJEU, the national court must take into consideration 'all the relevant factors . . . in each individual case, in particular the duration of each period of absence, the cumulative duration and the frequency of those absences, and the reasons why the person concerned left the host Member State'. The objective of this assessment is to ascertain 'whether those absences involve the transfer to another State of the centre of the personal, family or occupational interests of the person'. In effect, what the national court must determine is whether on the facts of the individual's case, the integrating links previously forged with the host Member State have been broken. This second finding appears to privilege substance over form.

In this assessment, the CJEU allows the national court to take into account the fact that the individual was the subject of a forced return to the host Member State to serve a prison sentence and the time spent in prison in addition to the other criteria. If the integrating links have not been broken then the individual is entitled to the highest level of protection against expulsion—meaning that there must be imperative grounds of public security to justify such a measure. The Court's test, while focused on the acquisition of enhanced protection under Article 28(3), seems to apply the same rule to the acquisition and loss of that status.[88] The CJEU added, for good measure, that where the national court finds that the integrating links have been broken and so the individual is no longer entitled to the Article 28(3) protection, it must then consider the case under Article 28(2) insofar as the individual had acquired permanent residence.

---

[88] Compare to the different rules in Art 16(3) and (4) for the acquisition and loss of permanent residence status: see Chapter 4.

In the second case on Article 28(3), the individual had lived in the host Member State from 1987 and had never moved, so the question of how to count the ten years did not arise, at least for the CJEU.[89] Implicitly, the Court's judgment rejected the Advocate-General's opinion in this case, which had argued that the person concerned could not qualify for protection under Article 28(3) despite his long period of residence, since this provision created 'a simple presumption of integration', which could be rebutted by the facts. In this case, the person concerned had begun to abuse a child before the five-year period for the acquisition of permanent residence status, and continued to abuse that child for eleven years afterward. According to the Advocate-General, this individual 'shows a total lack of desire to integrate into the society in which he finds himself and some of whose fundamental values he so conscientiously disregarded for years', and his residence was 'not interrupted because his conduct remained hidden'. In his view, '[a]n offence of that nature, just because it has lasted a long time, cannot create a right'; Article 35 was applicable, since the person's behaviour was fraudulent;[90] and the individual could not 'derive from his criminal conduct the right to the enhanced protection provided for in Article 28(2) and (3)', since this would 'conflict with the values on which citizenship of the Union is based'.

Presumably protection pursuant to Article 28(3) can be acquired in part during time periods which pre-date the transposition deadline of the Directive, or which occurred before the Member State of the person's nationality or residence acceded to the EU, by analogy with the case law on acquiring permanent residence status.[91] Indeed, the Court assumed as much in *Tsakouridis* and *PI*; otherwise the persons concerned (and all other EU citizens) could only benefit from Article 28(3) from 30 April 2016. Equally the interpretation of the permanent residence rules as regards the effect of imprisonment and/or expulsion should also apply to Article 28(3),[92] although the Court's ruling in *Tsakouridis* arguably casts doubt on that interpretation.

Finally, it is notable that unlike Article 16(1), there is no requirement in Article 28(3) that the prior residence must be legal or (unlike recital 17 in the preamble) that it must be in accordance with the Directive. In any event, there is no requirement to obtain permanent residence status before Article 28(3) is applicable, and so even if persons within the scope of the Directive cannot qualify for that status (for instance, even if an EU citizen's children and their parent carer who have the right

---

[89] Case C-348/09 *PI*, judgment of 22 May 2012, not yet reported.

[90] On that provision, see Chapter 7.

[91] See the commentary on Art 16 in Chapter 4, and particularly Case C-378/12 *Oneukwere*, pending. By analogy with the argument set out in Chapter 4, arguably an individual who had acquired EU citizenship by naturalization within the last ten years would also be covered by Art 28(3).

[92] See Case C-400/12 *MG*, pending, where the national court has asked questions about the calculation of the ten-year time period and the effect of imprisonment.

to reside pursuant to Article 12(3) cannot obtain permanent residence status), they could still obtain protection under Article 28(3). It can even be argued that any EU citizen with ten years' residence can obtain such protection, including persons who have only been permitted to reside on the basis of national law or persons who fall within the scope of Article 10 of Regulation 492/2011 (the children of migrant workers who are undertaking education).

Substance of Article 28(3)

First of all, the ground for expulsion set out in Article 28(3) is again exhaustive ('may *not* be taken against ... *except if* the decision ...'), as confirmed by the preamble ('only'). There is no definition provided for 'imperative' in the Directive or elsewhere in EU law. Further, expulsion action can be taken under this provision exclusively on grounds of 'public security', not 'public health' or 'public policy'. The CJEU held that the concept of 'imperative grounds of public security' is 'considerably stricter' than the concept of 'serious grounds' as set out in Article 28(2); it 'presupposes not only the existence of a threat to public security but also that such a threat is of a particularly high degree of seriousness'.[93] This is perhaps not as helpful as it might be.

In respect of the concept of 'public security', this also is not defined in the Directive. Again the CJEU was called upon to provide clarification for its meaning in the context of the Directive. It had regard to its previous jurisprudence in other fields and found that the term includes both the internal and external security of a Member State. It continued that 'a threat to the functioning of the institutions and essential public services and the survival of the population, as well as the risk of a serious disturbance to foreign relations or to the peaceful coexistence of nations, or a risk to military interests, may affect public security'.[94] However, having set out this tableau of public security interests, the CJEU added that it does not follow that objectives such as the fight against crime in connection with dealing in narcotics as part of an organized group are necessarily excluded from that concept. This provided the CJEU an opportunity to set out its views on dealing in narcotics which it states have 'devastating effects' and which, for that reason, is the subject of a Framework Decision.[95] On this basis it found that '[s]ince drug addiction represents a serious evil for the individual and is fraught with social and economic danger to mankind ... trafficking in narcotics as part of an organised group could reach a level of intensity that might directly threaten the calm and physical security of the population as a whole or a large part of it'.[96]

---

[93] Case C-145/09 *Tsakouridis* [2010] ECR I-11979, paras 40 and 41.
[94] Case C-145/09 *Tsakouridis* [2010] ECR I-11979, paras 43 and 44.
[95] 2004/757/JHA, [2004] OJ L 335/8.
[96] Case C-145/09 *Tsakouridis* [2010] ECR I-11979, paras 45–47.

In 2012 the CJEU provided further clarification of the meaning of 'imperative ground of public security', in a case involving repeated sexual offences against a young child. It affirmed its jurisprudence that the concept requires that the threat is of a particularly high degree of seriousness.[97] It added that the concept is limited, as stated in the recital, to exceptional circumstances. Reaffirming that EU law does not impose on Member States a uniform scale of values as regards the assessment of conduct which may be considered to be contrary to public security, the CJEU confirmed that 'imperative grounds of public security' is to be defined by the Member States. It further elaborated on this, stating that Member States retain the freedom to determine the requirements of public security in accordance with their national needs (which can vary from one Member State to another and from one era to another). However, as this is a justification for a derogation from the fundamental freedom of free movement of persons the requirements must be interpreted strictly. This means that their scope cannot be determined unilaterally by each Member State without control by the EU institutions (in other words, the Court itself).

In the case under consideration, the CJEU provided factors regarding criminal offences for the national court to take into account in determining whether the Member State could justify an expulsion decision on imperative grounds of public security. The offence was listed in Article 83(1) TFEU, which sets out the areas of particularly serious crime where there is a cross-border element which the EU can address by harmonizing substantive criminal law.[98] Presumably these are not the only crimes that could be relevant for applying Article 28(3) though, since Article 83(1) TFEU does not mention some other serious crimes like murder. A Directive adopted under the Article requires Member States to provide for maximum terms of imprisonment of 'at least' specific periods for the offences against children defined therein, with higher sentences possible where certain conditions are met.[99] Accordingly the CJEU held that it is open to Member States to regard criminal offences contained in the EU legislation as 'constituting a particularly serious threat to one of the fundamental interests of society, which might pose a direct threat to the calm and physical security of the population' and which would therefore be covered by the concept of 'imperative grounds of public security'. However, 'the manner in which such offences were committed must disclose particularly serious characteristics', which the national court must determine on the basis of the individual examination of the case before it.[100]

The CJEU confirmed that the national court must carry out the proportionality test set out in Article 28(1) examining the features of the individual's life in

---

[97] Case C-348/09 *PI*, judgment of 22 May 2012, not yet reported.
[98] The crimes in question are terrorism, trafficking in human beings and sexual exploitation of women and children, illicit drug trafficking, illicit arms trafficking, money laundering, corruption, counterfeiting of means of payment, computer crime, and organized crime.
[99] Directive 2011/93, [2011] OJ L 335/1.
[100] Case C-348/09 *PI*, judgment of 22 May 2012, not yet reported.

addition to ensuring that the conduct of the individual represents a genuine, present threat affecting one of the fundamental interests of society or of the host Member State which includes whether the individual has a propensity to act in the same way in the future. Also, an expulsion measure pursuant to Article 28(3) 'can be justified on imperative grounds of public security . . . only if, having regard to the exceptional seriousness of the threat, such a measure is necessary for the protection of the interests it aims to secure, provided that that objective cannot be attained by less strict means, having regard to the length of residence of the Union citizen in the host Member State and in particular to the serious negative consequences such a measure may have for Union citizens who have become genuinely integrated into the host Member State'. Moreover, 'a balance must be struck more particularly between the exceptional nature of the threat to public security as a result of the personal conduct of the person concerned . . . on the one hand, and, on the other hand, the risk of compromising the social rehabilitation of the Union citizen in the State in which he has become genuinely integrated, which . . . is not only in his interest but also in that of the [EU] in general'. A specific criminal sentence could only be one factor in that regard. Finally, account must be taken of human rights, in particular the right to protection of family life pursuant to Article 8 ECHR (and Article 7 of the EU Charter of Fundamental Rights).[101]

H. Evaluation—Article 28

Article 28 provides a high threshold of protection for EU citizens and (for the most part) their third-country national family members against expulsion from their host Member State. The Directive introduces a scale of increasing protection depending on the length of residence of the individual or in the event that he or she is a minor. The way this scale has been interpreted by the CJEU indicates that there are a series of proportionality assessments which must be undertaken by the national authorities and their courts. The starting point is that expulsion is an exception to the right of residence or permanent residence of any EU citizen or his or her family members and therefore must be justified. Where the State considers that such a measure is justified then the authorities must spell out the grounds. Once they have established the grounds then there is a proportionality test against those grounds. The level of seriousness of the grounds for expulsion rise by increments of five years—from one to five years it is the basic standard. From five to ten years (assuming the individual has acquired permanent residence) the threshold is 'serious grounds', and from ten years' residence onwards it is 'imperative grounds of public security'.

---

[101] Case C-145/09 *Tsakouridis* [2010] ECR I-11979, paras 49–52.

There seem to be a number of places, though where State authorities must carry out proportionality style assessments. The first is on the justification of expulsion, where the individual's circumstances must be examined. The second is in determining whether the individual has in fact clocked up ten years' residence and thus should enjoy the highest level of protection. Here the authorities must determine whether the integrating links have been broken on the basis of a similar kind of assessment.

The problem with the proportionality tests is that they may cloud the starting point of the issue: the individual has a right of residence unless the State can justify an interference with that right. It is particularly important that national authorities and courts do not simply transpose the proportionality assessments which they have developed in line with the jurisprudence of the European Court of Human Rights to this Directive, without (as discussed above) taking account of the existence of a right of entry under EU law.

Given the clear intention of the EU legislature to enshrine higher levels of protection against expulsion for EU citizens and their family members in the citizens' Directive, the case law on these provisions to date is, with great respect, disappointing. The basic problem is that the CJEU has indicated when people within the scope of Article 28(2) or (3) *can* still be expelled, but has said nothing concrete to indicate when they *cannot*. So there is nothing beyond vague rhetoric to indicate what additional protection actually exists.[102] Furthermore, the wording and context of Article 28(3) does not support the Court's interpretation of that provision, given its limitation to public security (as distinct from public policy),[103] and 'imperative' grounds of public security at that. Since the Directive was negotiated in the aftermath of the 9/11 terrorist attacks in the United States, the better view is that Article 28(3) only permits expulsion in the case of direct involvement in major terrorist offences.

While the Court has endorsed a wide personal scope but a narrow material scope of Article 28(2) and (3), the converse approach set out in the *PI* opinion must be rejected even more strongly. Having rejected reliance upon recital 24 in the preamble to bolster the position of the person concerned in the *Tsakouridis* case, the Court was right not to apply that recital against the person concerned in the *PI* case. In any event, there is nothing in the preamble to qualify the simple position that protection under Article 28(3) should be obtained based on ten years'

---

[102] As stated by N Rogers, R Scannell, and J Walsh, *Free Movement of Persons in the Enlarged European Union*, 2nd edn (Sweet and Maxwell, 2012), para 13-39: 'some real meaning must be given to the word "serious"'.

[103] As pointed out by L Azoulai and S Coutts, 'Restricting Union Citizens' Residence Rights on Grounds of Public Security. Where Union Citizenship and the AFSJ Meet: PI' (2013) 50 CMLRev 553 at 561: 'By framing the concept of public security in terms of society and its values, the Court removed any meaningful distinction as to its nature that may have existed between it and the notion of public policy.'

residence,[104] or to suggest that this provision creates a presumption only.[105] The fact that serious crimes are 'hidden' cannot alter that interpretation, since it is obvious that persons committing criminal offences will usually seek to hide their behaviour for as long as they can. The individual's right to benefit from Article 28(2) and (3) in this case is quite clearly *not* (as the opinion claims) created by or derived from his offences, but from his length of residence on the territory. More fundamentally, since Article 28(2) and (3) only apply to very serious criminal activity, anyone who would seek to assert the protection which they offer in practice would *necessarily* have violated the values held by most EU citizens; so the Advocate-General's approach would mean that *no one* could benefit from those provisions.

While the obvious intention of the EU legislature to increase the protection from expulsion for EU citizens who have resided for long periods in a host State ought to be more robustly respected by the EU judiciary, it should not be forgotten that the citizens' Directive in no way restricts the ability of Member States to penalize serious criminal offences through the means of imprisonment, as distinct from expulsion. Many EU citizens may be understandably disturbed that, in the *PI* case, eleven years of child abuse and rape merited only seven years in prison—but that sentence had nothing to do with EU law.

I. Analysis—Article 29

Article 29—Public Health

1. The only diseases justifying measures restricting freedom of movement shall be the diseases with epidemic potential as defined by the relevant instruments of the World Health Organisation and other infectious diseases or contagious parasitic diseases if they are the subject of protection provisions applying to nationals of the host Member State.
2. Diseases occurring after a three-month period from the date of arrival shall not constitute grounds for expulsion from the territory.
3. Where there are serious indications that it is necessary, Member States may, within three months of the date of arrival, require persons entitled to the right of residence to undergo, free of charge, a medical examination to certify that they are not suffering from any of the conditions referred to in paragraph 1. Such medical examinations may not be required as a matter of routine.

Article 29(1) and (2) are largely the same as Article 4(1) and (2) of Directive 64/221 though there are differences. In particular, the diseases covered by this rule were

---

[104] N Rogers, R Scannell, and J Walsh, *Free Movement of Persons in the Enlarged European Union*, 2nd edn (Sweet and Maxwell, 2012), para 13-40.

[105] As pointed out by Rogers, Scannell, and Walsh, n. 104, para 13-38, 'to review the quality of integration in every case as if this were a specific condition would be both difficult to administer and would rewrite the qualifying conditions'.

previously listed in an Annex to the Directive, whereas Article 29(1) refers to WHO instruments, and the three-month limit on expulsion on public health grounds replaced a possible six-month limit.[106] The prior references to 'disabilities', and a previous standstill rule, have also been removed.[107] As the Commission's proposal for the Directive states, the difference in wording in Article 29(1) reflects the fact that not all of the medical conditions which were included in the Annex to preceding Directive are still current,[108] the provision has been updated but retaining the principle that it is aligned to the WHO instruments. The WHO International Health Regulation 2005 is the one in force at the time of writing. It is the international legal instrument that is binding on 194 countries across the globe, including all the Member States of the WHO. According to the WHO, its aim is to help the international community prevent and respond to acute public health risks that have the potential to cross borders and threaten people worldwide.[109] The Directive links directly the meaning and use of the public health exception to the WHO standard. The objective is to limit strictly the grounds on which Member States may take decisions to exclude EU citizens and their family members from their territory on the grounds of public health to those which the international community has agreed are acute public health risks.

Article 29(2) limits the use of the public health exception to the three-month period following arrival in the host Member State. Clearly the meaning of the term 'arrival' must be different from the meaning of 'entry', as otherwise the EU citizen would be at risk of a public health exclusion every time he or she left the host State and returned even though that might be a matter of only days later. In light of the overall logic of the Directive, the three-month period referred to in Article 29(2) must be the same period referred to in Article 6. So once EU citizens or their family

---

[106] Art 4(2) of Directive 64/221 stated that diseases occurring after the issue of a first residence permit could not justify expulsion; Art 5(1) of that Directive required a residence permit to be issued as soon as possible after an application, and at the latest six months after.

[107] The standstill rule appeared in Art 4(3) of Directive 64/221. The Commission accepted amendments from the European Parliament as regards these two changes, on the grounds that 'only diseases may justify a measure restricting freedom of movement' and the standstill clause is 'not relevant' (amended proposal, COM(2003) 199).

[108] The Annex to Directive 64/221 stated:

   A. Diseases which might endanger public health:
     1. Diseases subject to quarantine listed in International Health Regulation No 2 of the World Health Organisation of 25 May 1951;
     2. Tuberculosis of the respiratory system in an active state or showing a tendency to develop;
     3. Syphilis;
     4. Other infectious diseases or contagious parasitic diseases if they are the subject of provisions for the protection of nationals of the host country.
   B. Diseases and disabilities which might threaten public policy or public security:
     1. Drug addiction;
     2. Profound mental disturbance; manifest conditions of psychotic disturbance with agitation, delirium, hallucinations or confusion.

[109] See the WHO mandate and website <http://www.who.int/ihr/en> visited on 7 October 2012.

members begin to exercise the longer-term right to reside defined in Article 7, they can no longer be expelled on public health grounds.[110]

Article 29(3) is an innovation of the Directive. The Commission proposed this in its initial draft of the Directive in 2001. The rationale was that the provision must be used only in exceptional circumstances where there are 'serious indications' that the person suffers from one of the diseases that can justify refusal of leave to enter or reside and provided that the host Member State bears the full cost of the examination. The three-month period matches the period set in Article 29(2).[111] According to the Commission (and as the Directive specifies) on no account can such examinations be carried out systematically, as this would undermine the purpose of the provisions on the issuing of registration certificates and cards in Articles 10 and 11.[112] The CJEU has never been asked to interpret the public health exception.

J. Function—Articles 30–33

The procedural guarantees of the Directive are critical to achieving its objectives, since the correct application of these guarantees is the mechanism by which the actions of the authorities of Member States can be tested by national judges against the obligations of the Directive. The guarantees are substantially strengthened as compared to the preceding measure, Directive 64/221. This is largely the consequence of a series of challenges before the CJEU, which interpreted the right to a remedy widely. The procedural remedies included in these Articles are the implementation in EU secondary legislation of the general principle of the EU right to an effective remedy, which is also now subject to Article 47 EU of the Charter of Fundamental Rights. They apply to all the rights contained in the Directive. Into the same category comes the limitation on exclusion bans of EU citizens or their family members from the territory of a Member State, to be found in Article 32. This ban results from the CJEU's jurisprudence, which requires a review of exclusion orders and prohibits life long exclusion orders.[113] There is also a prohibition (in Article 33) of using expulsion as a criminal penalty against an EU citizen or his or her family member, unless it conforms to the requirements of Articles 27, 28, and 29. This final Article in chapter VI (Article 33) also requires a potential host Member State to reassess the circumstances of a decision to expel an EU citizen or his or her family member where two years have passed since the decision was taken

---

[110] See the statement of reasons for the Council's Common Position 6/2003 ([2004] OJ C 54 E/12), which accepted a European Parliament amendment to set a three-month limit because this 'is more in keeping with the structure of the Directive'.

[111] See the Council's statement of reasons ([2004] OJ C 54 E/12): 'this is consistent with the text of the previous paragraph'.

[112] COM(2001) 257.

[113] Joined Cases 115/81 and 116/81 *Adoui and Cornuaille* [1982] ECR 1665; Case C-348/96 *Calfa* [1999] ECR I-11.

and the measure has still not been carried out. This also results from a reading of the CJEU jurisprudence which requires a reconsideration of fresh applications in which Member States are required to take into account any material changes in circumstance which justified the first expulsion.[114] Articles 32 and 33 are new in the form which they now take in the Directive.

K. Historical development

Directive 64/221 included notification requirements in Articles 6 and 7. It also provided at Article 8 that a person against whom action was being taken to refuse the issue or renewal of a residence document, or to exclude or expel him or her from the territory, had a right to the same legal remedies in respect of the decision as are available to nationals of the State in respect of acts of the administration. While this might be read as meaning that EU citizen's procedural rights should be subsumed into the general administrative law system of every Member State rather than into the immigration appeal system, this has not been a uniform practice. In fact in many Member States, remedies in respect of alleged violations of the rights of entry, residence, and expulsion of EU citizens are provided within the specialized tribunals which deal with third-country nationals' entry and residence status.

When Article 8 of Directive 64/221 was first considered by the CJEU in *Royer*,[115] the Court stated that the person concerned must at least have the opportunity of lodging an appeal and thus obtaining a stay of execution before the expulsion order is carried out. In *Pecastaing*[116] the CJEU held that a Member State cannot, without being in breach of the obligation imposed by Article 8, render the right of appeal for persons covered by the Directive conditional on particular requirements as to form or procedure which are less favourable than those pertaining to remedies available to nationals in respect of acts of the administration. A remedy must be available to any person covered by the Directive against any decision which may lead to expulsion before the decision is executed. This meant that a Member State could not, without being in breach of the obligation imposed by Article 8, organize, for persons covered by the Directive, legal remedies governed by special procedures affording lesser safeguards than those pertaining to remedies available to nationals in respect of acts of the administration.[117] Again relying on its finding in *Pecastaing*, the CJEU stated in *Shingara and Radiom*[118] that Article 8 does not govern the ways in which remedies are to be made available, for instance by

---

[114] Joined Cases 115/81 and 116/81 *Adoui and Cornuaille* [1982] ECR 1665.
[115] Case 48/75 [1976] ECR 497.
[116] Case 98/79 [1980] ECR 691.
[117] This finding was repeated without further elaboration in Case C-297/88 *Dzodzi* [1990] ECR I-3763.
[118] Joined Cases C-65/95 and C-111/95 [1997] ECR I-3343.

stipulating the courts from which such remedies may be sought, such details being dependent upon the organization of the courts in each Member State. However, the Court added that legal remedies with lesser safeguards than those applying to own nationals are inconsistent with Article 8. It also added in that case that in order to determine whether the remedies available to nationals of other Member States are to be assessed by reference to a specific appeal right, rather than that provided in respect of acts of the administration generally, it is necessary to see whether the circumstances in which nationals of the Member State concerned enjoy that remedy are sufficiently comparable to those mentioned in Article 8 of the Directive.

The UK authorities sought to argue that Article 8 did not apply in the circumstances of a person granted temporary admission. The CJEU was unimpressed. It held that a decision adopted by the authorities of a Member State refusing an EU citizen, not in possession of a residence permit, leave to enter its territory cannot be classified as a 'decision concerning entry' within the meaning of Article 8 thereof in a case where the person concerned was temporarily admitted to the territory of that Member State, pending a decision following the enquiries required for the investigation of her case, and therefore resided for almost seven months in that territory before that decision was notified to her.[119] The line of jurisprudence of the CJEU has been very consistent on Article 8 of Directive 64/221, and even after Directive 2004/38 had been adopted but before the end of its transposition period, the CJEU repeated and reaffirmed its findings in *Pecastaing* and *Dzodzi*.[120]

Article 9 of Directive 64/221 provided for the situation where there was no right of appeal to a court of law.[121] This possibility no longer exists. Article 9 of the previous Directive also made provision for the individual to submit his or her defence in person except where this would be contrary to the interests of national security. This is now incorporated in a form which provides more guarantees for the individual in Article 31(4) of the citizens' Directive.

According to the Commission, in its proposal for the Directive, Articles 32 and 33 bring into the Directive the interpretation which the CJEU has given to the expulsion power of the Member States.[122]

L. Interrelationship of Articles 30–33 with other provisions

These provisions are closely related to Articles 27 to 29, which provide for the grounds for exclusion or expulsion. There is also of course a close relationship with Articles 6 and 7 which set out the conditions for entry and stay by EU citizens and

---

[119] Case C-357/98 *Yiadom* [2000] ECR I-9265.
[120] Case C-136/03 *Dörr and Unal* [2005] ECR I-4759.
[121] See, for instance, Case C-175/94 *Gallagher* [1995] ECR I-4253 and Case 131/79 *Santillo* [1980] ECR 1585.
[122] COM(2001) 257.

their family members in a host Member State. As noted already, Articles 15(1) and 35 are subject to the procedural safeguards set out in Articles 30 and 31. However, due to the different subject matter of Articles 15(1) and 35 as compared to chapter VI, the procedural Articles apply to Articles 15(1) and 35 with some adaptations.[123]

M. Analysis—Article 30

Article 30—Notification of decisions

1. The persons concerned shall be notified in writing of any decision taken under Article 27(1), in such a way that they are able to comprehend its content and the implications for them.
2. The persons concerned shall be informed, precisely and in full, of the public policy, public security or public health grounds on which the decision taken in their case is based, unless this is contrary to the interests of State security.
3. The notification shall specify the court or administrative authority with which the person concerned may lodge an appeal, the time limit for the appeal and, where applicable, the time allowed for the person to leave the territory of the Member State. Save in duly substantiated cases of urgency, the time allowed to leave the territory shall be not less than one month from the date of notification.

This notification requirement is much expanded from that which appeared in Directive 64/221 (Articles 6–7). In particular, the citizens' Directive now specifies that the notification must be in writing, that the addressees must comprehend its content and implications, that information must be precise and in full, that the persons concerned must be told about appeals, and that there is a single deadline of one month to leave the territory. These changes largely reflect the jurisprudence of the CJEU on the notification requirements. In particular, in *Adoui and Cornuaille*[124] the CJEU indicated that people must be notified in a manner which makes the contents of the notice comprehensible for them, and 'the notification of the grounds must be sufficiently detailed and precise to enable the person concerned to defend his interests'. However, there are questions about the effective application of Article 30. In its report on implementation of the Directive, in 2008, the Commission found that only four Member States had correctly implemented Articles 30 to 31.[125] At that time one Member State still had not provided for written notifications to be issued, or a duty to inform the individual of the decision, or any right of appeal.

As for the interpretation of Article 30, first of all the Commission, in its proposal for the Directive, stated that Article 30(1) does not mean that the decision has to

---

[123] See the commentary on those provisions in Chapters 3 and 7.
[124] Joined Cases 115 and 116/81 [1982] ECR 1665, para 13. See also the earlier judgment in *Rutili* (Case 36/75 [1975] ECR 1219, para 39).
[125] COM(2008) 840.

be translated into the language of the person concerned. But it does mean that Member States must do what they can to make sure that the person understands what the decision is about and what it means for them.[126] It should be noted that if the decision follows a criminal conviction, separate EU legislation guarantees the right to interpretation and translation during the criminal proceedings, as well as information about charges and evidence during those proceedings.[127]

Moving on to Article 30(2) and (3), in its 2009 guidance on the application of the Directive, the Commission reminded the Member States that individuals must always be notified of any measure taken on public policy or public security grounds. Further, where the urgency ground is invoked under Article 30(3) by a Member State's authorities, the justification must be genuine and proportionate.[128] National authorities must take into account the impact of an urgent removal on the life of the person concerned, the assessment of urgency must be clearly and separately substantiated, and just because an expulsion measure is adopted on imperative or serious grounds, that does not necessarily mean it is urgent.

In the Court's view, the purpose of Article 30(2) is to enable 'the person concerned [to] make effective use of the redress procedures' which Member States are required to establish pursuant to Article 31 (see discussion below).[129] It was 'only by way of derogation' that Article 30(2) permitted Member States not to inform the person concerned fully of the reasons for the decision, and as a 'derogation from the rule . . . , this provision must be interpreted strictly, but without depriving it of its effectiveness'. So Articles 30 and 31 had to be interpreted in light of the right to an effective remedy, set out in Article 47 of the EU Charter of Fundamental Rights. While that right could be limited, Article 52(1) of the Charter requires 'any limitation must in particular respect the essence of the fundamental right in question and requires, in addition, that, subject to the principle of proportionality, the limitation must be necessary and genuinely meet objectives of general interest recognised by the European Union'.[130]

According to the Court's case law in other areas of EU law, for judicial review to be effective, 'the person concerned must be able to ascertain the reasons upon which the decision taken in relation to him is based, either by reading the decision itself or by requesting and obtaining notification of those reasons, without prejudice to the power of the court with jurisdiction to require the authority concerned to provide that information . . . so as to make it possible for him to defend

---

[126] COM(2001) 257.

[127] Directives 2010/64 ([2010] OJ L 280/1) and 2012/13 ([2012] OJ L 142/1).

[128] AG Stix-Hackl in Case C-441/02 *Commission v Germany* [2006] ECR I-3449.

[129] Case C-300/11 *ZZ*, judgment of 4 June 2013, para 48. See also the Commission's explanatory memorandum for the proposal for the Directive: 'so that the person is in a position to prepare their defence properly'. This reflects the previous judgments in *Rutili* [1975] ECR 1219 and *Adoui and Cornuaille* [1982] ECR 1665.

[130] Case C-300/11 *ZZ*, judgment of 4 June 2013, paras 49–52.

his rights in the best possible conditions and to decide, with full knowledge of the relevant facts, whether there is any point in his applying to the court with jurisdiction, and in order to put the latter fully in a position in which it may carry out the review of the lawfulness of the national decision in question'. While a refusal to disclose documents to the persons concerned might be justified in the interests of State security, the fundamental right to an effective remedy means that judicial decisions could not be 'founded on facts and documents which the parties themselves, or one of them, have not had an opportunity to examine and on which they have therefore been unable to state their views'. In the event that information was not disclosed to the persons concerned on security grounds, the relevant court 'must have at its disposal and apply techniques and rules of procedural law which accommodate, on the one hand, legitimate State security considerations regarding the nature and sources of the information taken into account in the adoption of such a decision and, on the other hand, the need to ensure sufficient compliance with the person's procedural rights, such as the right to be heard and the adversarial principle.' So national courts had to ensure 'effective judicial review both of the existence and validity of the reasons invoked by the national authority with regard to State security and of the legality of the decision taken under Article 27 of Directive 2004/38 and, second, to prescribe techniques and rules relating to that review'. The judicial review needs to assess 'whether those reasons stand in the way of precise and full disclosure of the grounds on which the decision in question is based and of the related evidence'. National authorities had to prove that 'State security would in fact be compromised by precise and full disclosure' of the relevant grounds and related evidence to the person concerned, and it could not be presumed that the reasons invoked by the authorities 'exist and are valid'. The national court 'must carry out an independent examination of all the matters of law and fact relied upon by the competent national authority' on this issue.[131]

If the national court found that the grounds and evidence ought to be disclosed, it had to give the authorities the choice to disclose those grounds and evidence to the person concerned. If the authorities did not wish to do so, then the national court would examine the legality of the decision 'on the basis of solely the grounds and evidence which have been disclosed'. If, on the other hand, the national court found that there were justified reasons for non-disclosure on grounds of State security, it would have to carry out its judicial review taking these special circumstances into account (see further the commentary on Article 31 below).

---

[131] Case C-300/11 *ZZ*, judgment of 4 June 2013, not yet reported, paras 53–62.

N. Analysis—Article 31

Article 31—Procedural safeguards

1. The persons concerned shall have access to judicial and, where appropriate, administrative redress procedures in the host Member State to appeal against or seek review of any decision taken against them on the grounds of public policy, public security or public health.

This first paragraph requires the Member States to provide a system of judicial redress as well as administrative redress in order to challenge a negative decision by the State authorities on the right of entry, exit, or residence (including challenges to expulsion) where those decisions are taken on the grounds of public policy, public security, or public health. As specified in Article 31(3), the appeal or review procedure must permit a consideration of both fact and law.

2. Where the application for appeal against or judicial review of the expulsion decision is accompanied by an application for an interim order to suspend enforcement of that decision, actual removal from the territory may not take place until such time as the decision on the interim order has been taken, except:
   – where the expulsion decision is based on a previous judicial decision; or
   – where the persons concerned have had previous access to judicial review; or
   – where the expulsion decision is based on imperative grounds of public security under Article 28(3).

According to the case law on the prior legislation, an appeal against a decision concerning refusal of a residence permit or expulsion should carry suspensive effect.[132] In those jurisdictions where this is not necessarily automatic, such as Germany where an application for suspensive effect must be made at the same time as the appeal, Article 31(2) requires the State authorities to permit the individual to continue to reside until such time as the application for suspension has been considered except in the very specific three circumstances set out. These circumstances are finite and cannot be augmented by other reasons at the behest of the host Member State ('may not take place...except').

The first situation is where there is already an expulsion decision which has been upheld by a previous judicial decision. But as discussed below (see the commentary on Article 33(2)), if two years or more have passed since the decision was made and the person has not yet been expelled, the Member State is required to reconsider the situation to determine whether the facts have changed. Secondly, where the person has already had access to a judicial remedy against the decision (judicial review) then there is not a right to recommence *de novo* the appeal procedure on the basis of the same decision of the authorities. Finally, where the decision is based on imperative grounds of public security the suspensive effect of the appeal procedure can be dispensed with (see the commentary on Article 28(3) above).

---

[132] Case C-357/98 *Yiadom* [2000] ECR I-9265.

3. The redress procedures shall allow for an examination of the legality of the decision, as well as of the facts and circumstances on which the proposed measure is based. They shall ensure that the decision is not disproportionate, particularly in view of the requirements laid down in Article 28.

This paragraph requires a full judicial inquiry into the law and facts of the situation which has given rise to the appeal. On appeal, the national court is required to carry out the proportionality test set out in Article 28; presumably this must take account of the different thresholds for expulsion set out in that Article (see the commentary above). The court cannot rely exclusively on the findings of fact by the State authorities, as the CJEU stated in *Pecastaing*.[133] The wording of the provision indicates that the judicial review can be limited to the facts and circumstances on which the proposed decision is based. However, any change of circumstances since the State authorities took the decision should also be relevant to the court's consideration of the matter before it. Because the issue is one of interference with a right of the individual to enter and reside under EU law the situation as at the date of hearing should be critical.

The interpretation of Article 31(3) has been developed by the CJEU in the recent *ZZ* judgment, which was introduced above in the context of Article 30.[134] Having explained the national court's obligations to examine a State's reasons not to disclose information on grounds of State security, pursuant to Article 30(2), the Court then set out the procedures which a national court should apply if it was not possible to disclose such information to the persons concerned. In that case, the judicial review of the legality of a decision 'must . . . be carried out in a procedure which strikes an appropriate balance between the requirements flowing from State security and the requirements of the right to effective judicial protection whilst limiting any interference with the exercise of that right to that which is strictly necessary'. First of all, 'to comply with Article 47 of the Charter', the court has to 'ensure, to the greatest possible extent, that the adversarial principle is complied with, in order to enable the person concerned to contest the grounds on which the decision in question is based and to make submissions on the evidence relating to the decision and, therefore, to put forward an effective defence'. So, '[i]n particular, the person concerned must be informed, in any event, of the essence of the grounds on which a decision refusing entry taken . . . is based, as the necessary protection of State security cannot have the effect of denying the person concerned his right to be heard and, therefore, of rendering his right of redress . . . ineffective'. Secondly, disclosure of the 'evidence underlying [these] grounds' was more problematic, since 'disclosure of that evidence is liable to compromise State security in a direct and specific manner, in that it may, in particular, endanger the life, health or freedom of persons or reveal the methods of investigation specifically used by

---

[133] Case 98/79 *Pecastaing* [1980] ECR 691.
[134] Case C-300/11, judgment of 4 June 2013, paras 64–68.

the national security authorities and thus seriously impede, or even prevent, future performance of the tasks of those authorities'. In that case, the national court has to assess 'whether and to what extent the restrictions on the rights of the defence arising in particular from' this non-disclosure 'are such as to affect the evidential value of the confidential evidence'. In summary, the national court has to 'ensure that the person concerned is informed of the essence of the grounds' for the decision, taking account of the 'the necessary confidentiality of the evidence', and to 'draw, pursuant to national law, the appropriate conclusions from any failure to comply with that obligation to inform him'.

> 4. Member States may exclude the individual concerned from their territory pending the redress procedure, but they may not prevent the individual from submitting his/her defence in person, except when his/her appearance may cause serious troubles to public policy or public security or when the appeal or judicial review concerns a denial of entry to the territory.

This paragraph is designed to ensure that Member States do not prevent individuals from fully presenting their defence against the State's action.[135] The only exceptions to the right of an individual to present his or her defence in person are,[136] first, where 'this appearance may cause serious troubles to public policy or public security'. This is a new phrase in the field of free movement of persons and has not been judicially considered yet. It would seem that 'serious troubles' are different from 'serious grounds of public policy' or 'imperative grounds of public security'. However, exactly where the difference lies is unclear. Since this is an exception to the right to present a defence in person, the burden of proof should fall upon the State to substantiate the grounds for using this exception. Presumably the procedural standards in Article 30 and the rest of Article 31 will apply, ie the State must notify its reasons and they must themselves be subject to effective judicial review. Substantively, since this rule must be interpreted strictly as an exception from a procedural right, the State should have to show that the personal appearance of the person concerned would be highly likely to lead to public disturbances which the State lacked the capacity to control.[137]

The second exception is where the appeal or judicial review concerns 'a denial of entry to the territory'. As can be seen in the *Yiadom* decision, where a person has been allowed into the State under temporary admission, he or she is no longer in a situation equivalent to waiting at the border for a decision, according to the CJEU. Such a person is present on the territory, so this second exception does not apply.[138]

---

[135] The CJEU interpreted the prior legislation to the effect that Member States were not obliged to let the person concerned remain for the duration of the proceedings, as long as he or she was able to have a fair hearing and present his or her defence in full: see Case 98/79 *Pecastaing* [1980] ECR 691, para 13.

[136] The list of exceptions is exhaustive ('may not prevent...except when'). There were no exceptions to the right in the Commission's proposal; they were introduced by the Council.

[137] See by analogy Case 231/83 *Cullet* [1985] ECR 305.

[138] Case C-357/98 *Yiadom* [2000] ECR I-9265.

O. Analysis—Article 32

Article 32—Duration of exclusion orders

1. Persons excluded on grounds of public policy or public security may submit an application for lifting of the exclusion order after a reasonable period, depending on the circumstances, and in any event after three years from enforcement of the final exclusion order which has been validly adopted in accordance with Community law, by putting forward arguments to establish that there has been a material change in the circumstances which justified the decision ordering their exclusion. The Member State concerned shall reach a decision on this application within six months of its submission.

This provision reflects the case law of the CJEU,[139] although the time frame for the right to challenge the exclusion order and the deadline to make a decision on the application are new.[140] The Council extended both time periods referred to in Article 32(1).[141] It should be noted that entry bans for third-country national family members of EU citizens can only be entered in the Schengen Information System and then enforced if they are compliant with the substantive and procedural rules of the Directive.[142] Also, according to Article 15(3), exclusion orders can only be made on grounds of public policy, public security, or public health.

Where a Member State has taken a decision of exclusion (which possibly followed an expulsion decision) against an EU citizen, the individual has the right to submit an application to lift the exclusion decision. The CJEU has ruled that Article 32 is also applicable to measures preventing a person from leaving his or her own Member State.[143] The Member State must consider the application unless it can argue that a 'reasonable period' of time has not passed since the decision was taken. However, such a decision to decline to consider lifting an exclusion order must be taken after a consideration of all the circumstances of the case. There is a long stop on the period during which a Member State can decline to consider lifting an exclusion order which is three years after it has been enforced (so long as the expulsion order was validly adopted in EU law in the first instance). The key element of

---

[139] Joined Cases 115/81 and 116/81 *Adoui and Cornuaille* [1982] ECR 1665, para 12.

[140] The Commission argued that the latter deadline was introduced 'so as not to undermine the purpose' of the right to apply for lifting the exclusion order (COM(2001) 257, explanatory memorandum).

[141] The original proposal (COM(2001) 257, explanatory memorandum) provided for an application after a maximum of two years, and a three-month deadline to decide on it. In its statement of reasons for Common Position 6/2003, [2004] OJ C 54 E/12, the Council stated that a six-month deadline was 'more realistic'. As noted in the commentary on Art 16(4) in Chapter 4, if a Member State validly excludes a person for more than two years, he or she will lose any permanent residence right which was acquired in the host State concerned.

[142] See Case C-503/03 *Commission v Spain* [2006] ECR I-1097, and now Art 25 of Reg 1987/2006 establishing the second-generation Schengen Information System ([2006] OJ L 381/4), which began operations on 9 April 2013.

[143] Case 249/11 *Byankov*, judgment of 4 October 2012, not yet reported, para 67.

an application for the lifting of an exclusion decision is that there has been a material change in circumstances which justify the lifting of the exclusion order.

The Commission originally proposed that this Article also expressly incorporate a prohibition on lifetime bans on EU citizens or their family members, but the Council decided to refer to this rule in the preamble (recital 27) instead. This prohibition, which is linked to the right to apply for reconsideration of an exclusion order (see again recital 27), arises from the *Calfa* judgment of the CJEU.[144] In that case the CJEU found that a life-long exclusion order on the basis of a criminal conviction was not consistent with Directive 64/221, as it did not take into account the personal conduct of the offender and her personal situation (the national law provided for exceptions for family reasons, but this was insufficient for the CJEU).

The interpretation of a 'material change in circumstances' is a matter for the appreciation of the national authorities in the first instance. However, in light of Article 47 of the Charter, the person concerned must have the right to appeal a negative decision to the courts, and Articles 30 and 31 apply *mutatis mutandis*.[145] The CJEU has not provided guidance on the interpretation of this concept yet.

In the event that the original exclusion order was *not* validly adopted, the CJEU has held that the person concerned cannot rely upon Article 32, but is still entitled to protection pursuant to EU law.[146] In particular, a national law which imposes exclusion orders for an unlimited period and does not provide for any other form of review, besides the possibility of challenging it within one month after it was adopted, is the 'antithesis' of free movement. So the exclusion order has to be open for challenge even after that one-month period, despite the principle of legal certainty.[147]

Finally, there is a time limit on the consideration of an application for the lifting of an exclusion order of six months, which corresponds to Articles 10 and 20, which set this as the maximum time limit for the issue of residence cards and permanent residence certificates (see Chapters 3 and 4). If a Member State fails to meet this deadline, it is arguable that Article 32(2) is no longer applicable, and that the person concerned is entitled to seek damages from the national authorities.

> 2. The persons referred to in paragraph 1 shall have no right of entry to the territory of the Member State concerned while their application is being considered.

An application for the lifting of an exclusion order does not have the effect of allowing the individual to enter the territory of the Member State concerned before a

---

[144] Case C-348/96 *Calfa* [1999] ECR I-21.

[145] See, as regards the prior legislation, Joined Cases C-65/95 and C-111/95 *Shingara and Radiom* [1997] ECR I-3343, at para 42. This judgment also makes clear (at para 43) that the same substantive grounds apply, and (at para 41) that a failure to challenge the prior decision does not bar a fresh application pursuant to Art 32.

[146] Case 249/11 *Byankov*, judgment of 4 October 2012, not yet reported, para 68.

[147] Case 249/11 *Byankov*, judgment of 4 October 2012, not yet reported, paras 69–82.

decision has been taken on the application. This provision, which also reflects the case law of the CJEU,[148] allows Member States to keep out the EU citizens or their family members against whom they have taken these draconian measures until a decision is made on their application. In practice, however, this may be somewhat more difficult within the Schengen area where there are no longer border controls among the participating States, so identifying people to be excluded at the border only takes place at the external borders of the Schengen States. As suggested above, arguably the Member State concerned can no longer rely on Article 32(2) if it fails to adhere to the deadline for making a decision set out in Article 32(1).

P. Analysis—Article 33

Article 33—Expulsion as a penalty or legal consequence

1. Expulsion orders may not be issued by the host Member State as a penalty or legal consequence of a custodial penalty, unless they conform to the requirements of Articles 27, 28 and 29.

This paragraph requires Member States to comply with all the substantive rules of the Directive governing the issue of an expulsion decision against EU citizens or their family members, even where the decision is associated with or arises as part of a penalty or legal consequence of a custodial penalty. There is no lighter procedural requirement just because the matter takes place within the criminal justice system rather than the administrative justice system.[149] Moreover, as noted already (see the commentary on Article 30), EU law prescribes minimum standards for defence rights in criminal proceedings, which have to be complied with by Member States.

2. If an expulsion order, as provided for in paragraph 1, is enforced more than two years after it was issued, the Member State shall check that the individual concerned is currently and genuinely a threat to public policy or public security and shall assess whether there has been any material change in the circumstances since the expulsion order was issued.

This paragraph is designed to protect EU citizens or their family members from being expelled on the basis of elderly expulsion decisions. It is not uncommon in some Member States that expulsion decisions are taken against individuals who are then not expelled for a significant period of time. This period of time may occur for many reasons such as a lack of travel documents, resistance from the individual etc. But most commonly it results from problems of execution of orders within State authorities. Expulsion is time consuming and costly. Often

---

[148] Joined Cases 115/81 and 116/81 *Adoui and Cornuaille* [1982] ECR 1665, para 12.

[149] Compare with the EU's Returns Directive (Directive 2008/115, [2008] OJ L 348/98), which governs the removal of third-country nationals (other than the family members of EU citizens) who are not entitled to stay in a Member State, and which permits Member States to exclude from its scope those persons who are being expelled as a result of a criminal conviction.

State authorities find themselves in a position where they must prioritize whom they will expel. Not infrequently, these same State authorities may also have efficiency targets to meet in the completion of their tasks. Thus a number of variables can creep into the expulsion process, which result in some people being expelled promptly and others kicking around for rather substantial periods of time after the taking of an expulsion decision in the host Member State and before any effort is made to carry it out. Where this occurs and there is a gap of two years or more between the issuing of the order and its enforcement, the Member State is required to make a new assessment of the person to ensure that the person is still a threat to public policy or public security, and whether there has been any material change in the circumstances since the expulsion order was issued (see the commentary on Article 32 above).

Article 33(2) is consistent with the ECtHR guidelines in *Uner*,[150] as well as the CJEU judgment in *Orfanopoulos and Oliveri*, which held that 'the requirement of the existence of a present threat must, as a general rule, be satisfied at the time of the expulsion'. While it was up to each Member State to elaborate the detailed rules for protection of EU law rights, such rules could not render the exercise of those rights 'virtually impossible or excessively difficult', which was the case for a German practice which prevented national courts from examining developments after the adoption of the expulsion decision at all.[151] Obviously such a rule would now also infringe the Directive, at least where two years had passed since the expulsion order was issued. However, it is problematic that unlike the Court's judgment, Article 33(2) only applies where the expulsion is connected to a criminal penalty, and allows for a two-year wait until the rule applies.[152]

Presumably for those persons within the scope of Article 28(2) or (3), the assessment pursuant to Article 33(2) must relate to the higher threshold for expulsion referred to in those paragraphs of Article 28, not the lower basic threshold for expulsion referred to in Article 28(1).[153] As noted above, the Directive does not expressly address the possibility that the person concerned might have qualified for the higher protection specified in Article 28(2) or (3)(a) in the meantime (or lost the protection of Article 28(3)(b) upon becoming an adult), but arguably the application of Article 33(2) must take account of such changes of status where relevant.

---

[150] *Uner v Netherlands* 18 October 2006—401-2,406.

[151] Joined Cases C-482/01 and C-493/01 [2004] ECR I-5257, paras 82–92.

[152] The Council introduced these changes as compared to the Commission's proposal (COM(2001) 257); see Common Position 6/2003, [2004] OJ C 54/12. In its statement of reasons the Council states that the assessment 'shall be made only' after a two-year period has passed.

[153] See the commentary on Art 28 above.

Q. Evaluation

The procedural rules designed to protect EU citizens and their family members from exclusion and expulsion are very comprehensive in comparison with the ECtHR's interpretation of the right to respect for private and family life in Article 8 ECHR. Not only are they based on a right of entry and interpreted as such, but they come with detailed procedural requirements which ensure that there is a full judicial consideration of the facts and law of each case. Individuals cannot be excluded indefinitely from a host Member State without the right to a review of their cases periodically at their request. The main concern about these rules is the use of proportionality tests in so many instances. These proportionality assessments allow for a substantial measure of flexibility in the application of the protections and need to be carefully considered in light of the overall objective of the procedural requirements which is to ensure that exit controls, exclusion, and expulsion are only ever used as exceptional actions which are subject to full scrutiny by the national courts.

As regards the issue of disclosure of evidence, the recent *ZZ* judgment of the CJEU places a heavy burden on the national courts. Yet, the reasoning of the CJEU is clear: the principle of disclosure necessary for the exercise of an effective remedy is paramount. Any exception or derogation from that duty of disclosure must be justified to a very high standard with the burden of proof on the State authorities to do so. While the CJEU does not strike out the national procedure being applied in that case, it does oblige the national judge to put the rights of the defence first, which means a presumption in favour of full and precise reasons and disclosure of evidence. It obliges the State to provide the national judge with the power to assess the strength of the State's national security claim in favour of non-disclosure against all the reasons and evidence and to disallow some or all of the claims if the national court considers they are less than absolutely necessary to protect concrete state security imperatives. So for instance, where a State refuses to provide reasons and evidence to a court on the grounds that it comes from a third country and the State has entered into an agreement with that third country never to reveal information emanating from it even to a national court, the national court is obliged to reject the State's argument for non-disclosure. The national court must always have access to the full reasons and evidence and the power to review whether the reasons and evidence are such as to justify non-disclosure. The appellant must always have access at the very least the essence of the grounds of the decision.

7

FINAL PROVISIONS

A. Function

The final provisions of the citizens' Directive do not concern a single specific issue, in the same way that the provisions on permanent residence (Chapter 4) or entry and exit (Chapter 2) do. Rather, they concern the effective implementation of the Directive as a whole. They include provisions which are absolutely essential for the Directive to have any legal effect at all (Articles 40–42, on transposition, entry into force, and addressees), as well as those deemed necessary to ensure its effective implementation in practice (concerning publicity, sanctions, and a report on implementation—Articles 34, 36, and 39). The intention of the Directive's drafters to 'codify' and 'simplify' the law in this area made it necessary to repeal much prior legislation (Article 38). Finally, while the Directive makes clear that Member States are free to set higher standards in their national law for the benefit of the persons concerned (Article 37), conversely it also aims to ensure that Member States need do no more than necessary to implement the Directive, providing for a rule concerning 'abuse of rights' (Article 35).

B. Historical development

The final provisions of the Directive have only a limited link to previous EU legislation in this area, although the Directive necessarily has the same 'boiler-plate' provisions that all other EU legislation has, namely, rules on transposition dates, entry into force, and addressees (Articles 40–42). It is also quite common for EU legislation to provide for reports on its application (Article 39), and the Directive's provision on this issue replaced other reporting obligations established by more recent free movement legislation which it repealed.[1]

---

[1] In particular, Art 4 of each of Directives 90/364 and 90/365 ([1990] OJ L 180/26 and 28) and Art 5 of Directive 93/96 ([1993] OJ L 317/59), provided for the Commission to produce a report on each Directive's application three years after its transposition date, and every three years thereafter. As regards Directive 93/96, the Commission's report had to 'pay particular attention to any

To the extent that the Directive is itself another stage in the development of EU legislation on citizenship and free movement, the repeal of prior legislation pursuant to Article 38 is a very significant step—as discussed in detail in the introductory chapter. Finally, at least some of the prior legislation in this area expressly provided for Member States to adopt higher standards for the persons concerned if they wished (Article 37). But there were no prior rules governing the issues of sanctions, abuse of rights, or publicity (Articles 34–36).

C. Interrelationship of Articles 34–42 with other provisions

First of all, Article 35 (abuse of rights) is implicitly linked with the provisions of the Directive on family members and on the scope of the Directive,[2] and is expressly linked to Articles 30 and 31, which set out the procedural rights which are applicable when a Member State seeks to restrict the rights in the Directive.[3] Article 37 (more favourable rules in national law) is implicitly linked to the rules in the Directive on the acquisition of permanent residence status,[4] because it raises the question as to whether periods spent on a Member State's territory pursuant to the rules referred to in Article 37 lead to the acquisition of such status. Similarly, Article 38 (repeal of prior measures) raises the question as to whether time spent pursuant to the legislation repealed by the Directive counts towards the acquisition of the same status. Next, Article 39 (reporting requirement) specifies that the Commission had to report in particular on the extension of the time period during which EU citizens can stay without conditions, which is provided for in Article 6. Finally, Article 40 (transposition date) also has a link to the provisions on permanent residence, and the other provisions in this Directive which provide for various qualifying periods, as it raises the questions as to whether time spent before the transposition date counts towards rights which a person seeks to exercise after that date.

D. Other relevant EU law rules

Article 38(1) leaves in place the remainder of Regulation 1612/68 on freedom of movement for workers, which it only partly repealed; that Regulation has itself now been replaced by a codified version.[5] Article 38(2) reduces the number of

---

difficulties to which the implementation of' the Directive 'might give rise in the Member States', and had to, 'if appropriate, submit proposals to the Council with the aim of remedying such difficulties'. The Commission produced three such reports, jointly covering all three Directives: COM(99) 127, 17 March 1999; COM(2003) 101, 5 March 2003; and COM(2006) 156, 5 April 2006.

[2] Arts 2 and 3; see Chapter 1.
[3] See Chapter 6.
[4] On those rules, see particularly Arts 16–18, discussed in Chapter 4.
[5] Reg 492/2011, [2011] OJ L 141/1.

other EU law rules concerning the free movement of persons, by repealing nine other measures. Article 38(3) also relates to other EU legislation, because it updates references to the legislation repealed by Article 38(2) that still appear in such other legislation.

E. Analysis

Article 34—Publicity

Member States shall disseminate information concerning the rights and obligations of Union citizens and their family members on the subjects covered by this Directive, particularly by means of awareness-raising campaigns conducted through national and local media and other means of communication.

This provision of the Directive was changed during negotiations, to add all of the particular examples of the forms of dissemination of information which the Article refers to; this list is clearly non-exhaustive, as evidenced by the word 'particularly'. While the text of Article 34 is clearly mandatory ('shall'), and so could presumably be the subject of infringement actions by the Commission if Member States' dissemination of information is non-existent or inadequate, it is harder to see how this provision could be enforceable in national courts. Certainly Article 34 does not provide for any rights which could be invoked by individuals, since it does not create any obligations to provide information as regards decision-making in individual cases (unlike, for instance, the rules in chapter VI of the Directive), but rather an obligation to inform the public as a whole about the subject matter of the Directive very generally.

There is no information available about the implementation of this provision. However, in principle it could make a useful contribution to public understanding and awareness of the important issues addressed by the citizens' Directive.

Article 35—Abuse of rights

Member States may adopt the necessary measures to refuse, terminate or withdraw any right conferred by this Directive in the case of abuse of rights or fraud, such as marriages of convenience. Any such measure shall be proportionate and subject to the procedural safeguards provided for in Articles 30 and 31.

This provision of the Directive was not in the Commission's proposal,[6] but was added by the Council during negotiations, 'in order to clarify that Member States may refuse, terminate or withdraw any right conferred by the Directive in the case of abuse of rights or fraud'.[7] It is clarified somewhat by recital 28 in the preamble, which states that '[t]o guard against abuse of rights or fraud, notably marriages of convenience or any other form of relationships contracted for the sole purpose of

---

[6] COM(2001) 257.
[7] Council Common Position 6/2004, [2004] OJ C 54 E/12, statement of reasons on Art 35.

enjoying the right of free movement and residence, Member States should have the possibility to adopt the necessary measures'.

The issues underlying Article 35 were first addressed by the CJEU in the *Singh* judgment, concerning the return of a UK citizen to the UK having spent several years in Germany with a third-country national spouse, when the Court stated that 'the facilities created by the Treaty cannot have the effect of allowing persons who benefit from them to evade the application of national legislation and of pro-hibiting Member States from taking measures necessary to prevent such abuse'.[8] Subsequently, in the *Akrich* judgment, concerning the position of a British citizen who moved to Ireland after the United Kingdom refused to admit her Moroccan husband, the Court stated that the motives leading to a stay in another Member State or the return to the home Member State were irrelevant, as long as the activity carried out there was genuine and effective. Furthermore, '[s]uch conduct can-not constitute an abuse... even if the spouse did not, at the time when the couple installed itself in another Member State, have a right to remain in the Member State of which the worker is a national'. But 'there would be an abuse if the facili-ties afforded by [EU] law in favour of migrant workers and their spouses were invoked in the context of marriages of convenience entered into in order to cir-cumvent the provisions relating to entry and residence of' third country nationals. If a marriage was 'genuine', the EU citizen in question was returning to his or her home Member State, and his or her family member was not lawfully resident in a Member State, the persons concerned would still be able to assert rights based on the ECHR.[9] However, it was not clear whether the latter point being made by the Court related to the concept of 'marriages of convenience' (ie 'genuine' marriages as a subset of 'marriages of convenience'), or whether the Court was simply trying to elaborate upon the legal position of family members whose EU citizen principal was returning with them to that citizen's home Member State even though the family members were not lawfully resident in a Member State—whose legal posi-tion was the main issue in the *Akrich* judgment. The point is important because the Court overturned this requirement of prior lawful residence in the later *Metock* judgment—which we will return to below.[10]

In the *Chen* judgment,[11] concerning a Chinese citizen's decision to give birth to a child in Northern Ireland (part of the UK), with the admitted intention of acquir-ing a residence right in the UK because her child would obtain Irish nationality, the CJEU rejected the UK government's argument that the persons concerned could not rely upon EU law because they were attempting to exploit it improperly.

---

[8] Case C-370/90 [1992] ECR I-4265, para 24. See further the discussion of Arts 2(2)(a) and 3(1) in Chapter 1.

[9] Case C-109/01 [2003] ECR I-9607, paras 55–58. See further the discussion of Art 3(1) in Chapter 1.

[10] Case C-127/08 [2008] ECR I-6241.

[11] Case C-200/02 [2004] ECR I-9925.

In the Court's view, this case was a simple application of the principle that each Member State had to recognize other Member States' grant of nationality.[12]

Next, in the *Metock* judgment, the CJEU briefly considered the content of Article 35. According to the Court, once a third-country national family member of an EU citizen acquires the right to enter and reside in a Member State on the basis of the Directive, that Member State may only restrict such rights in compliance with Articles 27 and 35. Even if the personal conduct of that individual did not justify taking measures on the basis of Article 27 (the 'public policy and public security' exception), the Member State could still 'impose other penalties on him [or her] which do not interfere with freedom of movement and residence, such as a fine, provided that they are proportionate'.[13] However, it was not clear whether the Court was interpreting Article 35 when it referred to the possibility of such other penalties. The Advocate-General's view in the *Metock* case was slightly more precise, stating that Article 35 'is obviously aimed at the possibility of marriages of convenience, but abuse of rights may also be deemed to cover the *Akrich* case of seeking to evade national immigration legislation illicitly'.[14]

In the opinion in the *PI* case,[15] an Advocate-General argued that there was 'fraud' for the purposes of Article 35 when an EU citizen who had moved to another Member State sought to rely upon the extra protection against expulsion for long-term residents in Article 28(2) and (3), since the EU citizen had begun to commit hidden and repellent crimes (not discovered until years later) before acquiring that extra protection. The CJEU implicitly did not accept this analysis in its judgment.

Finally, a pending case asks the CJEU to interpret Article 35, in order to determine whether that provision justifies a Member State (in effect) refusing to apply the rule in Article 5(2), which requires Member States to waive any visa requirement for third-country nationals who are family members of an EU citizen who has moved between Member States and who holds the residence card referred to in Article 10.[16]

The Commission's initial view on the interpretation of Article 35 was set out in its 2008 Report on the application of the Directive.[17] In its view, '[w]here there are doubts that the marriage is not genuine, Member States can investigate to determine whether the rights granted by the Directive are being abused, for example to circumvent national rules on immigration, and can refuse or withdraw the rights of entry or residence if abuse is proved'. Subsequently, due to the controversy caused

---

[12] See further the commentary on Art 2(1), in Chapter 1.

[13] Paras 95 and 97 of the *Metock* judgment.

[14] Para 14 of the view.

[15] Case C-348/09, judgment of 22 May 2012, not yet reported. See further the commentary on Art 28, in Chapter 6.

[16] Case C-202/13 *McCarthy*, pending. See further the commentary on Art 5 in Chapter 2.

[17] COM(2008) 840, 10 December 2008.

by the *Metock* judgment,[18] the interpretation of Article 35 formed a major part of the Commission's guidance to Member States on the application of the Directive, issued in 2009.[19] In this guidance, the Commission first of all stated that there was no abuse where EU citizens and their family members gain a right of residence in an EU Member State other than that of the citizen's nationality, since 'they are benefiting from an advantage inherent in the exercise of free movement protected by the Treaty, regardless of the purpose of their move'. EU law also 'protects EU citizens who return home after having exercised their free movement rights'.

The Commission's guidance then offered an interpretation of 'fraud', namely, 'deception or contrivance made to obtain the right of free movement and residence under the Directive'. For the purposes of the Directive, 'fraud is likely to be limited to forgery of documents or false representation of a material fact concerning the conditions attached to the right of residence'. If a person had obtained a residence document 'only as a result of fraudulent conduct in respect of which they have been convicted', they could 'have their rights under the Directive refused, terminated or withdrawn'. As for 'abuse', the Commission stated that it should be defined in the context of the Directive as 'as an artificial conduct entered into solely with the purpose of obtaining the right of free movement and residence under Community law which, albeit formally observing of the conditions laid down by Community rules, does not comply with the purpose of those rules'.

The Commission then addressed the particular issue of marriages of convenience in more detail, emphasizing that recital 28 in the preamble refers to a marriage for 'the sole purpose of enjoying the right of free movement and residence under the Directive that someone would not have otherwise'.[20] But a marriage was not a marriage of convenience 'simply because it brings an immigration advantage, or indeed any other advantage', and '[t]he quality of the relationship is immaterial to the application of Article 35'. The definition could be extended to other relationships contracted for the sole purpose of enjoying free movement rights, such as partnerships, fake adoptions, and false declarations of fatherhood.[21] But steps taken by Member States to combat such marriages could not 'deter' EU citizens and their family members from using free movement rights, or 'unduly encroach on their legitimate rights', 'undermine the effectiveness' of EU law, or 'discriminate on grounds of nationality'.

The concept of abuse in the context of the Directive was derived from EU law, not national law; Member States could investigate individual cases if there was a 'well-founded suspicion of abuse', but there could not be 'systematic checks'.

---

[18] See further the commentary on Art 3(1) in Chapter 1.

[19] COM(2009) 313, 9 July 2009.

[20] In fact, the words 'under the Directive that someone would not have otherwise' do not appear in recital 28.

[21] Indeed, recital 28 refers to 'any other form of relationship' on the same basis as marriages.

However, the Commission hinted that some kind of profiling was acceptable, stating that Member States 'could rely on previous analyses and experience showing a clear correlation between proven cases of abuse and certain characteristics of such cases'. The Commission then provided one list of criteria which would suggest that there was unlikely to be an abuse of rights (such as a long-standing marriage, or a lack of any immigration problems for the third country spouse), and another list of criteria which would suggest that there was a 'possible intention' to abuse such rights (no meetings before the marriage, or a past history of marriages of convenience). As regards procedural issues, the Commission took the view that Member States have the burden of proof if they wish to restrict rights under the Directive, investigations must be carried out in accordance with fundamental rights, and third-country nationals would still be entitled to exercise rights under the Directive while an investigation was ongoing.

As for 'other forms of abuse', the Commission believed that an abuse could also exist where an EU citizen moved to another Member State with the 'sole' purpose of evading national immigration law restrictions that prevent them being joined by their third-country national spouse. The test in such cases was whether the exercise of free movement rights in the Member State which the family initially moved to was 'genuine and effective'; if it was, then the motives which triggered the move were irrelevant. Again, the Commission suggested a list of criteria which would Member States should examine, such as the degree of effective residence in the host State, and the return to the Member State of origin immediately after the marriage. It could not be assumed that the move was abusive merely because the EU citizen maintains some ties to the home State.

Finally, the Commission offered guidance as to what 'necessary measures' Member States could take in the event of abuse of rights or fraud. These could entail the refusal to confer rights under EU free movement law or the termination or withdrawal of such rights. Member States could also take civil, administrative, or criminal sanctions, as long as those sanctions were effective, non-discriminatory, and proportionate.

Is the Commission's interpretation convincing? It should first of all be noted that the use of Article 35 is optional ('may'), so Member States cannot be criticized for refusing to apply it—although they could of course be criticized for infringing free movement rights by applying it too zealously, and it could be argued that since the application of Article 35 would limit free movement rights, its potential use would have to be 'prescribed by law', like a limit on a qualified ECHR right.[22] The Commission's interpretation of 'fraud' is surely correct; the underlying point is surely that 'fraud' can only exist for the purposes of Article 35 where the person

---

[22] The Commission's statement that 'Article 35 was not transposed by all Member States' in its 2008 Implementation Report must be seen in this light.

concerned does not have a right under the Directive at all, but is pretending to do so fraudulently.[23] This could take a number of different forms (for instance a false EU passport, or a false certificate of marriage to an EU citizen), and not every case of false documents would amount to fraud under the terms of the Directive. For example, an EU citizen might obtain a false passport from a Member State in order to avoid detection or prosecution for some reason; but a third-country national married to such a person would not be committing fraud for the purposes of Article 35. Of course, there might be serious consequences for obtaining a false passport, but as long as the third-country national is in fact married to a genuine EU citizen exercising free movement rights, he or she has rights under the Directive and Article 35 cannot be applied.[24] In the event that the third-country national genuinely (but wrongly) believed that the person they married was an EU citizen exercising free movement rights, then the former person is not guilty of fraud, but arguably there has been an abuse of rights (as distinct from fraud) even if one of the parties is blameless. In any event, the third-country national in question could not benefit from the Directive, since the conditions for its application would not have been genuinely satisfied. However, contrary to the *PI* opinion, the commission of hidden and appalling crimes unrelated to immigration law does not amount to 'fraud' which prevents the acquisition of any rights under the Directive. Such an approach would mean that the detailed provisions of chapter VI of the Directive, which are specifically focussed on persons committing criminal offences and which were moreover enhanced (as compared to the prior legislation) when the Directive was adopted, are otiose.[25]

The concept of 'abuse of rights' is more problematic, since (as distinct from fraud) it suggests that there are cases where people prima facie meet the criteria for the Directive to apply but nonetheless cannot benefit from it. It must be conceded that Article 35 at least applies to 'marriages of convenience', although it is not clear from the wording of the Directive whether such relationships should be regarded as 'fraud' or as 'abuse of rights'. Certainly fake adoptions and false declarations of fatherhood are prima facie fraudulent. Taking account of the underlying purpose of the Directive and the wording of recital 28, the Commission is correct to interpret the concept of 'marriages of convenience' (or equivalent relationships) as arrangements that were made purely to obtain free movement rights, not for any other purpose.[26] The fundamental test should be whether, despite meeting the formal legal requirements for a valid marriage, the persons concerned do not

---

[23] Of course, there are other forms of fraud, such as defrauding the EU budget, but logically these do not fall within the scope of Art 35.

[24] Unless, of course, the person concerned is actually a national of the '*host*' Member State, but falsely pretending to have (solely or additionally) the nationality of another Member State. In such a case, the Directive is not applicable at all (see Art 3(1), discussed in Chapter 1) and so Art 35 might then be relevant.

[25] See further the commentary on Art 28 in Chapter 6.

[26] This analysis would also apply to (for instance) registered partnerships of convenience.

have a genuine marital relationship and the only reason for that relationship is the invocation of free movement rights.

Next, are there 'other forms of abuse' of rights as the Commission claims, namely, a move within the EU by a couple whose marital relationship is not only legally valid but socially genuine, in order to avoid the constraints of national immigration law? While the Advocate-General in the *Metock* case interpreted Article 35 in this sense, the Court's judgment was vague. While the wording of Article 35 certainly envisages that fraud or abuse of rights can take forms other than 'marriages of convenience' (as evidenced by the words 'such as' in Article 35, and 'notably' in recital 28), this could be understood to refer to the use of false documents and other forms of fraud. In light of the Court's decision in *Metock* to overturn the prior lawful residence requirement for third-country national family members of EU citizens, it must be doubted whether this supposed additional category of 'abuse of rights' exists at all. If it does exist, then the Commission's suggested interpretation of the rule is correct (in light of the *Akrich* and *Chen* judgments) to the extent that the key issue is whether the exercise of activities in another Member State is genuine and effective. Arguably this test is satisfied as soon as the persons concerned can show that they have satisfied the criteria for a right of residence for over three months in that other Member State, pursuant to Article 7.[27]

The Commission's interpretation of the 'necessary measures' that Member States can take pursuant to Article 35 is correct in principle, in light of the wording of the Article ('to refuse, terminate or withdraw any right'). However, the Commission's analysis takes no real account of the express requirement that such actions 'shall be proportionate'. While an outright refusal of free movement rights is appropriate in cases where the conditions for free movement rights were fraudulently manufactured, this would not be appropriate where the persons concerned had a genuine marriage but moved to another Member State solely to avoid restrictions under national immigration law—assuming that Article 35 applies to such categories of cases at all. In such cases, it would be proportionate for the Member State concerned to insist that the family members concerned still had to comply with the conditions of national immigration law for entry (but not more than that, ie they should not be subject to an entry ban), without prejudice to the possibility that the EU citizen and his or her family members might still choose to exercise genuine and effective free movement rights in another Member State. In any event, in light of the wording and structure of the Directive, Article 35 clearly cannot justify a general derogation from its specific obligations,[28] but can apply only on a case-by-case basis.[29]

---

[27] See the commentary on Art 3(1), in Chapter 1.
[28] Cf the UK government's clearly incorrect application of the Directive in Case C-202/13 *McCarthy*, pending. See further the commentary on Art 5, in Chapter 2.
[29] See K E Sorensen, 'Abuse of Rights in Community Law: A Principle of Substance or Merely Rhetoric?' (2006) 43 CMLRev 423 at 452–454.

Finally, in light of the subject matter of Article 35, some of the exceptions from the procedural rules set out in Articles 30 and 31 should not be applicable.[30]

Article 36—Sanctions

Member States shall lay down provisions on the sanctions applicable to breaches of national rules adopted for the implementation of this Directive and shall take the measures required for their application. The sanctions laid down shall be effective and proportionate. Member States shall notify the Commission of these provisions not later than 30 April 2006 and as promptly as possible in the case of any subsequent changes.

This Article refers to the measures which Member States can take to enforce the Directive. The sanctions concerned are referred to in Articles 5(5), 8(2), 9(3), and 20(2), although as pointed out in the commentary on those Articles (Chapters 2, 3, and 4), the sanctions concerned cannot result in detention or expulsion, and the failure to register or obtain the proper documents is not a condition precedent for the exercise of the rights set out in the Directive (see Article 25, discussed in Chapter 5).

From the perspective of the enforcement of the Directive, Article 36 appears to be misdirected in principle. Since the application of the Directive is primarily in the hands of public authorities, EU citizens and their family members need effective remedies in the event that the Directive is wrongly applied by those authorities. While the general rules on remedies for enforcement of EU law, such as a right to damages and rules on effective and equal remedies (governing issues like time limits for bringing claims) are of course applicable to this area, it would be worth considering whether the Commission's recent proposal on enforcement of the remaining legislation on free movement of workers should also apply to this Directive.[31] That proposal would set out rules concerning defence of rights, time limits, actions by representative organizations, the powers of equal treatment bodies, and dialogue with social partners, which could easily be adapted to apply also to Directive 2004/38.[32]

Article 37—More favourable national provisions

The provisions of this Directive shall not affect any laws, regulations or administrative provisions laid down by a Member State which would be more favourable to the persons covered by this Directive.

This Article corresponds to recital 29 in the preamble, which states that '[t]his Directive should not affect more favourable national provisions'. There is no

---

[30] Ie exceptions specifically relating to public security. See, *mutatis mutandis*, the commentary on Art 15 in Chapter 3.

[31] COM(2013) 236, 26 April 2013.

[32] Arts 3–6 of the proposed Directive. It would only be necessary to amend the rules on the subject matter and scope of the proposal (Arts 1 and 2), and add references to Directive 2004/38 throughout. Art 7 of the proposal, on dissemination of information, largely overlaps with Art 34 of Directive 2004/38.

requirement that such higher standards need to be 'compatible' with the Directive or any other EU law, although any such national measures would have to comply with the cardinal primary law Treaty rule of non-discrimination on grounds of nationality. So any special advantages which a Member State wished to grant to nationals of one or more other Member State(s) would in principle have to be granted to the nationals of every Member State.[33]

Otherwise, the case law of the CJEU has made clear that any national law which sets higher standards, and therefore allows more EU citizens and their family members to stay on the territory without meeting the conditions of (in particular) Article 7, does not count towards the five-year period of legal residence which is usually necessary to acquire permanent residence status under the Directive. In the Court's view, just because Article 37 provides that more favourable national laws 'are not to be affected' by the Directive, this 'does not in any way mean that such provisions must be incorporated into the system introduced by the directive'. Furthermore, Article 37 'simply provides that the directive does not preclude the laws of the Member States from introducing a system' which is more favourable for the persons concerned, and 'it is for each Member State to decide not only whether it will adopt such a system but also the conditions and effects of that system, in particular as regards the legal consequences of a right of residence granted on the basis of national law alone'.[34] So residence solely pursuant to such national laws has no direct relationship with the Directive,[35] although such residence could indirectly make it easier for EU citizens and their family members to obtain rights under the Directive,[36] and the further legal stay would count, in the Member States concerned, toward the time period necessary to obtain long-term residence status pursuant to EU immigration law.[37]

Article 38—Repeals

1. Articles 10 and 11 of Regulation (EEC) No 1612/68 shall be repealed with effect from 30 April 2006.
2. Directives 64/221/EEC, 68/360/EEC, 72/194/EEC, 73/148/EEC, 75/34/EEC, 75/35/EEC, 90/364/EEC, 90/365/EEC and 93/96/EEC shall be repealed with effect from 30 April 2006.

---

[33] See, for instance, Case 235/87 *Matteucci* [1988] ECR 5589.

[34] Joined Cases C-424/10 and C-425/10 *Ziolkowski and Szeja*, judgment of 21 December 2011, not yet reported, paras 49 and 50.

[35] Note that the automatic admission of extended family members is the exercise of an option provided for in the Directive, and so cannot be regarded as admission pursuant to national law: see the commentary on Art 3(2) in Chapter 1.

[36] For instance, an EU citizen who is allowed to stay on the territory pursuant to national law even though he or she needs social assistance in circumstances which mean that the right of residence under the Directive is lost or not acquired at all (see Chapter 3) could have an easier time finding employment in that Member State (and therefore qualifying for the right of residence under the Directive) later on.

[37] Directive 2003/109, [2003] OJ L 16/44. See Case C-40/11 *Iida*, judgment of 8 November 2012, not yet reported.

3. References made to the repealed provisions and Directives shall be construed as being made to this Directive.

Article 38(1) repealed only in part the well-known Regulation 1612/68 on the freedom of movement of workers. Articles 10 and 11 of that Regulation defined in turn the family members who were entitled to install themselves with a worker, and certain family members' access to employment.[38] The rest of that Regulation—setting out the rights to free movement of workers (Articles 1–9),[39] the rights of access to education of migrant workers' children (Article 12),[40] and the rules on coordination of national employment offices (the remainder of the Regulation)—were *a contrario* not amended, and indeed, as noted above, the EU legislature decided to codify the Regulation (without further amendments) in 2011.[41] Furthermore, in 2013 the Commission proposed a Directive facilitating the effective exercise of the right to free movement of workers in the EU, which in effect concerns the enforcement of this Regulation.[42]

The case law on the citizens' Directive has made clear that the repeal of Articles 10 and 11 of Regulation 1612/68 leaves intact the other provisions of that Regulation, most notably Article 12 of that Regulation (now Article 10 of Regulation 492/2011), which confers rights not only as regards equal access to education for migrant workers' children, but also rights to residence and educational assistance for those children and rights of residence for their carer parents, even after the death or departure of the migrant worker.[43] However, like the national laws referred to in Article 37, such rights of residence pursuant solely to other EU legislation have no direct relationship with the Directive, as regards the acquisition of permanent residence rights.[44]

Article 38(2) provides for the complete repeal of nine additional measures. Of these, the most significant is perhaps Directive 64/221, which set out rules on the refusal of entry or expulsion of EU citizens and their family members on grounds of public policy, public security, or public health, and which has been integrated (with amendments) into chapter VI of the Directive. Directives 72/194 and 75/35 simply extended the application of Directive 64/221 so that it applied respectively to those who remained after employment or self-employment. Directive 68/360, which set out the necessary immigration law rules governing the free movement of workers and their families, has been integrated into chapter III, as has the parallel Directive

---

[38] See now respectively the commentary on Arts 2 and 3 in Chapter 1, and on Art 23 in Chapter 5.
[39] See further the commentary on Art 24 in Chapter 5.
[40] See further the commentary on Art 12(3) in Chapter 3.
[41] Reg 492/2011, [2011] OJ L 141/1.
[42] COM(2013) 236, 26 April 2013.
[43] See the commentary on Art 12(3) in Chapter 3. Art 7(2) of that Regulation is also still relevant: see the commentary on Art 24 in Chapter 5.
[44] See the commentary on Art 37 above, and furthermore Case C-529/11 *Alarape and Tijani*, judgment of 8 May 2013.

73/148, which set out equivalent rules for self-employed persons. The most recent measures, Directives 90/364, 90/365, and 93/96, extended free movement rights to those moving for non-economic reasons;[45] the relevant provisions have also been scattered across Chapter III, most notably Article 7(1)(b) and (c). Finally, Directive 75/34 set out rules on the right to remain after self-employment. A parallel measure, Regulation 1251/70 concerning the right to remain after employment, had to be repealed separately,[46] because it had been adopted by the Commission and therefore had to be repealed by the same institution.[47]

The case law on the rules in the Directive relating to the acquisition of permanent residence make clear that time spent in the territory of a Member State pursuant to the legislation repealed by Article 38(2), or those provisions of Regulation 1612/68 which were repealed by Article 38(1), still counts towards the acquisition of permanent residence status.[48] Presumably the same rule applies by analogy to the satisfaction of the time periods referred to in chapters III and VI of the Directive.

Article 38(3) avoids any lacuna in the application of EU law on free movement of persons by providing that references to the repealed legislation made in other measures must be construed as references to this Directive. Unusually, the Directive does not include a correlation table which specifies exactly which of its provisions correspond to the prior measures, perhaps because it goes far beyond a simple codification of the prior rules, not only amending them substantially but merging them into a single text.

Finally, it should be recalled that in accordance with recital 3 in the preamble, which refers to the legislative intention to 'simplify and strengthen' the free movement rights of EU citizens, the repeal of the prior legislation cannot have the impact of reducing the level of rights which EU citizens and their family members enjoy as compared to the prior rules.[49]

Article 39—Report

No later than 30 April 2006 the Commission shall submit a report on the application of this Directive to the European Parliament and the Council, together with any necessary proposals, notably on the opportunity to extend the period of time during which Union citizens and their family members may reside in the territory of the host Member State without any conditions. The Member States shall provide the Commission with the information needed to produce the report.

This Article corresponds to recital 30 in the preamble, which states that '[w]ith a view to examining how further to facilitate the exercise of the right of free

---

[45] Directive 90/365 applied to pensioners, Directive 93/96 applied to students, and Directive 90/364 applied to others who were self-sufficient.
[46] Reg 635/2006, [2006] OJ L 112/9.
[47] Directive 75/34 and Reg 1251/70 have been integrated into Art 17; see Chapter 4.
[48] See Chapter 4.
[49] See the case law starting with Case C-127/08 *Metock* [2008] ECR I-6241.

movement and residence, a report should be prepared by the Commission in order to evaluate the opportunity to present any necessary proposals to this effect, notably on the extension of the period of residence with no conditions'. The reference to the specific issue of extending the period of unconditional stay concerns Article 6. It should be recalled that in its original proposal, the Commission had suggested a six-month period of unconditional stay, rather than three months as provided for in the final Directive.[50]

It is striking that the Directive only requires one report on implementation of the Directive to be published, whereas some of the precursor legislation required reports to be published every three years.[51] The report required by Article 39 was published in 2008,[52] and in particular provided some useful information on whether, in the Commission's view, Member States were applying the Directive correctly or not.[53] Of course, while some of the Commission's interpretation of the Directive proved to be well-founded, according to the Court of Justice's later jurisprudence, conversely, some of its interpretation was not followed by the Court.[54]

In spite of the provisions of Article 39, the 2008 report paid no particular attention to the possibility of amending the Directive to provide for a longer period of unconditional stay, and indeed concluded that '[a]t this stage, it is not necessary to propose amendments to the Directive'. The Commission's rationale was that '[t]he Directive must be implemented by Member States more effectively', and that 'difficult issues of interpretation which have arisen so far can be addressed satisfactorily by issuing guidelines following further discussion and clarification'. However, the Commission did commit itself to issue a second report on the application of the Directive 'in due course'. Possibly, the real reason for the Commission's reluctance to propose amendments was its fear that Member States would not only reject any proposal which further strengthened the rights of EU citizens and their family members, but also that Member States would take the opportunity to *weaken* those rights, in particular in light of the controversy following the Court's then-recent judgment in *Metock*.[55] Indeed, the Commission's communication setting out these guidelines on the application of the Directive, issued in 2009,[56] is largely a response to the issues raised by the *Metock* judgment.

---

[50] See the commentary on Art 6 in Chapter 3.

[51] See Section B of this chapter.

[52] COM(2008) 840, 10 December 2008.

[53] For detail, see the other chapters of this book.

[54] For examples of each, see Joined Cases C-424/10 and C-425/10 *Ziolkowski and Szeja*, judgment of 21 December 2011, not yet reported. On the one hand, the Court accepted the Commission's interpretation as regards the acquisition of permanent residence status based on periods prior to accession, but on the other hand, it did not accept the Commission's interpretation that permanent residence status could be acquired based on stays pursuant to national law. See further the commentary on Art 16(1) in Chapter 4.

[55] Case C-127/08 [2008] ECR I-6241. See further the commentary on Art 3(1) in Chapter 1.

[56] COM(2009) 313, 9 July 2009. For the detail of these guidelines, see the other chapters of this book and the commentary on Art 35 in this chapter.

It would have been preferable if Article 39 had provided for reports on the application of the Directive at least every three years, in light of the requirements for regular reports set out in some of the previous legislation and the obvious significance of the Directive for the protection of the free movement rights of EU citizens and their family members. The Commission should commit itself to produce reports on its implementation at least this often. Most obviously, reports on the application of the Directive could be linked with the general reports on the citizenship of the Union, which Article 25 TFEU requires the Commission to produce every three years.[57]

But the more fundamental problem is the Commission's failure to follow up almost any of its complaints about wrongful implementation of the Directive with infringement actions brought to the Court of Justice. While some of the incorrect implementation will likely have been remedied in practice, either by national courts (perhaps following references to the Court of Justice) or by national administrations in the early stages of infringement proceedings, there is no way to be sure of this in the absence of another Commission report.[58] In any event, the case law of the Court of Justice indicates that some incorrect implementation did continue after the report. For instance, the refusal to count time periods before EU accession towards the acquisition of permanent residence status persisted until at least 2010, when the *Ziolkowski* case was referred to the Court of Justice. The Commission could—and should—have addressed this issue earlier, by bringing infringement actions on this point. Overall, it is remarkable that nine years after adoption of the Directive, and five years after a report which judged that 'the overall transposition' of the Directive 'is largely disappointing' and that '[n]ot one Article of the Directive has been transposed effectively and correctly by all Member States', the Commission has only brought a single infringement proceeding for incorrect application of the Directive to the Court of Justice.[59]

Article 40—Transposition

1. Member States shall bring into force the laws, regulations and administrative provisions necessary to comply with this Directive by 30 April 2006.
   When Member States adopt those measures, they shall contain a reference to this Directive or shall be accompanied by such a reference on the occasion of their official publication. The methods of making such reference shall be laid down by the Member States.
2. Member States shall communicate to the Commission the text of the provisions of national law which they adopt in the field covered by this Directive

---

[57] See most recently COM(2013) 270, 8 May 2013.

[58] However, there is some information on the progress of infringement actions brought since 2011 in the most recent report on EU citizenship (COM(2013) 270, 8 May 2013). But the previous such report was much vaguer on infringement issues (COM(2010) 602, 27 November 2010).

[59] Case C-75/11 *Commission v Austria*, judgment of 4 October 2012, not yet reported. See further the commentary on Art 24 in Chapter 5.

together with a table showing how the provisions of this Directive correspond to the national provisions adopted.

The most obvious issue arising as regards the transposition of the Directive is the question of how to calculate the acquisition of permanent residence status,[60] or other dates set out in the Directive as regards rights which it introduced for the first time.[61] However, this issue has been discussed above, in the context of Article 38.

Article 41—Entry into force

This Directive shall enter into force on the day of its publication in the Official Journal of the European Union.

This provision of the Directive is a 'boiler-plate' clause, which calls for no further comment, except to note that the Directive was published (and so entered into force) on 30 April 2004.

Article 42—Addressees

This Directive is addressed to the Member States.

This provision of the Directive is a 'boiler-plate' clause, which calls for no further comment.

F. Evaluation

The most significant provision in Chapter VII is Article 35, concerning fraud or abuse of rights. This Article is unobjectionable to the extent that it confirms prior case law,[62] and merely reiterates that persons who do not qualify for the rights in the Directive cannot rely upon it. But this statement begs the question as to who benefits from the rights in the first place. In the interests of legal certainty, it would be useful if the Court of Justice took an early opportunity to clarify the meaning of this clause.

---

[60] See the commentary on Art 16 in Chapter 4.

[61] See, for instance, the commentary on Arts 12(2) and 13(2) in Chapter 3.

[62] See K E Sorensen, 'Abuse of Rights in Community Law: A Principle of Substance or Merely Rhetoric?' (2006) 43 CMLRev 423 at 438: 'it must be expected that this provision will be interpreted to comply with how the principle has been interpreted previously'. Indeed, as the Court stated in *Metock* (Case C-127/08 [2008] ECR I-6241), the Directive does not lower standards as compared to the prior legislation.

APPENDIX

Directive 2004/38/EC of
The European Parliament and of
The Council of 29 April 2004

on the right of citizens of the Union and their family members
to move and reside freely within the territory of the Member States
amending Regulation (EEC) No 1612/68 and repealing Directives 64/221/EEC,
68/360/EEC, 72/194/EEC, 73/148/EEC, 75/34/EEC, 75/35/EEC,
90/364/EEC, 90/365/EEC and 93/96/EEC
(Text with EEA relevance)
[footnotes omitted]

THE EUROPEAN PARLIAMENT AND THE COUNCIL OF THE EUROPEAN UNION,

Having regard to the Treaty establishing the European Community, and in particular Articles 12, 18, 40, 44 and 52 thereof,

Having regard to the proposal from the Commission,

Having regard to the Opinion of the European Economic and Social Committee,

Having regard to the Opinion of the Committee of the Regions,

Acting in accordance with the procedure laid down in Article 251 of the Treaty,

Whereas:

(1) Citizenship of the Union confers on every citizen of the Union a primary and individual right to move and reside freely within the territory of the Member States, subject to the limitations and conditions laid down in the Treaty and to the measures adopted to give it effect.

(2) The free movement of persons constitutes one of the fundamental freedoms of the internal market, which comprises an area without internal frontiers, in which freedom is ensured in accordance with the provisions of the Treaty.

(3) Union citizenship should be the fundamental status of nationals of the Member States when they exercise their right of free movement and residence. It is therefore necessary to codify and review the existing Community instruments dealing separately with workers, self-employed persons, as well as students and other inactive persons in order to simplify and strengthen the right of free movement and residence of all Union citizens.

(4) With a view to remedying this sector-by-sector, piecemeal approach to the right of free movement and residence and facilitating the exercise of this right, there needs to be a single legislative act to amend Council Regulation (EEC) No 1612/68 of 15 October 1968 on freedom of movement for workers within the Community, and to repeal the following acts: Council Directive 68/360/EEC of 15 October 1968 on the abolition of restrictions on movement and residence within the Community for workers of Member States and their families, Council Directive 73/148/EEC of 21 May 1973 on the abolition of restrictions on movement and residence within the Community for nationals of Member States with regard to establishment and the provision of services, Council Directive 90/364/EEC of 28 June 1990 on the right of residence, Council Directive 90/365/EEC of 28 June 1990 on the right of residence for employees and self-employed persons who have ceased their occupational activity and Council Directive 93/96/EEC of 29 October 1993 on the right of residence for students.

(5) The right of all Union citizens to move and reside freely within the territory of the Member States should, if it is to be exercised under objective conditions of freedom and dignity, be also granted to their family members, irrespective of nationality. For the purposes of this Directive, the definition of "family member" should also include the registered partner if the legislation of the host Member State treats registered partnership as equivalent to marriage.

(6) In order to maintain the unity of the family in a broader sense and without prejudice to the prohibition of discrimination on grounds of nationality, the situation of those persons who are not included in the definition of family members under this Directive, and who therefore do not enjoy an automatic right of entry and residence in the host Member State, should be examined by the host Member State on the basis of its own national legislation, in order to decide whether entry and residence could be granted to such persons, taking into consideration their relationship with the Union citizen or any other circumstances, such as their financial or physical dependence on the Union citizen.

(7) The formalities connected with the free movement of Union citizens within the territory of Member States should be clearly defined, without prejudice to the provisions applicable to national border controls.

(8) With a view to facilitating the free movement of family members who are not nationals of a Member State, those who have already obtained a residence card should be exempted from the requirement to obtain an entry visa within the meaning of Council Regulation (EC) No 539/2001 of 15 March 2001 listing the third countries whose nationals must be in possession of visas when crossing the external borders and those whose nationals are exempt from that requirement or, where appropriate, of the applicable national legislation.

(9) Union citizens should have the right of residence in the host Member State for a period not exceeding three months without being subject to any conditions or any formalities other than the requirement to hold a valid identity card or passport, without prejudice to a more favourable treatment applicable to job-seekers as recognised by the case-law of the Court of Justice.

(10) Persons exercising their right of residence should not, however, become an unreasonable burden on the social assistance system of the host Member State during an initial period of residence. Therefore, the right of residence for Union citizens and their family members for periods in excess of three months should be subject to conditions.

(11) The fundamental and personal right of residence in another Member State is conferred directly on Union citizens by the Treaty and is not dependent upon their having fulfilled administrative procedures.

(12) For periods of residence of longer than three months, Member States should have the possibility to require Union citizens to register with the competent authorities in the place of residence, attested by a registration certificate issued to that effect.

(13) The residence card requirement should be restricted to family members of Union citizens who are not nationals of a Member State for periods of residence of longer than three months.

(14) The supporting documents required by the competent authorities for the issuing of a registration certificate or of a residence card should be comprehensively specified in order to avoid divergent administrative practices or interpretations constituting an undue obstacle to the exercise of the right of residence by Union citizens and their family members.

(15) Family members should be legally safeguarded in the event of the death of the Union citizen, divorce, annulment of marriage or termination of a registered partnership. With due regard for family life and human dignity, and in certain conditions to guard against abuse, measures should therefore be taken to ensure that in such circumstances family members already residing within the territory of the host Member State retain their right of residence exclusively on a personal basis.

(16) As long as the beneficiaries of the right of residence do not become an unreasonable burden on the social assistance system of the host Member State they should not be expelled. Therefore, an expulsion measure should not be the automatic consequence of recourse to the social assistance system. The host Member State should examine whether it is a case of temporary difficulties and take into account the duration of residence, the personal circumstances and the amount of aid granted in order to consider whether the beneficiary has become an unreasonable burden on its social assistance system and to proceed to his expulsion. In no case should an expulsion measure be adopted against workers, self-employed persons or job-seekers as defined by the Court of Justice save on grounds of public policy or public security.

(17) Enjoyment of permanent residence by Union citizens who have chosen to settle long term in the host Member State would strengthen the feeling of Union citizenship and is a key element in promoting social cohesion, which is one of the fundamental objectives of the Union. A right of permanent residence should therefore be laid down for all Union citizens and their family members who have resided in the host Member State in compliance with the conditions laid down in this Directive during a continuous period of five years without becoming subject to an expulsion measure.

(18) In order to be a genuine vehicle for integration into the society of the host Member State in which the Union citizen resides, the right of permanent residence, once obtained, should not be subject to any conditions.

(19) Certain advantages specific to Union citizens who are workers or self-employed persons and to their family members, which may allow these persons to acquire a right of permanent residence before they have resided five years in the host Member State, should be maintained, as these constitute acquired rights, conferred by Commission Regulation (EEC) No 1251/70 of 29 June 1970 on the right of workers to remain in the territory of a Member State after having been employed in that State and Council Directive 75/34/EEC of 17 December 1974 concerning the right of nationals of a Member State to remain in the territory of another Member State after having pursued therein an activity in a self-employed capacity.

(20) In accordance with the prohibition of discrimination on grounds of nationality, all Union citizens and their family members residing in a Member State on the basis of this Directive should enjoy, in that Member State, equal treatment with nationals in areas covered by the Treaty, subject to such specific provisions as are expressly provided for in the Treaty and secondary law.

(21) However, it should be left to the host Member State to decide whether it will grant social assistance during the first three months of residence, or for a longer period in the case of job-seekers, to Union citizens other than those who are workers or self-employed persons or who retain that status or their family members, or maintenance assistance for studies, including vocational training, prior to acquisition of the right of permanent residence, to these same persons.

(22) The Treaty allows restrictions to be placed on the right of free movement and residence on grounds of public policy, public security or public health. In order to ensure a tighter definition of the circumstances and procedural safeguards subject to which Union citizens and their family members may be denied leave to enter or may be expelled, this Directive should replace Council Directive 64/221/EEC of 25 February 1964 on the coordination of special measures concerning the movement and residence of foreign nationals, which are justified on grounds of public policy, public security or public health.

(23) Expulsion of Union citizens and their family members on grounds of public policy or public security is a measure that can seriously harm persons who, having availed themselves of the rights and freedoms conferred on them by the Treaty, have become genuinely integrated into the host Member State. The scope for such measures should therefore be limited in accordance with the principle of proportionality to take account of the degree of integration of the persons concerned, the length of their residence in

the host Member State, their age, state of health, family and economic situation and the links with their country of origin.

(24) Accordingly, the greater the degree of integration of Union citizens and their family members in the host Member State, the greater the degree of protection against expulsion should be. Only in exceptional circumstances, where there are imperative grounds of public security, should an expulsion measure be taken against Union citizens who have resided for many years in the territory of the host Member State, in particular when they were born and have resided there throughout their life. In addition, such exceptional circumstances should also apply to an expulsion measure taken against minors, in order to protect their links with their family, in accordance with the United Nations Convention on the Rights of the Child, of 20 November 1989.

(25) Procedural safeguards should also be specified in detail in order to ensure a high level of protection of the rights of Union citizens and their family members in the event of their being denied leave to enter or reside in another Member State, as well as to uphold the principle that any action taken by the authorities must be properly justified.

(26) In all events, judicial redress procedures should be available to Union citizens and their family members who have been refused leave to enter or reside in another Member State.

(27) In line with the case-law of the Court of Justice prohibiting Member States from issuing orders excluding for life persons covered by this Directive from their territory, the right of Union citizens and their family members who have been excluded from the territory of a Member State to submit a fresh application after a reasonable period, and in any event after a three year period from enforcement of the final exclusion order, should be confirmed.

(28) To guard against abuse of rights or fraud, notably marriages of convenience or any other form of relationships contracted for the sole purpose of enjoying the right of free movement and residence, Member States should have the possibility to adopt the necessary measures.

(29) This Directive should not affect more favourable national provisions.

(30) With a view to examining how further to facilitate the exercise of the right of free and residence, a report should be prepared by the Commission in order to evaluate the opportunity to present any necessary proposals to this effect, notably on the extension of the period of residence with no conditions.

(31) This Directive respects the fundamental rights and freedoms and observes the principles recognised in particular by the Charter of Fundamental Rights of the European Union. In accordance with the prohibition of discrimination contained in the Charter, Member States should implement this Directive without discrimination between the beneficiaries of this Directive on grounds such as sex, race, colour, ethnic or social origin, genetic characteristics, language, religion or beliefs, political or other opinion, membership of an ethnic minority, property, birth, disability, age or sexual orientation,

HAVE ADOPTED THIS DIRECTIVE:

CHAPTER I
General provisions

Article 1
Subject

This Directive lays down:

(a) the conditions governing the exercise of the right of free movement and residence within the territory of the Member States by Union citizens and their family members;

(b) the right of permanent residence in the territory of the Member States for Union citizens and their family members;

(c) the limits placed on the rights set out in (a) and (b) on grounds of public policy, public security or public health.

Article 2
Definitions

For the purposes of this Directive:

1) "Union citizen" means any person having the nationality of a Member State;

2) "Family member" means:

    (a) the spouse;

    (b) the partner with whom the Union citizen has contracted a registered partnership, on the basis of the legislation of a Member State, if the legislation of the host Member State treats registered partnerships as equivalent to marriage and in accordance with the conditions laid down in the relevant legislation of the host Member State;

    (c) the direct descendants who are under the age of 21 or are dependants and those of the spouse or partner as defined in point (b);

    (d) the dependent direct relatives in the ascending line and those of the spouse or partner as defined in point (b);

3) "Host Member State" means the Member State to which a Union citizen moves in order to exercise his/her right of free movement and residence.

Article 3
Beneficiaries

1. This Directive shall apply to all Union citizens who move to or reside in a Member State other than that of which they are a national, and to their family members as defined in point 2 of Article 2 who accompany or join them.

2. Without prejudice to any right to free movement and residence the persons concerned may have in their own right, the host Member State shall, in accordance with its national legislation, facilitate entry and residence for the following persons:

    (a) any other family members, irrespective of their nationality, not falling under the definition in point 2 of Article 2 who, in the country from which they have come, are dependants or members of the household of the Union citizen having the primary right of residence, or where serious health grounds strictly require the personal care of the family member by the Union citizen;

    (b) the partner with whom the Union citizen has a durable relationship, duly attested.

The host Member State shall undertake an extensive examination of the personal circumstances and shall justify any denial of entry or residence to these people.

Chapter II
Right of exit and entry

Article 4
Right of exit

1. Without prejudice to the provisions on travel documents applicable to national border controls, all Union citizens with a valid identity card or passport and their family members who are not nationals of a Member State and who hold a valid passport shall have the right to leave the territory of a Member State to travel to another Member State.

2. No exit visa or equivalent formality may be imposed on the persons to whom paragraph 1 applies.

3. Member States shall, acting in accordance with their laws, issue to their own nationals, and renew, an identity card or passport stating their nationality.

4. The passport shall be valid at least for all Member States and for countries through which the holder must pass when travelling between Member States. Where the law of a Member

State does not provide for identity cards to be issued, the period of validity of any passport on being issued or renewed shall be not less than five years.

Article 5
Right of entry

1. Without prejudice to the provisions on travel documents applicable to national border controls, Member States shall grant Union citizens leave to enter their territory with a valid identity card or passport and shall grant family members who are not nationals of a Member State leave to enter their territory with a valid passport.

   No entry visa or equivalent formality may be imposed on Union citizens.

2. Family members who are not nationals of a Member State shall only be required to have an entry visa in accordance with Regulation (EC) No 539/2001 or, where appropriate, with national law. For the purposes of this Directive, possession of the valid residence card referred to in Article 10 shall exempt such family members from the visa requirement.

   Member States shall grant such persons every facility to obtain the necessary visas. Such visas shall be issued free of charge as soon as possible and on the basis of an accelerated procedure.

3. The host Member State shall not place an entry or exit stamp in the passport of family members who are not nationals of a Member State provided that they present the residence card provided for in Article 10.

4. Where a Union citizen, or a family member who is not a national of a Member State, does not have the necessary travel documents or, if required, the necessary visas, the Member State concerned shall, before turning them back, give such persons every reasonable opportunity to obtain the necessary documents or have them brought to them within a reasonable period of time or to corroborate or prove by other means that they are covered by the right of free movement and residence.

5. The Member State may require the person concerned to report his/her presence within its territory within a reasonable and non-discriminatory period of time. Failure to comply with this requirement may make the person concerned liable to proportionate and non-discriminatory sanctions.

CHAPTER III
Right of residence

Article 6
Right of residence for up to three months

1. Union citizens shall have the right of residence on the territory of another Member State for a period of up to three months without any conditions or any formalities other than the requirement to hold a valid identity card or passport.

2. The provisions of paragraph 1 shall also apply to family members in possession of a valid passport who are not nationals of a Member State, accompanying or joining the Union citizen.

Article 7
Right of residence for more than three months

1. All Union citizens shall have the right of residence on the territory of another Member State for a period of longer than three months if they:
   (a) are workers or self-employed persons in the host Member State; or
   (b) have sufficient resources for themselves and their family members not to become a burden on the social assistance system of the host Member State during their period of residence and have comprehensive sickness insurance cover in the host Member State; or

(c) – are enrolled at a private or public establishment, accredited or financed by the host Member State on the basis of its legislation or administrative practice, for the principal purpose of following a course of study, including vocational training; and – have comprehensive sickness insurance cover in the host Member State and assure the relevant national authority, by means of a declaration or by such equivalent means as they may choose, that they have sufficient resources for themselves and their family members not to become a burden on the social assistance system of the host Member State during their period of residence; or

(d) are family members accompanying or joining a Union citizen who satisfies the conditions referred to in points (a), (b) or (c).

2. The right of residence provided for in paragraph 1 shall extend to family members who are not nationals of a Member State, accompanying or joining the Union citizen in the host Member State, provided that such Union citizen satisfies the conditions referred to in paragraph 1(a), (b) or (c).

3. For the purposes of paragraph 1(a), a Union citizen who is no longer a worker or self-employed person shall retain the status of worker or self-employed person in the following circumstances:

(a) he/she is temporarily unable to work as the result of an illness or accident;

(b) he/she is in duly recorded involuntary unemployment after having been employed for more than one year and has registered as a job-seeker with the relevant employment office;

(c) he/she is in duly recorded involuntary unemployment after completing a fixed-term employment contract of less than a year or after having become involuntarily unemployed during the first twelve months and has registered as a job-seeker with the relevant employment office. In this case, the status of worker shall be retained for no less than six months;

(d) he/she embarks on vocational training. Unless he/she is involuntarily unemployed, the retention of the status of worker shall require the training to be related to the previous employment.

4 By way of derogation from paragraphs 1(d) and 2 above, only the spouse, the registered partner provided for in Article 2(2)(b) and dependent children shall have the right of residence as family members of a Union citizen meeting the conditions under 1(c) above. Article 3(2) shall apply to his/her dependent direct relatives in the ascending lines and those of his/her spouse or registered partner.

Article 8
Administrative formalities for Union citizens

1. Without prejudice to Article 5(5), for periods of residence longer than three months, the host Member State may require Union citizens to register with the relevant authorities.

2. The deadline for registration may not be less than three months from the date of arrival. A registration certificate shall be issued immediately, stating the name and address of the person registering and the date of the registration. Failure to comply with the registration requirement may render the person concerned liable to proportionate and non-discriminatory sanctions.

3. For the registration certificate to be issued, Member States may only require that

   – Union citizens to whom point (a) of Article 7(1) applies present a valid identity card or passport, a confirmation of engagement from the employer or a certificate of employment, or proof that they are self-employed persons;

   – Union citizens to whom point (b) of Article 7(1) applies present a valid identity card or passport and provide proof that they satisfy the conditions laid down therein;

   – Union citizens to whom point (c) of Article 7(1) applies present a valid identity card or passport, provide proof of enrolment at an accredited establishment and of comprehensive sickness insurance cover and the declaration or equivalent means referred to in point (c) of Article 7(1). Member States may not require this declaration to refer to any specific amount of resources.

4. Member States may not lay down a fixed amount which they regard as "sufficient resources", but they must take into account the personal situation of the person concerned. In all cases this amount shall not be higher than the threshold below which nationals of the host Member State become eligible for social assistance, or, where this criterion is not applicable, higher than the minimum social security pension paid by the host Member State.

5. For the registration certificate to be issued to family members of Union citizens, who are themselves Union citizens, Member States may require the following documents to be presented:

(a) a valid identity card or passport;

(b) a document attesting to the existence of a family relationship or of a registered partnership;

(c) where appropriate, the registration certificate of the Union citizen whom they are accompanying or joining;

(d) in cases falling under points (c) and (d) of Article 2(2), documentary evidence that the conditions laid down therein are met;

(e) in cases falling under Article 3(2)(a), a document issued by the relevant authority in the country of origin or country from which they are arriving certifying that they are dependants or members of the household of the Union citizen, or proof of the existence of serious health grounds which strictly require the personal care of the family member by the Union citizen;

(f) in cases falling under Article 3(2)(b), proof of the existence of a durable relationship with the Union citizen.

Article 9
Administrative formalities for family members
who are not nationals of a Member State

1. Member States shall issue a residence card to family members of a Union citizen who are not nationals of a Member State, where the planned period of residence is for more than three months.

2. The deadline for submitting the residence card application may not be less than three months from the date of arrival.

3. Failure to comply with the requirement to apply for a residence card may make the person concerned liable to proportionate and non-discriminatory sanctions.

Article 10
Issue of residence cards

1. The right of residence of family members of a Union citizen who are not nationals of a Member State shall be evidenced by the issuing of a document called "Residence card of a family member of a Union citizen" no later than six months from the date on which they submit the application. A certificate of application for the residence card shall be issued immediately.

2. For the residence card to be issued, Member States shall require presentation of the following documents:

(a) a valid passport;

(b) a document attesting to the existence of a family relationship or of a registered partnership;

(c) the registration certificate or, in the absence of a registration system, any other proof of residence in the host Member State of the Union citizen whom they are accompanying or joining;

(d) in cases falling under points (c) and (d) of Article 2(2), documentary evidence that the conditions laid down therein are met;

(e) in cases falling under Article 3(2)(a), a document issued by the relevant authority in the country of origin or country from which they are arriving certifying that they are dependants or members of the household of the Union citizen, or proof of the existence of serious health grounds which strictly require the personal care of the family member by the Union citizen;

(f) in cases falling under Article 3(2)(b), proof of the existence of a durable relationship with the Union citizen.

Article 11
Validity of the residence card

1 The residence card provided for by Article 10(1) shall be valid for five years from the date of issue or for the envisaged period of residence of the Union citizen, if this period is less than five years.

2 The validity of the residence card shall not be affected by temporary absences not exceeding six months a year, or by absences of a longer duration for compulsory military service or by one absence of a maximum of twelve consecutive months for important reasons such as pregnancy and childbirth, serious illness, study or vocational training, or a posting in another Member State or a third country.

Article 12
Retention of the right of residence by family members
in the event of death or departure of the Union citizen

1. Without prejudice to the second subparagraph, the Union citizen's death or departure from the host Member State shall not affect the right of residence of his/her family members who are nationals of a Member State.

Before acquiring the right of permanent residence, the persons concerned must meet the conditions laid down in points (a), (b), (c) or (d) of Article 7(1).

2. Without prejudice to the second subparagraph, the Union citizen's death shall not entail loss of the right of residence of his/her family members who are not nationals of a Member State and who have been residing in the host Member State as family members for at least one year before the Union citizen's death.

Before acquiring the right of permanent residence, the right of residence of the persons concerned shall remain subject to the requirement that they are able to show that they are workers or self-employed persons or that they have sufficient resources for themselves and their family members not to become a burden on the social assistance system of the host Member State during their period of residence and have comprehensive sickness insurance cover in the host Member State, or that they are members of the family, already constituted in the host Member State, of a person satisfying these requirements. "Sufficient resources" shall be as defined in Article 8(4).

Such family members shall retain their right of residence exclusively on a personal basis.

3. The Union citizen's departure from the host Member State or his/her death shall not entail loss of the right of residence of his/her children or of the parent who has actual custody of the children, irrespective of nationality, if the children reside in the host Member State and are enrolled at an educational establishment, for the purpose of studying there, until the completion of their studies.

Article 13
Retention of the right of residence by family members in the event of
divorce, annulment of marriage or termination of registered partnership

1. Without prejudice to the second subparagraph, divorce, annulment of the Union citizen's marriage or termination of his/her registered partnership, as referred to in point 2(b) of Article 2 shall not affect the right of residence of his/her family members who are nationals of a Member State.

Before acquiring the right of permanent residence, the persons concerned must meet the conditions laid down in points (a), (b), (c) or (d) of Article 7(1).

2. Without prejudice to the second subparagraph, divorce, annulment of marriage or termination of the registered partnership referred to in point 2(b) of Article 2 shall not entail loss of the right of residence of a Union citizen's family members who are not nationals of a Member State where:

   (a) prior to initiation of the divorce or annulment proceedings or termination of the registered partnership referred to in point 2(b) of Article 2, the marriage or registered partnership has lasted at least three years, including one year in the host Member State; or

   (b) by agreement between the spouses or the partners referred to in point 2(b) of Article 2 or by court order, the spouse or partner who is not a national of a Member State has custody of the Union citizen's children; or

   (c) this is warranted by particularly difficult circumstances, such as having been a victim of domestic violence while the marriage or registered partnership was subsisting; or

   (d) by agreement between the spouses or partners referred to in point 2(b) of Article 2 or by court order, the spouse or partner who is not a national of a Member State has the right of access to a minor child, provided that the court has ruled that such access must be in the host Member State, and for as long as is required.

   Before acquiring the right of permanent residence, the right of residence of the persons concerned shall remain subject to the requirement that they are able to show that they are workers or self-employed persons or that they have sufficient resources for themselves and their family members not to become a burden on the social assistance system of the host Member State during their period of residence and have comprehensive sickness insurance cover in the host Member State, or that they are members of the family, already constituted in the host Member State, of a person satisfying these requirements. "Sufficient resources" shall be as defined in Article 8(4).

   Such family members shall retain their right of residence exclusively on personal basis.

Article 14
Retention of the right of residence

1. Union citizens and their family members shall have the right of residence provided for in Article 6, as long as they do not become an unreasonable burden on the social assistance system of the host Member State.

2. Union citizens and their family members shall have the right of residence provided for in Articles 7, 12 and 13 as long as they meet the conditions set out therein.

   In specific cases where there is a reasonable doubt as to whether a Union citizen or his/her family members satisfies the conditions set out in Articles 7, 12 and 13, Member States may verify if these conditions are fulfilled. This verification shall not be carried out systematically.

3. An expulsion measure shall not be the automatic consequence of a Union citizen's or his or her family member's recourse to the social assistance system of the host Member State.

4. By way of derogation from paragraphs 1 and 2 and without prejudice to the provisions of Chapter VI, an expulsion measure may in no case be adopted against Union citizens or their family members if:

   (a) the Union citizens are workers or self-employed persons, or

   (b) the Union citizens entered the territory of the host Member State in order to seek employment.

   In this case, the Union citizens and their family members may not be expelled for as long as the Union citizens can provide evidence that they are continuing to seek employment and that they have a genuine chance of being engaged.

Procedural safeguards

1. The procedures provided for by Articles 30 and 31 shall apply by analogy to all decisions restricting free movement of Union citizens and their family members on grounds other than public policy, public security or public health.

2. Expiry of the identity card or passport on the basis of which the person concerned entered the host Member State and was issued with a registration certificate or residence card shall not constitute a ground for expulsion from the host Member State.

3. The host Member State may not impose a ban on entry in the context of an expulsion decision to which paragraph 1 applies.

CHAPTER IV
Right of permanent residence

Section I
Eligibility

Article 16
General rule for Union citizens
and their family members

1. Union citizens who have resided legally for a continuous period of five years in the host Member State shall have the right of permanent residence there. This right shall not be subject to the conditions provided for in Chapter III.

2. Paragraph 1 shall apply also to family members who are not nationals of a Member State and have legally resided with the Union citizen in the host Member State for a continuous period of five years.

3. Continuity of residence shall not be affected by temporary absences not exceeding a total of six months a year, or by absences of a longer duration for compulsory military service, or by one absence of a maximum of twelve consecutive months for important reasons such as pregnancy and childbirth, serious illness, study or vocational training, or a posting in another Member State or a third country.

4. Once acquired, the right of permanent residence shall be lost only through absence from the host Member State for a period exceeding two consecutive years.

Article 17
Exemptions for persons no longer working in
the host Member State and their family members

1. By way of derogation from Article 16, the right of permanent residence in the host Member State shall be enjoyed before completion of a continuous period of five years of residence by:

   (a) workers or self-employed persons who, at the time they stop working, have reached the age laid down by the law of that Member State for entitlement to an old age pension or workers who cease paid employment to take early retirement, provided that they have been working in that Member State for at least the preceding twelve months and have resided there continuously for more than three years.

   If the law of the host Member State does not grant the right to an old age pension to certain categories of self-employed persons, the age condition shall be deemed to have been met once the person concerned has reached the age of 60;

   (b) workers or self-employed persons who have resided continuously in the host Member State for more than two years and stop working there as a result of permanent incapacity to work.

   If such incapacity is the result of an accident at work or an occupational disease entitling the person concerned to a benefit payable in full or in part by an institution in the host Member State, no condition shall be imposed as to length of residence;

(c) workers or self-employed persons who, after three years of continuous employment and residence in the host Member State, work in an employed or self-employed capacity in another Member State, while retaining their place of residence in the host Member State, to which they return, as a rule, each day or at least once a week.

For the purposes of entitlement to the rights referred to in points (a) and (b), periods of employment spent in the Member State in which the person concerned is working shall be regarded as having been spent in the host Member State.

Periods of involuntary unemployment duly recorded by the relevant employment office, periods not worked for reasons not of the person's own making and absences from work or cessation of work due to illness or accident shall be regarded as periods of employment.

2. The conditions as to length of residence and employment laid down in point (a) of paragraph 1 and the condition as to length of residence laid down in point (b) of paragraph 1 shall not apply if the worker's or the self-employed person's spouse or partner as referred to in point 2(b) of Article 2 is a national of the host Member State or has lost the nationality of that Member State by marriage to that worker or self-employed person.

3. Irrespective of nationality, the family members of a worker or a self-employed person who are residing with him in the territory of the host Member State shall have the right of permanent residence in that Member State, if the worker or self-employed person has acquired himself the right of permanent residence in that Member State on the basis of paragraph 1.

4. If, however, the worker or self-employed person dies while still working but before acquiring permanent residence status in the host Member State on the basis of paragraph 1, his family members who are residing with him in the host Member State shall acquire the right of permanent residence there, on condition that:

(a) the worker or self-employed person had, at the time of death, resided continuously on the territory of that Member State for two years; or

(b) the death resulted from an accident at work or an occupational disease; or

(c) the surviving spouse lost the nationality of that Member State following marriage to the worker or self-employed person.

Article 18
**Acquisition of the right of permanent residence by certain
family members who are not nationals of a Member State**

Without prejudice to Article 17, the family members of a Union citizen to whom Articles 12(2) and 13(2) apply, who satisfy the conditions laid down therein, shall acquire the right of permanent residence after residing legally for a period of five consecutive years in the host Member State.

**Section II
Administrative formalities**

Article 19
Document certifying permanent residence for Union citizens

1. Upon application Member States shall issue Union citizens entitled to permanent residence, after having verified duration of residence, with a document certifying permanent residence.

2. The document certifying permanent residence shall be issued as soon as possible.

Article 20
Permanent residence card for family members
who are not nationals of a Member State

1. Member States shall issue family members who are not nationals of a Member State entitled to permanent residence with a permanent residence card within six months of the submission of the application. The permanent residence card shall be renewable automatically every ten years.

2. The application for a permanent residence card shall be submitted before the residence card expires. Failure to comply with the requirement to apply for a permanent residence card may render the person concerned liable to proportionate and non-discriminatory sanctions.

3. Interruption in residence not exceeding two consecutive years shall not affect the validity of the permanent residence card.

Article 21
Continuity of residence

For the purposes of this Directive, continuity of residence may be attested by any means of proof in use in the host Member State. Continuity of residence is broken by any expulsion decision duly enforced against the person concerned.

Chapter V
Provisions common to the right of residence
and the right of permanent residence

Article 22
Territorial scope

The right of residence and the right of permanent residence shall cover the whole territory of the host Member State. Member States may impose territorial restrictions on the right of residence and the right of permanent residence only where the same restrictions apply to their own nationals.

Article 23
Related rights

Irrespective of nationality, the family members of a Union citizen who have the right of residence or the right of permanent residence in a Member State shall be entitled to take up employment or self-employment there.

Article 24
Equal treatment

1. Subject to such specific provisions as are expressly provided for in the Treaty and secondary law, all Union citizens residing on the basis of this Directive in the territory of the host Member State shall enjoy equal treatment with the nationals of that Member State within the scope of the Treaty. The benefit of this right shall be extended to family members who are not nationals of a Member State and who have the right of residence or permanent residence.

2. By way of derogation from paragraph 1, the host Member State shall not be obliged to confer entitlement to social assistance during the first three months of residence or, where appropriate, the longer period provided for in Article 14(4)(b), nor shall it be obliged, prior to acquisition of the right of permanent residence, to grant maintenance aid for studies, including vocational training, consisting in student grants or student loans to persons other than workers, self-employed persons, persons who retain such status and members of their families.

Article 25

General provisions concerning residence documents

1. Possession of a registration certificate as referred to in Article 8, of a document certifying permanent residence, of a certificate attesting submission of an application for a family member residence card, of a residence card or of a permanent residence card, may under no circumstances be made a precondition for the exercise of a right or the completion of an administrative formality, as entitlement to rights may be attested by any other means of proof.

2. All documents mentioned in paragraph 1 shall be issued free of charge or for a charge not exceeding that imposed on nationals for the issuing of similar documents.

Article 26

Checks

Member States may carry out checks on compliance with any requirement deriving from their national legislation for non-nationals always to carry their registration certificate or residence card, provided that the same requirement applies to their own nationals as regards their identity card.

In the event of failure to comply with this requirement, Member States may impose the same sanctions as those imposed on their own nationals for failure to carry their identity card.

CHAPTER VI

Restrictions on the right of entry and the right of residence on grounds of public policy, public security or public health

Article 27

General principles

1. Subject to the provisions of this Chapter, Member States may restrict the freedom of movement and residence of Union citizens and their family members, irrespective of nationality, on grounds of public policy, public security or public health. These grounds shall not be invoked to serve economic ends.

2. Measures taken on grounds of public policy or public security shall comply with the principle of proportionality and shall be based exclusively on the personal conduct of the individual concerned.

   Previous criminal convictions shall not in themselves constitute grounds for taking such measures. The personal conduct of the individual concerned must represent a genuine, present and sufficiently serious threat affecting one of the fundamental interests of society. Justifications that are isolated from the particulars of the case or that rely on considerations of general prevention shall not be accepted.

3. In order to ascertain whether the person concerned represents a danger for public policy or public security, when issuing the registration certificate or, in the absence of a registration system, not later than three months from the date of arrival of the person concerned on its territory or from the date of reporting his/her presence within the territory, as provided for in Article 5(5), or when issuing the residence card, the host Member State may, should it consider this essential, request the Member State of origin and, if need be, other Member States to provide information concerning any previous police record the person concerned may have. Such enquiries shall not be made as a matter of routine. The Member State consulted shall give its reply within two months.

4. The Member State which issued the passport or identity card shall allow the holder of the document who has been expelled on grounds of public policy, public security, or public health from another Member State to re-enter its territory without any formality even if the document is no longer valid or the nationality of the holder is in dispute.

Article 28
Protection against expulsion

1. Before taking an expulsion decision on grounds of public policy or public security, the host Member State shall take account of considerations such as how long the individual concerned has resided on its territory, his/her age, state of health, family and economic situation, social and cultural integration into the host Member State and the extent of his/her links with the country of origin.

2. The host Member State may not take an expulsion decision against Union citizens or their family members, irrespective of nationality, who have the right of permanent residence on its territory, except on serious grounds of public policy or public security.

3. An expulsion decision may not be taken against Union citizens, except if the decision is based on imperative grounds of public security, as defined by Member States, if they:

    (a) have resided in the host Member State for the previous ten years; or
    (b) are a minor, except if the expulsion is necessary for the best interests of the child, as provided for in the United Nations Convention on the Rights of the Child of 20 November 1989.

Article 29
Public health

1. The only diseases justifying measures restricting freedom of movement shall be the diseases with epidemic potential as defined by the relevant instruments of the World Health Organisation and other infectious diseases or contagious parasitic diseases if they are the subject of protection provisions applying to nationals of the host Member State.

2. Diseases occurring after a three-month period from the date of arrival shall not constitute grounds for expulsion from the territory.

3. Where there are serious indications that it is necessary, Member States may, within three months of the date of arrival, require persons entitled to the right of residence to undergo, free of charge, a medical examination to certify that they are not suffering from any of the conditions referred to in paragraph 1. Such medical examinations may not be required as a matter of routine.

Article 30
Notification of decisions

1. The persons concerned shall be notified in writing of any decision taken under Article 27(1), in such a way that they are able to comprehend its content and the implications for them.

2. The persons concerned shall be informed, precisely and in full, of the public policy, public security or public health grounds on which the decision taken in their case is based, unless this is contrary to the interests of State security.

3. The notification shall specify the court or administrative authority with which the person concerned may lodge an appeal, the time limit for the appeal and, where applicable, the time allowed for the person to leave the territory of the Member State. Save in duly substantiated cases of urgency, the time allowed to leave the territory shall be not less than one month from the date of notification.

Article 31
Procedural safeguards

1. The persons concerned shall have access to judicial and, where appropriate, administrative redress procedures in the host Member State to appeal against or seek review of any decision taken against them on the grounds of public policy, public security or public health.

2. Where the application for appeal against or judicial review of the expulsion decision is accompanied by an application for an interim order to suspend enforcement of that

decision, actual removal from the territory may not take place until such time as the decision on the interim order has been taken, except:

- where the expulsion decision is based on a previous judicial decision; or
- where the persons concerned have had previous access to judicial review; or
- where the expulsion decision is based on imperative grounds of public security under Article 28(3).

3. The redress procedures shall allow for an examination of the legality of the decision, as well as of the facts and circumstances on which the proposed measure is based. They shall ensure that the decision is not disproportionate, particularly in view of the requirements laid down in Article 28.

4. Member States may exclude the individual concerned from their territory pending the redress procedure, but they may not prevent the individual from submitting his/her defence in person, except when his/her appearance may cause serious troubles to public policy or public security or when the appeal or judicial review concerns a denial of entry to the territory.

Article 32
Duration of exclusion orders

1. Persons excluded on grounds of public policy or public security may submit an application for lifting of the exclusion order after a reasonable period, depending on the circumstances, and in any event after three years from enforcement of the final exclusion order which has been validly adopted in accordance with Community law, by putting forward arguments to establish that there has been a material change in the circumstances which justified the decision ordering their exclusion.

The Member State concerned shall reach a decision on this application within six months of its submission.

2. The persons referred to in paragraph 1 shall have no right of entry to the territory of the Member State concerned while their application is being considered.

Article 33
Expulsion as a penalty or legal consequence

1. Expulsion orders may not be issued by the host Member State as a penalty or legal consequence of a custodial penalty, unless they conform to the requirements of Articles 27, 28 and 29.

2. If an expulsion order, as provided for in paragraph 1, is enforced more than two years after it was issued, the Member State shall check that the individual concerned is currently and genuinely a threat to public policy or public security and shall assess whether there has been any material change in the circumstances since the expulsion order was issued.

Chapter VII
Final provisions

Article 34
Publicity

Member States shall disseminate information concerning the rights and obligations of Union citizens and their family members on the subjects covered by this Directive, particularly by means of awareness-raising campaigns conducted through national and local media and other means of communication.

Article 35
Abuse of rights

Member States may adopt the necessary measures to refuse, terminate or withdraw any right conferred by this Directive in the case of abuse of rights or fraud, such as marriages of convenience. Any such measure shall be proportionate and subject to the procedural safeguards provided for in Articles 30 and 31.

Article 36
Sanctions

Member States shall lay down provisions on the sanctions applicable to breaches of national rules adopted for the implementation of this Directive and shall take the measures required for their application. The sanctions laid down shall be effective and proportionate. Member States shall notify the Commission of these provisions not later than 30 April 2006 and as promptly as possible in the case of any subsequent changes.

Article 37
More favourable national provisions

The provisions of this Directive shall not affect any laws, regulations or administrative provisions laid down by a Member State which would be more favourable to the persons covered by this Directive.

Article 38
Repeals

1. Articles 10 and 11 of Regulation (EEC) No 1612/68 shall be repealed with effect from 30 April 2006.
2. Directives 64/221/EEC, 68/360/EEC, 72/194/EEC, 73/148/EEC, 75/34/EEC, 75/35/EEC, 90/364/EEC, 90/365/EEC and 93/96/EEC shall be repealed with effect from 30 April 2006.
3. References made to the repealed provisions and Directives shall be construed as being made to this Directive.

Article 39
Report

No later than 30 April 2008 the Commission shall submit a report on the application of this Directive to the European Parliament and the Council, together with any necessary proposals, notably on the opportunity to extend the period of time during which Union citizens and their family members may reside in the territory of the host Member State without any conditions. The Member States shall provide the Commission with the information needed to produce the report.

Article 40
Transposition

1. Member States shall bring into force the laws, regulations and administrative provisions necessary to comply with this Directive by 30 April 2006.

   When Member States adopt those measures, they shall contain a reference to this Directive or shall be accompanied by such a reference on the occasion of their official publication. The methods of making such reference shall be laid down by the Member States.

2. Member States shall communicate to the Commission the text of the provisions of national law which they adopt in the field covered by this Directive together with a table showing how the provisions of this Directive correspond to the national provisions adopted.

Article 41
Entry into force

This Directive shall enter into force on the day of its publication in the Official Journal of the European Union.

Article 42
Addressees

This Directive is addressed to the Member States.

BIBLIOGRAPHY

S Acierno, 'The *Carpenter* judgment: fundamental rights and the limits of the Community legal order' (2003) 28 CMLRev 393

S Adam and P van Elsuwege, 'Citizenship rights and the Federal Balance between the European Union and its Member States: Comment on *Dereci*' (2012) 37 ELRev 176

L Azoulai and S Coutts, 'Restricting Union Citizens' Residence Rights on Grounds of Public Security. Where Union Citizenship and the AFSJ Meet: *PI*' (2013) 50 CMLRev 553

G Barrett, 'Family Matters: European Community Law and Third-Country Family Members' (2003) 40 CMLRev 369

W Bohning, *The Migration of Workers in the United Kingdom and Western Europe* (OUP, Oxford, 1972)

S Breitenmoser, 'Sectoral Agreements between the EC and Switzerland: Contents and Context' (2003) 40 CMLRev 1137

J Y Carlier, *La condition des personnes dans l'union européene* (Larcier, Brussels, 2007)

R Cholewinski, R Perruchaud, E MacDonald, *International Migration Law: Developing Paradigms and key challenges* (T M C Asser, The Hague, 2007)

S Choudhury, 'Article 9', in S Peers, T Hervey, J Kenner, and A Ward, eds, *Commentary on the EU Charter of Fundamental Rights* (Hart, Oxford, 2014)

M Condinanzi, A Lang, and B Nascimbene, *Citizenship of the Union and Freedom of Movement of Persons* (Martinus Nijhoff, Leiden, 2008)

C Costello, '*Metock*: Free Movement and "Normal Family Life" in the Union' (2009) 46 CMLRev 587

S Currie, *Migration, Work and Citizenship in the Enlarged European Union: Law and Migration* (Ashgate, Farnham, 2008)

S Currie, 'Accelerated Justice or a Step Too Far? Residence Rights of Non-EU Family Members and the Court's Ruling in *Metock v Minister for Justice, Equality and Law Reform*' (2009) 34 ELRev 310

C Dautricourt and S Thomas, 'Reverse Discrimination and Free Movement of Persons Under Community Law: All for Ulysses, Nothing for Penelope?' (2009) 34 ELRev 433

M Dougan and E Spaventa, '"Wish you weren't here"... New Models of Social Solidarity in the European Union', in M Dougan and E Spaventa, eds, *Social Welfare and EU Law* (Hart, Oxford, 2005), 181

M Elsmore and P Starup, case note on *Jia* (2007) 44 CMLRev 787

P van Elsuwege, 'Shifting the Boundaries? European Union citizenship and the Scope of Application of EU Law' (2011) 38 LIEI 262

E Fahey, 'Going Back to Basics: Re-embracing the Fundamentals of the Free Movement of Persons in *Metock*' (2009) 36 LIEI 83

E Fahey, 'Interpretive Legitimacy and the Distinction Between "Social Assistance" and "Work-Seekers' Allowance": Comment on *Vatsouras*' (2009) 34 ELRev 933

N Fennelly, 'The European Union and Protection of Aliens from Expulsion' (1999) 3 EJML 313

H Graubner, 'Comparing People or Institutions? Sexual Orientation Discrimination and the Court of Justice of the European Union', in K Boele-Woelki and A Fuchs, eds, *Legal Recognition of Same-Sex Relationships in Europe: National, Cross-Border and European Perspectives*, 2nd edn (Intersentia, Cambridge, 2012) 271

C A Groenendijk, E Guild, and R Barzilay, *The Legal Status of Third Country Nationals who are Long Term Residents in a Member State of the European Union*, Brussels 2001, European Commission

C A Groenendijk, E Guild, and H Dogan, *Security of residence of long-term migrants, A comparative study of law and practice in European countries*, Strasbourg 1998, Council of Europe

E Guild, *European Immigration Law* (Kluwer Law International, The Hague 2000)

L Hantrais, 'What is a Family or Family Life in the European Union?', in E Guild, ed, *The Legal Framework and Social Consequences of Free Movement of Persons in the European Union* (Kluwer, The Hague, 1999), 19

B Hofstotter, 'A Cascade of Rights, or Who Shall Care for Little Catherine? Some Reflections on the *Chen* Case' (2005) 30 ELRev 548

G F Mancini, 'The Free Movement of Workers in the Case Law of the European Court of Justice', in *Constitutional Adjudication in European Community and National Law, Essays for the Hon. Mr Justice T. F. O'Higgins*, D Curtin and D O'Keeffe, eds (Butts, London, 1992)

D Martin, case note on *Jia* (2007) 9 EJML 457

D Martin, 'La libre circulation des personnes: au-delà de l'évolution et des revolutions, la perpétuelle quête de sens' (2012) 1 Rev Aff Eur 85

A P van der Mei, case note on *Akrich* (2004) 6 EJML (2004) 277

K Neunreither, 'Citizens and the Exercise of Power in the European Union', in *A Citizens' Europe: In search of a New Order*, Alan Rosas and Esko Antola, eds (Sage Publications, London, 1995)

N Nic Shiubhne, 'Free Movement of Persons and the Wholly Internal Rule: Time to Move On?' (2002) 39 CMLRev 763

N Nic Shiubhne, 'Derogating from the Free Movement of Persons: When can EU Citizens be Deported?' (2005–6) 8 CYELS 187

N Nic Shuibhne and M Maci, *Proving Public Interest: The Growing Impact of Evidence in Free Movement Case-Law* (publication forthcoming)

C O'Brien, 'Real links, abstract rights and false alarms: the relationship between the ECJ's "real link" case law and national solidarity' (2008) 33 ELRev 643

S O'Leary, *The Evolving Concept of Community Citizenship—from the Free Movement of Persons to Union citizenship* (Kluwer Law International, The Hague, 1996)

S O'Leary, 'The Options for the Reform of EU Citizenship', in *Citizenship and Nationality Status in the New Europe*, S O'Leary and T Tiilikainen, eds (Sweet & Maxwell, London, 1998) 83–86

S O'Leary, 'Developing an Ever Closer Union between the People's of Europe? A reappraisal of the case-law of the Court of Justice on the free movement of persons and EU citizenship' (2008) 27 YEL 167–194

B Olivier and J H Reestman, case note on *Jia* (2007) 3 EUConst 463

D Pearl and W F Menski, *Muslim Family Law*, 3rd edn (Sweet and Maxwell, London, 1998)

S Peers, 'The EC-Switzerland Agreement on Free Movement of Persons: Overview and Analysis' (2000) 2 EJML 127

S Peers, 'Family Reunion and Community Law', in N Walker, ed, *Towards an Area of Freedom, Security and Justice* (OUP, Oxford, 2004), 143

S Peers et al, *EU Immigration and Asylum Law: Text and Commentary*, 2nd edn (3 volumes: Brill 2012–2013)

S Peers, 'Article 52', in S Peers, T Hervey, J Kenner, and A Ward, eds, *Commentary on the EU Charter of Fundamental Rights* (Hart, 2014)

N Reich and S Harbacevica, 'Citizenship and Family on Trial: A Fairly Optimistic Overview of Recent Court Practice with Regard to Free Movement of Persons' (2003) 40 CMLRev 615

N Rogers, R Scannell, and J Walsh, *Free Movement of Persons in the Enlarged European Union*, 2nd edn (Sweet and Maxwell, London, 2012)

D-M Sandru, C-M Banu, and D A Calin, 'The Preliminary Reference in the Jipa case and the Case Law of the Romanian Courts on the Restriction on the Free Movement of Persons' (2012) 18 EPL 623

C Schlitz, '*Akrich*: A Clear Delimitation without Limits' (2005) 12 MJ 241

J Shaw, 'The Interpretation of EU citizenship' (1998) 6(3) *The Modern Law Review* 295

J Shaw, 'Citizenship: Contrasting Dynamics at the Interface of Integration and Constitutionalism', in P Craig and G de Burca, eds, *The Evolution of EU Law*, 2nd edn (OUP, Oxford, 2011) 575

K E Sorensen, 'Abuse of Rights in Community Law: A Principle of Substance or Merely Rhetoric?' (2006) 43 CMLRev 423

C Urbano de Sousa 'Le droit des membres de la famille du citoyen de l'Union europeéne de circuler et de séjourner sur le territoire des états membres, dans la directive 2004/38/CE' in J-Y Carlier and E Guild, *The Future of Free Movement of Persons in the EU* (Bruylant, Brussels, 2006) 103–126

E Spaventa, case note on *Akrich* (2005) 42 CMLRev 225

E Spaventa, 'Article 45', in S Peers, T Hervey, J Kenner, and A Ward, eds, *Commentary on the EU Charter of Fundamental Rights* (Hart, Oxford, 2014)

P Starup and M Elsmore, 'Taking a Logical or Giant Step Forward? Comment on *Ibrahim* and *Teixeira*' (2010) 35 ELRev 571

H Toner, 'Migration Rights and Same-Sex Couples in EU Law: A Case Study', in K Boele-Woelki and A Fuchs, eds, *Legal Recognition of Same-Sex Relationships in Europe: National, Cross-Border and European Perspectives*, 2nd edn (Intersentia, Cambridge, 2012) 285

A Travis, 'Stark choice under new immigration rules: exile or family breakup', *The Guardian*, 8 June 2012

A Tryfonidou, 'Jia or "Carpenter II": The Edge of Reason' (2007) 32 ELRev 908

A Tryfonidou, 'Family Reunification Rights of (Migrant) Union Citizens: Towards a More Liberal Approach' (2009) 15 ELJ 634

A Tryfonidou, 'Redefining the Outer Boundaries of EU Law: The *Zambrano, McCarthy* and *Dereci* Trilogy' (2012) 18 EPL 493

R White, 'Conflicting Competences: Free Movement Rules and Immigration Laws' (2004) 29 ELRev 385

INDEX